A DOCUMENTARY HISTORY OF AMERICAN LIFE

General Editor: **David Donald,** *The Johns Hopkins University*

PROGRESSIVISM AND POSTWAR DISILLUSIONMENT:

1898–1928

Edited by DAVID A. SHANNON

University of Maryland

Volume 6

A Documentary History of American Life

General Editor: David Donald

The Johns Hopkins University

McGRAW-HILL BOOK COMPANY

New York   St. Louis   San Francisco   Toronto   London   Sydney

PROGRESSIVISM AND POSTWAR

DISILLUSIONMENT: 1898–1928

FOREWORD

The history of the United States is more a matter of record than is that of any other major world power that has ever existed. The beginnings of our nation are not shrouded in myth or in medieval obscurity, for they can be traced in the precise and explicit directives which the English sovereigns gave their subjects who went to explore or inhabit the New World. At the other end of the time scale, the government of the United States has swiftly moved to declassify and to help publish even the "top secret" papers of World War II and after. For every intervening period the documentary record is voluminous and comprehensive.

A Documentary History of American Life presents an extensive, representative sampling of that vast record. It differs in a number of important ways from the several collections of documents already available to teachers and students. In the first place, it provides the most extensive coverage yet attempted for the entire history of America, from the first expedition of Walter Raleigh through the "Great Society" message to Congress by President Lyndon B. Johnson. The eight volumes of this series, containing approximately 2 million words, afford for the first time a canvas of sufficient size on which to present the panorama of the American past in its full complexity and detail. Moreover, the scope of the series allows the publication of all the significant portions of each document, not merely of selected snippets. Of course, not even a work of this size can include every document relating to American history, but for most students there is abundance here, and each teacher can choose those writings which best fit the needs of his particular courses.

A second major feature of the series is its variety. The seven editors, who have worked closely together during the preparation of these books, agree in rejecting the old notion that a document is necessarily a law, a treaty, or a Supreme Court decision. All these, to be sure, are here present, but so are diary accounts, contemporary letters, essays, poems, and cartoons. All the volumes include documents to illustrate our social, economic, and intellectual, as well as our political and diplomatic, history.

The series is further distinguished by its pedagogical usefulness. Teachers themselves, the seven editors are alert to the problems of college teaching in an age when classes are large and much of the actual instruction must be done by beginning instructors often only a few steps ahead of their pupils. Not just documents are needed, but documents whose relevance is explained and whose implications are explored. For each document, or group of documents, in this series, therefore, there is a full editorial introduction and a brief bibliographical note.

As a result, *A Documentary History of American Life* offers a rich fare to both beginning and advanced students who seek to know our country's history. The editors present these volumes in the profound conviction that only if our citizens understand the past can they intelligently face the future.

The Johns Hopkins University   *David Donald*

The American people have been wondrously dynamic, and one could make a strong argument that any thirty-year period in their history has been one of enormous change. Few would contend, however, that any such period saw a more fundamental change of pace and direction than the one between the War with Spain in 1898 and the stock market crash of 1929. After a half-century of peace with foreign nations, the United States within only a few years twice became engaged in war with European powers. After decades of only fitful and generally unfruitful attempts to adjust their society to the basic fact of industrialism, the American people made their first sustained political effort to adapt their institutions to the age of factories and corporations.

Every college library has thousands of documents that date from this first generation of this century. One could select an utterly different but still relevant group of documents from the storehouses of the past. Why, then, these particular selections? By what criteria did the editor choose these and reject others? Aside from personal preference—and we must not minimize the personal role of the historical writer and editor—his main considerations in selecting a particular document were its importance and its inherent interest. There may be disagreement over what is important, but surely there is a consensus that the questions of foreign policy in the first and third parts of this book and the political and economic matters treated in the second and fourth parts are basic. The inclusion of documents from the pens of men who wrote with distinction—Rudyard Kipling, Mark Twain, Sinclair Lewis, and H. L. Mencken are represented here—was an effort to excite the interest of literate readers. The editor endeavored also to provide a diversity of kinds of documents and of points of view. When the editor was a student, collections of historical documents consisted almost exclusively of judicial opinions and party platforms, and he was eager to include other material. Here the student will find congressional debates, editorials, speeches, a poem, diplomatic messages, and a chapter from a novel, as well as the product of a platform committee and a limited group of Supreme Court decisions. Finally, diversity of point of view was a consideration because differences of opinion provide historical drama. But the rather common either-or, pro-and-con approach is not satisfactory. Annoyed beyond his low boiling point by someone's failure to see that historical matters may be viewed from a great variety of positions, a remarkably crusty American historian of a few years ago declared, "Fatuous equivocators chirp the sententious banality that there are two sides to every question." Here, on most questions, the student will find several sides, few of them fatuous or stated equivocally, and none of them chirped.

David A. Shannon

PART **THREE** War and Peace

PART **FOUR** The New Era and the Old Complacency

PART *ONE*

Imperialism and Anti-imperialism

s Albert Beveridge stressed in one of the following documents, the American flag marched across the continent during the eighteenth and nineteenth centuries; but not until 1898 was it planted beyond the continental limits of North America. Then, with dazzling suddenness, an outburst of expansionist activity established a United States colonial empire in the Caribbean and the Pacific. Like other major powers, the United States had become imperialist.

Between the War with Spain and World War I, the United States, again like other major powers, employed at least three different kinds of expansionist or imperialist methods. Some areas, notably the Philippine Islands, the nation annexed outright, as the British had acquired most of India, as the French had taken Indochina, and so forth. It was to this colonialism that anti-imperialists such as William Jennings Bryan and Mark Twain objected most vigorously. An arrangement quite different was that by which the United States extended effective control over Cuba. In 1901 the Platt amendment to an army appropriations bill stipulated that Cuba agree to a treaty that in effect made it a protectorate of the United States, establishing a relationship similar to that between Great Britain and Egypt. Still more informal was the kind of influence the United States extended into other nations when American investors controlled important industries or financial institutions—"dollar diplomacy," as it came to be called while William Howard Taft occupied the White House.

The documents in Part One have to do with the imperialist impulse, the debate between advocates and opponents of colonialism, and each of the three kinds of expansionism practiced by the United States at the end of the last century and the beginning of this one.

"The White Man's Burden"

This widely quoted poem by Rudyard Kipling (1865–1936) first appeared in McClure's Magazine, volume 12, pages 290–291, the first two pages of the February, 1899, issue. Kipling, the writer of the English language most closely identified with imperialism, was born in Bombay and lived in India until he was in his mid-twenties, and many of his poems and stories have an Indian background. He married an American and lived in Vermont in the 1890s. This poem, the advice of an experienced imperialist to his American friends, reflects a great deal of the thought and attitudes of both British and American imperialists. Already widely published and recognized when this poem appeared, Kipling went on to even greater eminence, receiving the Nobel prize for literature in 1907, the first Englishman to do so.

Take up the White Man's burden—
    Send forth the best ye breed—
Go, bind your sons to exile
    To serve your captives' need;
To wait, in heavy harness,
    On fluttered folk and wild—
Your new-caught sullen peoples,
    Half devil and half child.

Take up the White Man's burden—
    In patience to abide,
To veil the threat of terror
    And check the show of pride;
By open speech and simple,
    An hundred times made plain,
To seek another's profit
    And work another's gain.

Take up the White Man's burden—
    The savage wars of peace—
Fill full the mouth of Famine,
    And bid the sickness cease;
And when your goal is nearest
    (The end for others sought)
Watch sloth and heathen folly
    Bring all your hope to nought.

Take up the White Man's burden—
    No iron rule of kings,
But toil of serf and sweeper—
    The tale of common things.

The ports ye shall not enter,
  The roads ye shall not tread,
Go, make them with your living
  And mark them with your dead.

Take up the White Man's burden,
  And reap his old reward—
The blame of those ye better
  The hate of those ye guard—
The cry of hosts ye humour
  (Ah, slowly!) toward the light:—
"Why brought ye us from bondage,
  Our loved Egyptian night?"

Take up the White Man's burden—
  Ye dare not stoop to less—
Nor call too loud on Freedom
  To cloke your weariness.
By all ye will or whisper,
  By all ye leave or do,
The silent sullen peoples
  Shall weigh your God and you.

Take up the White Man's burden!
  Have done with childish days—
The lightly-proffered laurel,
  The easy ungrudged praise:
Comes now, to search your manhood
  Through all the thankless years,
Cold, edged with dear-bought wisdom,
  The judgment of your peers.

SELECTION

A Spread-eagle Imperialist Orator:
Albert J. Beveridge, "The March of the Flag"

On April 20, 1898, Congress passed a resolution of war against Spain and President William McKinley signed it. Slightly more than three months later, the Spanish government requested the United States to name its peace terms, and on August 12 Spanish and American representatives signed a protocol that brought an end to all fighting, ceded Puerto Rico to the United States, freed Cuba from Spanish rule, and called for a peace conference to be held in Paris. The protocol provided that American forces would continue to occupy Manila (American forces did not control the rest of the Philippines) but deferred the whole question of the islands until the conference at Paris. Almost immediately after hostilities ceased, imperialists and anti-imperialists began campaigns for their positions. The ensuing debate is one of the more important debates in the history of American foreign policy.

"The March of the Flag" was very much a campaign speech, an emotional oratorical exercise designed to whip Republican enthusiasm to fever pitch as well as to persuade the uncommitted voter. Thus a considerable part of the speech, which Beveridge used to open the campaign in Indianapolis on September 16, 1898, was a condemnation of the Democratic free-silver plank of 1896. The voters had rejected free silver when McKinley defeated William Jennings Bryan, and apparently Albert J. Beveridge was unwilling to discard a popular, although not entirely timely, issue. Beveridge had a personal stake in a Republican victory in Indiana in 1898. If Republicans controlled the new Legislature, they would choose him to represent the state in the United States Senate. The Republicans did win, in fact, and sent Beveridge to Washington.

But "The March of the Flag" was above all a plea for imperialism, and this quite apart from its partisanship. Republicans were by no means unanimous for annexation of the Philippines and building an imperial system. Beveridge used his powers in the campaign to advance imperialist sentiment both within his party and with the public at large. In this speech Beveridge offered his audience many arguments for imperialism. He used the economic argument explicitly and rode it hard, but he was equally vigorous and a good bit more poetic with the argument that Americans had a responsibility to govern the Philippines, a responsibility that devolved upon them as Anglo-Saxons, as developers of liberal governmental institutions, as builders of a "soap-and-water, common school civilization of energy and industry." And besides the arguments of duty and commercial desire there was destiny, an argument long favored by American expansionists. America's planting the flag in the Philippines was as much the work of fate as had been its expansion from the Atlantic to the Pacific. When to this formula was added an appeal to racial superiority, the resulting mixture became heady indeed. In one sentence Beveridge touched upon most of his noneconomic arguments: "And the burning question of this campaign is, whether the American people will accept the gifts of events;

whether they will rise, as lifts their soaring destiny; whether they will proceed upon the lines of national development surveyed by the statesmen of our past, or whether, for the first time, the American people doubt their mission, question fate, prove apostate to the spirit of their race, and halt the ceaseless march of free institutions." Little wonder that Beveridge, in the words of a contemporary newspaper account, "literally carried the house by storm" and that frequently "his auditors felt their emotions overpowering them."

Born in 1862, Beveridge had graduated from Asbury College (now DePauw University) and had practiced law in Indianapolis. During his two terms in the Senate, from 1899 to 1911, he became nationally known as an outstanding progressive. He was one of the organizers of the Progressive party in 1912 and gave the keynote address at the convention that nominated ex-President Theodore Roosevelt. Beveridge was an unsuccessful candidate for governor of Indiana in that election. He turned then to the writing of biography. His four-volume life of John Marshall, published from 1916 to 1919, remains a standard work. His life of Abraham Lincoln, although unfinished at Beveridge's death in 1927, was published in two volumes the next year.

"The March of the Flag" is reprinted here as it first appeared in print in the Indianapolis Journal *on September 17, 1898. Beveridge subsequently shortened it a little, principally by reducing the economic references to a minimum, and polished it by changing a few words here and there. The slightly different version appears in a volume of Beveridge speeches,* The Meaning of the Times and Other Speeches *(Indianapolis: Bobbs-Merrill, 1908), pages 47–57. The standard biography of Beveridge is Claude Bowers,* Beveridge and the Progressive Era *(Boston: Houghton Mifflin, 1932).*

Fellow-citizens—It is a noble land that God has given us; a land that can feed and clothe the world; a land whose coast lines would inclose half the countries of Europe; a land set like a sentinel between the two imperial oceans of the globe; a greater England with a nobler destiny. It is a mighty people that He has planted on this soil; a people sprung from the most masterful blood of history; a people perpetually revitalized by the virile workingfold of all the earth; a people imperial by virtue of their power, by right of their institutions, by authority of their heaven-directed purposes, the propagandists and not the misers of liberty. It is a glorious history our God has bestowed upon His chosen people; a history whose keynote was struck by Liberty Bell; a history heroic with faith in our mission and our future; a history of statesmen, who flung the boundaries of the Republic out into unexplored lands and savage wildernesses; a history of soldiers, who carried the flag across blazing deserts and through the ranks of hostile mountains, even to the gates of sunset; a history of a multiplying people, who overrun a continent in half a century; a history divinely logical, in the process of whose tremendous reasoning we find ourselves to-day.

Therefore, in this campaign the question is larger than a party question. It is an American question. It is a world question. Shall the American people continue their resistless march toward the commercial supremacy of the world? Shall free institutions broaden their blessed reign as the children of liberty wax in strength until the empire of our principles is established over the hearts of all mankind? Have we no mission to perform —no duty to discharge to our fellow-man? Has the Almighty Father endowed us with gifts beyond our deserts, and marked us as the people of His peculiar favor, merely to rot in our own selfishness, as men and nations must who take cowardice for their companion and self for their deity—as China has, as India has, as Egypt has? Shall we be as the man who had one talent and hid it, or as he who had ten talents and used them until they grew to riches? And shall we reap the reward that waits on the discharge of our high duty as the sovereign power of earth; shall we occupy new markets for what our farmers raise, new markets for what our factories make, new markets for what our merchants sell—aye, and, please God, new markets for what our ships shall carry? Shall we avail ourselves of new sources of supply of what we do not raise or make, so that what are luxuries to-day will be necessities to-morrow? Shall we conduct the mightiest commerce of history with the best money known to man, or shall we use the pauper money of Mexico, China and the Chicago platform? Shall we be worthy of our mighty past of progress, brushing aside, as we have always done, the spider webs of technicality, and march ever onward upon the highway of development, to the doing of real deeds, the achievement of real things, and the winning of real victories?

The Leading Question

In a sentence, shall the American people indorse at the polls the American administration of William McKinley, which, under the guidance of Divine Providence, has started the Republic on its noblest career of prosperity, duty and glory; or shall the American people rebuke that administration, reverse the wheels of history, halt the career of the flag and turn to that purposeless horde of criticism and carping that is assailing the government at Washington? Shall it be McKinley, sound money and a world-conquering commerce, or Bryan, Bailey, Bland and Blackburn, a bastard currency and a policy of commercial retreat? In the only foreign war this Nation has had in two generations, will you, the voters of this Republic and the guardians of its good repute, give the other nations of the world to understand that the American people do not approve and indorse the administration that conducted it? These are the questions you must answer at the polls, and I well know how you will answer them. The thunder of American guns at Santiago and Manila will find its answer in the approval of the voters of the Republic. For the administration of William McKinley, in both peace and war, will receive the mightiest indorsement of a grateful people ever registered. In both peace and war, for we rely on the new birth of national prosperity as well as on the new birth of national glory. Think of both! Think of our country two years ago and think of it to-day!

Two years and more ago American labor begged for work; to-day employment calls for mine, factory and field. Two years and more ago money fled from the fingers of enterprise; to-day money is as abundant as demand and interest is at the lowest point in all the history of trade. Two years and more ago bonds were sold to syndicates in sudden emergencies to save the Nation's credit; in 1898, bonds were sold to the people in the emergency of war, to rescue the oppressed and redeem benighted lands. In 1896, we exported gold in obedience to the natural laws of finance; in 1898, we exported bayonets in obedience to the natural law of liberty. In 1894, the American people fought each other in strikes and insurrections because of misunderstandings born of the desperation of the times; in 1898, united and resistless, capitalist and workingman, side by side, in trench and charge, the American people fought the last great pirate of the world, in a war holy as righteousness. Two years and more ago, error-blinded and hatred-maddened men sought to create classes among the people, declared the decadence of American manhood and proclaimed the beginning of the end of the Republic; to-day proves that patriots are the only class this country knows, that American manhood is as virile under Santiago's sun as it was among the snows of Valley Forge, despite its slanderers, and that the real career of history's greatest Republic has only just begun.

A moment ago I said that the administration of William McKinley had been guided by a providence divine. That was no sacrilegious sentence. The signature of events proves it. This man of destiny has amazed the world. He was nominated as the apostle of protection; in two months, he was the standard bearer of the Nation's honor. He was elected as the representative of the conservative force of the Republic; in two years he filled the world with the thunder of the Republic's guns and the heavens with the unfurled flag of liberty. This man, whom the world regarded as a single-issue statesmen, as a tariff-schedule expert, gave to his countrymen the ablest argument in finance since Hamilton; rebuked the silver pirates of the Senate with utterance rich with the eloquence of truth; caught up the tangled lines of a diplomatic situation, vexed with infinite complication and inherited blunders; gave mankind a noble example of patient tact; taught the nations their first lesson in the diplomacy of honest speech; refused to be stampeded into conflict until the thunderbolts of war were forged; launched them at last when time had sanctified our cause before the bar of history, and preparation had made them irresistible; and now, in the hour of victory, clear-eyed and unelate, marks out the lines of our foreign policy as the soon-to-be supreme power of the world, and gives to the flag its rightful dominion over the islands of the sea. From protection to foreign war! From the insular and isolated to the world-embracing and universal! From the temporary and incidental to the essential, the permanent and the eternal; Who dares say God's hand has not guided him? Who will fail to say amen with his vote to the administration and career of the last American President of the nineteenth century—McKinley, the master statesman of his day!

Some of the Facts

What are the great facts of this administration? Not a failure of revenue, not a perpetual battle between the executive and legislative departments of the government; not a rescue from dishonor by European syndicates at the price of tens of millions in cash and national humiliation unspeakable. But a war has marked it, the most holy ever waged by one nation against another; a war for civilization; a war for a permanent peace; a war which, under God, although we knew it not in the beginning, has swung open to the Republic the portals of the commerce of the world. And the first question you must answer with your vote is whether you indorse that war. We are told that all citizens and every platform indorse the war, and I admit, with the joy of patriotism, that this is true. But that is only among ourselves—and we are of and to ourselves no longer. This election takes place on the stage of the world, with all earth's nations for our auditors. If the administration is defeated at the polls, will England believe that we have accepted the results of the war? Will Germany, that sleepless searcher for new markets for her factories and fields, and therefore the effective meddler in all international complications—will Germany be discouraged from interfering with our settlement of the war, if the administration is defeated at the polls? Will Russia, that weaver of the webs of commerce into which province after province and people after people falls, regard us as a steadfast people if the administration is defeated at the polls? The world is observing us to-day. Not a foreign office in Europe that is not studying the American Republic and watching the American elections of 1898 as it never watched an American election before. Are the American people the chameleon of the nations? "If so, we can easily handle them," say the diplomats of the world. Which result, say you, will have the best effect for us upon the great powers that watch us with the jealousy strength always inspires—a defeat at the hands of the American people of the administration which has conducted our foreign war to a world-embracing success, and which has in hand the most important foreign problems since the revolution, or, such an indorsement of the administration by the American people as will swell to a national acclaim? No matter what your views on the Dingley or the Wilson laws; no matter whether you favor Mexican money or the standard of this Republic; we must deal from this day on with nations greedy of every market we are to invade; nations with statesmen trained in craft; nations with ships and guns and money and men. Will they sift out the motive for your vote, or will they consider the large result of the indorsement, or rebuke of the administration? I repeat, it is more than a party question. It is an American question. It is an issue in which history sleeps. It is a situation which will influence the destiny of the Republic.

There is an issue in the war which affects ourselves. Shall we indorse the administration on the conduct of the war? What of its conduct? Men declared that McKinley was too slow; he waited still. Politicians, willing to buy votes with some other man's blood, called him coward; unmoved, the President pleaded with Spain to let the oppressed go. Bass-drum orators and bowie-knife editors denounced him as apostate to liberty; he silently held his course. A great party's unwise leaders lifted the slogan of "On to Havana"; before the hour had struck, the chief magistrate pursued the policies of peace. But while, in and out of his party, men, powder-brained and politics-mad, stormed; while a solid opposition denounced; while the world looked on with inquiry, William McKinley silently prepared. He had been to war himself, and he knew you must have powder before you can fire a gun; you must have provisions before you can feed soldiers; you must have a cause before you can fling the flags of battle out before the eyes of men; and you must let time and events ripen your cause before you make your declaration on it. William McKinley meant it to be a war of victory. William McKinley meant that the record should be made up before the grim judgment was pronounced; and then— then, when the day was full, when ships were manned, and coasts defended, and powder purchased, and all was ready for battle—then, our soldier-President hurled the navy and army of the Republic upon the hosts of Spain and smote them West and East like the avenging hand of Fate. History will tell our children the result—Manila, Santiago, Dewey, Sampson, Schley and peace—peoples freed, new lands acquired, the geography of the earth remade by liberty, henceforth the master map-maker of the world.

And, yet, have we peace? Does not the cloud of war linger on the horizon? If it does not—if only the tremendous problems of peace now under solution remain, ought not the administration be supported in its fateful work by the indorsement of the American people? Think of England abandoning its Ministry at the moment it was securing the fruits of a successful war! Think of Germany rebuking Bismarck at the moment he was dictating terms of peace to France! What would America say of them if they should do such a deed of mingled insanity, perfidy and folly? What would the world say of America if, in the very midst of peace negotiations, upon which the nations are looking with jealousy, fear and hatred, the American people should rebuke the administration in charge of those peace negotiations and place a hostile House and Senate in Washington? God forbid! When a people show such inconstancy, such childish fickleness as that, their career as a power among nations is a memory.

No Change of Leaders

But, if possible, war lurks in the future, what then? Shall we forsake our leaders at the close of a campaign of glory and on the eve of new campaigns for which it has prepared? Yet, that is what the success of the opposition to the government means. What is that old saying about the idiocy of him who changed horses while crossing a stream? It would be like discharging a workman because he was efficient and true. It would be like court-martialing Grant and dismissing his heroes in dishonor because they took Vicksburg.

Ah! The heroes of Vicksburg and Peace Tree Creek, Atlanta, Mission Ridge, the Wilderness and all those fields of glory, of suffering and of death. Soldiers of '61! A generation has passed and you have reared a race of heroes worthy of your blood—heroes of El Caney, San Juan and Cavite, of Santiago and Manila! Aye, and two hundred thousand more as brave as they who waited in their camps with an agony of impatience the call to battle, ready to count the hellish hardship of the trenches—the very sweets of fate—if they could only fight for the flag. For every tented field was full of Hobsons, Roosevelts, Wheelers and their men; full of the kind of soldiers that, in regiments of rags, starving, with bare feet in the snows of winter, made Valley Forge immortal; full of the same kind of boys that endured the hideous hardships of the civil war, drank from filthy roadside pools as they marched through swamps of death, ate food alive with weevils, and even corn picked from the horses' camps, slept in the blankets of the blast with sheets of sleet for covering, breakfasted with danger and dined with death and came back—those who did come back—with a laugh and a shout and a song of joy, true American soldiers, pride of their country and envy of the world. For that is the kind of boys the soldiers of 1898 are, notwithstanding the slanders of politicians and the infamy of a leprous press which try to make the world believe that our soldiers are suckling babes and womanish weaklings, and our government in war a corrupt machine, fattening off the suffering of our armies. In the name of patriotism I arraign these maligners of the soldierhood of our Nation. I call to the witness stand that Bayard of our armies, General Joe Wheeler. I call that Hotspur of the South, Fitzhugh Lee. I call the 200,000 men, themselves, who went to war for the business of war. And I put all these against the vandals of politics who are blackening their fame as soldiers and as men. I call history to the witness stand. In the Mexican war the loss from every cause was 25 per cent, and this is on incomplete returns; in the present war the loss from every cause is only 3 per cent. In the Mexican war the sick lay naked on the ground with only blankets over them, and were buried with only a blanket around them. Of the volunteer force 5,423 were discharged for disability and 3,229 died from disease. When Scott marched to Mexico only 96 men were left out of one regiment of 1,000. The average of a Mississippi company was reduced from 90 to 30 men. From Vera Cruz to Mexico a trail of sick and dying marked his line of march. General Taylor publicly declared that in his army five men died from sickness for every man killed in battle. The three months men lost nearly 9 per cent.; the six months men lost 14 per cent., the 12 months men, 29 per cent.; the men enlisted for the war lost 37 per cent.; 31,914 soldiers enlisted for the war and 11,914 of these were lost, of whom 7,369 are unaccounted for. In the war for the Union—no, there is no need of figures here. Go to the fields of Gettysburg and ask. Go ask that old veteran how fever's fetid breath breathed on them and disease rotted their blood. But in the present war, thank God, the loss and suffering is less than in any war in all the history of the world.

And if any needless suffering there has been, any deaths from criminal neglect, any hard condition not a usual incident of sudden war by a peaceful people has been permitted, William McKinley will see that the responsible ones are punished. Although our loss was less than the world ever knew before, although the condition of our troops was better than in any conflict of our history, McKinley, the just, has appointed from both parties a commission of the most eminent men in the Nation to lay the facts before him. Let the investigation go on; and when the report is made the people of America will know how black as midnight is the sin of those who, for purposes of politics, have shamed the hardihood of the American soldiers before the world, demoralized our army in the face of the enemy, and libeled the government at Washington to delighted and envious nations. And think of what was done! Two hundred and fifty thousand men suddenly called to arms; men unused to the life of camps; men fresh from the soft comforts of the best homes of the richest nation on earth. Those men equipped, transported to camps convenient for instant call to battle; waiting there the command which any moment might have brought; supplies purchased in every quarter of the land and carried hundreds, even thousands of miles; uniforms procured, arms purchased, ammunition bought, citizens drilled into the finest soldiery on the globe; a war fought in the deadliest climate in the world, beneath a sun whose rays means madness, and in Spanish surroundings, festering with fever—and yet the least suffering and the lowest loss ever known in the chronicles of war. What would have been the result if those who would have plunged us into war before we could have prepared at all could have had their way? What would have happened if those warriors of peace who denounced the President as a traitor when he would not send the flower of our youth against Havana, with its steaming swamps of fever, its splendid outworks and its 150,000 desperate defenders—what would have happened if they could have had their way? The mind shrinks and sickens at the thought. Those regiments which we greeted the other day with our cheers of pride would not have marched back again. All over this weeping land the tender song, "We shall meet but we shall miss him, there will be one vacant chair," would have risen once again from desolated homes. And the men who would have done this are the men who are assailing the government at Washington to-day and blaspheming the reputation of the American soldier. But the wrath of the people will pursue them. The scorpion whips of the furies will be as a caress to the deep damnation of those who seek a political issue in defaming the manhood of the Republic. God bless the soldiers of '98, children of the heroes of '61, descendants of the heroes of '76. In the halls of history they will stand side by side with those sons of glory, and the opposition to the government at Washington shall not deny them.

None Shall Be Robbed

No! they shall not be robbed of the honor due them nor shall the Republic be robbed of what they won for their country. For William McKinley is continuing the policy that Jefferson began, Monroe continued, Seward advanced, Grant promoted, Harrison championed, and the growth of the Republic has demanded. Hawaii is ours; Porto Rico is to be ours; at the prayer of its people Cuba will finally be ours; in the islands of the east, even to the gates of Asia, coaling stations are to be ours; at the very least the flag of a liberal government is to float over the Philippines, and it will be the stars and stripes of glory. And the burning question of this campaign is, whether the American people will accept the gifts of events; whether they will rise, as lifts their soaring destiny; whether they will proceed upon the lines of national development surveyed by the statesmen of our past, or whether, for the first time, the American people doubt their mission, question fate, prove apostate to the spirit of their race, and halt the cease-less march of the institutions?

The opposition tells us that we ought not to govern a people without their consent. I answer, the rule of liberty that all just government derives its authority from the consent of the governed, applies only to those who are capable of self-government. We govern the Indians without their consent; we govern our Territories without their consent; we govern our children without their consent. I answer, would not the natives of the Philippines prefer the just, humane, civilizing government of this Republic to the savage, bloody rule of pillage and extortion from which we have rescued them? Do not the blazing fires of joy and the ringing bells of gladness in Porto Rico prove the welcome of our flag? And, regardless of this formula of words made only for enlightened, self-governing peoples, do we owe no duty to the world? Shall we turn these peoples back to the reeking hands from which we have taken them? Shall we abandon them to their fate with the wolves of conquest all about them? Shall we save them from those nations, to give them a self-rule of tragedy? It would be like giving a razor to a babe and telling it to shave itself. It would be like giving a typewriter to an Esquimau and telling him to publish one of the great dailies of the world.

They ask us how we will govern these new possessions. I answer, out of local conditions and the necessities of the case methods of government will grow. If England can govern foreign lands so can America. If Germany can govern foreign lands so can America. If they can supervise protecto-rates so can America. Why is it more difficult to administer Hawaii than New Mexico or California? Both had a savage and an alien population; both were more remote from the seat of government when they came under our domination than Hawaii is to-day. Will you say by your vote that American ability to govern has decayed, that you are an infidel to American vigor and practical sense? Or that we are of the ruling race of the world; that ours is the blood of government; ours the heart of dominion; ours the brain and the genius of administration? We do but what our fathers did—but pitch the tents of liberty farther westward, farther south-ward; we only continue the march of the flag.

The march of the flag! In 1789 the flag of the Republic waved over 4,000,000 souls in thirteen States, and this a savage territory which stretched to the Mississippi, to Canada, to the Floridas. The timid minds of that day said that no new territory was needed, and for the hour they were right. But under the lead of Jefferson we acquired the territory which sweeps from the Mississippi to the mountains, from Texas to the British possessions, and the march of the flag began. The infidels to the gospel of liberty raved, but the flag swept on. The title to that noble land out of which Oregon, Washington, Idaho and Montana have been carved was uncertain. Jefferson obeyed the Anglo-Saxon impulse within him and an-other empire was added to the Republic and the march of the flag went on. Those who deny the power of free institutions to expand urged every argument, and more, that we hear to-day, but the march of the flag went on. A screen of land from New Orleans to Florida shut us from the gulf, and over this and the everglade peninsula waved the saffron flag of Spain. Andrew Jackson seized both, the American people stood at his back, and under Monroe the Floridas came under the dominion of the Republic, and the march of the flag went on. The Cassandras prophesied every prophecy of despair we hear to-day, but the march of the flag went on. Then Texas responded to the bugle calls of liberty and the march of the flag went on. And at last we waged war with Mexico and the flag swept over the southwest, over peerless California, past the gate of gold to Oregon on the north, and from ocean to ocean its folds of glory blazed. And now, obeying the same voice that Jefferson, Jackson, Seward heard and obeyed, Grant and Harrison heard and obeyed, William McKinley plants the flag over the islands of the sea, and the march of the flag goes on.

Discarded Arguments

Distance and oceans are no longer arguments. The fact that all the territory our fathers bought and seized is contiguous is no longer argument. In 1819 Florida was further from New York than Porto Rico is from Chicago to-day; Texas further from Washington in 1845 than Hawaii is from Boston in 1898; California more inaccessible in 1847 than the Philippines are now. Gibraltar is further from London than Havana is from Washington; Melbourne is further from Liverpool than Manila is from San Francisco. The ocean does not separate us from the lands of our duty and desire—the ocean to join us, a river never to be dredged, a canal never to be repaired. Steam joins us; electricity joins us—the very elements are in league with our destiny. Cuba not contiguous! Porto Rico not contiguous! Hawaii and the Philippines not contiguous! Our navy will make them contiguous. Dewey and Sampson and Schley have made them contiguous and American speed, American guns, American heart and brain and nerve will keep them contiguous forever.

But there is a difference. We did not need the western Mississippi valley when we acquired it, nor Florida, nor Texas, nor California, nor the royal provinces of the far Northwest. We had no emigrants to people this vast wilderness, no money to develop it, even no highways to cover it. No trade awaited us in its savage fastnesses. Our productions were not greater than our internal trade. There was not one reason for the land lust of our statesmen from Jefferson to Harrison other than the prophet and the Saxon within them. But, to-day, we are raising more than we can use. Therefore, we must find new markets for our produce, new occupation for our capital, new work for our labor. And so, while we did not need the territory taken during the past century at the time it was acquired, we do need what we have taken in 1898, and we need it now. Think of the thousands of Americans who will invade the Philippines when a liberal government shall establish order and equity there. Think of the hundreds of thousands of Americans who will build a soap-and-water, common school civilization of energy and industry in Cuba, when a government of law replaces the double reign of anarchy and tyranny. Think of the prosperous millions that empress of islands will support when, obedient to the law of political gravitation, her people ask for the highest honor liberty can bestow—the sacred order of the stars and stripes, the citizenship of the great Republic!

How will all this help each one of us? Our trade with Porto Rico and

Hawaii will be as free as between the States of the Union, because they are American soil, while every other nation must pay our tariff before they can compete with us. Our trade with Cuba and the Philippines will, at the very least, be like the preferential trade of Canada with England— a trade which will give the Republic the preference over the rest of the world—a trade which will apply the principle of protection to colonial commerce. That and the excellence of our goods and products will give the monopoly of these markets to the American people. And, then, the factories, and mills, and shops will call again to their hearts of fire the workingmen of the Republic, to receive once more the wages and eat once more the bread of prosperous times; then the farmer will find at his door once more the golden home market of those who work in factory and mill, and who want flour, and meat, and butter, and eggs, and garments of wool, and who have once more the money to pay for it all. It means new employment and better wages for every laboring man in the Union. It means higher prices for every item the farmers of this Republic produce. It means active investment for every dollar of moldy capital in the land. It means all this, to-morrow, and all this forever because it means, not only the trade of these prize provinces, but the beginning of the commercial empire of the Republic.

Great Fact of the Future

The commercial empire of the Republic! That is the greatest fact of the future. And that is why these islands involve considerations larger than their own commerce. The commercial supremacy of the Republic means that this Nation is to be the sovereign factor in the peace of the world. For the conflicts of the future are to be conflicts of trade—struggles for markets—commercial wars for existence. And the golden rule of peace is impregnability of position and invincibility of preparation. So we see England, the greatest strategist of history, plant her flag and her cannon on Gibraltar, at Quebec, the Bermudas, Vancouver—everywhere—until from every point of vantage her royal banner flashes in the sun. So Hawaii furnishes us a naval base in the heart of the Pacific; the Ladrones of sunset and of commerce; Manila, another, at the gates of Asia—Asia, to the trade of whose hundreds of millions American merchants, American manufacturers, American farmers have as good a right as those of Germany, or France, or Russia, or England; Asia, whose commerce with England alone amounts to hundreds of millions of dollars every year; Asia, to whom Germany looks to take the surplus of her factories, and foundries, and mills; Asia, whose doors shall not be shut against American trade! Within two decades the bulk of Oriental commerce will be ours—the richest commerce in the world. In the light of that golden future our chain of new-won stations rise like ocean sentinels from the night of waters—Porto Rico, a nobler Gibraltar; the Isthmian canal, a greater Suez; Hawaii, the Ladrones, the Philippines, commanding the Pacific! Ah! as our commerce spreads, the flag of liberty will circle the globe and the highways of the ocean-carrying trade of all mankind be guarded by the guns of the Republic. Shall this future of the race be left with those who, under God, began this career of sacred duty and immortal glory; or, shall we risk it to those who would build a dam in the current of destiny's large designs? We are enlisted in the cause of American supremacy, which will never end until American commerce has made the conquest of the world; until American citizenship has become the lord of civilization, and the stars and stripes the flag of flags throughout the world.

No wonder that in the shadow of coming events, so great, free silver is already a memory. Men understand to-day that the greatest commerce of the world must be conducted with the steadiest standard of value and most convenient medium of exchange human ingenuity can devise. Time, that unerring reasoner, has settled the silver question. Profit is an unanswerable argument. In a year or two thousands of Democratic investors will be making fortunes developing our Island interest; tens of thousands of Democratic farmers will be selling their pork and beef and wheat to the teeming millions that will pour into the Antilles and the gardens of the Pacific and to the home market our foreign trade will create; tens of thousands of Democratic workingmen will be at work in our factories and not a Democrat of them will consent to be paid in any money but the best. Silver is to-day as innocuous as fiat paper money.

Silver Fiatism

And why should not free silver be as dead as fiat paper money? It is the same proposition in a different form. If the government stamp can make a piece of silver which you can buy for 45 cents pass for 100 cents, that stamp can make a piece of paper worth a fraction of a cent pass for 100 cents. Free silver is the principle of fiat money applied to metal. And the American people have learned the fallacy of fiat money. If the government can create value out of nothing, why is all taxation not abolished? If revenue can be turned out of a printing press or stamp machine, why have a tariff for either revenue or protection? If the government can fix the ratio between gold and silver at 16 to 1 by law, when it is 35 or 40 to 1 in the market, why not fix the ratio at 1 to 1, make the silver dollar a more convenient size and sixteen times more plentiful? If free coinage makes 45 cents' worth of silver really worth 100 cents, how will that raise the price of anything but silver? And how will that help anybody but the silver mine owner? And if free coinage will not make 45 cents of silver really worth 100 cents, if that piece of silver still remains worth only 45 cents, is that the kind of a dollar you want your wages paid in? Is that the kind of a dollar you want to sell your crops for? And if it is not the stamp of the government which raises the value, but the demand which free coinage creates, why has the value of silver gone down at a time when more silver is coined by the government than ever before? And if the people want more silver, why do they refuse to use what we already have? And if free silver makes money more plentiful, how will you get any of it? Will the silver mine owner give it to you? Will the government give or loan it to you? Where do you or I come in on this free silver proposition?

Apply the principle to yourself as well as to the government. If you are to be paid in a dollar worth two-fifths of its face, why not slip a false bottom into your bushel measure and sell two-fifths of a bushel for a full bushel of grain? Why not work three hours and call it a day if they give you 45 cents' worth of silver and call it a dollar? And if the government lies two-fifths in declaring that 45 cents is 100 cents, why not lie three-thirds and declare that nothing at all is 100 cents? Why not make a fiat dollar? And if they pay you a fiat dollar why not give a fiat bushel of wheat or a fiat day of labor? Why not just quit altogether; make money, like hell's pavements, out of good resolutions; stamp ourselves rich; pitch silver and gold into the sea; abolish hunger by statute and solve the money question by the imagination and the will?

Do you think it safe to trust the precious business prosperity of this country to men who believe that this Nation should go to the silver standard of the Aztec republic? Is it safe to tamper with the standard to which the vast and delicate machinery of our commercial civilization is adjusted? Is it safe to disturb the measure with reference to which every contract is made, every policy of insurance issued, every value estimated? Is it safe to again experiment with our returning prosperity? Have we not learned our lesson well enough in the terrible school of a people's woes.

And yet I thank God for the financial baptism of fire the American people passed through in 1896. Why? Because it started them to thinking and the American people never start to thinking and stop half way through the syllogism. And the American people are going to think this money question clear through and settle it forever. If the American laborer wants his wages paid and the farmer the price of his products paid in the best money, he wants that fact fixed in the laws of the Nation. No man wants any mistake about the kind of standard we have. Therefore we want it written in the laws of the Republic that a dollar of gold is this Nation's standard of value, which nothing but the sovereign people can change. To-day we have nothing but a resolution that all our money shall be kept as good as gold—a resolution no President is bound to obey. When Cleveland was President, Stevenson was Vice President, and Olney was secretary of state. Our whole financial system rested on the life of Grover Cleveland. If he had died, Stevenson, a free-silver man, would have become President, and would have hurled us to a silver basis in a day. If Stevenson had died, Olney, a gold man, would have become President, and would have lifted us to a gold standard in the dip of a pen. No people on earth could endure that. And now, the American people are aroused to their danger, and they will fix their standard by law where no conspiracy of mine owners and demagogues will ever be tempted to dislodge it by the election of a President; they will fix their standard by law where no power can alter it but the people themselves. And whoever is opposed to that proposition is opposed to a "government of the people, for the people and by the people."

Basis of Our Finances

The heart of our financial system, to-day, is the Nation's resolution to keep all our money just as good as gold. Back of that resolution stands the government's reserve of gold, ready to make that resolution good, just as the reserve of cash in your bank makes good its promise to pay your check. That gold reserve and the Nation's pledge to maintain it, gives the whole world confidence in all the variegated money of the Republic, just as your bank's reserve gives you confidence in its present solvency. When you can no longer get gold for your greenbacks or treasury notes, they are no longer good as gold. To-day, practically, a gold dollar ultimately stands back of every dollar of the Republic's money. And so, upon that gold reserve— upon the government's ability to pay out gold upon demand—rests the honor of the Nation and the safety of every dollar in the land.

And yet that gold reserve is, to-day, in danger from every buccaneer of finance in the world. For when greenbacks are redeemed in gold at the treasury, they must be issued again in payment of the government's expenses, and so they go back, finally, to the hands of the man who drew gold out of the treasury with them. And when the gold reserve goes down by redeeming those greenbacks, the government must sell bonds to get gold to replace that which the greenbacks have drawn out, unless the tariff puts enough gold into the treasury to keep the reserve intact. And so, when the financial spiders of the world see our revenue so reduced that it cannot keep our gold reserve full if attached, they gather the greenbacks into their hands, get gold for them at the treasury, force the government to borrow gold on the Nation's bonds to replace the gold they have just drawn out with that very gold, and so secure the best investment known to man. And then those greenbacks once more go into circulation, once more get into the pirates' hands, and once more serve as the tools of financial villainy. William McKinley says that condition shall not continue; that if any man gets gold out of the treasury, by paying in a greenback, he shall not get that greenback out again, until he pays gold back into the treasury for it. William McKinley says that the revenue laws of the Nation shall be so framed that a ceaseless stream of gold, pouring into the treasury, will prove to the gamblers in the Nation's honor that any raid on the Nation's gold will meet inevitable defeat. He favors such a tariff as will prevent the Bill Sykes, and the Fagins of finance from trying to open the Republic's treasury with a greenback for a jimmy.

Now on the threshold of our career as the first power of earth, is the time to permanently adjust our system of finance. The American people have the most tremendous tasks of history to perform. They have the mightiest commerce of the world to conduct. They cannot halt their progress of wealth and power to unsettle their money system at the command of ignorance. Think of Great Britain becoming the commercial monarch of the world with her financial system periodically assailed! Think of Holland or Germany or France yet sending their flag in every sea, with their money at the mercy of politicians seeking for an issue! Sixteen to one is passed in our career. Why go back to it like the victim of opium to his deadly pipe? Now, when new rivers of gold are pouring through the fields of business, the foundation of all silver-standard argument that there is not enough gold, is swept away. Why mumble the meaningless phrases of a tale that is told when the golden future is before us, the world calls us, its wealth awaits us and God's command is on us? There are so many real things to be done—canals to be dug, railways to be laid, forests to be felled, cities to be built, unviolated fields to be tilled, priceless markets to be won, ships to be launched, peoples to be saved, civilization to be proclaimed and the flag of liberty flung to the eager air of every sea. Is this an hour to waste upon triflers with Nature's laws? Is this a season to give our destiny over to word mongers and prosperity wreckers? No! It is an hour to remember your duty to the home. It is a moment to realize the opportunities Fate has opened to this favored people and to you. It is a time to bethink you of the conquering march of the flag. It is a time to bethink you of your Nation and its sovereignty of the seas. It is a time to remember that the God of our fathers is our God and that the gifts and the duties He gave to them, enriched and multiplied. He renews to us, their children. It is a time to sustain that devoted man, servant of the people and of the most high God, who is guiding the Republic out into the ocean of infinite possibilities. It is a time to cheer the beloved President of God's chosen people, till the whole world is vocal with American loyalty to the American government and William McKinley, its head and chief.

Fellow-Americans, we are God's chosen people. Yonder at Bunker Hill and Yorktown His providence was above us. At New Orleans and on ensanguined seas His hand sustained us. Abraham Lincoln was His minister; and His was the altar of freedom the boys in blue set up on a hundred smoking battlefields. His power directed Dewey in the east, and He delivered the Spanish fleet into our hands on Liberty's natal day as He delivered the elder Armada into the hands of our English sires two centuries ago. His great purposes are revealed in the progress of the flag, which surpasses the intentions of Congresses and Cabinets, and leads us, like a holier pillar of cloud by day and pillar of fire by night, into situations unforeseen by finite wisdom and duties unexpected by the unprophetic heart of selfishness. The American people cannot use a dishonest medium of exchange; it is ours to set the world its example of right and honor. We cannot fly from our world of duties; it is ours to execute the purpose of a fate that has driven us to be greater than our small intentions. We cannot retreat from any soil where Providence has unfurled our banner; it is ours to save that soil for liberty and civilization. For liberty and civilization and God's promises fulfilled, the flag must henceforth be the symbol and the sign to all mankind.

SELECTION

McKinley's Postmaster General on Economic Expansion

In his 1898 speech "The March of the Flag," Albert Beveridge dwelt at least briefly upon most, if not all, of the various arguments for an expansionist foreign policy. Among them was the economic argument: Foreign markets, more

*particularly the markets of Asia, were necessary to absorb American produc-
tion, both industrial and agricultural. In the following pamphlet, a document
of the campaign of 1900, Charles Emory Smith, Postmaster General, concerned
himself almost exclusively with the economic argument. That there were obligations, responsibilities, duties, "burdens" imposed upon Americans by "the new
peoples who have come under our flag" Smith did not deny; but it was fortunate, he said, that the path of America's duty coincided with the path of
America's economic advantage. As he saw it, " . . . the moral mandate and the
material interest completely blend. . . ."*

*Postmaster General Smith gave his readers a quick lesson in American
economic history from the Civil War to the end of the century. Just after
Appomattox, American production had been vastly inferior to that of the leading powers of the Old World. But in the course of one generation American
industry had grown so rapidly that its production was considerably greater
than that of any other nation. Indeed, it was already equal to the combined
manufactures of Great Britain, France, and Germany and was growing twice
as fast. The United States had once been dependent upon imports for manufactured goods, but by the end of the century the nation had come to export more
manufactured goods than it imported. When the nation's manufactured exports
first exceeded its manufactured imports, the country's concern for foreign
markets became critical. Larger foreign markets became a prerequisite for full
production and continued industrial growth. As Smith put it, "Either we must
halt our growth, limit our production, bank our fires and stop our spindles,
reduce our labor and restrict our capital, with all the hardship that this involves,
or else we must find broader markets and expanded consumption." China was
the most promising place to search for new markets, and control of the Philippines was necessary for economic penetration of the Asian mainland.*

*Postmaster General Smith produced his pamphlet as a campaign document,
and it was imperative that he make its message clear to all. Consequently, he
spelled out the economic advantage that lay in expanding foreign markets for
the most numerous sections of the electorate, farmers and industrial workers.
He reminded farmers that they, like industrialists, produced more than the
domestic market could absorb. Further, he said, the farmers' domestic market
depended upon the prosperity of the nation's mills and factories, which in
turn rested upon foreign trade. For industrial wage earners the lessons were
plain: Expanding markets meant full production, and full production meant
steady employment at good wages.*

*Charles Emory Smith is no memorable figure of the American past, but he
had a skill that made him a useful person to his colleagues in the Republican
party: the ability to write clearly and forcefully for a wide audience. Born
in Connecticut in 1842, he grew up in Albany, New York, and became a newspaper editor there. In the 1870s he did the actual writing of the New York
Republican platforms and in 1876 was the primary author of the GOP national
platform, a role he played again in 1896. In 1880 he became editor of the influential* Philadelphia Press. *In 1890 President Harrison appointed him Minister
to Russia, from which office he resigned in June, 1892. He returned to public
office in 1898 when President McKinley named him Postmaster General, apparently to have him near at hand as a political adviser during the Spanish-*

American War period. He remained in this post for the remainder of the McKinley administration and the first few months of President Roosevelt's first term.

Smith's pamphlet, here reproduced in shortened form, bears no place or date of publication. Internal evidence, however, establishes 1900 as the year of publication, and the first page bears the "bug," or union label, of the Allied Printing Trades Council of Cleveland.

"THE WORLD'S MARKETS HAVE BEEN OPENED TO
AMERICAN PRODUCTS."—WILLIAM MCKINLEY.

AMERICAN INDUSTRIAL EXPANSION.

WE HAVE OUTSTRIPPED THE OLD WORLD AND HAVE
THE GREATEST MARKETS IN OUR GRASP.

SHALL WE BANK OUR FIRES?

VAST FOREIGN TRADE IS POSSIBLE—OF HIGHEST IMPORTANCE TO FARMERS AND
WAGE-EARNERS—EVENTS HAVE RULED US AND IT IS FOR
US TO RULE THE RESULTS.

The great overmastering fact in the material development of the world during the past quarter of a century is the marvelous industrial expansion of the United States. Our country had long been foremost among nations in agricultural products. Whether cotton or wheat or corn was king, in any case we held the scepter. Our great domain, our fertile soil and our varied climate gave us the unrivaled mastery.

But in everything outside of the earth's rich bounty the young Republic had yet its commanding place to make. Thirty years ago we were only at the threshold of our wonderful material growth. We had just emerged from the struggle and sacrifices and burdens of a long civil war, and had just entered upon the promise and the fruits of a regenerated Union and a peaceful development. We had achieved our political independence, but our economic independence was yet to be secured. Our manufactures were to be built up, our mines to be opened, our railroads to be constructed. We applied a true American policy, directed to the defence and advancement of American interests, and under its banner we proceeded to the great work of internal upbuilding.

Have Outstripped the Old World

The result is the mightiest industrial expansion the world has ever seen. This is the miracle-working age of steam and electricity. Under the potent application of these magic forces the whole civilized world has been bounding forward with astonishing strides. The great nations of the Old World had a long start in the race. They possessed accumulated capital and established industries and fixed markets. And yet, notwithstanding these advantages, they have been far outstripped by the puissant young Republic of the New World.

Among the industrial powers of the earth we now stand pre-eminent and unrivaled. We have gained a manufacturing supremacy which is altogether unapproached. We first aimed at the full control of our home market, which is the best of all markets, and when we had made ourselves its uncontested masters, when we produced enough and more than enough to supply its requirements, we were compelled to take the outward look. The moment our manufactured exports exceeded our manufactured imports that moment we passed beyond the possession of our domestic field to the demand for foreign markets. It showed that at length we had a surplus which must find its outlet. The pregnant hour when our exports of manufactures passed our imports came in 1898, and in the striking march of events that are not ruled by any mere chance, that very year witnessed the war with Spain which, as its unexpected and unavoidable result brought us the great opportunity of commercial outlet for which the princes of business had already begun to look, but which the keenest vision had never foreseen.

Moral Duty Paramount

The first and paramount obligation connected with the war is the moral duty growing out of it. Above all other considerations are the moral responsibilities of our new position. We owe a duty to our American character and honor. We owe a duty to the new peoples who have come under our flag. We must above all things be true to the principles of liberty and justice and right. These obligations have been and will be thoroughly considered, but it does not fall within my present purpose to discuss them. Recognizing the moral duty as supreme, I do not hesitate to say that President McKinley has made it his guiding rule in dealing with all the transcendent questions which have grown out of our new possessions.

But when we have met the highest requirement of the moral standard, there is no code of ethics and no rule of statesmanship which excludes consideration of the commercial interests involved in our public policy. It is the obligation of the Government first of all to be right; it is also its obligation to promote the advantage and welfare of its own people; and when the two fully coincide and harmonize, when the moral mandate and the material interest completely blend, the policy is doubly wise and the duty doubly commanding. Such is our present position. We should be recreant to our American manhood if we did not bravely fulfill the mission of humanity and civilization which the war has bequeathed to us. We should be strangely blind to our American interests if we did not recognize the requirements of our phenomenal industrial expansion and see the marvelous opportunity of commercial expansion thus made necessary which is opened before us.

American Economic Superiority

Let me ask your attention to our remarkable position of economic superiority and to the imperative demands which grow out of it. Familiar as we are with the legend of our national growth, we do not realize its stupendous proportions until we analyze and measure it by comparison. In 1870 the annual value of our manufactures was $3,700,000,000; now it is about $12,000,000,000. For half a century England had been the workshop of the world, and we had only just begun. Still we had got such a start that in 1870 the manufactures of the United States just about equaled those of Great Britain. But since then our growth has been so prodigious that now our manufactures amount to two and a half times the total volume of British manufactures, and equal those of Great Britain, Germany and France put together. The increase in the annual American product within thirty years has been double the combined increase of those three great nations of Europe. In other words, if you match the United States against Great Britain, Germany and France together, our manufactures are now equal to all theirs and are growing twice as fast. We are manufacturing nearly two-thirds as much as all Europe, with its 380,000,000 people, and more than one-third of all that is manufactured in the world.

If you take the whole range of industries, including agriculture, mining, transportation and even commerce, wherein alone we are behind, the proportions stand about the same. The aggregate value of all American industries is more than double that of Great Britain, three times that of France and two and a half times that of Germany. It is one-half that of all Europe combined. With this enormous industrial expansion the national wealth of the United States grows proportionately. In 1860 our aggregate wealth was but little more than half that of Great Britain, less than half that of France, and only about half that of the nations that made up the German Empire. Now it is a third greater than Great Britain's, double Germany's and nearly double that of France. Within forty years the United States has gained over 67,000 millions in wealth, while Great Britain, France and Germany together have gained less than 60,000 millions.

National Earnings of the United States

The figures of our national earnings dazzle the imagination. Last year we earned about 14,500 million dollars, of which more than one-half was the wages of labor. The earnings of labor in the United States to-day are greater than the combined earnings of capital and labor together in Great Britain. Labor was never as well rewarded as in this prosperous year. As compared with the years 1893, 1894 and 1895, the average earnings of labor now are in the ratio of 127 to 81. That is, they are nearly 60 per cent. greater than they were five years ago. The whole country is striding forward by leaps and bounds. The twenty million dollars granted to Spain in connection with the Philippines was paid by what the country earns in half a day. The nation's earnings in a single year like the present are equivalent to more than one-half its entire accumulated wealth in 1870; that is, to more than one-half of all that it had saved and put into all forms of property during the first eighty years of its existence as a nation.

If we did not spend more freely than other peoples, if we did not maintain a higher general standard of comfort, education and good living, our savings would be stupendous. But, on the other hand, under such limitations we should not have such power of earning. As it is, our annual gain is two thousand million dollars, and every succeeding working day sees the United States over $6,000,000 better off that it was the day before. We have multiplied our capital more than threefold since 1870, and to its present vast proportions we shall in the next ten years add as much as the entire capital of the nation was in 1870. With this rapid and tremendous expansion of capital and of the product of labor, is there to be no expansion of its opportunity and its outlets?

When we pass from these broad outlines to the particular factors, the astonishing growth and the superior position of the United States are emphasized. Iron and steel are everywhere recognized as the basic fabrics and the surest index of industrial power. Fifteen years ago the United States made only half as much pig iron as Great Britain, and only a little more than Germany. Within that short period our gain has been equal to the combined gain of the two great iron nations of Europe; we now make 50 per cent. more than either, and we have leaped so far to the front that we make more than one-third of all the iron that is made in the world. The same thing is true of steel. Last year we produced twice as much steel as Great Britain, though fifteen years ago our product was less than hers; and while Germany has outstripped Great Britain, we are 60 per cent. ahead of Germany. We make half as much steel as all other nations put together.

America Commands the Future

Not only do we hold the present mastery, but we command the future because we possess the elements of continued industrial supremacy. Our unused resources are even more remarkable and significant than our present achievements. Coal and iron ore are the raw material and the foundation of iron and steel production. The coal fields of Great Britain embrace 9,300 square miles, and those of Germany 3,000 square miles. But how mighty seem the potentialities of the United States when we remember that our total coal area covers 200,000 square miles, and that even when we limit it to the quantity of coal which enters into the manufacture of iron, it still reaches the stupendous figures of more than 70,000 square miles, or 20,000 square miles more than the entire area of England! Our coal production has rapidly advanced until we now mine as much as Great Britain and nearly one-third of all that is mined in the world. Great Britain exports 40,000,000 tons, or one-fifth of her entire product, while we consume practically all of ours and export only 4,000,000 tons. As our illimitable fields are opened and foreign fields are reduced, our capability of supplying the world will become more and more marked. Even now we are reading in the public press of the coal famine in Europe, and of the great demand for American coal.

The facts as to iron ore are much the same. Great Britain used about 18,000,000 tons in 1898, but she had to import one-third of it, or 6,000,000 tons. On the other hand, the United States produced 19,000,000 tons, and used all of it within her borders. In the lake regions we have a wealth of ore beds which are practically inexhaustible, and which, with our boundless coal fields, assure our increasing and enduring supremacy as an industrial power. We have not yet gained the same lead in textiles. But, though we began fifty years ago with a valued product only one-seventh of Great Britain's, only one-fifth of France's and only one-half of Germany's, we have now caught up to Great Britain and nearly equal France and Germany combined. Our predominance will become as signal in this field as in metals. English authorities point out the fact that there is a serious depreciation in cotton mills at Manchester, that no new capital enters the trade and that employment is decreasing. But in South Carolina alone twenty-six new cotton mills have been established within the past year, many more being doubled in capacity, while in the whole South 5,000,000 spindles have been set up, standing for an investment of $125,000,000. Much of this new development springs from the new opportunity in the East, for which alone 1,000,000 spindles have been added.

American Genius and Invention

Nor does American superiority end here. When England was rising to her industrial leadership she had the advantage of new mechanical forces. The continent was paralyzed and prostrate for a quarter of a century under the blight of the Napoleonic wars. While thus free from all competitive rivalry England, through the skill of her Watts and Arkwrights and Stephensons, applied new mechanical power to the productive processes and became the unchallenged workshop of the world. It was estimated at that time that one pair of hands in England, with these efficient agencies, had the productive energy and value of ten pairs of hands on the continent. The United States has a similar, though less signal advantage now. American genius and invention and adaptability have given our industries a completeness and perfection of mechanical equipment which greatly multiply their productive power. A single broad fact demonstrates the superiority. In Europe 45,000,000 operatives and artisans were employed in 1895 in producing the annual aggregate of manufactured articles valued at seventeen thousand million dollars, or $380 apiece. In the United States at the same time 6,000,000 operatives produced goods worth ten thousand millions, or about $1,666 apiece, or more than four times as much as an operative in Europe.

This superior equipment and producing power, man for man, explains why we can pay higher wages and still compete with the nations of the Old World on their own ground and in their own markets. It is the secret of the comfort of American labor, the key of American enterprise, and the talisman of American expansion. It explains why, within a few months, American shops have placed a goodly number of locomotives on English railways. It explains why we are sending American machinery to Sheffield and Birmingham, and why our rails are found in Manchuria and Siberia, in India and Africa. The antiquity which enshrines the Pyramids looks down through forty centuries on the American electric road that carries the troops of visitors to their base, and the mystery of the silent Sphinx must now well-nigh yield its secret in wonder at the new riddle of the youngest civilization and people peacefully invading and conquering the oldest. The British Government needed a great steel bridge nearly a quarter of a mile long, across the Abbarra for Kitchener, and needed it at once; the British manufacturers required seven months to build it; American constructors asked seven weeks, and Philadelphia sent the bridge. This superior alertness, adaptability and equipment distinguish general American enterprise. It has a plant which beats the world, and it must find the market for its product. . . .

Since 1870, while our population has doubled, our manufactures have quadrupled. Our producing capacity is up to and beyond the measure of our consuming ability and is increasing faster. Though we are foremost in industrial growth, yet all the great nations have been advancing rapidly, and it is estimated that, under the application of modern forces and of improved machinery, the producing capacity of the world is such that, if operated to its full extent ten hours a day, enough would be produced in six months to supply the world's demand for a year. Just now, with the great revival of business following the depression and the depletion which went on from 1893 to 1897, the production may not outrun the demand. But it is the part of prudence to deal with broad and lasting conditions, and to prepare to-day for the requirements of to-morrow.

What, then, are we to do? Are we to restrict production? Are we to run mill and factory on reduced time, with the necessary sequences of lower wages, smaller profits and wide discontent? Or are we to provide for this enormous and expanding output by supplementing our own vast, but unequal measure of consumption with new outlets and new markets? Under this stress and in this rivalry the other great nations are struggling for empire and making opportunities for trade. They are eagerly extending their colonial dependencies in order to make new regions tributary to their commerce. England has raised her flag over 16,000,000 square miles of domain, with more than 300,000,000 people; France holds 2,500,000 square miles, with a population of nearly 50,000,000, and Germany has secured 1,600,000 square miles, with more than 7,000,000 inhabitants.

The Open Door in China

The United States has no need to engage in this territorial rivalry with the object of commercial opportunity. We have made an opportunity larger than all these in securing the open door in China. There we find the greatest potential new market in the world. There we find a population of three to four hundred millions who are just breaking away from their old barriers and coming into the sphere of the world's trade. The annual imports of China are less than fifty cents a head. When Japan entered upon her new career her imports did not exceed that small ratio, but within a few years and under her new impulse they have increased to six dollars a head. Let China advance in the same proportion and her imports will rise to $1,500,000,000 a year—more than the United States now sends to all the nations of the world. Give us an equal chance and a merchant marine, and we shall secure a large share of that coming traffic. The open door gives us an equal chance; the merchant marine should become a great feature of our public policy, and every other advantage we already have. We are nearest China; we hold the other coast of the Pacific; we have secured natural stations on the way across, and that great ocean is our legitimate highway of commerce.

Our exports to China and Japan have increased 256 per cent. in the last ten years. The largest part of that increase has come within the last three years. The movement thus inaugurated can, with care and wise direction, be multiplied tenfold. China wants our wheat and flour; she wants our cotton goods; she wants our oil; she wants our fabrics of iron and steel; she wants our rails and locomotives and equipment for the thousands of miles of railroads she will construct within the coming period. The Southern States have a special interest in the acquisition of this market. It offers the most important outlet for their growing cotton industries. In nine months of last year China imported from the United States 182,875,000 yards of plain American cotton goods against 112,480,000 yards for the same period of 1898. The imports from England for the same time showed an actual decline. In 1898 the cotton imports into China from the United States were 37 per cent. of those from England. In 1899 they were 61 per cent. At that rate of increase how long, if we rightly use our opportunity, will it take the United States to become foremost in the Chinese market? The possibilities of that market are incalculable. In 1886 Japan purchased foreign goods to the value of only $16,000,000. Last year her purchases rose to $137,000,000. What boundless fields lie before us in China and all the Orient, if we are not so weak and blind as to throw them away!

A Vast Trade Is Possible

The open door in China is the open sesame of this vast possible trade, and the American accomplishment of the open door, with the consent and pledge of all the great nations, and without the necessity of entering into any territorial division, is the greatest of all recent achievements of diplomacy. It secures for the United States a commercial opportunity which is immeasurable. It provides one of the great outlets which our industrial supremacy and our enormous producing capacity require. And that achievement is the great and magnificent fruit of our triumph at Manila and our possession of the Philippines. It comes because we have established our footing in the Orient, because we have planted ourselves for a thousand miles along the front of China, and because we have taken a new position as a world power. Such a demand on our part two years ago would have been impotent and fruitless. Three years ago England proposed the policy of the open door in China and failed, and was compelled in protection of her interests to declare that she would join the scheme of division and claim her sphere of influence. But when the United States unfurled her flag in the Philippines and made the world resound with the echoes of her swift success and her brilliant triumphs on the sea, and then put forward the same demand of an open door it met with a prompt and full acceptance. Nay, more, it is not too much to say that our possession of the Philippines has stayed the threatened dismemberment of China, and has perhaps altogether averted that danger. But whether China is to be divided and parcelled among the struggling and competing nations, or whether she is to remain intact with the possibilities of a great development, the guarantee of the open door which has been given to us, secures our rights and our interests in the coming time. No fancy can overestimate the value of that achievement in its relations to our future commercial advancement. The potency of that commercial opportunity is worth immeasurably more than all the cost of the Spanish war and all the cost of the subsequent conflict in the Philippines.

I might dwell upon the value of the Philippines themselves. I might speak of the enlarged trade which is offered in their own fertility and their own richness when once brought under the peaceful sway of good government and of civilizing development. But valuable as they are, their highest significance lies in the fact that they give us a foothold in the Orient and constitute a commercial and naval base, at the very vestibule of China, for a commercial opportunity and expansion which were far beyond our wildest dreams two years ago. If we were to falter in the policy we have undertaken, if we were to shrink from the responsibility which, without our seeking, has come upon us, we should lose all the prestige of that splendid triumph and should sacrifice all that we have gained as its precious fruit. We should find that the door which has been opened to us would soon be closed, for a nation which does not respect itself, and which does not appreciate its own destiny, will not be respected by others. We should find ourselves with the almost unbounded producing capacity which I have imperfectly described, a capacity already beyond our consuming ability and growing much faster, and at the same time cut off in large measure from the new outlets and new markets which it requires and without which it must be curtailed and crippled.

Our Farming Interests Concerned

The great farming interests of the country have a vital concern in this question. We outstrip the world in industrial equipment, but other nations have land as fertile and productive. As recently as 1885, Argentina produced only 14,000,000 bushels of wheat a year; now she grows 60,000,000. Our wheat fields find export rivals in Argentina, Russia and India. Our farmers thus have need, as well as our manufacturers, of the new outlet of China. Every bushel of wheat and every barrel of flour shipped from the Pacific coast across the western ocean relieves the competition at Liverpool, which fixes the price. Above all, the farmers are supremely interested that our industrial power shall be maintained at its highest capacity. They are prosperous when our manufactures are prosperous; they find the best demand when our mills and factories are busiest, and any failure of our industrial production to find full consumption would be a disastrous blow to their welfare. In the same way the interests of the workingmen are bound up with this great national movement to secure new outlets. Make new markets and keep your productive power fully employed, and labor gets its highest reward; but restrict your production because you will not seek or accept new channels of consumption, and labor suffers with the rest.

Highest Importance to Wage-earners

It is of the highest importance to the workingmen of our country that they should thoroughly understand the vital relation of this policy of commercial expansion to their immediate welfare. No portion of our people are more directly interested in it than they are. What they want is the most active and constant operation of our industrial machinery. That means steady employment for labor; that means good wages; that means comfort and happiness for themselves and their families. If we can produce more than we can consume at home, if we should have a surplus that would be unsalable unless we could find markets for it abroad, then it follows that the labor which produces that surplus is deeply concerned in a national policy which opens such outlets. Capital can stand restriction; labor cannot. The manufacturer can live, with reduced product; but reduced product means idle hands for the workingman. What labor wants and must have, then, is the largest field and opportunity for American enterprise everywhere. . . .

Shall We Bank Our Fires?

Either we must halt our growth, limit our production, bank our fires and stop our spindles, reduce our labor and restrict our capital, with all the hardship that this involves, or else we must find broader markets and expanded consumption. Do you tell me there is cost and possible difficulty in this extension abroad? But is there not greater cost and loss in a paralyzing restriction at home with its diminished employment and wide discontent? Do you tell me there are risks and perplexities in this policy of commercial expansion? But are there not greater and graver perplexities and dangers, which may only be suggested, in a policy of industrial contraction with its direct hardships? Which is the better—to accept the expansion which has come to us as the result of the Spanish war, which is the natural continuation of our former expansions, and which is on the direct line of a new and necessary commercial development, or to reject it and to declare that we will shut ourselves up within ourselves, with all its inevitable consequences of impaired prestige, lost markets, restricted trade, reduced labor and unhappy conflict?

Let us fully realize the mighty facts of our national situation. Had there been no war with Spain, had the new and glorious May morn of American liberty never shed its luster over the Bay of Manila, had no victory of Santiago brought a brilliant triumph of peace charged with great responsibilities, we should still have been compelled to look beyond our continental bounds. It was inevitable that we should advance out of our isolation and turn our faces outward to the world. Our transcendent industrial growth and its imperative need of outlets demanded it. . . .

SELECTION

William Jennings Bryan, "Imperialism"

As this document makes abundantly clear, imperialists had no monopoly on eloquence or on the disposition to appeal to their listeners' emotions. And although an imperialist such as Beveridge appealed to American traditions to buttress his argument, the anti-imperialist Bryan to an even greater extent drew upon American history to justify his diametrically opposed position. Indeed, one of the major anti-imperialist arguments, an argument which Bryan dwelt upon at length in his speech, was that to embark upon an imperialist course would be to betray the traditions of the American Revolution. The Revolutionary fathers, he argued, had not revolted from one empire in order to establish another. Bryan cited earlier opponents of the Democratic party, such as the Whigs Webster and Clay and the Republican Lincoln, with full approval; but the contemporary Republicans, the Democratic standard-bearer asserted, had deserted American tradition. "The Republican party has accepted the European idea and planted itself upon the ground taken by George III and by every ruler who distrusts the capacity of the people for self-government, or denies them a voice in their own affairs." Another often-employed anti-imperialist argument that Bryan used in this speech was opposition to militarism, which anti-imperialists held was inherent in colonialism. But much of Bryan's speech—and much of the effort of the anti-imperialists generally—was devoted merely to replying to imperialist arguments. Here the advocates of annexation and expansion had an advantage: Beveridge, Charles Emory Smith, and others thrust; Bryan only parried. Bryan was capable of a telling sentence —"Destiny is the subterfuge of the invertebrate who, lacking the courage to oppose error, seeks some plausible excuse for supporting it"—but Beveridge had already set the general terms of the debate, had introduced destiny as an argument, and had stirred imaginations more than Bryan's counteractions ever were able to.

Bryan and the Democratic party were at another disadvantage in the debate on imperialism: They accepted the economic goals of expansionists and only argued that territorial annexation was not necessary to achieve commercial success. Bryan could refer to the Republican position as "sordid," but he could not even appear to be against profitable trade. "The Democratic party is in favor of the expansion of trade. It would extend our trade by every legitimate and peaceful means; but it is not willing to make merchandise of human blood."

Near the beginning of this speech Bryan raised the complicated matter of his support of the Treaty of Paris when it was before the Senate for ratification and of the Bacon Resolution. This requires clarification. The United States and Spain concluded the treaty on December 10, 1898. Under the terms of the treaty, Spain ceded the Philippines to the United States for a payment of 20 million dollars. The Senate considered ratification of the treaty early in 1899. In January there was introduced the Bacon Resolution, to which Bryan referred in this speech. It declared that the United States would grant the Philippines independence as soon as order prevailed in the islands. The Senate took no action on the proposed resolution before the Filipino nationalists, led by Emilio Aguinaldo, on February 4, 1889, began an insurrection against Ameri-. can control of the archipelago. On February 6, 1899, the Senate ratified the Treaty of Paris by a vote of 57 to 27, exceeding by 2 votes the two-thirds majority necessary for ratification. Despite Bryan's opposition to annexation of the Philippines, he went to Washington, as he explained in the following selection, and urged his followers to vote for ratification. His argument was that the treaty was acceptable despite its failure to provide Philippine independence and that independence could be granted after ratification. On February 14 the proposal to grant Philippine independence came to a Senate vote for the first time. The voting resulted in a tie, and the Republican Vice President, Garret A. Hobart, cast the deciding ballot against independence. Subsequently the Senate adopted the McEnery Resolution, which stated that the United States had not permanently annexed the Philippines and would "in due time" make such arrangements in the islands "as will best promote the interests of the citizens of the United States and the inhabitants of said islands."

This speech, which Bryan delivered in Indianapolis upon formal notification that the Democratic party had again nominated him for the Presidency, is reproduced as it appeared in the Indianapolis Journal *on August 9, 1900. During the campaign the Democrats issued the speech in pamphlet form under the title* Imperialism.

Mr. Chairman and Members of the Notification Committee—I shall, at an early date and in a more formal manner, accept the nomination which you tender, and I shall at that time discuss the various questions covered by the Democratic platform. It may not be out of place, however, to submit a few observations at this time upon the general character of the contest before us and upon the question which is declared to be of paramount importance in this campaign.

When I say that the contest of 1900 is a contest between democracy on the one hand and plutocracy on the other, I do not mean to say that all our opponents have deliberately chosen to give to organized wealth a predominating influence in the affairs of the government, but I do assert that on the important issues of the day the Republican party is dominated by those influences which constantly tend to elevate pecuniary considerations and ignore human rights. In 1859 Lincoln said that the Republican party believed in the man and the dollar, but that in case of conflict it believed in the man before the dollar. This is the proper relation which should exist between the two. Man, the handiwork of God, comes first; money, the handiwork of man, is of inferior importance. Man is the master, money is the servant, but upon all important questions to-day Republican legislation tends to make money the master and the man the servant. The maxim of Jefferson, "Equal rights to all and special privileges to none," and the doctrine of Lincoln that this should be a government "of the people, by the people, and for the people" are being disregarded and the instrumentalities of government are being used to advance the interests of those who are in a position to secure favors from the government.

The Democratic party is not making war upon the honest acquisition of wealth; it has no desire to discourage industry, economy and thrift. On the contrary, it gives to every citizen the greatest possible stimulus to honest toil when it promises him protection in the enjoyment of the proceeds of his labor. Property rights are most secure when human rights are respected. Democracy strives for a civilization in which every member of society will share according to his merits. No one has a right to expect from society more than a fair compensation for the service which he renders to society. If he secures more it is at the expense of someone else. It is no injustice to him to prevent his doing injustice to another. To him who would, either through class legislation, or in the absence of necessary legislation, trespass upon the rights of another, the Democratic party says, "Thou shalt not."

The Opposition

Against us are arrayed a comparatively small but politically and financially powerful number who really profit by Republican policies, but with them are associated a large number who because of their attachment to the party name are giving their support to doctrines antagonistic to the former teachings of their own party. Republicans who used to advocate bimetallism now try to convince themselves that the gold standard is good; Republicans who were formerly attached to the greenback are now seeking an excuse for giving national banks control of the Nation's paper money; Republicans who used to boast that the Republican party was paying off the national debt are now looking for reasons to support a perpetual and increasing debt; Republicans who formerly abhorred a trust now beguile themselves with the delusion that there are good trusts and bad trusts, while in their minds the line between the two is becoming more and more obscure; Republicans who in times past congratulated the country upon the small expense of our standing army are now making light of the objections which are urged against a large increase in the permanent military establishment; Republicans who gloried in our independence when the Nation was less powerful now look with favor upon a foreign alliance; Republicans who three years ago condemned "forcible annexation" as immoral and even criminal are now sure that it is both immoral and criminal to oppose forcible annexation. That partisanship has already blinded many to present dangers is certain; how large a portion of the Republican party can be drawn over to the new policies remains to be seen.

For a time Republican leaders were inclined to deny to opponents the right to criticise the Philippine policy of the administration, but upon investigation they found that both Lincoln and Clay asserted and exercised the right to criticise a President during the progress of the Mexican war. Instead of meeting the issue boldly and submitting a clear and positive plan for dealing with the Philippine question, the Republican convention adopted a platform, the larger part of which was devoted to boasting and self-congratulation. In attempting to press economic questions upon the country to the exclusion of those which involve the very structure of our government, the Republican leaders give new evidence of their abandonment of the earlier ideals of the party and of their complete subserviency to pecuniary considerations.

Why He Favored the Treaty

But they will not be permitted to evade the stupendous and far-reaching issue which they have deliberately brought into the arena of politics. When the President, supported by a practically unanimous vote of the House and Senate, entered upon a war with Spain for the purpose of aiding the struggling patriots of Cuba, the country, without regard to party, applauded. Although the Democrats recognized that the administration would necessarily gain a political advantage from the conduct of a war which, in the very nature of the case, must soon end in a complete victory, they vied with the Republicans in the support which they gave to the President. When the war was over and the Republican leaders began to suggest the propriety of a colonial policy, opposition at once manifested itself. When the President finally laid before the Senate a treaty which recognized the independence of Cuba, but provided for the cession of the Philippine islands to the United States, the menace of imperialism became so apparent that many preferred to reject the treaty and risk the ills that might follow rather than take the chance of correcting the errors of the treaty by the independent action of the country.

I was among those who believed it better to ratify the treaty and end the war, release the volunteers, remove the excuse for war expenditures, and then give to the Filipinos the independence which might be forced from Spain by a new treaty. In view of the criticism which my action aroused in some quarters I take this occasion to restate the reasons given at that time. I thought it safer to trust the American people to give independence to the Filipinos than to trust the accomplishment of that purpose to diplomacy with an unfriendly nation. Lincoln embodied an argument in the question when he asked, "Can aliens make treaties easier than friends can make laws?" I believe that we are now in a better position to wage a successful contest against imperialism than we would have been had the treaty been rejected. With the treaty ratified a clean-cut issue is presented between a government by consent and a government by force, and imperialists must bear the responsibility for all that happens until the question is settled. If the treaty had been rejected the opponents of imperialism would have been held responsible for any international complications which might have arisen before the ratification of another treaty. But whatever differences of opinion may have existed as to the best method of opposing the colonial policy there never was any difference as to the great importance of the question, and there is no difference now as to the course to be pursued.

The Bacon Resolution

The title of Spain being extinguished, we were at liberty to deal with the Filipinos according to American principles. The Bacon resolution, introduced a month before hostilities broke out at Manila, promised independence to the Filipinos on the same terms that it was promised to the Cubans. I supported this resolution, and believe that its adoption prior to the breaking out of hostilities would have prevented bloodshed, and that its adoption at any subsequent time would have ended hostilities. If the treaty had been rejected, considerable time would have necessarily elapsed before a new treaty could have been agreed upon and ratified, and during that time the question would have been agitating the public mind. If the Bacon resolution had been adopted by the Senate and carried out by the President, either at the time of the ratification of the treaty or at any time afterward, it would have taken the question of imperialism out of politics and left the American people free to deal with their domestic problems. But the resolution was defeated by the vote of the Republican Vice President, and from that time to this a Republican Congress has refused to take any action whatever in the matter. When hostilities broke out at Manila, Republican speakers and Republican editors at once sought to lay the blame upon those who had delayed the ratification of the treaty, and during the progress of the war the same Republicans have accused the opponents of imperialism of having given encouragement to the Filipinos. This is a cowardly evasion of responsibility.

If it is right for the United States to hold the Philippine islands permanently and imitate European empires in the government of colonies, the Republican party ought to state its position and defend it, but it must expect the subject races to protest against such a policy and to resist to the extent of their ability. The Filipinos do not need any encouragement from Americans now living. Our whole history has been an encouragement, not only to the Filipinos but to all who are denied a voice in their own government. If the Republicans are prepared to censure all who have used language calculated to make the Filipinos hate foreign domination, let them condemn the speech of Patrick Henry. When he uttered that passionate appeal. "Give me liberty or give me death," he expressed a sentiment which still echoes in the hearts of men. Let them censure Jefferson; of all the statesmen of history, none have used words so offensive to those who would hold their fellows in political bondage. Let them censure Washington, who declared that the colonists must choose between liberty and slavery. Or, if the statue of limitations has run against the sins of Henry and Jefferson and Washington, let them censure Lincoln, whose Gettysburg speech will be quoted in defense of popular government when the present advocates of force and conquest are forgotten.

Evils of Conquest

Someone has said that a truth once spoken can never be recalled. It is true. It goes on and on, and no one can set a limit to its ever widening influence. But if it were possible to obliterate every word written or spoken in defense of the principles set forth in the Declaration of Independence, a war of conquest would still leave its legacy of perpetual hatred, for it was God himself who placed in every human heart the love of liberty. He never made a race of people so low in the scale of civilization or intelligence that it would welcome a foreign master. Those who would have this nation enter upon a career of empire must consider not only the effect of imperialism on the Filipinos, but they must also calculate its effect upon our own nation. We cannot repudiate the principle of self-government in the Philippines without weakening that principle here. Lincoln said that the safety of this nation was not in its fleets, its armies or its forts, but in the spirit which prizes liberty and the heritage of all men, in all lands, everywhere; and he warned his countrymen that they could not destroy this spirit without planting the seeds of despotism at their own doors.

Now we are beginning to see the paralyzing influence of imperialism. Heretofore, this Nation has been prompt to express its sympathy with those who were fighting for civil liberty. While our sphere of activity has been limited to the western hemisphere, our sympathies have not been bounded by the seas. We have felt it due to ourselves and to the world, as well as to those who were struggling for the right to govern themselves, to proclaim the interest which our people have, from the date of their own independence, felt in every contest between human rights and arbitrary power. Three-quarters of a century ago, when our Nation was small, the struggles of Greece aroused our people and Webster and Clay gave eloquent expression to the universal desire for Grecian independence. In 1896, all parties manifested a lively interest in the success of the Cubans, but now when a war is in progress in South Africa, which must result in the extension of the monarchical idea or in the triumph of a republic, the advocates of imperialism in this country dare not say a word in behalf of the Boers. Sympathy for the Boers does not arise from any unfriendliness toward England; the American people are not unfriendly toward the people of any nation. This sympathy is due to the fact that, as stated in our platform, we believe in the principle of self-government and reject, as did our forefathers, the claims of monarchy. If this Nation surrenders its belief in the universal application of the principles set forth in the Declaration of Independence, it will lose the prestige and influence which it has enjoyed among the nations as an exponent of popular government.

Jefferson's Views

Our opponents, conscious of the weakness of their cause, seek to confuse imperialism with expansion, and have even dared to claim Jefferson as a supporter of their policy. Jefferson spoke so freely and used language with such precision that no one can be ignorant of his views. On one occasion he declared: "If there be one principle more deeply rooted than any other in the mind of every American it is that we should have nothing to do with conquest." And again he said: "Conquest is not in our principles; it is inconsistent with our government."

The forcible annexation of territory to be governed by arbitrary power differs as much from the acquisition of territory to be built up into States as a monarchy differs from a democracy. The Democratic party does not oppose expansion when expansion enlarges the area of the Republic and incorporates land which can be settled by American citizens, or adds to our population people who are willing to become citizens and are capable of discharging their duties as such. The acquisition of the Louisiana territory, Florida, Texas and other tracts which have been secured from time to time enlarged the Republic, and the Constitution followed the flag into the new territory. It is now proposed to seize upon distant territory already more densely populated than our own country, and to force upon the people a government for which there is no warrant in our Constitution or our laws. Even the argument that this earth belongs to those who desire to cultivate it and have the physical power to acquire it cannot be invoked to justify the appropriation of the Philippine islands by the United States. If the islands were uninhabited American citizens would not be willing to go there and till the soil. The white race will not live so near the equator. Other nations have tried to colonize in the same latitude. The Netherlands have controlled Java for 300 years, and yet to-day there are less than 60,000 people of European birth scattered among 25,000,000 natives. After a century and a half of English domination in India less than one-twentieth of 1 per cent. of the people of India are of English birth, and it requires an army of 70,000 British soldiers to take care of the tax collectors. Spain has asserted title to the Philippine islands for three centuries, and yet, when our fleet entered Manila bay, there were less than 10,000 Spaniards residing in the Philippines.

Meaning of Colonial Policy

A colonial policy means that we shall send to the Philippines a few traders, a few task masters and a few officeholders and an army large enough to support the authority of a small fraction of the people while they rule the natives. If we have an imperial policy we must have a large standing army as its natural and necessary complement. The spirit which will justify the forcible annexation of the Philippine islands will justify the seizure of other islands and the domination of other people, and with wars of conquest we can expect a certain if not rapid growth of our military establishment. That a large permanent increase in our regular army is intended by the Republican leaders is not a mere matter of conjecture but a matter of fact. In his message of Dec. 5, 1898, the President asked for authority to increase the standing army to 100,000. In 1896 the army contained about 25,000 men. Within two years the President asked for four times that many and a Republican House of Representatives complied with the request after the Spanish treaty had been signed and no country was at war with the United States. If such an army is demanded when an imperial policy is contemplated but not openly avowed what may be expected if the people encourage the Republican party by indorsing its policy at the polls? A large standing army is not only a pecuniary burden to the people and, if accompanied by compulsory service, a constant source of irritation, but it is ever a menace to a Republican form of government. The army is the personification of force, and militarism will inevitably change the ideals of the people and turn the thoughts of our young men from the arts of peace to the science of war. The government which relies for its defense upon its citizens is more likely to be just than one which has at call a large body of professional soldiers. A small standing army and a well equipped and well disciplined State militia are sufficient in ordinary times, and in an emergency the Nation should in the future as in the past place its dependence upon the volunteers who come from all occupations at their country's call and return to productive labor when their services are no longer required—men who fight when the country needs fighters and work when the country needs workers.

Demands Discussion

The Republican platform assumes that the Philippine islands will be retained under American sovereignty, and we have a right to demand of the Republican leaders a discussion of the future status of the Filipino. Is he to be a citizen or a subject? Are we to bring into the body politic eight or ten million Asiatics, so different from us in race and history that amalgamation is impossible? Are they to share with us in making the laws and shaping the destiny of this nation? No Republican of prominence has been bold enough to advocate such a proposition. The McEnery resolution, adopted by the Senate immediately after the ratification of the treaty, expressly negatives this idea. The Democratic platform described the situation when it says that the Filipinos cannot be citizens without endangering our civilization. Who will dispute it? And what is the alternative? If the Filipino is not to be a citizen, shall we make him a subject? On that question the Democratic platform speaks with emphasis. It declares that the Filipino cannot be a subject without endangering our form of government. A republic can have no subjects. A subject is possible only in a government resting upon force, he is unknown in a government deriving its just powers from the consent of the governed. The Republican platform says that "the largest measure of self-government consistent with their welfare and our duties shall be secured to them (the Filipinos) by law." This is a strange doctrine for a government which owes its very existence to the men who offered their lives as a protest against government without consent and taxation without representation. In what respect does the position of the Republican party differ from the position taken by the English government in 1776? Did not the English government promise a good government to the colonists? What king ever promised a bad government to his people? Did not the English government promise that the colonists should have the largest measure of self-government with their welfare and English duties? Did not the Spanish government promise to given the Cubans the largest measure of self-government consistent with their welfare and Spanish duties? The whole difference between a monarchy and a republic may be summed up in one sentence. In a monarchy the king gives to the people what he believes to be a good government; in a republic the people secure for themselves what they believe to be a good government. The

Republican party has accepted the European idea and planted itself upon the ground taken by George III and by every ruler who distrusts the capacity of the people for self-government, or denies them a voice in their own affairs. . . .

The Title to the Philippines

What is our title to the Philippine islands? Do we hold them by treaty or by conquest? Did we buy them, or did we take them? Did we purchase the people? If not, how did we secure title to them? Were they thrown in with the land? Will the Republicans say that inanimate earth has value and when that earth is molded by the Divine hand and stamped with the likeness of the Creator it becomes a fixture and passes with the soil? If governments derive their just powers of the consent of the governed it is impossible to secure title to people either by force or by purchase. We could extinguish Spain's title by treaty, but if we hold title we must hold it by some method consistent with our ideas of government. When we made allies of the Filipinos and armed them to fight against Spain, we disputed Spain's title. If we buy Spain's title we are not innocent purchasers. But even if we had not disputed Spain's title, she could transfer no greater title than she had, and her title was based on force alone. We cannot defend such a title, but as Spain gave us a quit claim deed, we can honorably turn the property over to the party in possession. Whether any American official gave the Filipinos moral assurance of independence is not material. There can be no doubt that we accepted and utilized the services of the Filipinos and that when we did so we had full knowledge that they were fighting for their own independence, and I submit that history furnishes no example of turpitude baser than ours if we now substitute our yoke for the Spanish yoke.

Let us consider briefly the relations which have been given in support of an imperialistic policy. Some say it is our duty to hold the Philippine islands. But duty is not an argument; it is a conclusion. To ascertain what our duty is, in any emergency, we must apply well-settled and generally accepted principles. It is our duty to avoid stealing, no matter whether the thing be stolen is of great or little value. It is our duty to avoid killing a human being, no matter where the human being lives, or to what race or class he belongs. Every one recognizes the obligation imposed upon individuals to observe both the human and moral law, but as some deny the application of those laws to nations it may not be out of place to quote the opinion of others. Jefferson, than whom there is no higher political authority, said: "I know of but one code of morality for men, whether acting singly or collectively."

Franklin, whose learning, wisdom and virtue are a part of the priceless legacy bequeathed to us from the revolutionary days, expressed the same idea in even stronger language when he said: "Justice is as strictly due between neighbor nations as between neighbor citizens. A highwayman is as much a robber when he plunders in a gang as when singly; and the nation that makes an unjust war is only a great gang."

Morals and Numbers

Men may dare to do in crowds what they would not dare to do as individuals, but the moral character of an act is not determined by the number of those who join in it. Force can defend a right, but force has never yet created a right. If it was true, as declared in the resolution of intervention, that the Cubans "are and of right ought to be free and independent" (language taken from the Declaration of Independence), it is equally true that the Filipinos "are and of right ought to be free and independent." The right of the Cubans to freedom was not based upon their proximity to the United States, nor upon the language which they spoke, nor yet upon the race or races to which they belonged. Congress by a practically unanimous vote declared that the principles enunciated at Philadelphia in 1776 were still alive and applicable to the Cubans.

Who will draw a line between the natural rights of the Cubans and the Filipinos? Who will say that the former have a right to liberty and the latter have no rights which we are bound to respect? And if the Filipinos "are and of right ought to be free and independent," what right have we to force our government upon them without their consent? Before our duty can be ascertained, and when their rights are once determined, it is as much our duty to respect those rights as it was the duty of Spain to respect the rights of the people of Cuba, or the duty of England to respect the rights of the American colonists. Rights never conflict; duties never clash. Can it be our duty to kill those who, following the example of our forefathers, love liberty well enough to fight for it? Some poet has described the terror which overcame a soldier who, in the midst of battle, discovered that he had slain his brother. It is written, "All ye are brethren." Let us hope for the coming of the day when human life—which when once destroyed cannot be restored—will be so sacred that it will never be taken, except when necessary to punish a crime already committed, or to prevent a crime about to be committed.

The Highest Obligation

If it is said that we have assumed before the world obligations which make it necessary for us to permanently maintain a government in the Philippine islands. I reply, first, that the highest obligation of this Nation is to be true to itself. No obligation to any particular nation or to all nations combined can require the abandonment of our theory of government and the substitution of doctrines against which our whole national life has been a protest. And, second, that our obligations to the Filipinos who inhabit the islands are greater than any obligation which we can owe to foreigners who have a temporary residence in the Philippines or desire to trade there.

It is argued by some that the Filipinos are incapable of self-government and that therefore we owe it to the world to take control of them. Admiral Dewey in an official report to the Navy Department declared the Filipinos more capable of self-government than the Cubans and said that he based his opinion upon a knowledge of both races. But I will not rest the case upon the relative advancement of the Filipinos. Henry Clay in defending the rights of the people of South America to self-government said:

> It is the doctrine of thrones that man is too ignorant to govern himself. Their partisans assert his incapacity in reference to all nations; if they cannot command universal assent to the proposition, it is then remanded to particular nations; and our pride and our presumption too often make converts of us. I contend that it is to arraign the disposition of Providence himself, to suppose that he has created beings incapable of governing themselves, and to be trampled on by kings. Self-government is the natural government of man.

Clay was right. There are degrees of proficiency in the art of self-government, but it is a reflection upon the Creator to say that He denied to any people the capacity of self-government. Once admit that some people are capable of self-government, and that others are not, and that the capable people have a right to seize upon and govern the incapable, and you make force—brute force—the only foundation of government and invite the reign of the despot. I am not willing to believe that an all-wise and an all-loving God created the Filipinos, and then left them thousands of years helpless until the islands attracted the attention of the European nations.

Government of Colonies

Republicans ask: "Shall we haul down the flag that floats over our dead in the Philippines?" The same question might have been asked when the American flag floated over Chapultepec and waved over the dead who fell there; but the tourist who visits the City of Mexico finds there a national cemetery owned by the United States and cared for by an American citizen. Our flag still floats over our dead, but when the treaty with Mexico was signed, American authority withdrew to the Rio Grande, and I venture the opinion that during the last fifty years the people of Mexico have made more progress under the stimulus of independence and self-government than they would have made under a carpet-bag government held in place by bayonets. The United States and Mexico, friendly republics, are each stronger and happier than they would have been had the former been cursed and the latter crushed by an imperialistic policy disguised as "benevolent assimilation." . . .

Education Will Not Help

Some argue that American rule in the Philippine islands will result in the better education of the Filipinos. Be not deceived. If we expect to maintain a colonial policy we shall not find it to our advantage to educate the people. The educated Filipinos are now in revolt against us, and the most ignorant ones have made the least resistance to our domination. If we are to govern them without their consent and give them no voice in determining the taxes which they must pay we dare not educate them, lest they learn to read the Declaration of Independence and the Constitution of the United States and mock us for our inconsistency.

The principal arguments, however, advanced by those who enter upon a defense of imperialism are:

First—That we must improve the present opportunity to become a world power and enter into international politics.

Second—That our commercial interests in the Philippine islands and in the Orient make it necessary for us to hold the islands permanently.

Third—That the spread of the Christian religion will be facilitated by a colonial policy.

Fourth—That there is no honorable retreat from the position which the Nation has taken.

The first argument is addressed to the Nation's pride and the second to the Nation's pocketbook. The third is intended for the church member and the fourth for the partisan.

It is a sufficient answer to the first argument to say that for more than a century this nation has been a world power. For ten decades it has been the most potent influence in the world. Not only has it been a world power, but it has done more to affect the politics of the human race than all the other nations of the world combined. Because our Declaration of Independence was promulgated, others have been promulgated; because the patriots of 1776 fought for liberty, others have fought for it; because our Constitution was adopted, other constitutions have been adopted. The growth of the principle of self-government, planted on American soil, has been the overshadowing political fact of the nineteenth century. It has made this Nation conspicuous among the nations and given it a place in history such as no other nation has ever enjoyed. Nothing has been able to check the onward march of this idea. I am not willing that this Nation shall cast aside the omnipotent weapon of truth to seize the weapon of physical warfare. I would not exchange the glory of this Republic for the glory of all the empires that have risen and fallen since time began.

The Commercial Argument

The permanent chairman of the last Republican national convention presented the pecuniary argument in all its baldness when he said:

We make no hypocritical pretenses of being interested in the Philippines solely on account of others. While we regard the welfare of those people as a sacred trust we regard the welfare of the American people first. We see our duty to ourselves as well as to others. We believe in trade expansion. By every legitimate means within the province of government and Constitution we mean to stimulate the expansion of our trade and open new markets.

This is the commercial argument. It is based upon the theory that war can be rightly waged for pecuniary advantage and that it is profitable to purchase trade by force and violence. Franklin denied both of these propositions. When Lord Howe asserted that the acts of Parliament which brought on the revolution were necessary to prevent American trade from passing into foreign channels Franklin replied:

> To me it seems that neither the obtaining nor retaining of any trade, how valuable soever is an object for which men may justly spill each other's blood; that the true and sure means of extending and securing commerce are the goodness and cheapness of commodities, and that the profits of no trade can ever be equal to the expense of compelling it and holding it by fleets and armies. I consider this war against us, therefore, as both unjust and unwise.

I place the philosophy of Franklin against the sordid doctrine of those who would put a price upon the life of an American soldier and justify a war of conquest upon the ground that it will pay. The Democratic party is in favor of the expansion of trade. It would extend our trade by every legitimate and peaceful means; but it is not willing to make merchandise of human blood.

But a war of conquest is as unwise as it is unrighteous. A harbor and coaling station in the Philippines would answer every trade and military necessity, and such a concession could have been secured at any time without difficulty. It is not necessary to own people in order to trade with them. We carry on trade to-day with every part of the world, and our commerce has expanded more rapidly than the commerce of any European empire. We do not own Japan or China, but we trade with their people. We have not absorbed the republics of Central and South America, but we trade with them. It has not been necessary to have any political connections with Canada or the nations of Europe in order to trade with them. Trade cannot be permanently profitable unless it is voluntary. When trade is secured by force the cost of securing it and retaining it must be taken out of the profits, and the profits are never large enough to cover the expense. Such a system would never be defended but for the fact that the expense is borne by all the people, while the profits are enjoyed by the few.

Who Would Profit

Imperialism would be profitable to the army contractors; it would be profitable to the ship owners, who would carry live soldiers to the Philippines and bring dead soldiers back; it would be profitable to those who would seize upon the franchises, and it would be profitable to the officials whose salaries would be fixed here and paid over there, but to the farmer, to the laboring man and to the vast majority of those engaged in other occupations it would bring expenditure without return and risk without reward.

Farmers and laboring men have, as a rule, small incomes, and, under systems which place the tax upon consumption, pay more than their fair share of the expenses of government. Thus the very people who receive least benefit from imperialism will be injured most by the military burdens which accompany it.

In addition to the evils which he and the farmer share in common, the laboring man will be the first to suffer if Oriental subjects seek work in the United States; the first to suffer if American capital leaves our shores to employ Oriental labor in the Philippines to supply the trade of China and Japan; the first to suffer from the violence which the military spirit arouses, and the first to suffer when the methods of imperialism are applied to our own government. It is not strange, therefore, that the labor organizations have been quick to note the approach of these dangers and prompt to protest against both militarism and imperialism.

The pecuniary argument, though more effective with certain classes, is not likely to be used so often or presented with so much emphasis as the religious argument. If what has been termed the "gunpowder gospel" were urged against the Filipinos only, it would be a sufficient answer to say that a majority of the Filipinos are now members of one branch of the Christian Church; but the principle involved is one of much wider application and challenges serious consideration.

A Varying Argument

The religious argument varies in positiveness from a passive belief that Providence delivered the Filipinos into our hands, for their good and our glory, to the exultation of the minister who said that we ought to "thrash the natives (Filipinos) until they understand who we are," and that "every bullet sent, every cannon shot and every flag waved means righteousness." We cannot approve of this doctrine in one place unless we are willing to apply it everywhere. If there is poison in the blood of the hand it will ultimately reach the heart. It is equally true that forcible Christianity, if planted under the American flag in the far-away Orient, will sooner or later be transplanted upon American soil. If true Christianity consists in carrying out in our daily lives the teachings of Christ, who will say that we are commanded to civilize with dynamite and proselyte with the sword? He who would declare the divine will must prove his authority either by Holy Writ or by evidence of a special dispensation. The command "go ye into all the world and preach the gospel to every creature" has no Gatling-gun attachment. . . .

Defines His Position

There is an easy, honest, honorable solution of the Philippine question. It is set forth in the Democratic platform and it is submitted with confidence to the American people. This plan I unreservedly indorse. If elected I shall convene Congress in extraordinary session as soon as I am inaugurated, and recommend an immediate declaration of the Nation's purpose, first, to establish a stable form of government in the Philippine islands, just as we are now establishing a stable form of government in the island of Cuba; second, to give independence to the Filipinos, just as we have promised to give independence to the Cubans; third, to protect the Filipinos from outside interference while they work out their destiny, just as we have protected the republics of Central and South America, and are, by the Monroe doctrine, pledged to protect Cuba. A European protectorate often results in the exploitation of the ward by the guardian. An American protectorate gives to the nation protected the advantage of our strength, without making it the victim of our greed. For three-quarters of a century the Monroe doctrine has been a shield to neighboring republics, and yet it has imposed no pecuniary burden upon us. After the Filipinos had aided us in the war against Spain we could not honorably turn them over to their former masters; we could not leave them to be the victims of the ambitious designs of the European nations, and since we do not desire to make them a part of us or so hold them as subjects we propose the only alternative—namely, to give them independence and guard them against molestation from without.

The Talk of Destiny

When our opponents are unable to defend their position by argument they fall back upon the assertion that it is destiny and insist that we must submit to it no matter how much it violates moral precepts and our principles of government. This is a complacent philosophy. It obliterates the distinction between right and wrong and makes individuals and nations the helpless victims of circumstances. Destiny is the subterfuge of the invertebrate who, lacking the courage to oppose error, seeks some plausible excuse for supporting it. Washington said that the destiny of the republican form of government was deeply if not finally staked on the experiment intrusted to the American people. How different Washington's definition of destiny from the Republican definition. The Republicans say that this Nation is in the hands of destiny; Washington believed that not only the destiny of our own Nation but the destiny of the republican form of government throughout the world was intrusted to American hands. Washington was right. The destiny of this Republic is in the hands of its own people. Upon the success of the experiment here rests the hope of humanity. No exterior force can disturb this Republic and no foreign influence should be permitted to change its course. What the future has in store for this Nation no one has authority to declare, but each individual has his own idea of the Nation's mission and he owes it to his country as well as to himself to contribute as best he may to the fulfillment of that mission.

Republic of the Future

Mr. Chairman and gentlemen of the committee, I have never fully discharged the debt of gratitude which I owe to my countrymen for the honors which they have so generously bestowed upon me, but, sirs, whether it be my lot to occupy the high office for which the convention has named me or to spend the remainder of my days in private life it shall be my constant ambition and my controlling purpose to aid in realizing the high ideals of those whose wisdom and courage and sacrifices brought this Republic into existence.

I can conceive of a national destiny surpassing the glories of the present and the past—a destiny which meets the responsibilities of to-day, and measures up to the possibilities of the future. Behold a republic, resting securely upon the foundation stones quarried by revolutionary patriots from the mountain of eternal truth—a republic applying in practice and proclaiming to the world the self-evident proposition that all men are created equal; that they are endowed with inalienable rights; that governments are instituted among men to secure these rights; that governments derive their just powers from the consent of the governed. Behold a republic in which civil and religious liberty stimulate all to earnest endeavor and in which the law restrains every hand uplifted for a neighbor's injury —a republic in which every citizen is a sovereign, but in which no one cares to wear a crown. Behold a republic standing erect while empires all around are bowed beneath the weight of their own armaments—a republic whose flag is loved while other flags are only feared. Behold a republic increasing in population, in wealth, in strength and in influence, solving the problems of civilization and hastening the coming of a universal brotherhood—a republic which shakes thrones and dissolves aristocracies by its silent example and gives light and inspiration to those who sit in darkness. Behold a republic gradually but surely becoming the supreme moral factor in the world's progress and the accepted arbiter of the world's disputes—a republic whose history, like the path of the just, "is as the shining light that shineth more and more into the perfect day."

SELECTION

The Open Door Notes

Like the foreign-policy advice in Washington's Farewell Address and the Monroe Doctrine, the Open Door policy announced by Secretary of State John Hay in 1899 and 1900 became an object of popular patriotic sanctification. More widely genuflected toward than actually understood, the term "Open Door" was catchy but hardly fully descriptive of America's commercial policies in China.

In the years just previous to the Open Door notes, the government of the Chinese Empire demonstrated it was too weak effectively to rule or to defend itself from foreign aggressors. In the war of 1894–1895 Japan annexed the island of Formosa from China and forced the Chinese to recognize the independence of Korea. In 1897 and 1898 Germany demanded and received rights to establish a naval station in Kiaochow Bay and gained mining and railroad rights in Shantung province. France, having already wrested parts of the Indo-Chinese area from China in 1862 and 1885, now demanded special mining and railroad concessions in the southern part of China proper. Russia demanded and received a lease of naval and commercial ports at Port Arthur and Dairen as well as railroad and other economic rights in Manchuria. Great Britain gained a lease on the port of Weihaiwei on the Shantung Peninsula, across the strait from Port Arthur. Since 1844 the United States had enjoyed most-favored-nation status with China. That is to say, whatever benefits to another power China might grant through treaty automatically devolved upon the United States as well. Commercial privileges granted to Germany, for example, were also available to the United States—in short, the Open Door. Now, in the late 1890s, the United States feared that the Western imperialist powers might use their special privileges in their "spheres of influence" to discriminate against American commercial activity in favor of their own nationals.

This was the background of the first Open Door notes, which Hay dispatched September 6, 1899. The notes asked the American ambassadors in Berlin, London, and St. Petersburg (today, Leningrad) to seek assurances from the foreign ministers of the countries to which they were accredited that the countries would not discriminate against the commercial interests of other nations in their spheres of influence. Subsequent notes in November sought the same assurances from France, Italy, and Japan. Replies from the six governments, some of which were rather evasive and all of which said their acceptance was conditional upon agreement by all concerned, trickled in over the next several months. On March 20, 1900, Hay sent instructions mutatis mutandis *(with the necessary changes) to the six United States representatives concerned to notify the governments to which they were accredited that all the powers addressed on the subject had accepted the American proposals and that therefore the United States considered each assent "as final and definitive." Each government was furnished the replies of the other governments.*

At about the same time that Hay announced acceptance of the Open Door principle, a group of fanatically antiforeign Chinese, called Boxers by Westerners because of their clenched-fist emblem, undertook a campaign of violence to expel foreigners from China. The Boxer movement grew rapidly. By the beginning of the summer of 1900 the Boxers had many Westerners under siege in the legation area of Peking, the imperial Capital, cut off from communication with the rest of the world. An international rescue expedition of about twenty thousand men, to which the United States contributed twenty-five hundred, lifted the siege on August 14. Although the Boxer movement was a real danger to the surrounded Westerners in Peking (among them a young mining engineer and business organizer named Herbert Hoover), even before the rescue expedition reached Peking, Secretary Hay perceived that the presence of many Western soldiers constituted a greater danger to his policy in China. The danger was that the Western powers might regard the Boxer rebellion as sufficient provocation to dismember the Chinese Empire and annex critical parts of Chinese territory. Slamming the Open Door in a colony would be easier than in a sphere of influence. Therefore, on July 3, 1900, Hay dispatched the second round of Open Door notes to the representatives of the United States at Vienna, Berlin, London, Paris, Rome, St. Petersburg, and Tokyo. The messages of July 3 declared that the United States stood for the preservation of "Chinese territorial and administrative entity," which came in the future to be phrased usually as "territorial integrity," and for "the principle of equal and impartial trade with all parts of the Chinese Empire," not just within the spheres of influence. The messages made no request for replies, but several of the governments addressed did reply. In messages to Great Britain and Germany about a related matter, Hay on October 29, 1900, said that "all the powers held similar views."

Historians have differed widely in their interpretations of the Open Door notes. Widely heralded in its own time as a victory for fair play in foreign affairs, the Open Door policy received the plaudits of historians for years thereafter. A generation later, historians began to belittle the accomplishment of Secretary Hay, at least indirectly, when they emphasized that the idea was by no means new in 1899 and that a British subject who had worked for the Chinese customs service, A. E. Hippisley, had a major role in getting the Department of State to accept the idea of spelling out its Open Door policy with the notes to other powers. This tendency to discount the importance of the Open Door notes perhaps reached its ultimate in George F. Kennan's American Diplomacy, 1900–1950 *(Chicago: University of Chicago Press, 1951), especially the second and third chapters. William Appleman Williams, in* The Tragedy of American Diplomacy *(New York: Harcourt, Brace & World, 1959), saw the Open Door policy as a "brilliant strategic stroke" and of the greatest importance for subsequent American history, even though he was critical of the continued acceptance of the whole structure of foreign policy of which the Open Door was a major part.*

The documents reprinted here, except for the last one in the series, are from Papers Relating to the Foreign Relations of the United States, 1899 *(Washington: Government Printing Office, 1901), pages 128–143. Only one of the notes of the first round—September 6, 1899, and the following November—is reproduced here. There was no important difference in the content of the several messages sent. All the replies—from Germany, Great Britain, Italy, France, Japan, and Russia, in that order in this volume—are reproduced so that the reader may note the indirection of some of them. Following the replies from the six governments is Hay's note of March 20, 1900, announcing acceptance of the Open Door policy. The last document here—Hay to Herdliska, Washington, July 3, 1900—is one of the messages in the second round of notes during the Boxer uprising. It is from* Papers Relating to the Foreign Relations of the United States, 1900 *(Washington: Government Printing Office, 1902), page 299.*

The peculiar date in the note from Count Mouravieff, the Russian Foreign Minister, requires explanation. Russia stayed with the Julian, or Old Style, calendar until soon after the Bolshevik revolution. The Gregorian, or New Style, calendar, adopted in Roman Catholic countries in the late sixteenth century, was used in England and the British Colonies of North America after 1752. During the nineteenth century, twelve days separated the two calendar systems.

GERMANY

Mr. Hay to Mr. White

No. 927.]

Department of State,
Washington, September 6, 1899.

Sir:

At the time when the Government of the United States was informed by that of Germany that it had leased from His Majesty the Emperor of China the port of Kiao-chao and the adjacent territory in the province of Shantung, assurances were given to the ambassador of the United States at Berlin by the Imperial German minister for foreign affairs that the rights and privileges insured by treaties with China to citizens of the United States would not thereby suffer or be in anywise impaired within the area over which Germany had thus obtained control.

More recently, however, the British Government recognized by a formal agreement with Germany the exclusive right of the latter country to enjoy in said leased area and the contiguous "sphere of influence or interest" certain privileges, more especially those relating to railroads and mining enterprises; but as the exact nature and extent of the rights thus recognized have not been clearly defined, it is possible that serious conflicts of interest may at any time arise not only between British and German subjects within said area, but that the interests of our citizens may also be jeopardized thereby.

Earnestly desirous to remove any cause of irritation and to insure at the same time to the commerce of all nations in China the undoubted benefits which would accrue from a formal recognition by the various powers claiming "spheres of interest" that they shall enjoy perfect equality of treatment for their commerce and navigation within such "spheres," the Government of the United States would be pleased to see His German Majesty's Government give formal assurances, and lend its cooperation in securing like assurances from the other interested powers, that each, within its respective sphere of whatever influence—

First. Will in no way interfere with any treaty port or any vested interest within any so-called "sphere of interest" or leased territory it may have in China.

Second. That the Chinese treaty tariff of the time being shall apply to all merchandise landed or shipped to all such ports as are within said "sphere of interest" (unless they be "free ports"), no matter to what nationality it may belong, and that duties so leviable shall be collected by the Chinese Government.

Third. That it will levy no higher harbor dues on vessels of another nationality frequenting any port in such "sphere" than shall be levied on vessels of its own nationality, and no higher railroad charges over lines built, controlled, or operated within its "sphere" on merchandise belonging to citizens or subjects of other nationalities transported through such "sphere" than shall be levied on similar merchandise belonging to its own nationals transported over equal distances.

The liberal policy pursued by His Imperial German Majesty in declaring Kiao-chao a free port and in aiding the Chinese Government in the establishment there of a custom-house is so clearly in line with the proposition which this Government is anxious to see recognized that it entertains the strongest hope that Germany will give its acceptance and hearty support.

The recent ukase of His Majesty the Emperor of Russia declaring the port of Ta-lien-wan open during the whole of the lease under which it is held from China to the merchant ships of all nations, coupled with the categorical assurances made to this Government by His Imperial Majesty's representative at this capital at the time and since repeated to me by the present Russian ambassador, seem to insure the support of the Emperor to the proposed measure. Our ambassador at the Court of St. Petersburg has in consequence been instructed to submit it to the Russian Government and to request their early consideration of it. A copy of my instruction on the subject to Mr. Tower is herewith inclosed for your confidential information.

The commercial interests of Great Britain and Japan will be so clearly served by the desired declaration of intentions, and the views of the Governments of these countries as to the desirability of the adoption of measures insuring the benefits of equality of treatment of all foreign trade throughout China are so similar to those entertained by the United States, that their acceptance of the propositions herein outlined and their cooperation in advocating their adoption by the other powers can be confidently expected. I inclose herewith copy of the instruction which I have sent to Mr. Choate on the subject.

In view of the present favorable conditions, you are instructed to submit the above considerations to His Imperial German Majesty's Minister for Foreign Affairs, and to request his early consideration of the subject.

Copy of this instruction is sent to our ambassadors at London and at St. Petersburg for their information.   I have, etc.

                                                        JOHN HAY.

Inclosures.

To London, September 6, 1899.
To St. Petersburg, September 6, 1899.

Mr. Jackson to Mr. Hay

[Telegram.]

Embassy of the United States,
Berlin, December 4, 1899.

I have just had a conversation with secretary of state for foreign affairs, who stated that the politics of Germany in the extreme Orient are de facto the politics of the open door, and Germany proposes to maintain this principle in the future. Germany does not wish the question to become the subject of controversy between the different powers engaged in China. She thinks it would be advantageous for the United States Government to confer with other European Governments having interests in China. If the other cabinets adhere to the proposal of the United States Government, Germany will raise no objection, and Germany is willing to have the Government of the United States inform these other cabinets that no difficulty will come from her if the other cabinets agree.

JACKSON, *Chargé.*

Count von Bülow to Mr. White

[Translation.]

Foreign Office,
Berlin, February 19, 1900.

Mr. Ambassador:

Your excellency informed me, in a memorandum presented on the 24th of last month, that the Government of the United States of America had received satisfactory written replies from all the powers to which an inquiry had been addressed similar to that contained in your excellency's note of September 26 last, in regard to the policy of the open door in China. While referring to this, your excellency thereupon expressed the wish that the Imperial Government would now also give its answer in writing.

Gladly complying with this wish, I have the honor to inform your excellency, repeating the statements already made verbally, as follows: As recognized by the Government of the United States of America, according to your excellency's note referred to above, the Imperial Government has, from the beginning, not only asserted, but also practically carried out to the fullest extent, in its Chinese possessions, absolute equality of treatment of all nations with regard to trade, navigation, and commerce. The Imperial Government entertains no thought of departing in the future from this principle, which at once excludes any prejudicial or disadvantageous commercial treatment of the citizens of the United States of America, so long as it is not forced to do so, on account of considerations of reciprocity, by a divergence from it by other governments. If, therefore, the other powers interested in the industrial development of the Chinese Empire are willing to recognize the same principles, this can only be desired by the Imperial Government, which in this case upon being requested will gladly be ready to participate with the United States of America and the other powers in an agreement made upon these lines, by which the same rights are reciprocally secured.

I avail myself, etc.,
BÜLOW.

GREAT BRITAIN

Lord Salisbury to Mr. Choate

Foreign Office,
London, September 29, 1899.

Your Excellency:
I have read with great interest the communication which you handed me on the 23d instant, in which you inform me of the desire of the United States Government to obtain from the various powers claiming spheres of interest in China declarations as to their intentions in regard to the treatment of foreign trade and commerce therein.

I have the honor to inform your excellency that I will lose no time in consulting my colleagues in regard to a declaration by Her Majesty's Government and on the proposal that they should cooperate with the Government of the United States in obtaining similar declarations by the other powers concerned.

In the meantime, I may assure your excellency that the policy consistently advocated by this country is one of securing equal opportunity for the subjects and citizens of all nations in regard to commercial enterprise in China, and from this policy Her Majesty's Government have no intention or desire to depart.

I have, etc.,
SALISBURY.

Lord Salisbury to Mr. Choate

Foreign Office,
London, November 30, 1899.

Your Excellency:
With reference to my note of September 29 last, I have the honor to state that I have carefully considered, in communication with my colleagues, the proposal contained in your excellency's note of September 22 that a declaration should be made by foreign powers claiming "spheres of interest" in China as to their intentions in regard to the treatment of foreign trade and interest therein.

I have much pleasure in informing your excellency that Her Majesty's Government will be prepared to make a declaration in the sense desired by your Government in regard to the leased territory of Weihai Wei and all territory in China which may hereafter be acquired by Great Britain by lease or otherwise, and all spheres of interest now held or that may hereafter be held by her in China, provided that a similar declaration is made by other powers concerned.

I have, etc.
SALISBURY.

ITALY

Visconti Venosta to Mr. Draper

[Translation.]

Rome, January 7, 1900.

Mr. Ambassador:

Supplementary to what you had already done me the honor of communicating to me in your note of December 9, 1899, your excellency informed me yesterday of the telegraphic note received from your Government that all the powers consulted by the Cabinet of Washington concerning the suitability of adopting a line of policy which would insure to the trade of the whole world equality of treatment in China have given a favorable reply.

Referring to your communications and to the statements in my note of December 23 last, I take pleasure in saying that the Government of the King adheres willingly to the proposals set forth in said note of December 9.

I beg your excellency to kindly convey the notice of our adhesion to the Cabinet of Washington, and I avail myself of the occasion to renew to you, etc.

VISCONTI VENOSTA.

FRANCE

Mr. Delcassé to Mr. Porter

[Translation.]

Foreign Affairs.
(Received at United States embassy at Paris December 16, 1899.)

My Dear Ambassador:

I find your note awaiting me on my return. The declarations which I made in the Chamber on the 24th of November last, and which I have had occasion to recall to you since then, show clearly the sentiments of the Government of the Republic. It desires throughout the whole of China and, with the quite natural reservation that all the powers interested give an assurance of their willingness to act likewise, is ready to apply, in the territories which are leased to it, equal treatment to the citizens and subjects of all nations, especially in the matter of customs duties and navigation dues, as well as transportation tariffs on railways.

I beg you, my dear ambassador, to accept, etc.,
DELCASSÉ.

JAPAN

Viscount Aoki to Mr. Buck

[Translation.]

Department of Foreign Affairs,
Tokyo, the 26th day, the 12th month of the 32d year of Meiji,
(December 26, 1899).

Mr. Minister:

I have the honor to acknowledge the receipt of the note No. 176 of the 20th instant, in which, pursuing the instructions of the United States Government, your excellency was so good as to communicate to the Imperial Government the representations of the United States as presented in notes to Russia, Germany, and Great Britain on the subject of commercial interests of the United States in China.

I have the happy duty of assuring your excellency that the Imperial Government will have no hesitation to give their assent to so just and fair a proposal of the United States, provided that all the other powers concerned shall accept the same.

I avail myself, etc.,
VISCOUNT AOKI SIUZO,
Minister for Foreign Affairs.

RUSSIA

Count Mouravieff to Mr. Tower

[Translation.]

No. 761.]

Ministry of Foreign Affairs,
December 18–30, 1899.

Mr. Ambassador:

I had the honor to receive your excellency's note dated the 8th–20th of September last, relating to the principles which the Government of the United States would like to see adopted in commercial matters by the powers which have interests in China.

In so far as the territory leased by China to Russia is concerned, the Imperial Government has already demonstrated its firm intention to follow the policy of "the open door" by creating Dalny (Ta-lien-wan) a free port; and if at some future time that port, although remaining free itself, should be separated by a customs limit from other portions of the territory in question, the customs duties would be levied, in the zone subject to the tariff, upon all foreign merchandise without distinction as to nationality.

As to the ports now opened or hereafter to be opened to foreign commerce by the Chinese Government, and which lie beyond the territory leased to Russia, the settlement of the question of customs duties belongs to China herself, and the Imperial Government has no intention whatever of claiming any privileges for its own subjects to the exclusion of other foreigners. It is to be understood, however, that this assurance of the Imperial Government is given upon condition that a similar declaration shall be made by other powers having interests in China.

With the conviction that this reply is such as to satisfy the inquiry made in the aforementioned note, the Imperial Government is happy to have complied with the wishes of the American Government, especially as it attaches the highest value to anything that may strengthen and consolidate the traditional relations of friendship existing between the two countries.

I beg you to accept, etc.,
COUNT MOURAVIEFF.

Instructions Sent Mutatis Mutandis to the United States Ambassadors at London, Paris, Berlin, St. Petersburg, and Rome, and to the United States Minister at Tokyo

Department of State,
Washington, March 20, 1900.

Sir:

The ———— Government having accepted the declaration suggested by the United States concerning foreign trade in China, the terms of which I transmitted to you in my instruction No. ———— of ————, and like action having been taken by all the various powers having leased territory or so-called "spheres of interest" in the Chinese Empire, as shown by the notes which I herewith transmit to you, you will please inform the Government to which you are accredited that the condition originally attached to its acceptance—that all other powers concerned should likewise accept the proposals of the United States—having been complied with, this Government will therefore consider the assent given to it by ———— as final and definitive.

You will also transmit to the minister for foreign affairs copies of the present inclosures, and by the same occasion convey to him the expression of the sincere gratification which the President feels at the successful termination of these negotiations, in which he sees proof of the friendly spirit which animates the various powers interested in the untrammeled development of commerce and industry in the Chinese Empire, and a source of vast benefit to the whole commercial world.

I am, etc.
JOHN HAY.

Inclosures.

Mr. Delcassé to Mr. Porter (received December 16, 1899), translation.
Mr. Jackson to Mr. Hay, telegram, December 4, 1899.
Count von Bülow to Mr. White, February 19, 1900, translation.

Lord Salisbury to Mr. Choate, November 30, 1899.
Marquis Visconti Venosta to Mr. Draper, January 7, 1900, translation.
Viscount Aoki to Mr. Buck, December 26, 1899, translation.
Count Mouravieff to Mr. Tower, December 18, 1899, translation.

AUSTRIA-HUNGARY

Mr. Hay to Mr. Herdliska

[Circular Telegram.][1]

Department of State,
Washington, July 3, 1900.

In this critical posture of affairs in China it is deemed appropriate to define the attitude of the United States as far as present circumstances permit this to be done. We adhere to the policy initiated by us in 1857, of peace with the Chinese nation, of furtherance of lawful commerce, and of protection of lives and property of our citizens by all means guaranteed under extraterritorial treaty rights and by the law of nations. If wrong be done to our citizens we propose to hold the responsible authors to the uttermost accountability. We regard the condition at Pekin as one of virtual anarchy, whereby power and responsibility are practically devolved upon the local provincial authorities. So long as they are not in overt collusion with rebellion and use their power to protect foreign life and property we regard them as representing the Chinese people, with whom we seek to remain in peace and friendship. The purpose of the President is, as it has been heretofore, to act concurrently with the other powers, first, in opening up communication with Pekin and rescuing the American officials, missionaries, and other Americans who are in danger; secondly, in affording all possible protection everywhere in China to American life and property; thirdly, in guarding and protecting all legitimate American interests; and fourthly, in aiding to prevent a spread of the disorders to the other provinces of the Empire and a recurrence of such disasters. It is, of course, too early to forecast the means of attaining this last result; but the policy of the Government of the United States is to seek a solution which may bring about permanent safety and peace to China, preserve Chinese territorial and administrative entity, protect all rights guaranteed to friendly powers by treaty and international law, and safeguard for the world the principle of equal and impartial trade with all parts of the Chinese Empire.

You will communicate the purport of this instruction to the minister for foreign affairs.

HAY.

[1] Also sent to the representatives of the United States at Berlin, London, Paris, Rome, St. Petersburg, and Tokio.

SELECTION

Mark Twain on Imperialism
and "the Blessings of Civilization"

Although several American men of letters lent their talents to the campaign against imperialism—among them William Dean Howells, William Vaughn Moody, Thomas Bailey Aldrich, and Thomas Wentworth Higginson—none was more biting and bitter in his anti-imperialism than Mark Twain. Sixty-five years old the month McKinley defeated Bryan the second time, Mark Twain had come to have a sharp eye for sham and hypocrisy and had found much of them in Western civilization. When imperialists, whether European, British, or American, assumed they were morally superior to colonial and non-Christian people, they outraged the white-haired former Missourian. To Twain, "the Blessings-of-Civilization Trust" was a fraud because its blessings were at best dubious. But, "There is more money in it, more territory, more sovereignty, and other kinds of emolument, than there is in any other game that is played."

A close reading of the following article reveals that Twain was opposed to annexation of overseas territory, to colonialism, and to efforts to impose Western ways on non-Western people but that he was not necessarily opposed to American military ventures abroad or to overseas investment. Twain, like thousands of other anticolonialists, could accept the Open Door policy. He approved American policy in Cuba and went so far as to describe the Teller amendment to the war resolution of 1898, which disclaimed American intention of annexing Cuba, as "stirring words." (Twain warned, however, that imperialists would try to "slip out of our congressional contract with Cuba and give her something better in the place of it." He predicted well: The Platt amendment passed Congress just a month after publication of this article.) In his views upon what should have been United States policy in the Philippines, Twain clearly countenanced foreign investment there and came close to declaring himself for an anticolonial but Open Door policy in the islands. If the game in the Philippines "had been played according to the American rules, Dewey would have sailed away from Manila as soon as he had destroyed the Spanish fleet—after putting up a sign on shore guaranteeing foreign property and life against damage by the Filipinos, and warning the Powers that interference with the emancipated patriots would be regarded as an act unfriendly to the United States. The Powers cannot combine, in even a bad cause, and the sign would not have been molested."

This article was one of the last in the debate between imperialists and anti-imperialists. McKinley's and Roosevelt's victory over Bryan in 1900 was so overwhelming that anti-imperialism as a political force almost ceased to exist.

The standard works on the anti-imperialist movement are two articles by Fred Harvey Harrington, "The Anti-imperialist Movement in the United States, 1898–1900," Mississippi Valley Historical Review, volume 22, 1935, pages 211–230, and "Literary Aspects of Anti-imperialism," New England Quarterly, volume 10, December, 1937, pages 650–667.

The article by Twain, "To the Person Sitting in Darkness," is here reprinted in its entirety as it first appeared in The North American Review, *volume 172, February, 1901, pages 161–176.*

Christmas will dawn in the United States over a people full of hope and aspiration and good cheer. Such a condition means contentment and happiness. The carping grumbler who may here and there go forth will find few to listen to him. The majority will wonder what is the matter with him and pass on.   —*New York Tribune,* on Christmas Eve

From *The Sun,* of New York:

The purpose of this article is not to describe the terrible offences against humanity committed in the name of Politics in some of the most notorious East Side districts. *They could not be described, even verbally.* But it is the intention to let the great mass of more or less careless citizens of this beautiful metropolis of the New World get some conception of the havoc and ruin wrought to man, woman and child in the most densely populated and least known section of the city. Name, date and place can be supplied to those of little faith—or to any man who feels himself aggrieved. It is a plain statement of record and observation, written without license and without garnish.

Imagine, if you can, a section of the city territory completely dominated by one man, without whose permission neither legitimate nor illegitimate business can be conducted; *where illegitimate business is encouraged and legitimate business discouraged;* where the respectable residents have to fasten their doors and windows summer nights and sit in their rooms with asphyxiating air and 100-degree temperature, rather than try to catch the faint whiff of breeze in their natural breathing places, the stoops of their homes; *where naked women dance by night in the streets, and unsexed men prowl like vultures through the darkness on "business"* not only permitted but encouraged by the police; *where the education of infants begins with the knowledge of prostitution* and the training of little girls is training in the arts of Phryne; where *American* girls brought up with the refinements of *American* homes are imported from small towns up-State, Massachusetts, Connecticut and New Jersey, and kept as virtually prisoners as if they were locked up behind jail bars until they have lost all semblance of womanhood; *where small boys are taught to solicit for the women of disorderly houses;* where there is an organized society of young men *whose sole business in life is to corrupt young girls and turn them over to bawdy houses;* where men walking with their wives along the street are openly insulted; *where children that have adult diseases are the chief patrons of the hospitals and dispensaries;* where it is the rule, rather than the exception, that *murder, rape, robbery and theft go unpunished*—in short where the Premium of the most awful forms of Vice is the Profit of the politicians.

The following news from China appeared in *The Sun,* of New York, on Christmas Eve. The italics are mine:

The Rev. Mr. Ament, of the American Board of Foreign Missions, has returned from a trip which he made for the purpose of collecting indemnities for damages done by Boxers. *Everywhere he went he compelled the Chinese to pay.* He says that all his native Christians are now provided for. He had

700 of them under his charge, and 300 were killed. He has *collected* 300 *taels for each* of these murders, and has *compelled full payment for all the property belonging to Christians* that was destroyed. He also assessed *fines* amounting to THIRTEEN TIMES the amount of the indemnity. *This money will be used for the propagation of the Gospel.*

Mr. Ament declares that the compensation he has collected is *moderate,* when compared with the amount secured by the Catholics, who demand in addition to money, *head for head.* They collect 500 taels for each murder of a Catholic. In the Wenchiu country, 680 Catholics were killed, and for this the European Catholics here demand 750,000 strings of cash and 680 *heads.*

In the course of a conversation, Mr. Ament referred to the attitude of the missionaries toward the Chinese. He said:

"I deny emphatically that the missionaries are *vindictive,* that they *generally* looted, or that they have done anything *since* the siege that *the circumstances did not demand.* I criticise the Americans. *The soft hand of the Americans is not as good as the mailed fist of the Germans.* If you deal with the Chinese with a soft hand they will take advantage of it."

The statement that the French Government will return the loot taken by the French soldiers, is the source of the greatest amusement here. The French soldiers were more systematic looters than the Germans, and it is a fact that to-day *Catholic Christians,* carrying French flags and armed with modern guns, *are looting villages* in the Province of Chili.

By happy luck, we get all these glad tidings on Christmas Eve—just in time to enable us to celebrate the day with proper gaiety and enthusiasm. Our spirits soar, and we find we can even make jokes: Taels I win, Heads you lose.

Our Reverend Ament is the right man in the right place. What we want of our missionaries out there is, not that they shall merely represent in their acts and persons the grace and gentleness and charity and loving kindness of our religion, but that they shall also represent the American spirit. The oldest Americans are the Pawnees. Macallum's History says:

When a white Boxer kills a Pawnee and destroys his property, the other Pawnees do not trouble to seek *him* out, they kill any white person that comes along; also, they make some white village pay deceased's heirs the full cash value of deceased, together with full cash value of the property destroyed; they also make the village pay, in addition, *thirteen times* the value of that property into a fund for the dissemination of the Pawnee religion, which they regard as the best of all religions for the softening and humanizing of the heart of man. It is their idea that it is only fair and right that the innocent should be made to suffer for the guilty, and that it is better that ninety and nine innocent should suffer than that one guilty person should escape.

Our Reverend Ament is justifiably jealous of those enterprising Catholics, who not only get big money for each lost convert, but get "head for head" besides. But he should soothe himself with the reflection that the entirety of their exactions are for their own pockets, whereas he, less selfishly, devotes only 300 taels per head to that service, and gives the whole vast thirteen repetitions of the property-indemnity to the service of propagating the Gospel. His magnanimity has won him the approval of his

nation, and will get him a monument. Let him be content with these rewards. We all hold him dear for manfully defending his fellow missionaries
from exaggerated charges which were beginning to distress us, but which
his testimony has so considerably modified that we can now contemplate
them without noticeable pain. For now we know that, even before the
siege, the missionaries were not "generally" out looting, and that, "since
the siege," they have acted quite handsomely, except when "circumstances"
crowded them. I am arranging for the monument. Subscriptions for it can
be sent to the American Board; designs for it can be sent to me. Designs
must allegorically set forth the Thirteen Reduplications of the Indemnity,
and the Object for which they were exacted; as Ornaments, the designs
must exhibit 680 Heads, so disposed as to give a pleasing and pretty effect;
for the Catholics have done nicely, and are entitled to notice in the monument. Mottoes may be suggested, if any shall be discovered that will satisfactorily cover the ground.

Mr. Ament's financial feat of squeezing a thirteen-fold indemnity out of
the pauper peasants to square other people's offenses, thus condemning
them and their women and innocent little children to inevitable starvation
and lingering death, in order that the blood-money so acquired might be
"used for the propagation of the Gospel," does not flutter my serenity;
although the act and the words, taken together, concrete a blasphemy so
hideous and so colossal that, without doubt, its mate is not findable in the
history of this or of any other age. Yet, if a layman had done that thing
and justified it with those words, I should have shuddered, I know. Or, if
I had done the thing and said the words myself—however, the thought is
unthinkable, irreverent as some imperfectly informed people think me.
Sometimes an ordained minister sets out to be blasphemous. When this
happens, the layman is out of the running; he stands no chance.

We have Mr. Ament's impassioned assurance that the missionaries are
not "vindictive." Let us hope and pray that they will never become so,
but will remain in the almost morbidly fair and just and gentle temper
which is affording so much satisfaction to their brother and champion
to-day.

The following is from the *New York Tribune* of Christmas Eve. It comes
from that journal's Tokio correspondent. It has a strange and impudent
sound, but the Japanese are but partially civilized as yet. When they become wholly civilized they will not talk so:

> The missionary question, of course, occupies a foremost place in the dis-
> cussion. It is now felt as essential that the Western Powers take cognizance
> of the sentiment here, that religious invasions of Oriental countries by power-
> ful Western organizations are tantamount to filibustering expeditions, and
> should not only be discountenanced, but that stern measures should be
> adopted for their suppression. The feeling here is that the missionary organi-
> zations constitute a constant menace to peaceful international relations.

Shall we? That is, shall we go on conferring our Civilization upon the
peoples that sit in darkness, or shall we give those poor things a rest?
Shall we bang right ahead in our old-time, loud, pious way, and commit
the new century to the game; or shall we sober up and sit down and think

it over first? Would it not be prudent to get our Civilization-tools together, and see how much stock is left on hand in the way of Glass Beads and Theology, and Maxim Guns and Hymn Books, and Trade-Gin and Torches of Progress and Enlightenment (patent adjustable ones, good to fire villages with, upon occasion), and balance the books, and arrive at the profit and loss, so that we may intelligently decide whether to continue the business or sell out the property and start a new Civilization Scheme on the proceeds?

Extending the Blessings of Civilization to our Brother who Sits in Darkness has been a good trade and has paid well, on the whole; and there is money in it yet, if carefully worked—but not enough, in my judgment, to make any considerable risk advisable. The People that Sit in Darkness are getting to be too scarce—too scarce and too shy. And such darkness as is now left is really of but an indifferent quality, and not dark enough for the game. The most of those People that Sit in Darkness have been furnished with more light than was good for them or profitable for us. We have been injudicious.

The Blessings-of-Civilization Trust, wisely and cautiously administered, is a Daisy. There is more money in it, more territory, more sovereignty, and other kinds of emolument, than there is in any other game that is played. But Christendom has been playing it badly of late years, and must certainly suffer by it, in my opinion. She has been so eager to get every stake that appeared on the green cloth, that the People who Sit in Darkness have noticed it—they have noticed it, and have begun to show alarm. They have become suspicious of the Blessings of Civilization. More—they have begun to examine them. This is not well. The Blessings of Civilization are all right, and a good commercial property; there could not be a better, in a dim light. In the right kind of a light, and at a proper distance, with the goods a little out of focus, they furnish this desirable exhibit to the Gentlemen who Sit in Darkness:

LOVE,	LAW AND ORDER,
JUSTICE,	LIBERTY,
GENTLENESS,	EQUALITY,
CHRISTIANITY,	HONORABLE DEALING,
PROTECTION TO THE WEAK,	MERCY,
TEMPERANCE,	EDUCATION,

—and so on.

There. Is it good? Sir, it is pie. It will bring into camp any idiot that sits in darkness anywhere. But not if we adulterate it. It is proper to be emphatic upon that point. This brand is strictly for Export—apparently. *Apparently.* Privately and confidentially, it is nothing of the kind. Privately and confidentially, it is merely an outside cover, gay and pretty and attractive, displaying the special patterns of our Civilization which we reserve for Home Consumption, while *inside* the bale is the Actual Thing that the Customer Sitting in Darkness buys with his blood and tears and land and liberty. That Actual Thing is, indeed, Civilization, but it is only for Export. Is there a difference between the two brands? In some of the details, yes.

We all know that the Business is being ruined. The reason is not far to seek. It is because our Mr. McKinley, and Mr. Chamberlain, and the the Kaiser, and the Czar and the French have been exporting the Actual Thing *with the outside cover left off*. This is bad for the Game. It shows that these new players of it are not sufficiently acquainted with it.

It is a distress to look on and note the mismoves, they are so strange and so awkward. Mr. Chamberlain manufactures a war out of materials so inadequate and so fanciful that they make the boxes grieve and the gallery laugh, and he tries hard to persuade himself that it isn't purely a private raid for cash, but has a sort of dim, vague respectability about it somewhere, if he could only find the spot; and that, by and by, he can scour the flag clean again after he has finished dragging it through the mud, and make it shine and flash in the vault of heaven once more as it had shone and flashed there a thousand years in the world's respect until he laid his unfaithful hand upon it. It is bad play—bad. For it exposes the Actual Thing to Them that Sit in Darkness, and they say: "What! Christian against Christian? And only for money? Is *this* a case of magnanimity, forbearance, love, gentleness, mercy, protection of the weak—this strange and over-showy onslaught of an elephant upon a nest of field-mice, on the pretext that the mice had squeaked an insolence at him—conduct which 'no self-respecting government could allow to pass unavenged'? as Mr. Chamberlain said. Was that a good pretext in a small case, when it had not been a good pretext in a large one?—for only recently Russia had affronted the elephant three times and survived alive and unsmitten. Is this Civilization and Progress? Is it something better than we already possess? These harryings and burnings and desert-makings in the Transvaal—is this an improvement on our darkness? Is it, perhaps, possible that there are two kinds of Civilization—one for home consumption and one for the heathen market?"

Then They that Sit in Darkness are troubled, and shake their heads; and they read this extract from a letter of a British private, recounting his exploits in one of Methuen's victories, some days before the affair of Magersfontein, and they are troubled again:

> We tore up the hill and into the intrenchments, and the Boers saw we had them; so they dropped their guns and went down on their knees and put up their hands clasped, and begged for mercy. And we gave it them—*with the long spoon.*

The long spoon is the bayonet. See *Lloyd's Weekly,* London, of those days. The same number—and the same column—contained some quite unconscious satire in the form of shocked and bitter upbraidings of the Boers for their brutalities and inhumanities!

Next, to our heavy damage, the Kaiser went to playing the game without first mastering it. He lost a couple of missionaries in a riot in Shantung, and in his account he made an overcharge for them. China had to pay a hundred thousand dollars apiece for them, in money; twelve miles of territory, containing several millions of inhabitants and worth twenty million dollars; and to build a monument, and also a Christian church; whereas the people of China could have been depended upon to remember the missionaries without the help of these expensive memorials. This was all bad play. Bad, because it would not, and could not, and will not now or ever, deceive the Person Sitting in Darkness. He knows that it was an overcharge. He knows that a missionary is like any other man: he is worth merely what you can supply his place for, and no more. He is useful, but so is a doctor, so is a sheriff, so is an editor; but a just Emperor does not charge war-prices for such. A diligent, intelligent, but obscure missionary, and a diligent, intelligent country editor are worth much, and we know it; but they are not worth the earth. We esteem such an editor, and we are sorry to see him go; but, when he goes, we should consider twelve miles of territory, and a church, and a fortune, over-compensation for his loss. I mean, if he was a Chinese editor, and we had to settle for him. It is no proper figure for an editor or a missionary; one can get shop-worn kings for less. It was bad play on the Kaiser's part. It got this property, true; but it *produced the Chinese revolt*, the indignant uprising of China's traduced patriots, the Boxers. The results have been expensive to Germany, and to the other Disseminators of Progress and the Blessings of Civilization.

The Kaiser's claim was paid, yet it was bad play, for it could not fail to have an evil effect upon Persons Sitting in Darkness in China. They would muse upon the event, and be likely to say: "Civilization is gracious and beautiful, for such is its reputation; but can we afford it? There are rich Chinamen, perhaps they could afford it; but this tax is not laid upon them, it is laid upon the peasants of Shantung; it is they that must pay this mighty sum, and their wages are but four cents a day. Is this a better civilization than ours, and holier and higher and nobler? Is not this rapacity? Is not this extortion? Would Germany charge America two hundred thousand dollars for two missionaries, and shake the mailed fist in her face, and send warships, and send soldiers, and say: 'Seize twelve miles of territory, worth twenty millions of dollars, as additional pay for the missionaries; and make those peasants build a monument to the missionaries, and a costly Christian church to remember them by'? And later would Germany say to her soldiers: 'March through America and slay, *giving no quarter;* make the German face there, as has been our Hun-face here, a terror for a thousand years; march through the Great Republic and slay, slay, slay, carving a road for our offended religion through its heart and bowels'? Would Germany do like this to America, to England, to France, to Russia? Or only to China the helpless—imitating the elephant's assault upon the field-mice? Had we better invest in this Civilization—this Civilization which called Napoleon a buccaneer for carrying off Venice's bronze horses, but which steals our ancient astronomical instruments from our walls, and goes looting like common bandits—that is, all the alien soldiers except America's; and (Americans again excepted) storms frightened villages and cables the result to glad journals at home every day: 'Chinese losses, 450 killed; ours, *one officer and two men wounded.* Shall proceed against neighboring village to-morrow, where a *massacre* is reported.' Can we afford Civilization?"

And, next, Russia must go and play the game injudiciously. She affronts

England once or twice—with the Person Sitting in Darkness observing and noting; by moral assistance of France and Germany, she robs Japan of her hard-earned spoil, all swimming in Chinese blood—Port Arthur—with the Person again observing and noting; then she seizes Manchuria, raids its villages, and chokes its great river with the swollen corpses of countless massacred peasants—that astonished Person still observing and noting. And perhaps he is saying to himself: "It is yet *another* Civilized Power, with its banner of the Prince of Peace in one hand and its loot-basket and its butcher-knife in the other. Is there no salvation for us but to adopt Civilization and lift ourselves down to its level?"

And by and by comes America, and our Master of the Game plays it badly—plays it as Mr. Chamberlain was playing it in South Africa. It was a mistake to do that; also, it was one which was quite unlooked for in a Master who was playing it so well in Cuba. In Cuba, he was playing the usual and regular *American* game, and it was winning, for there is no way to beat it. The Master, contemplating Cuba, said: "Here is an oppressed and friendless little nation which is willing to fight to be free; we go partners, and put up the strength of seventy million sympathizers and the resources of the United States: play!" Nothing but Europe combined could call that hand: and Europe cannot combine on anything. There, in Cuba, he was following our great traditions in a way which made us very proud of him, and proud of the deep dissatisfaction which his play was provoking in Continental Europe. Moved by a high inspiration, he threw out those stirring words which proclaimed that forcible annexation would be "criminal aggression;" and in that utterance fired another "shot heard round the world." The memory of that fine saying will be outlived by the remembrance of no act of his but one—that he forgot it within the twelvemonth, and its honorable gospel along with it.

For, presently, came the Philippine temptation. It was strong; it was too strong, and he made that bad mistake: he played the European game, the Chamberlain game. It was a pity; it was a great pity, that error; that one grievous error, that irrevocable error. For it was the very place and time to play the American game again. And at no cost. Rich winnings to be gathered in, too; rich and permanent; indestructible; a fortune transmissible forever to the children of a flag. Not land, not money, not dominion—no, something worth many times more than that dross: our share, the spectacle of a nation of long harassed and persecuted slaves set free through our influence; our posterity's share, the golden memory of that fair deed. The game was in our hands. If it had been played according to the American rules, Dewey would have sailed away from Manila as soon as he had destroyed the Spanish fleet—after putting up a sign on shore guaranteeing foreign property and life against damage by the Filipinos, and warning the Powers that interference with the emancipated patriots would be regarded as an act unfriendly to the United States. The Powers cannot combine, in even a bad cause, and the sign would not have been molested.

Dewey could have gone about his affairs elsewhere, and left the competent Filipino army to starve out the little Spanish garrison and send it home, and the Filipino citizens to set up the form of government they might prefer, and deal with the friars and their doubtful acquisitions according to Filipino ideas of fairness and justice—ideas which have since been tested and found to be of as high an order as any that prevail in Europe or America.

But we played the Chamberlain game, and lost the chance to add another Cuba and another honorable deed to our good record.

The more we examine the mistake, the more clearly we preceive that it is going to be bad for the Business. The Person Sitting in Darkness is almost sure to say: "There is something curious about this—curious and unaccountable. There must be two Americas: one that sets the captive free, and one that takes a once-captive's new freedom away from him, and picks a quarrel with him with nothing to found it on; then kills him to get his land."

The truth is, the Person Sitting in Darkness *is* saying things like that; and for the sake of the Business we must persuade him to look at the Philippine matter in another and healthier way. We must arrange his opinions for him. I believe it can be done; for Mr. Chamberlain has arranged England's opinion of the South African matter, and done it most cleverly and successfully. He presented the facts—some of the facts—and showed those confiding people what the facts meant. He did it statistically, which is a good way. He used the formula: "Twice 2 are 14, and 2 from 9 leaves 35." Figures are effective; figures will convince the elect.

Now, my plan is a still bolder one than Mr. Chamberlain's, though apparently a copy of it. Let us be franker than Mr. Chamberlain; let us audaciously present the whole of the facts, shirking none, then explain them according to Mr. Chamberlain's formula. This daring truthfulness will astonish and dazzle the Person Sitting in Darkness, and he will take the Explanation down before his mental vision has had time to get back into focus. Let us say to him:

"Our case is simple. On the 1st of May, Dewey destroyed the Spanish fleet. This left the Archipelago in the hands of its proper and rightful owners, the Filipino nation. Their army numbered 30,000 men, and they were competent to whip out or starve out the little Spanish garrison; then the people could set up a government of their own devising. Our traditions required that Dewey should now set up his warning sign, and go away. But the Master of the Game happened to think of another plan—the European plan. He acted upon it. This was, to send out an army—ostensibly to help the native patriots put the finishing touch upon their long and plucky struggle for independence, but really to take their land away from them and keep it. That is, in the interest of Progress and Civilization. The plan developed, stage by stage, and quite satisfactorily. We entered into a military alliance with the trusting Filipinos, and they hemmed in Manila on the land side, and by their valuable help the place, with its garrison of 8,000 or 10,000 Spaniards, was captured—a thing which we could not have accomplished unaided at that time. We got their help by—by ingenuity. We knew they were fighting for their independence, and that they had been at it for two years. We knew they supposed that we also were fighting in their worthy cause—just as we had helped the Cubans fight for Cuban independence—and we allowed them to go on thinking so. *Until Manila was ours and we could get along without them.* Then we showed our hand. Of course, they were surprised—that was natural; surprised and disappointed; disappointed and grieved. To them it looked un-American; uncharacteristic; foreign to our established traditions. And this was natural, too; for we were only playing the American Game in public—in private it was the European. It was neatly done, very neatly, and it bewildered them. They could not understand it; for we had been so friendly—so affectionate, even—with those simple-minded patriots! We, our own selves, had brought back out of exile their leader, their hero, their hope, their Washington— Aguinaldo; brought him in a warship, in high honor, under the sacred shelter and hospitality of the flag; brought him back and restored him to his people, and got their moving and eloquent gratitude for it. Yes, we had been so friendly to them, and had heartened them up in so many ways! We had lent them guns and ammunition; advised with them; exchanged pleasant courtesies with them; placed our sick and wounded in their kindly care; entrusted our Spanish prisoners to their humane and honest hands; fought shoulder to shoulder with them against 'the common enemy' (our own phrase); praised their courage, praised their gallantry, praised their mercifulness, praised their fine and honorable conduct; borrowed their trenches, borrowed strong positions which they had previously captured from the Spaniard; petted them, lied to them—officially proclaiming that our land and naval forces came to give them their freedom and displace the bad Spanish Government—fooled them, used them until we needed them no longer; then derided the sucked orange and threw it away. We kept the positions which we had beguiled them of; by and by, we moved a force forward and overlapped patriot ground—a clever thought, for we needed trouble, and this would produce it. A Filipino soldier, crossing the ground, where no one had a right to forbid him, was shot by our sentry. The badgered patriots resented this with arms, without waiting to know whether Aguinaldo, who was absent, would approve or not. Aguinaldo did not approve; but that availed nothing. What we wanted, in the interest of Progress and Civilization, was the Archipelago, unencumbered by patriots struggling for independence; and War was what we needed. We clinched our opportunity. It is Mr. Chamberlain's case over again—at least in its motive and intention; and we played the game as adroitly as he played it himself."

At this point in our frank statement of fact to the Person Sitting in Darkness, we should throw in a little trade-taffy about the Blessings of Civilization—for a change, and for the refreshment of his spirit—then go on with our tale:

"We and the patriots having captured Manila, Spain's ownership of the Archipelago and her sovereignty over it were at an end—obliterated— annihilated—not a rag or shred of either remaining behind. It was then that we conceived the divinely humorous idea of *buying* both of these spectres from Spain! [It is quite safe to confess this to the Person Sitting in Darkness, since neither he nor any other sane person will believe it.] In buying those ghosts for twenty millions, we also contracted to take care of the friars and their accumulations. I think we also agreed to propagate leprosy and smallpox, but as to this there is doubt. But it is not important; persons afflicted with the friars do not mind other diseases.

"With our Treaty ratified, Manila subdued, and our Ghosts secured, we had no further use for Aguinaldo and the owners of the Archipelago. We forced a war, and we have been hunting America's guest and ally through the woods and swamps ever since."

At this point in the tale, it will be well to boast a little of our war-work and our heroisms in the field, so as to make our performance look as fine as England's in South Africa; but I believe it will not be best to emphasize this too much. We must be cautious. Of course, we must read the war-telegrams to the Person, in order to keep up our frankness; but we can throw an air of humorousness over them, and that will modify their grim eloquence a little, and their rather indiscreet exhibitions of gory exultation. Before reading to him the following display heads of the dispatches of November 18, 1900, it will be well to practice on them in private first, so as to get the right tang of lightness and gaiety into them:

ADMINISTRATION WEARY OF PROTRACTED HOSTILITIES!

REAL WAR AHEAD FOR FILIPINO REBELS!*

WILL SHOW NO MERCY!

KITCHENER'S PLAN ADOPTED!

Kitchener knows how to handle disagreeable people who are fighting for their homes and their liberties, and we must let on that we are merely imitating Kitchener, and have no national interest in the matter, further than to get ourselves admired by the Great Family of Nations, in which august company our Master of the Game has bought a place for us in the back row.

Of course, we must not venture to ignore our General MacArthur's reports—oh, why do they keep on printing those embarrassing things?—we must drop them trippingly from the tongue and take the chances:

> During the last ten months our losses have been 268 killed and 750 wounded; Filipino loss, *three thousand two hundred and twenty-seven killed,* and 694 wounded.

We must stand ready to grab the Person Sitting in Darkness, for he will swoon away at this confession, saying: "Good God, those 'niggers' spare their wounded, and the Americans massacre theirs!"

We must bring him to, and coax him and coddle him, and assure him that the ways of Providence are best, and that it would not become us to find fault with them; and then, to show him that we are only imitators, not originators, we must read the following passage from the letter of an American soldier-lad in the Philippines to his mother, published in *Public Opinion,* of Decorah, Iowa, describing the finish of a victorious battle:

"WE NEVER LEFT ONE ALIVE. IF ONE WAS WOUNDED, WE WOULD RUN OUR BAYONETS THROUGH HIM."

* "Rebels!" Mumble that funny word—don't let the Person catch it distinctly.

Having now laid all the historical facts before the Person Sitting in Darkness, we should bring him to again, and explain them to him. We should say to him:

"They look doubtful, but in reality they are not. There have been lies; yes, but they were told in a good cause. We have been treacherous; but that was only in order that real good might come out of apparent evil. True, we have crushed a deceived and confiding people; we have turned against the weak and the friendless who trusted us; we have stamped out a just and intelligent and well-ordered republic; we have stabbed an ally in the back and slapped the face of a guest; we have bought a Shadow from an enemy that hadn't it to sell; we have robbed a trusting friend of his land and his liberty; we have invited our clean young men to shoulder a discredited musket and do bandit's work under a flag which bandits have been accustomed to fear, not to follow; we have debauched America's honor and blackened her face before the world; but each detail was for the best. We know this. The Head of every State and Sovereignty in Christendom and ninety per cent. of every legislative body in Christendom, including our Congress and our fifty State Legislatures, are members not only of the church, but also of the Blessings-of-Civilization Trust. This world-girdling accumulation of trained morals, high principles, and justice, cannot do an unright thing, an unfair thing, an ungenerous thing, an unclean thing. It knows what it is about. Give yourself no uneasiness; it is all right."

Now then, that will convince the Person. You will see. It will restore the Business. Also, it will elect the Master of the Game to the vacant place in the Trinity of our national gods; and there on their high thrones the Three will sit, age after age, in the people's sight, each bearing the Emblem of his service: Washington, the Sword of the Liberator; Lincoln, the Slave's Broken Chains; the Master, the Chains Repaired.

It will give the Business a splendid new start. You will see.

Everything is prosperous, now; everything is just as we should wish it. We have got the Archipelago, and we shall never give it up. Also, we have every reason to hope that we shall have an opportunity before very long to slip out of our Congressional contract with Cuba and give her something better in the place of it. It is a rich country, and many of us are already beginning to see that the contract was a sentimental mistake. But now— right now—is the best time to do some profitable rehabilitating work— work that will set us up and make us comfortable, and discourage gossip. We cannot conceal from ourselves that, privately, we are a little troubled about our uniform. It is one of our prides; it is acquainted with honor; it is familiar with great deeds and noble; we love it, we revere it; and so this errand it is on makes us uneasy. And our flag—another pride of ours, our chiefest! We have worshipped it so; and when we have seen it in far lands —glimpsing it unexpectedly in that strange sky, waving its welcome and benediction to us—we have caught our breath, and uncovered our heads, and couldn't speak, for a moment, for the thought of what it was to us and the great ideals it stood for. Indeed, we *must* do something about these things; we must not have the flag out there, and the uniform. They are not needed there; we can manage in some other way. England manages, as regards the uniform, and so can we. We have to send soldiers—we can't get out of that—but we can disguise them. It is the way England does in South Africa. Even Mr. Chamberlain himself takes pride in England's honorable uniform, and makes the army down there wear an ugly and odious and appropriate disguise, of yellow stuff such as quarantine flags are made of, and which are hoisted to warn the healthy away from unclean disease and repulsive death. This cloth is called Khaki. We could adopt it. It is light, comfortable, grotesque, and deceives the enemy, for he cannot conceive of a soldier being concealed in it.

And as for a flag for the Philippine Province, it is easily managed. We can have a special one—our States do it: we can have just our usual flag, with the white stripes painted black and the stars replaced by the skull and cross-bones.

And we do not need that Civil Commission out there. Having no powers, it has to invent them, and that kind of work cannot be effectively done by just anybody; an expert is required. Mr. Croker can be spared. We do not want the United States represented there, but only the Game.

By help of these suggested amendments, Progress and Civilization in that country can have a boom, and it will take in the Persons who are Sitting in Darkness, and we can resume Business at the old stand.

SELECTION

Theodore Roosevelt and the Panama Canal Route

The following account of Colombian-American relations and the Panamanian revolution of 1903 from Theodore Roosevelt: An Autobiography, *originally published in 1913 by the Outlook Company, reproduced here from the Scribner edition of 1925, pages 520–527, is remarkable on several counts. It is remarkable for some of the things it says or at least implies, for some of the things it leaves unsaid, and for the way it says still other things. Studied closely after one has become familiar with the essential facts from another account, it can provide a good insight into the working of Roosevelt's mind. One of the best brief accounts of how the United States acquired the canal route is the twelfth chapter of William Henry Harbaugh,* Power and Responsibility: The Life and Times of Theodore Roosevelt *(New York: Farrar, Straus, & Giroux, 1961). For fuller treatments see Dwight C. Miner,* The Fight for the Panama Route: The Story of the Spooner Act and the Hay-Herrán Treaty *(New York: Columbia, 1940) and William David McCain,* The United States and the Republic of Panama *(Durham, N.C.: Duke, 1937).*

Some of the statements Roosevelt actually made in this published account were quite frank admissions. The revelation that by his own direction Secretary of State Hay and the United States officer at Bogotá "repeatedly warned Colombia that grave consequences might follow her rejection of the treaty" is startling. It is the more startling in that Roosevelt almost immediately after this sentence spelled out the consequences. If Colombia rejected the Hay-Herrán Treaty, which provided that for 10 million dollars and an annual rental of 250,000 dollars the United States would receive a ninety-nine-year lease on a canal zone in the Panama province of Colombia, "There would then be two possibilities." One was a Panamanian revolution, which in fact did occur. The other "was that Panama would remain quiet. In that case I was prepared to recommend to Congress that we should at once occupy the Isthmus anyhow, and proceed to dig the canal; and I had drawn out a draft of my message to this effect." In other words, Colombia faced either Panamanian revolution or United States force.

Roosevelt left unsaid some facts about Colombian-American diplomacy that may be relevant. The ex-President, for example, said nothing in his Autobiography about the Hay-Herrán Treaty, which the Colombian Congress rejected, other than that "if it erred at all, [it] erred in being overgenerous toward Colombia." The Colombians, at least, did not regard it as overgenerous. Tomás Herrán, the Colombian representative in Washington whose duty it was to get the best terms he could for his nation, signed the treaty only after he became persuaded that the United States was going to break off the negotiations altogether and build the canal across Nicaragua. Then, on January 22, 1903, three days after he had signed the treaty, he received word from his government in Bogotá not to sign it and to wait for new instructions. Nor did Roosevelt mention in this selection that the American minister in Bogotá reported that Colombian public opinion was "strongly against" the treaty.

And Roosevelt's account in his memoirs is unusual for the way that it says certain things about Panama. He went to some lengths to deny his or his government's complicity in the Panamanian revolution. "I did not lift my finger to incite the revolutionists." Yet, he reported with a touch of pride, "We gave to the people of Panama self-government, and freed them from subjection to alien oppressors."

In some of his personal letters Roosevelt was understandably more candid than in his published writings. In a letter to his English friend Cecil Arthur Spring Rice on January 18, 1904, he took a frankly imperialist position: "It was a good thing for Egypt and the Sudan, and for the world, when England took Egypt and the Sudan. It is a good thing for India that England should control it. And so it is a good thing, a very good thing, for Cuba and for Panama and for the world that the United States has acted as it has actually done during the last six years. The people of the United States and the people of the Isthmus and the rest of mankind will all be the better because we dig the Panama Canal and keep order in its neighborhood. And the politicians and revolutionists at Bogotá are entitled to precisely the amount of sympathy we extend to other inefficient bandits."

When we submitted to Colombia the Hay-Herran Treaty, it had been settled that the time for delay, the time for permitting any government of anti-social character, or of imperfect development, to bar the work, had passed. The United States had assumed in connection with the canal certain responsibilities not only to its own people, but to the civilized world which imperatively demanded that there should be no further delay in beginning the work. The Hay-Herran Treaty, if it erred at all, erred in being overgenerous toward Colombia. The people of Panama were delighted with the treaty, and the President of Colombia, who embodied in his own person the entire government of Colombia, had authorized the treaty to be made. But after the treaty had been made the Colombia Government thought it had the matter in its own hands; and the further thought, equally wicked and foolish, came into the heads of the people in control at Bogota that they would seize the French Company at the end of another year and take for themselves the forty million dollars which the United States had agreed to pay the Panama Canal Company.

President Maroquin, through his Minister, had agreed to the Hay-Herran Treaty in January, 1903. He had the absolute power of an unconstitutional dictator to keep his promise or break it. He determined to break it. To furnish himself an excuse for breaking it he devised the plan of summoning a Congress especially called to reject the canal treaty. This the Congress—a Congress of mere puppets—did, without a dissenting vote; and the puppets adjourned forthwith without legislating on any other subject. The fact that this was a mere sham, and that the President had entire power to confirm his own treaty and act on it if he desired, was shown as soon as the revolution took place, for on November 6 General Reyes, of Colombia, addressed the American Minister at Bogota, on behalf of President Maroquin, saying that "if the Government of the United States would land troops and restore the Colombian sovereignty" the Colombian President would "declare martial law; and, by virtue of vested constitutional authority, when public order is disturbed, would approve by decree the ratification of the canal treaty as signed; or, if the Government of the United States prefers, would call an extra session of the Congress—with new and friendly members—next May to approve the treaty." This, of course, is proof positive that the Colombian dictator had used his Congress as a mere shield, and a sham shield at that, and it shows how utterly useless it would have been further to trust his good faith in the matter.

When, in August, 1903, I became convinced that Colombia intended to repudiate the treaty made the preceding January, under cover of securing its rejection by the Colombian Legislature, I began carefully to consider what should be done. By my direction, Secretary Hay, personally and through the Minister at Bogota, repeatedly warned Colombia that grave consequences might follow her rejection of the treaty. The possibility of ratification did not wholly pass away until the close of the session of the Colombian Congress on the last day of October. There would then be two possibilities. One was that Panama would remain quiet. In that case I was prepared to recommend to Congress that we should at once occupy the Isthmus anyhow, and proceed to dig the canal; and I had drawn out a draft of my message to this effect. But from the information I received, I deemed it likely that there would be a revolution in Panama as soon as the Colombian Congress adjourned without ratifying the treaty, for the entire population of Panama felt that the immediate building of the canal was of vital concern to their well-being. Correspondents of the different newspapers on the Isthmus had sent to their respective papers widely published forecasts indicating that there would be a revolution in such event.

Moreover, on October 16, at the request of Lieutenant-General Young, Captain Humphrey and Lieutenant Murphy, two army officers who had returned from the Isthmus, saw me and told me that there would unquestionably be a revolution on the Isthmus, that the people were unanimous in their criticism of the Bogota Government and their disgust over the failure of that Government to ratify the treaty; and that the revolution would probably take place immediately after the adjournment of the Colombian Congress. They did not believe that it would be before October 20, but they were confident that it would certainly come at the end of October or immediately afterwards, when the Colombian Congress had adjourned. Accordingly I directed the Navy Department to station various ships within easy reach of the Isthmus, to be ready to act in the event of need arising.

These ships were barely in time. On November 3 the revolution occurred. Practically everybody on the Isthmus, including all the Colombian troops that were already stationed there, joined in the revolution, and there was no bloodshed. But on that same day four hundred new Colombian troops were landed at Colon. Fortunately, the gunboat *Nashville,* under Commander Hubbard, reached Colon almost immediately afterwards, and when the commander of the Colombian forces threatened the lives and property of the American citizens, including women and children, in Colon, Commander Hubbard landed a few score sailors and marines to protect them. By a mixture of firmness and tact he not only prevented any assault on our citizens, but persuaded the Colombian commander to reembark his troops for Cartagena. On the Pacific side a Colombian gunboat shelled the City of Panama, with the result of killing one Chinaman—the only life lost in the whole affair.

No one connected with the American Government had any part in preparing, inciting, or encouraging the revolution, and except for the reports of our military and naval officers, which I forwarded to Congress, no one connected with the Government had any previous knowledge concerning the proposed revolution, except such as was accessible to any person who read the newspapers and kept abreast of current questions and current affairs. By the unanimous action of its people, and without the firing of a shot, the state of Panama declared themselves an independent republic. The time for hesitation on our part had passed.

My belief then was, and the events that have occurred since have more than justified it, that from the standpoint of the United States it was imperative, not only for civil but for military reasons, that there should be the immediate establishment of easy and speedy communication by sea between the Atlantic and the Pacific. These reasons were not of convenience only, but of vital necessity, and did not admit of indefinite delay. The action of Colombia had shown not only that the delay would be indefinite, but that she intended to confiscate the property and rights of the French Panama Canal Company. The report of the Panama Canal Committee of the Colombian Senate on October 14, 1903, on the proposed treaty with the United States, proposed that all consideration of the matter should be postponed until October 31, 1904, when the next Colombian Congress would have convened, because by that time the new Congress would be in condition to determine whether through lapse of time the French company had not forfeited its property and rights. "When that time arrives," the report significantly declared, "the Republic, without any impediment, will be able to contract and will be in more clear, more definite and more advantageous possession, both legally and materially." The naked meaning of this was that Colombia proposed to wait a year, and then enforce a forfeiture of the rights and property of the French Panama Company, so as to secure the forty million dollars our Government had authorized as payment to this company. If we had sat supine, this would doubtless have meant that France would have interfered to protect the company, and we should then have had on the Isthmus, not the company, but France; and the gravest international complications might have ensued. Every consideration of international morality and expediency, of duty to the Panama people, and of satisfaction of our own national interests and honor, bade us take immediate action. I recognized Panama forthwith on behalf of the United States, and practically all the countries of the world immediately followed suit. The State Department immediately negotiated a canal treaty with the new Republic. One of the foremost men in securing the independence of Panama, and the treaty which authorized the United States forthwith to build the canal, was M. Philippe Bunau-Varilla, an eminent French engineer formerly associated with De Lesseps and then living on the Isthmus; his services to civilization were notable, and deserve the fullest recognition.

From the beginning to the end our course was straightforward and in absolute accord with the highest of standards of international morality. Criticism of it can come only from misinformation, or else from a sentimentality which represents both mental weakness and a moral twist. To have acted otherwise than I did would have been on my part betrayal of the interests of the United States, indifference to the interests of Panama, and recreancy to the interests of the world at large. Colombia had forfeited every claim to consideration; indeed, this is not stating the case strongly enough: she had so acted that yielding to her would have meant on our part that culpable form of weakness which stands on a level with wickedness. As for me personally, if I had hesitated to act, and had not in advance discounted the clamor of those Americans who have made a fetish of disloyalty to their country, I should have esteemed myself as deserving a place in Dante's inferno beside the faint-hearted cleric who was guilty of "il gran rifiuto." The facts I have given above are mere bald statements from the record. They show that from the beginning there had been acceptance of our right to insist on free transit, in whatever form was best, across the Isthmus; and that towards the end there had been a no less universal feeling that it was our duty to the world to provide this transit in the shape of a canal—the resolution of the Pan-American Congress was practically a mandate to this effect. Colombia was then under a one-man government, a dictatorship, founded on usurpation of absolute and irresponsible power. She eagerly pressed us to enter into an agreement with her, as long as there was any chance of our going to the alternative route through Nicaragua. When she thought we were committed, she refused to fulfill the agreement, with the avowed hope of seizing the French company's property for nothing and thereby holding us up. This was a bit of pure bandit morality. It would have achieved its purpose had I possessed as weak moral fiber as those of my critics who announced that I ought to have confined my action to feeble scolding and temporizing until the opportunity for action passed. I did not lift my finger to incite the revolutionists. The right simile to use is totally different. I simply ceased to stamp out the different revolutionary fuses that were already burning. When Colombia committed flagrant wrong against us, I considered it no part of my duty to aid and abet her in her wrongdoing at our expense, and also at the expense of Panama, of the French company, and of the world generally. There had been fifty years of continuous bloodshed and civil strife in Panama; because of my action Panama had now known ten years of such peace and prosperity as she never before saw during the four centuries of her existence—for in Panama, as in Cuba and Santo Domingo, it was the action of the American people, against the outcries of the professed apostles of peace, which alone brought peace. We gave to the people of Panama self-government, and freed them from subjection to alien oppressors. We did our best to get Colombia to let us treat her with a more than generous justice; we exercised patience to beyond the verge of proper forbearance. When we did act and recognize Panama, Colombia at once acknowledged her own guilt by promptly offering to do what we had demanded, and what she had protested it was not in her power to do. But the offer came too late. What we would gladly have done before, it had by that time become impossible for us honorably to do; for it would have necessitated our abandoning the people of Panama, our friends, and turning them over to their and our foes, who would have wreaked vengeance on them precisely because they had shown friendship to us. Colombia was solely responsible for her own humiliation; and she had not then, and has not now, one shadow of claim upon us, moral or legal; all the wrong that was done was done by her. If, as representing the American people, I had not acted precisely as I did, I would have been an unfaithful or incompetent representative; and inaction at that crisis would have meant not only indefinite delay in building the canal, but also practical admission on our part that we were not fit to play the part on the Isthmus which we had arrogated to ourselves. I acted on my own responsibility in the Panama matter. John Hay spoke of this action as follows: "The action of the President in the Panama matter is not only in the strictest accordance with the principles of justice and equity, and in line with all the best precedents of our public policy, but it was the only course he could have taken in compliance with our treaty rights and obligations."

I deeply regretted, and now deeply regret, the fact that the Colombian Government rendered it imperative for me to take the action I took; but I had no alternative, consistent with the full performance of my duty to my own people, and to the nations of mankind. (For, be it remembered, that certain other nations, Chile for example, will probably benefit even more by our action than will the United States itself.) I am well aware that the Colombian people have many fine traits; that there is among them a circle of highbred men and women which would reflect honor on the social life of any country; and that there has been an intellectual and literary development within this small circle which partially atones for the stagnation and illiteracy of the mass of the people; and I also know that even the illiterate mass possesses many sterling qualities. But unfortunately in international matters every nation must be judged by the action of its Government. The good people in Colombia apparently made no effort, certainly no successful effort, to cause the Government to act with reasonable good faith towards the United States; and Colombia had to take the consequences. If Brazil, or the Argentine, or Chile, had been in possession of the Isthmus, doubtless the canal would have been built under the governmental control of the nation thus controlling the Isthmus, with the hearty acquiescence of the United States and of all other powers. But in the actual fact the canal would not have been built at all save for the action I took. If men choose to say that it would have been better not to build it, than to build it as the result of such action, their position, although foolish, is compatible with belief in their wrong-headed sincerity. But it is hypocrisy, alike odious and contemptible, for any man to say both that we ought to have built the canal and that we ought not to have acted in the way we did act.

After a sufficient period of wrangling, the Senate ratified the treaty with Panama, and work on the canal was begun.

SELECTION

William Howard Taft and Dollar Diplomacy: Message to Congress, December 3, 1912

Article II, Section 3, of the Constitution, speaking of the President, says, "He shall from time to time give to the Congress Information of the State of the Union. . . ." From this injunction has come the annual State of the Union address. This selection is from President Taft's last such message, which he devoted exclusively to a consideration of foreign policy.

Historians have frequently referred opprobriously to Taft's foreign policies as "dollar diplomacy." It is a little difficult to see why Taft's policies especially should be thus labeled, because concern for commercial or financial advantage has been a consistent purpose of American foreign policy, well before Taft's administration and since, as well as a cardinal objective of the foreign policies of other nations. President Taft explicitly referred to the dollar, but he thought of it as an alternative to force: "substituting dollars for bullets." In Taft's eyes, "legitimate commercial aims" and "idealistic humanitarian sentiments" presented no conflicting values in the conduct of the nation's relations with other countries. In international relations, Taft seemed to agree with Alexander Pope that "self-love and social are the same." Thus, to use a Central American example, his administration "has been glad to encourage and support American bankers who were willing to lend a helping hand to the financial rehabilitation" of Nicaragua and Honduras because their financial rehabilitation and the "protection of their customhouses from being the prey of would-be dictators would remove at one stroke the menace of foreign [European] creditors and the menace of revolutionary disorder." Further, the "era of peace and prosperity" that was the expected result would be advantageous for "all the southern and Gulf ports and the business and industry of the South" of the United States as well as for the Nicaraguans and Hondurans. Everyone benefits.

This selection, which cuts Taft's message by about half, is from the Congressional Record, *Sixty-second Congress, third session, volume 49, part 1, pages 9–11, 14. For a general work on the relations of the United States with her southern neighbors, see Samuel Flagg Bemis,* The Latin American Policy of the United States: An Historical Interpretation *(New York: Harcourt, Brace and World, 1943). The standard work on Taft is Henry F. Pringle,* The Life and Times of William Howard Taft: A Biography *(New York: Holt, Rinehart and Winston, 1939), two volumes.*

The diplomacy of the present administration has sought to respond to modern ideas of commercial intercourse. This policy has been characterized as substituting dollars for bullets. It is one that appears alike to idealistic humanitarian sentiments, to the dictates of sound policy and strategy, and to legitimate commercial aims. It is an effort frankly directed to the increase of American trade upon the axiomatic principle that the Government of the United States shall extend all proper support to every legitimate and beneficial American enterprise abroad. How great have been the results of this diplomacy, coupled with the maximum and minimum provision of the tariff law, will be seen by some consideration of the wonderful increase in the export trade of the United States. Because modern diplomacy is commercial, there has been a disposition in some quarters to attribute to it none but materialistic aims. How strikingly erroneous is such an impression may be seen from a study of the results by which the diplomacy of the United States can be judged.

Successful Efforts in Promotion of Peace

In the field of work toward the ideals of peace this Government negotiated, but to my regret was unable to consummate, two arbitration treaties which set the highest mark of the aspiration of nations toward the substitution of arbitration and reason for war in the settlement of international disputes.

Through the efforts of American diplomacy several wars have been prevented or ended. I refer to the successful tripartite mediation of the Argentine Republic, Brazil, and the United States between Peru and Ecuador; the bringing of the boundary dispute between Panama and Costa Rica to peaceful arbitration; the staying of warlike preparations when Haiti and the Dominican Republic were on the verge of hostilities; the stopping of a war in Nicaragua; the halting of internecine strife in Honduras. The Government of the United States was thanked for its influence toward the restoration of amicable relations between the Argentine Republic and Bolivia. The diplomacy of the United States is active in seeking to assuage the remaining ill-feeling between this country and the Republic of Colombia. In the recent civil war in China the United States successfully joined with the other interested powers in urging an early cessation of hostilities. An agreement has been reached between the Governments of Chile and Peru whereby the celebrated Tacna-Arica dispute, which has so long embittered international relations on the west coast of South America, has at last been adjusted. Simultaneously came the news that the boundary dispute between Peru and Ecuador had entered upon a stage of amicable settlement. The position of the United States in reference to the Tacna-Arica dispute between Chile and Peru has been one of nonintervention, but one of friendly influence and pacific counsel throughout the period during which the dispute in question has been the subject of interchange of views between this Government and the two Governments immediately concerned. In the general easing of international tension on the west coast of South America the tripartite mediation, to which I have referred, has been a most potent and beneficent factor.

China

In China the policy of encouraging financial investment to enable that country to help itself has had the result of giving new life and practical application to the open-door policy. The consistent purpose of the present administration has been to encourage the use of American capital in the development of China by the promotion of those essential reforms to which China is pledged by treaties with the United States and other powers. The hypothecation to foreign bankers in connection with certain industrial enterprises, such as the Hukuang railways, of the national revenues upon which these reforms depended, led the Department of State early in the administration to demand for American citizens participation in such enterprises, in order that the United States might have equal rights and an equal voice in all questions pertaining to the disposition of the public revenues concerned. The same policy of promoting international accord among the powers having similar treaty rights as ourselves in the matters of reform, which could not be put into practical effect without the common consent of all, was likewise adopted in the case of the loan desired by China for the reform of its currency. The principle of international cooperation in matters of common interest upon which our policy had already been based in all of the above instances has admittedly been a great factor in that concert of the powers which has been so happily conspicuous during the perilous period of transition through which the great Chinese nation has been passing.

Central America Needs Our Help in Debt Adjustment

In Central America the aim has been to help such countries as Nicaragua and Honduras to help themselves. They are the immediate beneficiaries. The national benefit to the United States is twofold. First, it is obvious that the Monroe doctrine is more vital in the neighborhood of the Panama Canal and the zone of the Caribbean than anywhere else. There, too, the maintenance of that doctrine falls most heavily upon the United States. It is therefore essential that the countries within that sphere shall be removed from the jeopardy involved by heavy foreign debt and chaotic national finances and from the ever-present danger of international complications due to disorder at home. Hence the United States has been glad to encourage and support American bankers who were willing to lend a helping hand to the financial rehabilitation of such countries, because this financial rehabilitation and the protection of their customhouses from being the prey of would-be dictators would remove at one stroke the menace of foreign creditors and the menace of revolutionary disorder.

The second advantage to the United States is one affecting chiefly all the southern and Gulf ports and the business and industry of the South. The Republics of Central America and the Caribbean possess great natural wealth. They need only a measure of stability and the means of financial regeneration to enter upon an era of peace and prosperity, bringing profit and happiness to themselves and at the same time creating conditions sure to lead to a flourishing interchange of trade with this country. . . .

Increase of Foreign Trade

In my last annual message I said that the fiscal year ended June 30, 1911, was noteworthy as marking the highest record of exports of American products to foreign countries. The fiscal year 1912 shows that this rate of advance has been maintained, the total domestic exports having a valuation approximately of $2,200,000,000, as compared with a fraction over $2,000,000,000 the previous year. It is also significant that manufactured and partly manufactured articles continue to be the chief commodities forming the volume of our augmented exports, the demands of our own people for consumption requiring that an increasing proportion of our abundant agricultural products be kept at home. In the fiscal year 1911 the exports of articles in the various stages of manufacture, not including foodstuffs partly or wholly manufactured, amounted approximately to $907,500,000. In the fiscal year 1912 the total was nearly $1,022,000,000, a gain of $114,000,000.

Advantage of Maximum and Minimum Tariff Provision

The importance which our manufactures have assumed in the commerce of the world in competition with the manufactures of other countries again draws attention to the duty of this Government to use its utmost endeavors to secure impartial treatment for American products in all markets. Healthy commercial rivalry in international intercourse is best assured by the possession of proper means for protecting and promoting our foreign trade. It is natural that competitive countries should view with some concern this steady expansion of our commerce. If in some instances the measure taken by them to meet it are not entirely equitable, a remedy should be found. In former messages I have described the negotiations of the Department of State with foreign Governments for the adjustment of the maximum and minimum tariff as provided in section 2 of the tariff law of 1909. The advantages secured by the adjustment of our trade relations under this law have continued during the last year, and some additional cases of discriminatory treatment of which we had reason to complain have been removed. The Department of State has for the first time in the history of this country obtained substantial most-favored-nation treatment from all the countries of the world. There are, however, other instances which, while apparently not constituting undue discrimination in the sense of section 2, are nevertheless exceptions to the complete equity of tariff treatment for American products that the Department of State consistently has sought to obtain for American commerce abroad.

Necessity for Supplementary Legislation

These developments confirm the opinion conveyed to you in my annual message of 1911, that while the maximum and minimum provision of the tariff law of 1909 has been fully justified by the success achieved in removing previously existing undue discriminations against American products, yet experience has shown that this feature of the law should be amended in such way as to provide a fully effective means of meeting the varying degrees of discriminatory treatment of American commerce in foreign countries still encountered, as well as to protect against injurious treatment on the part of foreign Governments, through either legislative or administrative measures, the financial interests abroad of American citizens whose enterprises enlarge the market for American commodities.

I can not too strongly recommend to the Congress the passage of some such enabling measure as the bill which was recommended by the Secretary of State in his letter of December 13, 1911. The object of the proposed legislation is, in brief, to enable the Executive to apply, as the case may require, to any or all commodities, whether or not on the free list from a country which discriminates against the United States, a graduated scale of duties up to the maximum of 25 per cent ad valorem provided in the present law. Flat tariffs are out of date. Nations no longer accord equal tariff treatment to all other nations irrespective of the treatment from them received. Such a flexible power at the command of the Executive would serve to moderate any unfavorable tendencies on the part of those countries from which the importations into the United States are substantially confined to articles on the free list as well as of the countries which find a lucrative market in the United States for their products under existing customs rates. It is very necessary that the American Government should be equipped with weapons of negotiation adapted to modern economic conditions, in order that we may at all times be in a position to gain not only technically just but actually equitable treatment for our trade, and also for American enterprise and vested interests abroad.

Business Secured to Our Country by Direct Official Effort

As illustrating the commercial benefits to the Nation derived from the new diplomacy and its effectiveness upon the material as well as the more ideal side, it may be remarked that through direct official efforts alone there have been obtained in the course of this administration contracts from foreign Governments involving an expenditure of $50,000,000 in the factories of the United States. Consideration of this fact and some reflection upon the necessary effects of a scientific tariff system and a foreign service alert and equipped to cooperate with the business men of America carry the conviction that the gratifying increase in the export trade of this country is, in substantial amount, due to our improved governmental methods of protecting and stimulating it. It is germane to these observations to remark that in the two years that have elapsed since the successful negotiation of our new treaty with Japan, which at the time seemed to present so many practical difficulties, our export trade to that country has increased at the rate of over $1,000,000 a month. Our exports to Japan for the year ended June 30, 1910, were $21,959,310, while for the year ended June 30, 1912, the exports were $53,478,046, a net increase in the sale of American products of nearly 150 per cent. . . .

Necessity for Greater Governmental Effort in Retention and Expansion of Our Foreign Trade

It is not possible to make to the Congress a communication upon the present foreign relations of the United States so detailed as to convey an adequate impression of the enormous increase in the importance and activities of those relations. If this Government is really to preserve to the American people that free opportunity in foreign markets which will soon be indispensable to our prosperity, even greater efforts must be made. Otherwise the American merchant, manufacturer, and exporter will find many a field in which American trade should logically predominate preempted through the more energetic efforts of other governments and other commercial nations.

There are many ways in which through hearty cooperation the legislative and executive branches of this Government can do much. The absolute essential is the spirit of united effort and singleness of purpose. I will allude only to a very few specific examples of action which ought then to result. America can not take its proper place in the most important fields for its commercial activity and enterprise unless we have a merchant marine. American commerce and enterprise can not be effectively fostered in these fields unless we have good American banks in the countries referred to. We need American newspapers in those countries and proper means for public information about them. We need to assure the permanency of a trained foreign service. We need legislation enabling the members of the foreign service to be systematically brought in direct contact with the industrial, manufacturing, and exporting interests of this country in order that American business men may enter the foreign field with a clear perception of the exact conditions to be dealt with and the officers themselves may prosecute their work with a clear idea of what American industrial and manufacturing interests require.

Conclusion

Congress should fully realize the conditions which obtain in the world as we find ourselves at the threshold of our middle age as a Nation. We have emerged full grown as a peer in the great concourse of nations. We have passed through various formative periods. We have been self-centered in the struggle to develop our domestic resources and deal with our domestic questions. The Nation is now too mature to continue in its foreign relations those temporary expedients natural to a people to whom domestic affairs are the sole concern. In the past our diplomacy has often consisted, in normal times, in a mere assertion of the right to international existence. We are now in a larger relation with broader rights of our own and obligations to others than ourselves. A number of great guiding principles were laid down early in the history of this Government. The recent task of our diplomacy has been to adjust those principles to the conditions of to-day, to develop their corollaries, to find practical applications of the old principles expanded to meet new situations. Thus are being evolved bases upon which can rest the superstructure of policies which must grow with the destined progress of this Nation. The successful conduct of our foreign relations demands a broad and a modern view. We can not meet new questions nor build for the future if we confine ourselves to outworn dogmas of the past and to the perspective appropriate at our emergence from colonial times and conditions. The opening of the Panama Canal will mark a new era in our international life and create new and worldwide conditions which, with their vast correlations and consequences, will obtain for hundreds of years to come. We must not wait for events to overtake us unawares. With continuity of purpose we must deal with the problems of our external relations by a diplomacy modern, resourceful, magnanimous, and fittingly expressive of the high ideals of a great nation.

SELECTION

The Department of State, Mining Investors, and the Mexican Revolution, 1916

The most dramatic events in the relations of the United States and Mexico in early 1916 were the raids into the United States of Francisco (Pancho) Villa and the Punitive Expedition into Mexico led by Brigadier General John J. Pershing in futile pursuit of the bandit-revolutionist. Villa was in rebellion against the government of General Venustiano Carranza, and his raids north of the Rio Grande were apparently part of a strategy to provoke a United States invasion and thereby weaken Carranza. In the fall of 1915, after Carranza had successfully defeated a counterrevolutionary force, the Wilson administration had recognized the Carranza government as the de facto [in fact] government of Mexico, as opposed to the de jure [of right] government). Villa's strategy did not completely succeed. As Pershing's forces penetrated deeply into Mexico, tensions between the two nations became serious—war was quite conceivable in June, 1916—but Wilson was more anxious about the war in Europe and agreed to negotiate the differences between the two nations.

The United States was deeply concerned with the course of the Mexican revolution, which first erupted in 1911, was intense for the next few years, and then subsided, only to erupt into other periods of revolutionary tension in the 1920s and 1930s. The proximity of Mexico has been one important reason for United States concern with Mexican political affairs, as has been the recurring anticlericalism that has often alarmed Roman Catholics north of the border. But another important reason for concern, a reason often overlooked, has been the investments, particularly in oil and mining properties, that United States citizens and firms have in Mexico. This selection of correspondence between Department of State personnel has to do with representations made in behalf of United States investors in Mexican mines who objected to the taxes on their mines.

These communications tell a story of pressure and resistance that needs only a little explanation to be understood. The reader should remember always that the trouble with Villa was contemporary with these documents. (On January 10, 1916, Villa's men removed eighteen American engineers from a Mexican train and executed them on the spot. His raid on Columbus, New Mexico, was March 9. General Pershing and the expedition crossed into Mexico on March 15.) A pertenencia was a unit of land measurement used in mining; it was equal to a hectare, or "metric acre," the equivalent of 2.471 Anglo-American acres. A tercio was a tax period. Luis Cabrera was Minister of Finance in the Carranza government. John R. Silliman had been a special agent of the State Department to Carranza, serving as a communications channel between Washington and the general, since July, 1914, long before Carranza was recognized as the de facto head of state. James L. Rodgers was named a special representative to the de facto government February 28, 1916, after this exchange of correspondence had begun. *Lansing, the sender of many of these letters and telegrams, was, of course, Secretary of State Robert Lansing, who served in that office from 1915 to 1920. Secretary Lansing, incidentally, was a son-in-law of John Watson Foster, President Benjamin Harrison's Secretary of State, and was an uncle by marriage of John Foster Dulles, Secretary of State under President Eisenhower.*

This selection is taken from Papers Relating to the Foreign Relations of the United States, 1916 *(Washington: Government Printing Office, 1925), pages 710–715, 718–719. For an account of Mexican-American relations during the Wilson years, see Arthur S. Link,* Woodrow Wilson and the Progressive Era, 1910–1917 *(New York: Harper & Row, 1954); for a valuable general work see Howard F. Cline.* The United States and Mexico *(Cambridge, Mass.: Harvard, 1953).*

The Secretary of State to Special Agent Silliman

Department of State,
Washington, February 21, 1916.

Sir:

You are instructed to bring the following statement personally to the attention of General Carranza, handing him a copy thereof:

The Government of the United States is cognizant and mindful of all that is transpiring in Mexico, particularly is this so in relation to events pertaining to the revolution, and it has taken into deep and friendly consideration the incontrollable bounds which the excesses of the fratricidal strife, at times, assumed, to the consequent cost of American lives, property, and rights. This Government has consistently shown its friendly interest for the Mexican people in numerous and manifest ways, and it has no desire or thought of altering its well-known attitude of good will. In the capacity of a friend it wishes to continue to lend such assistance as it appropriately can, to enable the Mexican people to attain the greatest measure of liberty, peace and happiness.

During the earlier period of the revolution, because of there being no recognized government, and because of the existence of different factions, many untoward incidents occurred in Mexico, affecting the rights of Americans and other foreigners, even going to the extreme of a deplorable sacrifice of human life, and giving the deepest concern to this Government; all the more so because of its earnest and kindly inclinations toward the Mexican nation.

Since the recognition of the *de facto* Government, on October 19, 1915, this Government has extended its friendship in an even more tangible manner, and, in numerous ways has assisted, cooperated with, and supported the *de facto* Government, realizing full well that the work of pacification is no light task, and that, in the pursuance of that object, the *de facto* Government would have, at times, to face bewildering circumstances and to solve difficult problems.

Moved by its sincere desire to be helpful, and in accordance with the spirit which this desire excites, this Government invites the attention of the *de facto* Government to the unfortunate, and, it may be said, disastrous effect of a number of decrees recently promulgated by the *de facto* Government. These decrees were probably issued with the best of intentions. It appears, however, that in taking into account the underlying causes which probably prompted their issuance, a studious consideration of their probable effect was, unfortunately, not given before official pronouncement. In many cases decrees, designed to be remedial to the exchequer of the *de facto* Government, have had, and will continue to have, the contrary effect. The imposition of arbitrary and excessive taxes, practically confiscatory in their nature, tends to stifle industry and to stagnate business. On the other hand, if the cooperation of the industrial agencies which formerly operated in Mexico were invited, with assurances of protection while their plants were being rehabilitated, and in their subsequent operation; and if, at the same time, the *de facto* Government should announce that it wished them to assist it in the work of restoring peace and reviving prosperity, and that the old rates of taxation to which they were formerly accustomed would be applied, it is reasonably certain that such a blend of friendliness and economic wisdom would result in establishing wholesome confidence and would instill a new-born strength into the country. Millions of dollars would drift rapidly into Mexico, and, before it would be realized, the flood-tide of prosperity would have set in. Such a policy would logically have had an immediate effect on the paper money issued by the *de facto* Government, and would have been, and would still be, of wonderful aid to it in solving its perplexing problems, and of removing many of them forthwith.

Decrees like those of Governor Caballero, of Tamaulipas, of January 14, 1914, just now being put into effect; of the Governor of Chihuahua, of December 31, 1915; of Governor Aguilar, of Vera Cruz, of January 15, 1916; of Governor Triana, of Aguascalientes, of January 21, 1916; of Governor Calles, of Sonora, of January 27, 1916; and the circular of the Secretary of Justice, of February 18, 1916, all of which affect property rights, with clauses, or phraseology, which make it plain that they are aimed at foreigners; the decree prohibiting the exportation of cotton, and that applying the same restriction to hides, can produce only ill effects. They are all in direct violation of the Constitution of Mexico and advertise to the world, all too plainly, facts which certainly should not be made so patent. Some of these decrees, it appears, were issued without the knowledge of General Carranza; but the fact that they remain in force, after his attention has been called to them, tends to show that they have his approval.

Four months have elapsed since this Government recognized the *de facto* Government, of which General Carranza is the Chief Executive. During that time a number of decrees have been issued, and the provisions of previous decrees insisted upon, which have seriously affected American property and rights, and if some of these decrees emanating from General Carranza continue to be enforced by him, they will assume proportions of very grave concern, for, aside from the nature of the decrees, the spirit shown throughout is not reciprocally in consonance with that shown by this Government. Owing to the importance of the case, this Government was constrained, on June 30, 1915, to take a stand relative to the increased taxes imposed by the mining decree of March 1, 1915. On December 28, 1915, this Government reiterated its stand of June 30. Since that time this Government was informed that upon the return of Señor Luis Cabrera it was expected that certain modifications would be made in this decree. Señor Cabrera returned to Querétaro the early part of the present month, and it was then stated that the excessive taxes imposed by this decree, in many cases confiscatory, should be paid on March 1, but that certain modifications would be considered for the taxes falling due on July 1, 1916. This Government regards the matter as one of such grave import that it most earnestly desires the *de facto* Government to give this subject full and conscientious reconsideration. In fact, it asks that the annulment of this degree, before March 1, be taken under serious advisement. It may here be stated that the operation of the decree of March 1, 1915, has already caused the threatened abandonment of certain mining properties; and when such measures begin to be adopted, it will be difficult to foresee how far they will go, or what effects they may produce.

This Administration feels assured that the broad circumspection of the *de facto* Government will make evident to it the fact that failure to adopt measures to win the confidence of the people at home and of foreign nations will have the effect of keeping the currency of the *de facto* Government at its present depreciated figure, or of still further depressing it. That condition of the currency, together with others so closely correlated that they cannot be regarded separately from it, makes the very delicate task before the *de facto* Government one which should be approached, in all of its phases, with the greatest caution as to means and considerateness as to consequences.

I am [etc.]
ROBERT LANSING

Special Agent Silliman to the Secretary of State

[Telegram]

Guadalajara, February 24, 1916, 4 p. m.

4. Pending written reply to my representation conveying Department's February 21, 6 p. m., mining decrees.

Foreign Secretary said on the train this afternoon:

First, the Mexican Government cannot comply with the request of the Government of the United States to annul the present mining decree nor can it modify the decree at this time. Second, the Mexican Government does not consider the Department's construction of the Mexican constitution in the matter as tenable. Third, the Mexican Government must consider payments made for mining taxes due and receipts given therefor as a complete liquidation.

SILLIMAN

The Secretary of State to Special Agent Silliman

[Telegram—Extract]

Department of State,
Washington, February 26, 1916, 4 p. m.

Your 4, February 24, 4 p. m. You will say to General Carranza that this Government is deeply disappointed at his attitude toward the representations of this Government in a matter so vitally affecting a vast amount of American owned property. You will also say to him that this Government, while not wishing to add to the many difficulties confronting the *de facto* Government, feels it to be its duty towards its own citizens very earnestly but respectfully to reaffirm the tenor of its telegrams on this subject, of June 30, and December 28 last, and the 21st instant.

LANSING

The Secretary of State to Special Representative Rodgers

[Telegram]

Department of State,
Washington, March 13, 1916, 6 p. m.

Mining decree. Refer to Department's telegrams June 30, December 28, February 21 and 26 to Silliman, and to memorandums given you in person. You are instructed to take up with General Carranza, at first favorable and early opportunity, the annulment of the mining decree of March 1, 1915. If, after earnest representations, you find that abrogation is impossible at present, you should then use every effort to convince General Carranza that the ruling for the payment of taxes for the last tercio, namely, at rate of eight pesos per annum per pertenencia, be made to apply to taxes now due. Also the metal export duties fixed by said decree should be reduced by one half. Failing in your efforts, endeavor to obtain an extension of 30 days after March 31, for payment of taxes now due.

You will call General Carranza's attention to the assurances given Silliman, set forth in latter's telegram of January 5.

LANSING

Department of State,
Washington, March 24, 1916, 6 p. m.

6. If annulment or modification of mining decree has not yet been accomplished in accordance with Department's March 13, 6 p. m., you will, in view present unusual circumstances, and impossibility for many interested Americans to pay their taxes before April 1, immediately con-

centrate your best efforts to secure, as a temporary expedient, longest possible extension in time for payment of this tercio's tax, in order that more time may be available for negotiations.

Telegraph status and prospects.

LANSING

Special Representative Rodgers to the Secretary of State

[Telegram]

Querétaro, March 28, 1916, 1 a. m.

8. In reply to Department's March 24, 6 p. m. Mining decree. Authorized to state by the Secretary of the Treasury that extension time payment mining taxes present tercio will be given until May 1, and that no forfeitures will occur before July 1 in any event. Meanwhile further careful consideration will be given whole matter with view absolutely fair action in view conditions both sides of the question. Invited by the Secretary of the Treasury consult with him frequently about this subject and to study same in conjunction with Mexican authorities. Secretary of the Treasury stated frankly Mexico needs revenue but would proceed fairly and justly in all things. Believe mining matter safely can be left in abeyance for the present.

RODGERS

The Secretary of State to Special Representative Rodgers

[Telegrams]

Department of State,
Washington, March 31, 1916, 4 p. m.

19. Your 8, March 28, 1 a. m. It is suggested that you convey to *de facto* Government Department's appreciation of extension time-limit within which mining taxes may be paid.

LANSING

Department of State,
Washington, April 11, 1916, 5 p. m.

34. American mining representative in Mexico City telegraphs:
"No decree exists relative extension May 1 without fine."

Ascertain and telegraph whether or not those taking advantage extension time to pay mining taxes will be subjected to fines or penalties.

LANSING

Special Representative Rodgers to the Secretary of State

[Telegrams]

Mexico City, April 12, 1916, noon.

4. In reply to Department's April 11, 5 p. m. Cabrera said Monday, instructions to collectors taxes allowing extension time for payment mining taxes would be issued at once, press other matters delayed this action. Will ask for further time. Any fine or penalty paid will be credited on payment taxes present tercio. Few such cases. Have explained all this to mining representatives here. Will be little action until new law announced.

RODGERS

Mexico City, April 19, 1916, noon.

21. Mining taxes. New taxes effective July 1. Precious metal mines. One to ten pertenencias six pesos Mexican gold each per annum; eleven to fifty, twelve pesos; fifty-one to hundred, eighteen pesos; over hundred, twenty-four pesos.

Nonprecious metal mines. One to fifty pertenencias, six pesos Mexican gold each; fifty-one to two hundred, twelve pesos; two hundred to five hundred, eighteen pesos; above five hundred, twenty-four. Export tax gold and silver ten per cent *ad valorem*. State tax raised to maximum of two per cent. Cabrera states intent new law develop small holdings and places prohibitive rates upon undeveloped large holdings. Justifies increase export tax by necessity for revenue.

Mining interests while not satisfied are acquiescent some extent. Disinterested people assert new taxes rather fair. Do not think much, if any, amendment possible.

RODGERS

The Secretary of State to Special Representative Rodgers

[Telegram]

Department of State,
Washington, April 24, 1916. 6 p. m.

58. Your 21, April 19. American mining companies disappointed in proposed new rates. They claim new decree more severe, in some respects, than present decree, and request Department to insist on position taken in its June 30 last, that taxes should be collected in accordance with laws emanating from Constitution, and contend that this Government should not recognize forfeitures resulting from inability to pay the present high rates, in view prostrate condition mining and smelting industry in Mexico. Companies also desire to know whether you can effect compromise, on basis of last November payment, namely, eight pesos per pertenencia.

Department does not consider that new decree in any way meets suggestions of this Government. You will therefore renew your best efforts to obtain consent of *de facto* Government to accept payment present and last tercio's tax, on basis eight pesos, and to effect material modification in proposed decree. Telegraph soon as possible.

Mining companies believe persons mentioned last paragraph your telegram probably not *bona fide* representatives of mining interests.

LANSING

Special Representative Rodgers to the Secretary of State

[Telegram—Extract]

Mexico City, April 25, 1916, 7 p. m.

30. In reply to Department's 58, April 22, 6 p. m. Had extended conference with Cabrera on proposed mining taxes to-day. He stated, first, that Mexico has undoubtedly right to institute, apply and maintain its own revenue measures and that in this instance such measures are instituted in regular manner by *de facto* Government. Second, that Mexico Government determined to apply principle high tax to large holdings, mineral lands and low to small, this being for general benefit and in the interest of overvalues. Third, that proposed taxes not high, but only fair, and especially so to Government which needs revenue for rehabilitation after disastrous period civil disturbance. Fourth, that proposed taxes when reduced to average basis will appear low for privilege given. Fifth, that mining companies and encumbents of nationality other than American have not objected to pertenencia taxes but apparently have accepted that in good spirit. Sixth, that advisability increasing export tax should be open to question. Seventh, that intent proposed decree to develop mining industry and not to retard it. Eighth, that Mexican Government thinks proposed decree all right and will adhere to it and it remains for mining operators to say whether they desire to work under it or not.

Suggestions of compromise tax eight pesos per pertenencia and was informed would not be considered as sliding scale proposed meets view Mexican Government.

Some slight modifications in minor details proposed decree probable and perhaps export tax may be lowered after trial but think announced taxes will be maintained absolutely and that nothing more can be done at present.

RODGERS

PART TWO

The Progressive Era

D uring the Presidencies of Theodore Roosevelt (1901–1909), William Howard Taft (1909–1913), and Woodrow Wilson (1913–1921), or at least until the 1917 war declaration, the ferment for reform of various kinds was so strong that we commonly refer to those years as the Progressive Era. Progressivism was pervasive. The passion for orderly, rationally directed, "progressive" change focused most sharply, perhaps, upon problems of government economic policy, both state and national, but it affected municipal administration, education, law, business administration, and religion as well.

Most of the problems that challenged progressives were directly or indirectly a result of the industrialization of the nation that had developed rapidly in the last half of the nineteenth century. Through the first six selections in Part Two (up to and including Senator La Follette's speech) run two threads: the question of the nature of government in general and the Federal government in particular, its powers, and its proper role in an industrial society; and the problem of how to use governmental powers, however conceived, in the best interests of the nation and society in general in dealing with the economic power of large and strong corporations, which had developed with industrialism. Each of these six selections, explicitly or implicitly, directly or indirectly, treats one or both of these questions. The authors did not agree in their analyses or their solutions; they agreed only that the problems were basic and their solution necessary.

The selection by Lincoln Steffens has to do with urban corruption, which was largely a result of industrialization, and the problems before the Supreme Court in Selection 17 would not have arisen in an agrarian society. The selections by Jane Addams and Randolph Bourne, on immigrants and their role in America, likewise consider a problem that derived from the nation's becoming industrialized.

An Intellectual Formulates the New Nationalism:
Herbert Croly in "The Promise of American Life" (1909)

In conventional accounts of the split in the Republican party from about 1910 to 1916, one reads that the vigorous and young ex-President Theodore Roosevelt got the idea for his New Nationalism from Herbert Croly's book The Promise of American Life. *Thus, Croly had the idea, Roosevelt translated it into partisan political terms, and the result was the Bull Moose movement of 1912 and its galvanizing of progressive sentiment. Clearly, Roosevelt did read the book, and he was enthusiastic about it. Croly probably sharpened and clarified some of TR's thinking, and he certainly provided him the term "New Nationalism." But there is much evidence that Roosevelt was already thinking along the Hamiltonian Federalist, or nationalist, lines that Croly urged. However, to qualify the book's direct influence upon the ex-President and later political developments is not to minimize its importance. The volume had an enormous impact, both directly and indirectly, upon popular political thought. It still has an effect. One hears even today about applying Hamiltonian methods to Jeffersonian purposes, which was the essence of Croly's argument.*

Virtually unknown when this book appeared, the forty-year-old Croly had been editor of The Architectural Record *and the author of two books on architecture. With the success of* The Promise of American Life, *he devoted the rest of his life to political writing. In 1914, together with Walter Lippmann, Walter Weyl, Willard Straight, and others, he founded* The New Republic, *and he remained as its main editor until 1930.*

One of the striking aspects of Croly's work is the great number of his insights. Reading him, one's attention is likely to lag a little for a few paragraphs and then be snapped back brightly by a sentence that gets at the root of a subject, in this case reformers and reform movements. Different readers, of course, will be struck by different thoughts of Croly's, depending upon their interests and experiences. But almost anyone who has read much of early-twentieth-century politics or observed the contemporary scene closely will be impressed by some of the passages in this selection: the comments upon some reformers who represent "a higher species of conservatism"; the observation that "reform exclusively as a moral protest and awakening is condemned to sterility"; and the animadversions upon the personalities of many reformers.

Reading The Promise *today, after nationalism has brought horrible wars and denials of freedom and dignity, one cannot but wonder that Croly did not qualify his enthusiasm about nationalism or at least make some distinctions between the kind of nationalism he advocated and what became nationalistic totalitarianism. In his later work Croly changed his mind considerably. In* Progressive Democracy *(1914) he shifted his emphasis a little, and during World War I and immediately thereafter he became acutely, though belatedly, aware that nationalism was an extremely powerful force that could be used for evil as well as for good.*

Those who have not read extensively in late-nineteenth- and early-twentieth-century political history may wish some of the more forgotten of these reformers to be identified. People today are not likely to remember the publisher William Randolph Hearst (1863–1951) as a reformer, but he regarded himself as such early in the century and was a persistent, if unsuccessful, seeker of public office. William Travers Jerome (1859–1934) was a racket-busting prosecutor in Manhattan in the first decade of the century, and Seth Low (1850–1916) was first a reform mayor of Brooklyn before it was joined politically to the City of New York in 1898, then president of Columbia University, and then reform mayor of the City of New York. George B. McClellan (1865–1940) was a son of the Civil War general of the same name, a mayor of New York just before Croly published this book, and later a professor of economic history at Princeton.

An interesting book in which Croly is considered at length is Charles Forcey, The Crossroads of Liberalism: Croly, Weyl, Lippmann and the Progressive Era, 1900–1925 *(Fair Lawn, N.J.: Oxford University Press, 1961). The present selection is from chapter VI, "Reform and the Reformers," of* The Promise of American Life *(New York: Macmillan, 1909).*

Sensible and patriotic Americans have not, of course, tamely and ignobly submitted to the obvious evils of their political and economic condition. There was, indeed, a season when the average good American refused to take these evils seriously. He was possessed by the idea that American life was a stream, which purified itself in the running, and that reformers and critics were merely men who prevented the stream from running free. He looked upon the first spasmodic and ineffective protests with something like contempt. Reformers he appraised as busybodies, who were protesting against the conditions of success in business and politics. He nicknamed them "mugwumps" and continued to vote the regular tickets of his party. There succeeded to this phase of contemptuous dislike a few years, in which he was somewhat bewildered by the increasing evidences of corruption in American politics and lawlessness in American business methods, and during which he occasionally supported some favorite among the several reforming movements. Then a habit of criticism and reform increased with the sense that the evils were both more flagrant and more stubborn than he imagined, until at the present time average well-intentioned Americans are likely to be reformers of one kind or another, while the more intelligent and disinterested of them are pretty sure to vote a "reform" ticket. To stand for a programme of reform has become one of the recognized roads to popularity. The political leaders with the largest personal followings are some kind of reformers. They sit in presidential chairs; they occupy executive mansions; they extort legislation from unwilling politicians; they regulate and abuse the erring corporations; they are coming to control the press; and they are the most aggressive force in American public opinion. The supporters and beneficiaries of existing abuses still control much of the official and practically all the unofficial political and business machinery; but they are less domineering and self-confident than they were. The reformers have both scared and bewildered them. They begin to realize that reform has come to stay, and perhaps even to conquer, while reform itself is beginning to pay the penalty of success by being threatened with deterioration. It has had not only its hero in Theodore Roosevelt, but its specter in William R. Hearst.

In studying the course of the reforming movement during the last twenty-five years, it appears that, while reform has had a history, this history is only beginning. Since 1880, or even 1895 or 1900, it has been transformed in many significant ways. In the beginning it was spasmodic in its outbursts, innocent in its purposes, and narrow in its outlook. It sprang up almost spontaneously in a number of different places and in a number of different detached movements; and its adherents did not look much beyond a victory at a particular election, or the passage of a few remedial laws. Gradually, however, it increased in definiteness, persistence, and comprehensiveness of purpose. The reformers found the need of permanent organization, of constant work, and even within limits, of a positive programme. Their success and their influence upon public opinion increased just in proportion as they began to take their job seriously. Indeed, they have become extremely self-conscious in relation to their present standing and their future responsibilities. They are beginning to predict the most abundant results from the "uplift" movement, of which they are the leaders. They confidently anticipate that they are destined to make a much more salient and significant contribution to the history of their country than has been made by any group of political leaders since the Civil War.

It is in a sense a misnomer to write of "Reform" as a single thing. Reform is, as a matter of fact, all sorts of things. The name has been applied to a number of separate political agitations, which have been started by different people at different times in different parts of the country, and these separate movements have secured very different kinds of support, and have run very different courses. Tariff reform, for instance, was an early and popular agitation whose peculiarity has consisted in securing the support of one of the two national parties, but which in spite of that support has so far made little substantial progress. Civil service reform, on the other hand, was the first agitation looking in the direction of political purification. The early reformers believed that the eradication of the spoils system would deal a deadly blow at political corruption and professional politics. But although they have been fairly successful in establishing the "merit" system in the various public offices, the results of the reform have not equaled the promises of its advocates. While it is still an important part of the programme of reform from the point of view of many reformers, it has recently been over-shadowed by other issues. It does not provoke either as much interest as it did or as much opposition. Municipal reform has, of course, almost as many centers of agitation as there are centers of corruption—that is, large municipalities in the United States. It began as a series of local non-partisan movements for the enforcement of the laws, the dispossession of the "rascals," and the businesslike, efficient administration of municipal affairs; but the reformers discovered in many cases that municipal corruption could not be eradicated without the reform of state politics, and without some drastic purging of the local public service corporations. They have consequently in many cases enlarged the area of their agitation; but in so doing they have become divided among themselves, and their agitation has usually lost its non-partisan character. Finally the agitation against the trusts has developed a confused hodge-podge of harmless and deadly, overlapping and mutually exclusive, remedies, which are the cause of endless disagreements. Of course they are all for the People and against the Octopus, but beyond this precise and comprehensive statement of the issue, the reformers have endlessly different views about the nature of the disease and the severity of the necessary remedy.

If reform is an ambiguous and many-headed thing, the leading reformers are as far as possible from being a body of men capable of mutual coöperation. They differ almost as widely among themselves as they do from the beneficiaries or supporters of the existing abuses. William R. Hearst, William Travers Jerome, Seth Low, and George B. McClellan are all in their different ways reformers; but they would not constitute precisely a happy family. Indeed, Mr. Hearst, who in his own opinion is the only immaculate reformer, is, in the eyes of his fellow-reformers, as dangerous a public enemy as the most corrupt politician or the most unscrupulous millionaire. Any reformer who, like Mr. William Jennings Bryan, proclaims views which are in some respects more than usually radical, comes in for heartier denunciation from his brothers in reform than he does from the conservatives. Each of our leading reformers is more or less a man on horseback, who is seeking to popularize a particular brand of reform, and who is inclined to doubt whether the other brands are available for public consumption without rigid inspection. Consequently, the party of reform is broken up into a number of insurgent personalities. "The typical reformer," says the late Alfred Hodder in a book written in praise of Mr. William Travers Jerome, "The typical reformer is a 'star,' and a typical reform administration is usually a company of stars," and a most amusing piece of special pleading is the reasoning whereby the same author seeks to prove that Mr. Jerome himself is or was not a "star" performer. The preference which individual performers have shown for leading parts is in itself far from being a bad thing, but the lack of "team play" has none the less diminished the efficiency of reform as a practical and prosperous political agitation.

These disagreements are the more significant, because the different "star" reformers are sufficiently united upon their statement of fundamental principles. They all of them agree to conceive of reform as at bottom a moral protest and awakening, which seeks to enforce the violated laws and to restore the American political and economic system to its pristine purity and vigor. From their point of view certain abuses have become unwholesomely conspicuous, because the average American citizen has been a little lethargic, and allowed a few of his more energetic and unscrupulous fellow-citizens to exploit for selfish purposes the opportunities of American business and politics. The function of reform, consequently, is to deprive these parasites of their peculiar opportunities. Few reformers anticipate now that this task will be easily or quickly accomplished. They are coming to realize that the abuses are firmly intrenched, and a prolonged siege as well as constant assaults are necessary for final success. Some reformers are even tending to the opinion that a tradition of reform and succession of reformers will be demanded for the vigilant protection of the American political and economic system against abuse. But the point is the agreement among practical reformers that reform means at bottom no more than moral and political purification. It may, indeed, bring with it the necessity of a certain amount of reorganization; but such reorganization will aim merely at the improvement of the existing political and economic machinery. Present and future reformers must cleanse, oil, and patch a piece of economic and political machinery, which in all essentials is adequate to its purpose. The millionaire and the trust have appropriated too many of the economic opportunities formerly enjoyed by the people. The corrupt politician has usurped too much of the power which should be exercised by the people. Reform must restore to the people the opportunities and power of which they have been deprived.

An agitation of this kind, deriving as it does its principles and purposes from the very source of American democracy, would seem to deserve the support of all good Americans: and such support was in the beginning expected. Reformers have always tended to believe that their agitation ought to be and essentially was non-partisan. They considered it inconceivable either that patriotic American citizens should hesitate about restoring the purity and vigor of American institutions, or such an object should not appeal to every disinterested man, irrespective of party. It was a fight between the law and its violators, between the Faithful and the Heretic, between the Good and the Wicked. In such a fight there was, of course, only one side to take. It was not to be doubted that the honest men, who constitute, of course, an enormous majority of the "plain people," would rally to the banners of reform. The rascals would be turned out; the people would regain their economic opportunities and political rights; and the American democracy would pursue undefiled its triumphant career of legalized prosperity.

These hopes have never been realized. Reform has rarely been non-partisan—except in the minds of its more innocent advocates. Now and then an agitation for municipal reform in a particular city will suffer a spasm of non-partisanship; but the reformers soon develop such lively differences among themselves, that they separate into special groups or else resume their regular party ties. Their common conception of reform as fundamentally a moral awakening, which seeks to restore the American political and economic system to its early purity and vigor, does not help them to unity of action or to unity in the framing of a remedial policy. Different reformers really mean something very different by the traditional system, from which American practice has departed and which they propose to restore. Some of them mean thereby a condition of spiritual excellence, which will be restored by a sort of politico-moral revivalism and which will somehow make the results of divine and popular election coincide. Others mean nothing more than the rigid enforcement of existing laws. Still others mean a new legal expression of the traditional democratic principle, framed to meet the new political and social conditions; but the reformers who agree upon this last conception of reform disagree radically as to what the new legal expression should be. The traditional system, which they seek to restore, assumes almost as many shapes as there are leading reformers; and as the reforming movement develops, the disagreements among the reformers become more instead of less definite and acute.

The inability of the reformers to coöperate in action or to agree as to the application of their principles is in part merely a natural result of their essential work. Reformers are primarily protestants; and protestants are naturally insubordinate. They have been protesting against the established order in American business and politics. Their protest implies a certain degree of moral and intellectual independence, which makes them dislike to surrender or subordinate their own personal opinions and manner of action. Such independence is a new and refreshing thing, which has suddenly made American politics much more interesting and significant than it has been at any time since the Civil War. It has a high value wholly apart from its immediate political results. It means that the American people are beginning a new phase of their political experience,—a phase in which there will be room for a much freer play of individual ability and character. Inevitably the sudden realization by certain exceptional politicians that they have a right to be individuals, and that they can take a strong line of their own in politics without being disqualified for practical political association with their fellow-countrymen—such a new light could hardly break without tempting the performers to over-play the part. The fact that they have over-played their parts, and have wasted time and energy over meaningless and unnecessary disagreements is not in itself a matter of much importance. The great majority of them are disinterested and patriotic men, who will not allow in the long run either personal ambition or political crotchets to prevent them from coöperating for the good of the cause.

Unfortunately, however, neither public spirit nor patriotism will be sufficient to bring them effectively together—any more than genuine excellence of intention and real public spirit enabled patriotic Americans to coöperate upon a remedial policy during the years immediately preceding the Civil War. The plain fact is that the traditional American political system, which so many good reformers wish to restore by some sort of reforming revivalism, is just as much responsible for the existing political and economic abuses as the Constitution was responsible for the evil of slavery. As long, consequently, as reform is considered to be a species of higher conservatism, the existing abuses can no more be frankly faced and fully understood than the Whig leaders were able to face and understand the full meaning and consequences of any attempt on the part of a democracy to keep house with slavery. The first condition of a better understanding and a more efficient coöperation among the reforming leaders is a better understanding of the meaning of reform and the function of reformers. They will never be united on the basis of allegiance to the traditional American political creed, because that creed itself is overflowing with inconsistencies and ambiguities, which afford a footing for almost every extreme of radicalism and conservatism; and in case they persist in the attempt to reform political and economic abuses merely by a restoration of earlier conditions and methods, they will be compromising much that is good in the present economic and political organization without recovering that which was good in the past.

The prevailing preconception of the reformers, that the existing evils and abuses have been due chiefly to the energy and lack of scruple with which business men and politicians have taken advantage of the good but easy-going American, and that a general increase of moral energy, assisted by some minor legal changes, will restore the balance,—such a conception of the situation is less than half true. No doubt, the "plain people" of the United States have been morally indifferent, and have allowed unscrupulous special interests to usurp too much power; but that is far from being the whole story. The unscrupulous energy of the "Boss" or the "tainted" millionaire is vitally related to the moral indifference of the "plain people." Both of them have been encouraged to believe by the nature of our traditional ideas and institutions that a man could be patriotic without being either public-spirited or disinterested. The democratic state has been conceived as a piece of political machinery, which existed for the purpose of securing certain individual rights and opportunities—the expectation being that the greatest individual happiness would be thereby promoted, and one which harmonized with the public interest. Consequently when the "Boss" and the "tainted" millionaire took advantage of this situation to secure for themselves an unusually large amount of political and economic power, they were putting into practice an idea which traditionally had been entirely respectable, and which during the pioneer period had not worked badly. On the other hand, when the mass of American voters failed to detect the danger of such usurpation until it had gone altogether too far, they, too, were not without warrant for their lethargy and callousness. They, too, in a smaller way had considered the American political and economic system chiefly as a system framed for their individual benefit, and it did not seem sportsmanlike to turn and rend their more successful competitors, until they were told that the "trusts" and the "Bosses" were violating the sacred principle of equal rights. Thus the abuses of which we are complaining are not weeds which have been allowed to spring up from neglect, and which can be eradicated by a man with a hoe. They are cultivated plants, which, if not precisely specified in the plan of the American political and economic garden, have at least been encouraged by traditional methods of cultivation.

The fact that this dangerous usurpation of power has been accomplished partly by illegal methods has blinded many reformers to two considerations, which have a vital relation to both the theory and the practice of reform. Violation of the law was itself partly the result of conflicting and unwise state legislation, and for this reason did not seem very heinous either to its perpetrators or to public opinion. But even if the law had not been violated, similar results would have followed. Under the traditional American system, with the freedom permitted to the individual, with the restriction placed on the central authority, and with its assumption of a substantial identity between the individual and the public interest—under such a system unusually energetic and unscrupulous men were bound to seize a kind and an amount of political and economic power which was not entirely wholesome. They had a license to do so; and if they had failed to take advantage thereof, their failure would have been an indication, not of disinterestedness or moral impeccability, but of sheer weakness and inefficiency.

How utterly confusing it is, consequently, to consider reform as equivalent merely to the restoration of the American democracy to a former condition of purity and excellence! Our earlier political and economic condition was not at its best a fit subject for any great amount of complacency. It cannot be restored, even if we would; and the public interest has nothing to gain by its restoration. The usurpation of power by "trusts" and "Bosses" is more than anything else an expression of a desirable individual initiative and organizing ability—which have been allowed to become dangerous and partly corrupt, because of the incoherence and the lack of purpose and responsibility in the traditional American political and economic system. A "purification" might well destroy the good with the evil; and even if it were successful in eradicating certain abuses, would only prepare the way for the outbreak in another form of the tendency towards individual aggrandizement and social classification. No amount of moral energy, directed merely towards the enforcement of the laws, can possibly avail to accomplish any genuine or lasting reform. It is the laws themselves which are partly at fault, and still more at fault is the group of ideas and traditional practices behind the laws.

Reformers have failed for the most part to reach a correct diagnosis of existing political and economic abuses, because they are almost as much the victim of perverted, confused, and routine habits of political thought as is the ordinary politician. They have eschewed the tradition of partisan conformity in reference to controverted political questions, but they have not eschewed a still more insidious tradition of conformity—the tradition that a patriotic American citizen must not in his political thinking go beyond the formulas consecrated in the sacred American writings. They adhere to the stupefying rule that the good Fathers of the Republic relieved their children from the necessity of vigorous, independent, or consistent thinking in political matters,—that it is the duty of their loyal children to repeat the sacred words and then await a miraculous consummation of individual and social prosperity. Accordingly, all the leading reformers begin by piously reiterating certain phrases about equal rights for all and special privileges for none, and of government of the people, by the people, and for the people. Having in this way proved their fundamental political orthodoxy, they proceed to interpret the phrases according to their personal, class, local, and partisan preconceptions and interests. They have never stopped to inquire whether the principle of equal rights in its actual embodiment in American institutional and political practice has not been partly responsible for some of the existing abuses, whether it is either a safe or sufficient platform for a reforming movement, and whether its continued proclamation as the fundamental political principle of a democracy will help or hinder the higher democratic consummation. Their unquestioning orthodoxy in this respect has made them faithless both to their own personal interest as reformers and to the cause of reform. Reform exclusively as a moral protest and awakening is condemned to sterility. Reformers exclusively as moral protestants and purifiers are condemned to misdirected effort, to an illiberal puritanism, and to personal self-stultification. Reform must necessarily mean an intellectual as well as a moral challenge; and its higher purposes will never be accomplished unless it is accompanied by a masterful and jubilant intellectual awakening.

All Americans, whether they are professional politicians or reformers, "predatory" millionaires or common people, political philosophers or schoolboys, accept the principle of "equal rights for all and special privileges for none" as the absolutely sufficient rule of an American democratic political system. . . .

In this respect the good American finds himself in a situation similar to that with which he was confronted before the Civil War. At that time, also, Abolitionist and slave-holder, Republican and pioneer Democrat, each of them declared himself to be the interpreter of the true democratic doctrine; and no substantial progress could be made towards the settlement of the question, until public opinion had been instructed as to the real meaning of democracy in relation to the double-headed problem of slavery and states' rights. It required the utmost intellectual courage and ability to emancipate the conception of democracy from the illusions and confusions of thought which enabled Davis, Douglas, and Garrison all to pose as impeccable democrats; and at the present time reformers need to devote as much ability and more courage to the task of framing a fitting creed for a reformed and reforming American democracy.

The political lessons of the anti-slavery and states' rights discussions may not be of much obvious assistance in thinking out such a creed; but they should at least help the reformers to understand the methods whereby the purposes of a reformed democracy can be achieved. No progress was made towards the solution of the slavery question until the question itself was admitted to be national in scope, and its solution a national responsibility. No substantial progress had been made in the direction of reform until it began to be understood that here, also, a national responsibility existed, which demanded an exercise of the powers of the central government. Reform is both meaningless and powerless unless the Jeffersonian principle of non-interference is abandoned. The experience of the last generation plainly shows that the American economic and social system cannot be allowed to take care of itself, and that the automatic harmony of the individual and the public interest, which is the essence of the Jeffersonian democratic creed, has proved to be an illusion. Interference with the natural course of individual and popular action there must be in the public interest; and such interference must at least be sufficient to accomplish its purposes. The house of the American democracy is again by way of being divided against itself, because the national interest has not been consistently asserted as against special and local interests; and again, also, it can be reunited only by being partly reconstructed on better foundations.

If reform does not and cannot mean restoration, it is bound to mean reconstruction.

The reformers have come partly to realize that the Jeffersonian policy of drift must be abandoned. They no longer expect the American ship of state by virtue of its own righteous framework to sail away to a safe harbor in the Promised Land. They understand that there must be a vigorous and conscious assertion of the public as opposed to private and special interests, and that the American people must to a greater extent than they have in the past subordinate the latter to the former. They behave as if the American ship of state will hereafter require careful steering; and a turn or two at the wheel has given them some idea of the course they must set. On the other hand, even the best of them have not learned the name of its ultimate destination, the full difficulties of the navigation, or the stern discipline which may eventually be imposed upon the ship's crew. They do not realize, that is, how thoroughly Jeffersonian individualism must be abandoned for the benefit of a genuinely individual and social consummation; and they do not realize how dangerous and fallacious a chart their cherished principle of equal rights may well become. In reviving the practice of vigorous national action for the achievement of a national purpose, the better reformers have, if they only knew it, been looking in the direction of a much more trustworthy and serviceable political principle. The assumption of such a responsibility implies the rejection of a large part of the Jeffersonian creed, and a renewed attempt to establish in its place the popularity of its Hamiltonian rival. On the other hand, it involves no less surely the transformation of Hamiltonianism into a thoroughly democratic political principle. None of these inferences have, however, as yet been generally drawn, and no leading reformer has sought to give reform its necessary foundation of positive political principle.

Only a very innocent person will expect reformers to be convinced of such a novel notion of reform by mere assertion, no matter how emphatic, or by argument, no matter how conclusive. But if, as I have said, reform actually implies a criticism of traditional American ideas, and a more responsible and more positive conception of democracy, these implications will necessarily be revealed in the future history of the reforming agitation. The reformers who understand will be assisted by the logic of events, whereas those who cannot and will not understand will be thwarted by the logic of events. Gradually (it may be anticipated) reformers, who dare to criticise and who are not afraid to reconstruct will be sharply distinguished from reformers who believe reform to be a species of higher conservatism. The latter will be forced where they belong into the ranks of the supporters and beneficiaries of the existing system; and the party of genuine reform will be strengthened by their departure. On the other hand, the sincere and thorough-going reformers can hardly avoid a division into two divergent groups. One of these groups will stick faithfully to the principle of equal rights and to the spirit of the true Jeffersonian faith. It will seek still further to undermine the representative character of American institutions, to deprive official leadership of any genuine responsibility, and to cultivate individualism at the expense of individual and national integrity. The second group, on the other hand, may learn from experience that the principle of equal rights is a dangerous weapon in the hands of factious and merely revolutionary agitators, and even that such a principle is only a partial and poverty-stricken statement of the purpose of a democratic polity. The logic of its purposes will compel it to favor the principle of responsible representative government, and it will seek to forge institutions which will endow responsible political government with renewed life. Above all, it may discover that the attempt to unite the Hamiltonian principle of national political responsibility and efficiency with a frank democratic purpose will give a new meaning to the Hamiltonian system of political ideas and a new power to democracy. . . .

It is fortunate, consequently, that one reformer can be named whose work has tended to give reform the dignity of a constructive mission. Mr. Theodore Roosevelt's behavior at least is not dictated by negative conception of reform. During the course of an extremely active and varied political career he has, indeed, been all kinds of a reformer. His first appearance in public life, as a member of the Legislature of New York, coincided with an outbreak of dissatisfaction over the charter of New York City; and Mr. Roosevelt's name was identified with the bills which began the revision of that very much revised instrument. Somewhat later, as one of the Federal Commissioners, Mr. Roosevelt made a most useful contribution to the more effective enforcement of the Civil Service Law. Still later, as Police Commissioner of New York City, he had his experience of reform by means of unregenerate instruments and administrative lies. Then, as Governor of the State of New York, he was instrumental in securing the passage of a law taxing franchises as real property and thus faced for the first time and in a preliminary way the many-headed problems of the trusts. Finally, when an accident placed him in the Presidential chair, he consistently used the power of the Federal government and his own influence and popularity for the purpose of regulating the corporations in what he believed to be the public interest. No other American has had anything like so varied and so intimate an acquaintance with the practical work of reform as has Mr. Roosevelt; and when, after more than twenty years of such experience, he adds to the work of administrative reform the additional task of political and economic reconstruction, his originality cannot be considered the result of innocence. Mr. Roosevelt's reconstructive policy does not go very far in purpose or achievement, but limited as it is, it does tend to give the agitation for reform the benefit of a much more positive significance and a much more dignified task.

Mr. Roosevelt has imparted a higher and more positive significance to reform, because throughout his career he has consistently stood for an idea, from which the idea of reform cannot be separated—namely, the national idea. He has, indeed, been even more of a nationalist than he has a reformer. His most important literary work was a history of the beginning of American national expansion. He has treated all public questions from a vigorous, even from an extreme, national standpoint. No American politician was more eager to assert the national interest against an actual or a possible foreign enemy; and not even William R. Hearst was more resolute to involve his country in a war with Spain. Fortunately, however, his aggressive nationalism did not, like that of so many other statesmen, faint from exhaustion as soon as there were no more foreign enemies to defy. He was the first political leader of the American people to identify the national principle with an ideal of reform. He was the first to realize that an American statesman could no longer really represent the national interest without becoming a reformer. Mr. Grover Cleveland showed a glimmering of the necessity of this affiliation; but he could not carry it far, because, as a sincere traditional Democrat, he could not reach a clear understanding of the meaning either of reform or of nationality. Mr. Roosevelt, however, divined that an American statesman who eschewed or evaded the work of reform came inevitably to represent either special and local interests or else a merely Bourbon political tradition, and in this way was disqualified for genuinely national service. He divined that the national principle involved a continual process of internal reformation; and that the reforming idea implied the necessity of more efficient national organization. Consequently, when he became President of the United States and the official representative of the national interest of the country, he attained finally his proper sphere of action. He immediately began the salutary and indispensable work of nationalizing the reform movement.

The nationalization of reform endowed the movement with new vitality and meaning. What Mr. Roosevelt really did was to revive the Hamiltonian ideal of constructive national legislation. During the whole of the nineteenth century that ideal, while by no means dead, was disabled by associations and conditions from active and efficient service. Not until the end of the Spanish War was a condition of public feeling created, which made it possible to revive Hamiltonianism. That war and its resulting policy of extra-territorial expansion, so far from hindering the process of domestic amelioration, availed, from the sheer force of the national aspirations it aroused, to give a tremendous impulse to the work of national reform. It made Americans more sensitive to a national idea and more conscious of their national responsibilities, and it indirectly helped to place in the Presidential chair the man who, as I have said, represented both the national idea and the spirit of reform. The sincere and intelligent combination of those two ideas is bound to issue in the Hamiltonian practice of constructive national legislation.

Of course Theodore Roosevelt is Hamiltonian with a difference. Hamilton's fatal error consisted in his attempt to make the Federal organization not merely the effective engine of the national interest, but also a bulwark against the rising tide of democracy. The new Federalism or rather new Nationalism is not in any way inimical to democracy. On the contrary, not only does Mr. Roosevelt believe himself to be an unimpeachable democrat in theory, but he has given his fellow-countrymen a useful example of the way in which a college-bred and a well-to-do man can become by somewhat forcible means a good practical democrat. The whole tendency of his programme is to give a democratic meaning and purpose to the Hamiltonian tradition and method. He proposes to use the power and the resources of the Federal government for the purpose of making his countrymen a more complete democracy in organization and practice; but he does not make these proposals, as Mr. Bryan does, gingerly and with a bad conscience. He makes them with a frank and full confidence in an efficient national organization as the necessary agent of the national interest and purpose. He has completely abandoned that part of the traditional democratic creed which tends to regard the assumption by the government of responsibility, and its endowment with power adequate to the responsibility as inherently dangerous and undemocratic. He realizes that any efficiency of organization and delegation of power which is necessary to the promotion of the American national interest must be helpful to democracy. More than any other American political leader, except Lincoln, his devotion both to the national and to the democratic ideas is thorough-going and absolute.

As the founder of a new national democracy, then, his influence and his work have tended to emancipate American democracy from its Jeffersonian bondage. They have tended to give a new meaning to popular government by endowing it with larger powers, more positive responsibilities, and a better faith in human excellence. Jefferson believed theoretically in human goodness, but in actual practice his faith in human nature was exceedingly restricted. Just as the older aristocratic theory had been to justify hereditary political leadership by considering the ordinary man as necessarily irresponsible and incapable, so the early French democrats, and Jefferson after them, made faith in the people equivalent to a profound suspicion of responsible official leadership. Exceptional power merely offered exceptional opportunities for abuse. He refused, as far as he could, to endow special men, even when chosen by the people, with any opportunity to promote the public welfare proportionate to their abilities. So far as his influence has prevailed the government of the country was organized on the basis of a cordial distrust of the man of exceptional competence, training, or independence as a public official. To the present day this distrust remains the sign by which the demoralizing influence of the Jeffersonian democratic creed is most plainly to be traced. So far as it continues to be influential it destroys one necessary condition of responsible and efficient government, and it is bound to paralyze any attempt to make the national organization adequate to the promotion of the national interest. Mr. Roosevelt has exhibited his genuinely national spirit in nothing so clearly as in his endeavor to give to men of special ability, training, and eminence a better opportunity to serve the public. He has not only appointed such men to office, but he has tried to supply them with an administrative machinery which would enable them to use their abilities to the best public advantage; and he has thereby shown a faith in human nature far more edifying and far more genuinely democratic than that of Jefferson or Jackson.

Mr. Roosevelt, however, has still another title to distinction among the brethren of reform. He has not only nationalized the movement, and pointed it in the direction of a better conception of democracy, but he has rallied to its banner the ostensible, if not the very enthusiastic, support of the Republican party. He has restored that party to some sense of its historic position and purpose. As the party which before the War had insisted on making the nation answerable for the solution of the slavery problem, it has inherited the tradition of national responsibility for the national good; but it was rapidly losing all sense of its historic mission, and, like the Whigs, was constantly using its principle and its prestige as a cloak for the aggrandizement of special interests. At its worst it had, indeed, earned some claim on the allegiance of patriotic Americans by its defense of the fiscal system of the country against Mr. Bryan's well-meant but dangerous attack, and by its acceptance after the Spanish War of the responsibilities of extra-territorial expansion; but there was grave danger that its alliance with the "vested" interests would make it unfaithful to its past as the party of responsible national action. It escaped such a fate only by an extremely narrow margin; and the fact that it did escape is due chiefly to the personal influence of Theodore Roosevelt. The Republican party is still very far from being a wholly sincere agent of the national reform interest. Its official leadership is opposed to reform; and it cannot be made to take a single step in advance except under compulsion. But Mr. Roosevelt probably prevented it from drifting into the position of an anti-reform party—which if it had happened would have meant its ruin, and would have damaged the cause of national reform. A Republican party which was untrue to the principle of national responsibility would have no reason for existence; and the Democratic party, as we have seen, cannot become the party of national responsibility without being faithless to its own creed.

SELECTION 11

An Intellectual Criticizes the Antitrust Tradition: Walter Lippmann in "Drift and Mastery"

Since the early Wilson administration, almost everyone with a modicum of political literacy has at least heard of Walter Lippmann. Lippmann has been read by more people more frequently and over a longer time than has perhaps any other political writer in the history of the Republic. A remarkable clarity of thought and lucidity of expression are Lippmann's chief characteristics and the basic reasons for his wide following.

Lippmann's career was brilliant even in his youth. He graduated from Harvard in 1909, Phi Beta Kappa, when not quite twenty years old and after only three years in Cambridge. Professors sought his opinion. A visiting English lecturer, Graham Wallas, dedicated a book to the young man. A leader of the Socialist group among the students, Lippmann in 1912 became an assistant to the Socialist mayor of Schenectady, New York. After only a few months, Lippmann abandoned both Marxism and an active political role. The rest of his career has been in the library, the study, and the editorial office.

In 1912 Lippmann was one of the founders of The New Republic, *with which he remained until 1917, when he became an assistant to the Secretary of War. After the war he became an editorial writer and subsequently editor of the*

New York World, *the most influential Democratic newspaper in the nation and probably its liveliest newspaper of quality. The* World *ceased publication in 1931, as a result of the Depression, and Lippmann went to the* Herald Tribune, *with which he remained until the early 1960s, when he shifted his base to the Washington Post. After he went to the* Herald Tribune, *he was very widely syndicated. A prolific writer, Lippmann has turned out numerous books on subjects ranging from foreign policy to public education in addition to his newspaper work. This selection, chapter 7 of* Drift *and* Mastery: An Attempt to Diagnose the Current Unrest *(New York: Mitchell Kennerly, 1914), pages 121–148, is too clearly written to require explanation. The selection has not been shortened; the ellipses were in the original 1914 publication.*

A nation of villagers—BERNARD SHAW

It has been said that no trust could have been created without breaking the law. Neither could astronomy in the time of Galileo. If you build up foolish laws and insist that invention is a crime, well—then it is a crime. That is undeniably true, but not very interesting. Of course, you can't possibly treat the trusts as crimes. First of all, nobody knows what the trust laws mean. The spectacle of an enlightened people trying in vain for twenty-five years to find out the intention of a statute that it has enacted—that is one of those episodes that only madmen can appreciate. You see, it is possible to sympathize with the difficulties of a scholar trying to decipher the hieroglyphics of some ancient people, but when statesmen can't read the things they've written themselves, it begins to look as if some imp had been playing pranks. The men who rule this country to-day were all alive, and presumably sane, when the Sherman Act was passed. They all say in public that it is a great piece of legislation—an "exquisite instrument" someone called it the other day. The highest paid legal intelligence has concentrated on the Act. The Supreme Court has interpreted it many times, ending with the enormous assumption that reason had something to do with the law. The Supreme Court was denounced for this: the reformers said that if there was any reason in the law, the devil himself had got hold of it. As I write, Congress is engaged in trying to define what it thinks it means by the Act. . . .

That uncertainty hasn't prevented a mass of indictments, injunctions, lawsuits. It has, if anything, invited them. But of course, you can't enforce the criminal law against every "unfair" business practice. Just try to imagine the standing army of inspectors, detectives, prosecutors, and judges, the city of courthouses and jails, the enormous costs, and the unremitting zeal—if you cannot see the folly, at least see the impossibility of the method. To work with it seriously would not only bring business to a standstill, it would drain the energy of America more thoroughly than the bitterest foreign war. Visualize life in America, if you can, when the government at Washington and forty-eight state governments really undertook not our present desultory pecking, but a systematic enforcement of the criminal law. The newspapers would enjoy it for a week, and everybody would be excited; in two weeks it would be a bore; in six, there would be

such a revolt that everyone, radical and conservative, would be ready
to wreck the government and hang the attorney-general. For these "criminal" practices are so deep in the texture of our lives; they affect so many,
their results are so intimate that anything like a "surgical" cutting at evil
would come close to killing the patient.

If the anti-trust people really grasped the full meaning of what they
said, and if they really had the power or the courage to do what they
propose, they would be engaged in one of the most destructive agitations
that America has known. They would be breaking up the beginning of a
collective organization, thwarting the possibility of coöperation, and in-
sisting upon submitting industry to the wasteful, the planless scramble of
little profiteers. They would make impossible any deliberate and constructive use of our natural resources, they would thwart any effort to form the
great industries into coordinated services, they would preserve commercialism as the undisputed master of our lives, they would lay a premium on
the strategy of industrial war,—they would, if they could. For these antitrust people have never seen the possibilities of organized industries. They
have seen only the obvious evils, the birth-pains, the undisciplined strut
of youth, the bad manners, the greed, and the trickery. The trusts have
been ruthless, of course. No one tried to guide them; they have broken the
law in a thousand ways, largely because the law was such that they
had to.

At any rate, I should not like to answer before a just tribunal for the
harm done this country in the last twenty-five years by the stupid hostility
of anti-trust laws. How much they have perverted the constructive genius
of this country it is impossible to estimate. They have blocked any policy
of welcome and use, they have concentrated a nation's thinking on inessen-
tials, they have driven creative business men to underhand methods, and
put a high money value on intrigue and legal cunning, demagoguery and
waste. The trusts have survived it all, but in mutilated form, the battered
makeshifts of a trampled promise. They have learned every art of evasion
—the only art reformers allowed them to learn.

It is said that the economy of trusts is unreal. Yet no one has ever tried
the economies of the trust in any open, deliberate fashion. The amount
of energy that has had to go into repelling stupid attack, the adjustments
that had to be made underground—it is a wonder the trusts achieved what
they did to bring order out of chaos, and forge an instrument for a nation's
business. You have no more right to judge the trusts by what they are than
to judge the labor movement by what it is. Both of them are in that preliminary state where they are fighting for existence, and any real outburst
of constructive effort has been impossible for them.

But revolutions are not stopped by blind resistance. They are only
perverted. And as an exhibition of blind resistance to a great promise, the
trust campaign of the American democracy is surely unequalled. Think
of contriving correctives for a revolution, such as ordering business men to
compete with each other. It is as if we said: "Let not thy right hand
know what thy left hand doeth; let thy right hand fight thy left hand,
and in the name of God let neither win." Bernard Shaw remarked several
years ago that "after all, America is not submitting to the Trusts without

a struggle. The first steps have already been taken by the village constable. He is no doubt preparing a new question for immigrants" . . . after asking them whether they are anarchists or polygamists, he is to add " 'Do you approve of Trusts?' but pending this supreme measure of national defense he has declared in several states that trusts will certainly be put in the stocks and whipped."

There has been no American policy on the trust question: there has been merely a widespread resentment. The small local competitors who were wiped out became little centers of bad feeling: these nationally organized industries were looked upon as foreign invaders. They were arrogant, as the English in Ireland or the Germans in Alsace, and much of the feeling for local democracy attached itself to the revolt against these national despotisms. The trusts made enemies right and left: they squeezed the profits of the farmer, they made life difficult for the shopkeeper, they abolished jobbers and travelling salesmen, they closed down factories, they exercised an enormous control over credit through their size and through their eastern connections. Labor was no match for them, state legislatures were impotent before them. They came into the life of the simple American community as a tremendous revolutionary force, upsetting custom, changing men's status, demanding a readjustment for which people were unready. Of course, there was anti-trust feeling; of course, there was a blind desire to smash them. Men had been ruined and they were too angry to think, too hard pressed to care much about the larger life which the trusts suggested.

This feeling came to a head in Bryan's famous "cross of gold" speech in 1896. "When you come before us and tell us that we shall disturb your business interests, we reply that you have disturbed our business interests by your action. . . . The man who is employed for wages is as much a business man as his employers. The attorney in a country town is as much a business man as the corporation counsel in a great metropolis. The merchant at the crossroads store is as much a business man as the merchant of New York. The farmer . . . is as much a business man as the man who goes upon the Board of Trade and bets upon the price of grain. The miners . . . It is for these that we speak . . . we are fighting in the defense of our homes, our families, and posterity." What Bryan was really defending was the old and simple life of America, life that was doomed by the great organization that had come into the world. He thought he was fighting the plutocracy: as a matter of fact he was fighting something much deeper than that; he was fighting the larger scale of human life. The Eastern money power controlled the new industrial system, and Bryan fought it. But what he and his people hated from the bottom of their souls were the economic conditions which had upset the old life of the prairies, made new demands upon democracy, introduced specialization and science, had destroyed village loyalties, frustrated private ambitions, and created the impersonal relationships of the modern world.

Bryan has never been able to adjust himself to the new world in which he lives. That is why he is so irresistibly funny to sophisticated newspaper men. His virtues, his habits, his ideas, are the simple, direct, shrewd qualities of early America. He is the true Don Quixote of our politics, for he moves in a world that has ceased to exist.

He is a more genuine conservative than some propertied bigot. Bryan stands for the popular tradition of America, whereas most of his enemies stand merely for the power that is destroying that tradition. Bryan is what America was; his critics are generally defenders of what America has become. And neither seems to have any vision of what America is to be.

Yet there has always been great power behind Bryan, the power of those who in one way or another were hurt by the greater organization that America was developing. The Populists were part of that power. La Follette and the insurgent Republicans expressed it. It was easily a political majority of the American people. The Republican Party disintegrated under the pressure of the revolt. The Bull Moose gathered much of its strength from it. The Socialists have got some of it. But in 1912 it swept the Democratic Party, and by a combination of circumstances, carried the country. The plutocracy was beaten in politics, and the power that Bryan spoke for in 1896, the forces that had made muckraking popular, captured the government. They were led by a man who was no part of the power that he represented.

Woodrow Wilson is an outsider capable of skilled interpretation. He is an historian, and that has helped him to know the older tradition of America. He is a student of theory, and like most theorists of his generation he is deeply attached to the doctrines that swayed the world when America was founded.

But Woodrow Wilson at least knows that there is a new world. "There is one great basic fact which underlies all the questions that are discussed on the political platform at the present moment. That singular fact is that nothing is done in this country as it was done twenty years ago. We are in the presence of a new organization of society. . . . We have changed our economic conditions, absolutely, from top to bottom; and, with our economic society, the organization of our life." You could not make a more sweeping statement of the case. The President is perfectly aware of what has happened, and he says at the very outset that "our laws still deal with us on the basis of the old system . . . the old positive formulas do not fit the present problems."

You wait eagerly for some new formula. The new formula is this: "I believe the time has come when the governments of this country, both state and national, have to set the stage, and set it very minutely and carefully, for the doing of justice to men in every relationship of life." Now that is a new formula, because it means a willingness to use the power of government much more extensively.

But for what purpose is this power to be used? There, of course, is the rub. It is to be used to "*restore* our politics to their full spiritual vigor *again*, and our national life, whether in trade, in industry, or in what concerns us only as families and individuals, to its purity, its self-respect, and its *pristine* strength and freedom." The ideal is the old ideal, the ideal of Bryan, the method is the new one of government interference.

That, I believe, is the inner contradiction of Woodrow Wilson. He knows that there is a new world demanding new methods, but he dreams of an older world. He is torn between the two. It is a very deep conflict in him between what he knows and what he feels.

His feeling is, as he says, for "the man on the make." "For my part,

I want the pigmy to have a chance to come out" . . . "Just let some of the youngsters I know have a chance and they'll give these gentlemen points. Lend them a little money. They can't get any now. See to it that when they have got a local market they can't be squeezed out of it." Nowhere in his speeches will you find any sense that it may be possible to organize the fundamental industries on some deliberate plan for national service. He is thinking always about somebody's chance to build up a profitable business; he likes the idea that somebody can beat somebody else, and the small business man takes on the virtues of David in a battle with Goliath.

"Have you found trusts that thought as much of their men as they did of their machinery?" he asks, forgetting that few people have ever found competitive textile mills or clothing factories that did. There isn't an evil of commercialism that Wilson isn't ready to lay at the door of the trusts. He becomes quite reckless in his denunciation of the New Devil—Monopoly—and of course, by contrast the competitive business takes on a halo of light. It is amazing how clearly he sees the evils that trusts do, how blind he is to the evils that his supporters do. You would think that the trusts were the first oppressors of labor; you would think they were the first business organization that failed to achieve the highest possible efficiency. The pretty record of competition throughout the Nineteenth Century is forgotten. Suddenly all that is a glorious past which we have lost. You would think that competitive commercialism was really a generous, chivalrous, high-minded stage of human culture.

"We design that the limitations on private enterprise shall be removed, so that the next generation of youngsters, as they come along, will not have to become protégés of benevolent trusts, but will be free to go about making their own lives what they will; so that we shall taste again the full cup, not of charity, but of liberty,—the only wine that ever refreshed and renewed the spirit of a people." That cup of liberty—we may well ask him to go back to Manchester, to Paterson to-day, to the garment trades of New York, and taste it for himself.

The New Freedom means the effort of small business men and farmers to use the government against the larger collective organization of industry. Wilson's power comes from them; his feeling is with them; his thinking is for them. Never a word of understanding for the new type of administrator, the specialist, the professionally trained business man; practically no mention of the consumer—even the tariff is for the business man; no understanding of the new demands of labor, its solidarity, its aspiration for some control over the management of business; no hint that it may be necessary to organize the fundamental industries of the country on some definite plan so that our resources may be developed by scientific method instead of by men "on the make"; no friendliness for the larger, collective life upon which the world is entering, only a constant return to the commercial chances of young men trying to set up in business. That is the push and force of this New Freedom, a freedom for the little profiteer, but no freedom for the nation from the narrowness, the poor incentives, the limited vision of small competitors,—no freedom from clamorous advertisement, from wasteful selling, from duplication of plants, from unnecessary enterprise, from the chaos, the welter, the strategy of industrial war.

There is no doubt, I think, that President Wilson and his party represent primarily small business in a war against the great interests. Socialists speak of his administration as a revolution within the bounds of capitalism. Wilson doesn't really fight the oppressions of property. He fights the evil done by large property-holders to small ones. The temper of his administration was revealed very clearly when the proposal was made to establish a Federal Trade Commission. It was suggested at once by leading spokesmen of the Democratic Party that corporations with a capital of less than a million dollars should be exempted from supervision. Is that because little corporations exploit labor or the consumer less? Not a bit of it. It is because little corporations are in control of the political situation.

But there are certain obstacles to the working out of the New Freedom. First of all, there was a suspicion in Wilson's mind, even during the campaign, that the tendency to large organization was too powerful to be stopped by legislation. So he left open a way of escape from the literal achievement of what the New Freedom seemed to threaten. *"I am for big business,"* he said, *"and I am against the trusts."* That is a very subtle distinction, so subtle, I suspect, that no human legislation will ever be able to make it. The distinction is this: big business is a business that has survived competition; a trust is an arrangement to do away with competition. But when competition is done away with, who is the Solomon wise enough to know whether the result was accomplished by superior efficiency or by agreement among the competitors or by both?

The big trusts have undoubtedly been built up in part by superior business ability, and by successful competition, but also by ruthless competition, by underground arrangements, by an intricate series of facts which no earthly tribunal will ever be able to disentangle. And why should it try? These great combinations are here. What interests us is not their history but their future. The point is whether you are going to split them up, and if so into how many parts. Once split, are they to be kept from coming together again? Are you determined to prevent men who could coöperate from cooperating? Wilson seems to imply that a big business which has survived competition is to be let alone, and the trusts attacked. But as there is no real way of distinguishing between them, he leaves the question just where he found it: he must choose between the large organization of business and the small.

It's here that his temperament and his prejudices clash with fact and necessity. He really would like to disintegrate large business. "Are you not eager for the time," he asks, "when your sons shall be able to look forward to becoming not employees, but heads of some small, it may be, but hopeful business . . .?" But to what percentage of the population can he hold out that hope? How many small but hopeful steel mills, coal mines, telegraph systems, oil refineries, copper mines, can this country support? A few hundred at the outside. And for these few hundred sons whose "best energies . . . are inspired by the knowledge that they are their own masters with the paths of the world before them," we are asked to give up the hope of a sane, deliberate organization of national industry brought under democratic control.

I submit that it is an unworthy dream. I submit that the intelligent men of my generation can find a better outlet for their energies than in making themselves masters of little businesses. They have the vast opportunity of introducing order and purpose into the business world, of devising administrative methods by which the great resources of the country can be operated on some thought-out plan. They have the whole new field of industrial statesmanship before them, and those who prefer the egotism of some little business are not the ones whose ambitions we need most to cultivate.

But the disintegration which Wilson promised in the New Freedom is not likely to be carried out. One year of public office has toned down the audacity of the campaign speeches so much that Mr. Dooley says you can play the President's messages on a harp. Instead of a "radical reconstruction" we are engaged in signing a "constitution of peace." These big business men who a few months ago showed not the "least promise of disinterestedness" are to-day inspired by "a spirit of accommodation." The President's own Secretary of Commerce, Mr. Redfield, has said to the National Chamber of Commerce that the number of trusts still operating "is conspicuously small." Was ever wish the father to a pleasanter thought? Was ever greater magic wrought with less effort? Or is it that politicians in office have to pretend that what they can't do has happened anyway?

Wilson is against the trusts for many reasons: the political economy of his generation was based on competition and free trade; the Democratic Party is by tradition opposed to a strong central government, and that opposition applies equally well to strong national business,—it is a party attached to local rights, to village patriotism, to humble but ambitious enterprise; its temper has always been hostile to specialization and expert knowledge, because it admires a very primitive man-to-man democracy. Wilson's thought is inspired by that outlook. It has been tempered somewhat by contact with men who have outgrown the village culture, so that Wilson is less hostile to experts, less oblivious to administrative problems than is Bryan. But at the same time his speeches are marked with contempt for the specialist: they play up quite obviously to the old democratic notion that any man can do almost any job. You have always to except the negro, of course, about whom the Democrats have a totally different tradition. But among white men, special training and expert knowledge are somewhat under suspicion in Democratic circles.

Hostility to large organization is a natural quality in village life. Wilson is always repeating that the old personal relationships of employer and employee have disappeared. He deplores the impersonal nature of the modern world. Now that is a fact not to be passed over lightly. It does change the nature of our problems enormously. Indeed, it is just this breakdown of the old relationships which constitutes the modern problem. So the earlier chapters of this book were devoted to showing how in response to new organization the psychology of business men had changed; how the very nature of property had been altered; how the consumer has had to develop new instruments for controlling the market, and how labor is compelled to organize its power in order not to be trodden by gigantic economic forces.

Nobody likes the present situation very much. But where dispute arises is over whether we can by legislation return to a simpler and more direct stage of civilization. Bryan really hopes to do that, Wilson does too, but his mind is too critical not to have some doubts, and that is why he is against trusts but not against big business. But there is a growing body of opinion which says that communication is blotting out village culture, and opening up national and international thought. It says that bad as big business is to-day, it has a wide promise within it, and that the real task of our generation is to realize it. It looks to the infusion of scientific method, the careful application of administrative technique, the organization and education of the consumer for control, the discipline of labor for an increasing share of the management. Those of us who hold such a belief are pushed from behind by what we think is an irresistible economic development, and lured by a future which we think is possible.

We don't imagine that the trusts are going to drift naturally into the service of human life. We think they can be made to serve it if the American people compel them. We think that the American people may be able to do that if they can adjust their thinking to a new world situation, if they apply the scientific spirit to daily life, and if they can learn to coöperate on a large scale. Those, to be sure, are staggering *ifs*. The conditions may never be fulfilled entirely. But in so far as they are not fulfilled we shall drift along at the mercy of economic forces that we are unable to master. Those who cling to the village view of life may deflect the drift, may batter the trusts about a bit, but they will never dominate business, never humanize its machinery, and they will continue to be the playthings of industrial change.

At bottom the issue is between those who are willing to enter upon an effort for which there is no precedent, and those who aren't. In a real sense it is an adventure. We have still to explore the new scale of human life which machinery has thrust upon us. We have still to invent ways of dealing with it. We have still to adapt our abilities to immense tasks. Of course, men shudder and beg to be let off in order to go back to the simpler life for which they were trained. Of course, they hope that competition will automatically produce the social results they desire. Of course, they see all the evils of the trust and none of its promise. They can point to the failure of empires and the success of little cities. They can say that we are obliterating men in the vast organizations we are permitting.

But they are not the only people who realize that man as he is to-day is not big enough to master the modern world. It is this realization which has made men speculate on the development of what they call a "collective mind." They hope that somehow we shall develop an intelligence larger than the individual.

I see no evidence for that. There are no minds but human minds so far as our problems go. It seems to me that this notion of a collective mind over and above men and women is simply a myth created to meet difficulties greater than men and women are as yet capable of handling. It is a *deus ex machina* invented to cover an enormous need,—a hope that something outside ourselves will do our work for us. It would be infinitely easier if such a power existed. But I can't see any ground for relying upon it. We shall have, it seems to me, to develop within men and women themselves the power they need. It is an immense ambition, and each man who approaches it must appear presumptuous. But it is the problem of our generation: to analyze the weakness, to attack the obstacles, to search for some of the possibilities, to realize if we can the kind of effort by which we can face the puzzling world in which we live.

SELECTION **12**

A Political Leader Formulates the New Nationalism: Theodore Roosevelt at Osawatomie, Kansas, August 31, 1910

William Howard Taft, whom Theodore Roosevelt had designated as his successor, had hardly settled into the White House when natural, historic differences within the Republican party began to widen and threaten division. The strength and, especially, the intensity of the insurgents, as those most critical of the status quo within the Republican camp were known, increased dramatically. Taft stood with the standpatters. Many of the insurgents looked to Midwestern Republicans such as Robert M. La Follette and George W. Norris for leadership, but all watched eagerly to see what ex-President Roosevelt would do when he returned from his trip to Africa and Europe and observed the party strife at first hand. He did not return until June 18, 1910. For the first several weeks at home he was uncharacteristically quiet, even subdued.

Although political insiders could see some evidence of antagonism between the President and the ex-President in July and August, the public at large could not be sure of the situation until TR gave his speech at Osawatomie, reproduced here almost in its entirety, on the last day of August. The occasion was the dedication of a state park where the abolitionist John Brown had massacred some proslavery men in 1856, two years before Roosevelt's birth. For some months before his speech in Kansas, the Rough Rider tried to prevent an open break within the Republican party, but after that speech and others he made in the West in late August and early September, it was clear that Roosevelt and Taft no longer stood together. No one was surprised when the animosity between the two became open and they vied with one another for the 1912 Presidential nomination.

In this speech Roosevelt translated the central idea of Croly's nationalism into the language of the political stump. In one sense, Roosevelt's speech was a radical document for its day, with its strong assertion of human rights and its argument that the community may regulate the use of private property "to whatever degree the public welfare may require it." But in another sense, Roosevelt's version of the New Nationalism was what Croly had called "a higher species of conservatism." "If the reactionary man, who thinks of nothing but the rights of property, could have his way, he would bring about a revolution;

and one of my chief fears in connection with progress comes because I do not want to see our people, for lack of proper leadership, compelled to follow men whose intentions are excellent, but whose eyes are a little too wild to make it really safe to trust them." Reform to prevent revolution; progress in order to conserve.

In late 1910 the Outlook Company published a collection of the TR speeches of August and September, edited by Ernest H. Abbott, under the title The New Nationalism. *The Osawatomie speech was the first in the volume, pages 3–33. Some introductory material, pages 3–7 of the 1910 volume, and one extraneous footnote have been removed.*

We come here to-day to commemorate one of the epoch-making events of the long struggle for the rights of man—the long struggle for the uplift of humanity. Our country—this great republic—means nothing unless it means the triumph of a real democracy, the triumph of popular government, and, in the long run, of an economic system under which each man shall be guaranteed the opportunity to show the best that there is in him. That is why the history of America is now the central feature of the history of the world; for the world has set its face hopefully toward our democracy; and, O my fellow citizens, each one of you carries on your shoulders not only the burden of doing well for the sake of your own country, but the burden of doing well and of seeing that this nation does well for the sake of mankind. . . .

I do not speak of this struggle of the past merely from the historic standpoint. Our interest is primarily in the application to-day of the lessons taught by the contest of half a century ago. It is of little use for us to pay lip loyalty to the mighty men of the past unless we sincerely endeavor to apply to the problems of the present precisely the qualities which in other crises enabled the men of that day to meet those crises. It is half melancholy and half amusing to see the way in which well-meaning people gather to do honor to the men who, in company with John Brown, and under the lead of Abraham Lincoln, faced and solved the great problems of the nineteenth century, while, at the same time, these same good people nervously shrink from, or frantically denounce, those who are trying to meet the problems of the twentieth century in the spirit which was accountable for the successful solution of the problems of Lincoln's time.

Of that generation of men to whom we owe so much, the man to whom we owe most is, of course, Lincoln. Part of our debt to him is because he forecast our present struggle and saw the way out. He said:

I hold that while man exists it is his duty to improve not only his own condition, but to assist in ameliorating mankind.

And again:—

Labor is prior to, and independent of, capital. Capital is only the fruit of labor, and could never have existed if labor had not first existed. Labor is the superior of capital, and deserves much the higher consideration.

If that remark was original with me, I should be even more strongly denounced as a communist agitator than I shall be anyhow. It is Lincoln's. I am only quoting it; and that is one side; that is the side the capitalist should hear. Now, let the workingman hear his side.

> Capital has its rights, which are as worthy of protection as any other rights. . . . Nor should this lead to a war upon the owners of property. Property is the fruit of labor; . . . property is desirable; is a positive good in the world.

And then comes a thoroughly Lincolnlike sentence:—

> Let not him who is houseless pull down the house of another, but let him work diligently and build one for himself, thus by example assuring that his own shall be safe from violence when built.

It seems to me that, in these words, Lincoln took substantially the attitude that we ought to take; he showed the proper sense of proportion in his relative estimates of capital and labor, of human rights and property rights. Above all, in this speech, as in many others, he taught a lesson in wise kindliness and charity; an indispensable lesson to us of to-day. But this wise kindliness and charity never weakened his arm or numbed his heart. We cannot afford weakly to blind ourselves to the actual conflict which faces us to-day. The issue is joined, and we must fight or fail.

In every wise struggle for human betterment one of the main objects, and often the only object, has been to achieve in large measure equality of opportunity. In the struggle for this great end, nations rise from barbarism to civilization, and through it people press forward from one stage of enlightenment to the next. One of the chief factors in progress is the destruction of special privilege. The essence of any struggle for healthy liberty has always been, and must always be, to take from some one man or class of men the right to enjoy power, or wealth, or position, or immunity, which has not been earned by service to his or their fellows. That is what you fought for in the Civil War, and that is what we strive for now.

At many stages in the advance of humanity, this conflict between the men who possess more than they have earned and the men who have earned more than they possess is the central condition of progress. In our day it appears as the struggle of free men to gain and hold the right of self-government as against the special interests, who twist the methods of free government into machinery for defeating the popular will. At every stage, and under all circumstances, the essence of the struggle is to equalize opportunity, destroy privilege, and give to the life and citizenship of every individual the highest possible value both to himself and to the commonwealth. That is nothing new. All I ask in civil life is what you fought for in the Civil War. I ask that civil life be carried on according to the spirit in which the army was carried on. You never get perfect justice, but the effort in handling the army was to bring to the front the men who could do the job. Nobody grudged promotion to Grant, or Sherman, or Thomas, or Sheridan, because they earned it. The only complaint was when a man got promotion which he did not earn.

Practical equality of opportunity for all citizens, when we achieve it, will have two great results. First, every man will have a fair chance to make of himself all that in him lies; to reach the highest point to which his capacities, unassisted by special privilege of his own and unhampered by the special privilege of others, can carry him, and to get for himself and his family substantially what he has earned. Second, equality of opportunity means that the commonwealth will get from every citizen the highest service of which he is capable. No man who carries the burden of the special privileges of another can give to the commonwealth that service to which it is fairly entitled.

I stand for the square deal. But when I say that I am for the square deal, I mean not merely that I stand for fair play under the present rules of the game, but that I stand for having those rules changed so as to work for a more substantial equality of opportunity and of reward for equally good service. One word of warning, which, I think, is hardly necessary in Kansas. When I say I want a square deal for the poor man, I do not mean that I want a square deal for the man who remains poor because he has not got the energy to work for himself. If a man who has had a chance will not make good, then he has got to quit. And you men of the Grand Army, you want justice for the brave man who fought, and punishment for the coward who shirked his work. Is not that so?

Now, this means that our government, national and state, must be freed from the sinister influence or control of special interests. Exactly as the special interests of cotton and slavery threatened our political integrity before the Civil War, so now the great special business interests too often control and corrupt the men and methods of government for their own profit. We must drive the special interests out of politics. That is one of our tasks to-day. Every special interest is entitled to justice—full, fair, and complete,—and, now, mind you, if there were any attempt by mob violence to plunder and work harm to the special interest, whatever it may be, that I most dislike, and the wealthy man, whomsoever he may be, for whom I have the greatest contempt, I would fight for him, and you would if you were worth your salt. He should have justice. For every special interest is entitled to justice, but not one is entitled to a vote in Congress, to a voice on the bench, or to representation in any public office. The Constitution guarantees protection to property, and we must make that promise good. But it does not give the right of suffrage to any corporation.

The true friend of property, the true conservative, is he who insists that property shall be the servant and not the master of the commonwealth; who insists that the creature of man's making shall be the servant and not the master of the man who made it. The citizens of the United States must effectively control the mighty commercial forces which they have themselves called into being.

There can be no effective control of corporations while their political activity remains. To put an end to it will be neither a short nor an easy task, but it can be done.

We must have complete and effective publicity of corporate affairs, so that the people may know beyond peradventure whether the corporations obey the law and whether their management entitles them to the confidence of the public. It is necessary that laws should be passed to prohibit the use of corporate funds directly or indirectly for political purposes; it is still more necessary that such laws should be thoroughly enforced. Corporate expenditures for political purposes, and especially such expenditures by public service corporations, have supplied one of the principal sources of corruption in our political affairs.

It has become entirely clear that we must have government supervision of the capitalization, not only of public service corporations, including, particularly, railways, but of all corporations doing an interstate business. I do not wish to see the nation forced into the ownership of the railways if it can possibly be avoided, and the only alternative is thoroughgoing and effective regulation, which shall be based on a full knowledge of all the facts, including a physical valuation of property. This physical valuation is not needed, or, at least, is very rarely needed, for fixing rates; but it is needed as the basis of honest capitalization.

We have come to recognize that franchises should never be granted except for a limited time, and never without proper provision for compensation to the public. It is my personal belief that the same kind and degree of control and supervision which should be exercised over public service corporations should be extended also to combinations which control necessaries of life, such as meat, oil, and coal, or which deal in them on an important scale. I have no doubt that the ordinary man who has control of them is much like ourselves. I have no doubt he would like to do well, but I want to have enough supervision to help him realize that desire to do well.

I believe that the officers, and, especially, the directors, of corporations should be held personally responsible when any corporation breaks the law.

Combinations in industry are the result of an imperative economic law which cannot be repealed by political legislation. The effort at prohibiting all combination has substantially failed. The way out lies, not in attempting to prevent such combinations, but in completely controlling them in the interest of the public welfare. For that purpose the Federal Bureau of Corporations is an agency of first importance. Its powers, and, therefore, its efficiency, as well as that of the Interstate Commerce Commission, should be largely increased. We have a right to expect from the Bureau of Corporations and from the Interstate Commerce Commission a very high grade of public service. We should be as sure of the proper conduct of the interstate railways and the proper management of interstate business as we are now sure of the conduct and management of the national banks, and we should have as effective supervision in one case as in the other. The Hepburn Act, and the amendment to the Act in the shape in which it finally passed Congress at the last session, represent a long step in advance, and we must go yet further.

There is a widespread belief among our people that, under the methods of making tariffs which have hitherto obtained, the special interests are too influential. Probably this is true of both the big special interests and the little special interests. These methods have put a premium on selfishness, and, naturally, the selfish big interests have gotten more than their smaller, though equally selfish, brothers. The duty of Congress is to provide a method by which the interest of the whole people shall be all that receives consideration. To this end there must be an expert tariff commission, wholly removed from the possibility of political pressure or of improper business influence. Such a commission can find the real difference between cost of production, which is mainly the difference of labor cost here and abroad. As fast as its recommendations are made, I believe in revising one schedule at a time. A general revision of the tariff almost inevitably leads to log-rolling and the subordination of the general public interest to local and special interests.

The absence of effective state, and, especially, national, restraint upon unfair money getting has tended to create a small class of enormously wealthy and economically powerful men, whose chief object is to hold and increase their power. The prime need is to change the conditions which enable these men to accumulate power which it is not for the general welfare that they should hold or exercise. We grudge no man a fortune which represents his own power and sagacity, when exercised with entire regard to the welfare of his fellows. Again, comrades over there, take the lesson from your own experience. Not only did you not grudge, but you gloried in the promotion of the great generals who gained their promotion by leading the army to victory. So it is with us. We grudge no man a fortune in civil life if it is honorably obtained and well used. It is not even enough that it should have been gained without doing damage to the community. We should permit it to be gained only so long as the gaining represents benefit to the community. This, I know, implies a policy of a far more active governmental interference with social and economic conditions in this country than we have yet had, but I think we have got to face the fact that such an increase in governmental control is now necessary.

No man should receive a dollar unless that dollar has been fairly earned. Every dollar received should represent a dollar's worth of service rendered —not gambling in stocks, but service rendered. The really big fortune, the swollen fortune, by the mere fact of its size acquires qualities which differentiate it in kind as well as in degree from what is possessed by men of relatively small means. Therefore, I believe in a graduated income tax on big fortunes, and in another tax which is far more easily collected and far more effective—a graduated inheritance tax on big fortunes, properly safeguarded against evasion and increasing rapidly in amount with the size of the estate.

The people of the United States suffer from periodical financial panics to a degree substantially unknown among the other nations which approach us in financial strength. There is no reason why we should suffer what they escape. It is of profound importance that our financial system should be promptly investigated, and so thoroughly and effectively revised as to make it certain that hereafter our currency will no longer fail at critical times to meet our needs.

It is hardly necessary for me to repeat that I believe in an efficient army and a navy large enough to secure for us abroad that respect which is the surest guarantee of peace. A word of special warning to my fellow citizens who are as progressive as I hope I am. I want them to keep up their interest in our internal affairs; and I want them also continually to remember Uncle Sam's interests abroad. Justice and fair dealing among nations rest upon principles identical with those which control justice and fair dealing among the individuals of which nations are composed, with the vital exception that each nation must do its own part in international police work. If you get into trouble here, you can call for the police; but if Uncle Sam gets into trouble, he has got to be his own policeman, and I want to see him strong enough to encourage the peaceful aspirations of other peoples in connection with us. I believe in national friendships and heartiest good will to all nations; but national friendships, like those between men, must be founded on respect as well as on liking, on forbearance as well as upon trust. I should be heartily ashamed of any American who did not try to make the American government act as justly toward the other nations in international relations as he himself would act toward any individual in private relations. I should be heartily ashamed to see us wrong a weaker power, and I should hang my head forever if we tamely suffered wrong from a stronger power.

Of conservation I shall speak more at length elsewhere. Conservation means development as much as it does protection. I recognize the right and duty of this generation to develop and use the natural resources of our land; but I do not recognize the right to waste them, or to rob, by wasteful use, the generations that come after us. I ask nothing of the nation except that it so behave as each farmer here behaves with reference to his own children. That farmer is a poor creature who skins the land and leaves it worthless to his children. The farmer is a good farmer who, having enabled the land to support himself and to provide for the education of his children, leaves it to them a little better than he found it himself. I believe the same thing of a nation.

Moreover, I believe that the natural resources must be used for the benefit of all our people, and not monopolized for the benefit of the few, and here again is another case in which I am accused of taking a revolutionary attitude. People forget now that one hundred years ago there were public men of good character who advocated the nation selling its public lands in great quantities, so that the nation could get the most money out of it, and giving it to the men who could cultivate it for their own uses. We took the proper democratic ground that the land should be granted in small sections to the men who were actually to till it and live on it. Now, with the water power, with the forests, with the mines, we are brought face to face with the fact that there are many people who will go with us in conserving the resources only if they are to be allowed to exploit them for their benefit. That is one of the fundamental reasons why the special interests should be driven out of politics. Of all the questions which can come before this nation, short of the actual preservation of its existence in a great war, there is none which compares in importance with the great central task of leaving this land even a better land for our descendants than it is for us, and training them into a better race to inhabit the land and pass it on. Conservation is a great moral issue, for it involves the patriotic duty of insuring the safety and continuance of the nation. Let me add that the health and vitality of our people are at least as well worth conserving as their forests, waters, lands, and minerals, and in this great work the national government must bear a most important part.

I have spoken elsewhere also of the great task which lies before the farmers of the country to get for themselves and their wives and children not only the benefits of better farming, but also those of better business methods and better conditions of life on the farm. The burden of this great task will fall, as it should, mainly upon the great organizations of the farmers themselves. I am glad it will, for I believe they are all well able to handle it. In particular, there are strong reasons why the Departments of Agriculture of the various states, the United States Department of Agriculture, and the agricultural colleges and experiment stations should extend their work to cover all phases of farm life, instead of limiting themselves, as they have far too often limited themselves in the past, solely to the question of the production of crops. And now a special word to the farmer. I want to see him make the farm as fine a farm as it can be made; and let him remember to see that the improvement goes on indoors as well as out; let him remember that the farmer's wife should have her share of thought and attention just as much as the farmer himself.

Nothing is more true than that excess of every kind is followed by reaction; a fact which should be pondered by reformer and reactionary alike. We are face to face with new conceptions of the relations of property to human welfare, chiefly because certain advocates of the rights of property as against the rights of men have been pushing their claims too far. The man who wrongly holds that every human right is secondary to his profit must now give way to the advocate of human welfare, who rightly maintains that every man holds his property subject to the general right of the community to regulate its use to whatever degree the public welfare may require it.

But I think we may go still further. The right to regulate the use of wealth in the public interest is universally admitted. Let us admit also the right to regulate the terms and conditions of labor, which is the chief element of wealth, directly in the interest of the common good. The fundamental thing to do for every man is to give him a chance to reach a place in which he will make the greatest possible contribution to the public welfare. Understand what I say there. Give him a chance, not push him up if he will not be pushed. Help any man who stumbles; if he lies down, it is a poor job to try to carry him; but if he is a worthy man, try your best to see that he gets a chance to show the worth that is in him. No man can be a good citizen unless he has a wage more than sufficient to cover the bare cost of living, and hours of labor short enough so that after his day's work is done he will have time and energy to bear his share in the management of the community, to help in carrying the general load. We keep countless men from being good citizens by the conditions of life with which we surround them. We need comprehensive workmen's compensation acts, both state and national laws to regulate child labor and work for women, and, especially, we need in our common schools not merely education in book learning, but also practical training for daily life and work. We need to enforce better sanitary conditions for our workers and to extend the use of safety appliances for our workers in industry and commerce, both within and between the states. Also, friends, in the interest of the workingman himself we need to set our faces like flint against mob violence just as against corporate greed; against violence and injustice and lawlessness by wage workers just as much as against lawless cunning and greed and selfish arrogance of employers. If I could ask but one thing of my fellow countrymen, my request would be that, whenever they go in for reform, they remember the two sides, and that they always exact justice from one side as much as from the other. I have small use for the public servant who can always see and denounce the corruption of the capitalist, but who cannot persuade himself, especially before election, to say a word about lawless mob violence. And I have equally small use for the man, be he a judge on the bench, or editor of a great paper, or wealthy and influential private citizen, who can see clearly enough and denounce the lawlessness of mob violence, but whose eyes are closed so that he is blind when the question is one of corruption in business on a gigantic scale. Also remember what I said about excess in reformer and reactionary alike. If the reactionary man, who thinks of nothing but the rights of property, could have his way, he would bring about a revolution; and one of my chief fears in connection with progress comes because I do not want to see our people, for lack of proper leadership, compelled to follow men whose intentions are excellent, but whose eyes are a little too wild to make it really safe to trust them. Here in Kansas there is one paper which habitually denounces me as the tool of Wall Street, and at the same time frantically repudiates the statement that I am a Socialist on the ground that that is an unwarranted slander of the Socialists.

National efficiency has many factors. It is a necessary result of the principle of conservation widely applied. In the end it will determine our failure or success as a nation. National efficiency has to do, not only with natural resources and with men, but it is equally concerned with institutions. The state must be made efficient for the work which concerns only the people of the state; and the nation for that which concerns all the people. There must remain no neutral ground to serve as a refuge for lawbreakers, and especially for lawbreakers of great wealth, who can hire the vulpine legal cunning which will teach them how to avoid both jurisdictions. It is a misfortune when the national legislature fails to do its duty in providing a national remedy, so that the only national activity is the purely negative activity of the judiciary in forbidding the state to exercise power in the premises.

I do not ask for overcentralization; but I do ask that we work in a spirit of broad and far-reaching nationalism when we work for what concerns our people as a whole. We are all Americans. Our common interests are as broad as the continent. I speak to you here in Kansas exactly as I would speak in New York or Georgia, for the most vital problems are those which affect us all alike. The national government belongs to the whole American people, and where the whole American people are interested, that interest can be guarded effectively only by the national government.

The betterment which we seek must be accomplished, I believe, mainly through the national government.

The American people are right in demanding that New Nationalism, without which we cannot hope to deal with new problems. The New Nationalism puts the national need before sectional or personal advantage. It is impatient of the utter confusion that results from local legislatures attempting to treat national issues as local issues. It is still more impatient of the impotence which springs from overdivision of governmental powers, the impotence which makes it possible for local selfishness or for legal cunning, hired by wealthy special interests, to bring national activities to a deadlock. This New Nationalism regards the executive power as the steward of the public welfare. It demands of the judiciary that it shall be interested primarily in human welfare rather than in property, just as it demands that the representative body shall represent all the people rather than any one class or section of the people.

I believe in shaping the ends of government to protect property as well as human welfare. Normally, and in the long run, the ends are the same; but whenever the alternative must be faced, I am for men and not for property, as you were in the Civil War. I am far from underestimating the importance of dividends; but I rank dividends below human character. Again, I do not have any sympathy with the reformer who says he does not care for dividends. Of course, economic welfare is necessary, for a man must pull his own weight and be able to support his family. I know well that the reformers must not bring upon the people economic ruin, or the reforms themselves will go down in the ruin. But we must be ready to face temporary disaster, whether or not brought on by those who will war against us to the knife. Those who oppose all reform will do well to remember that ruin in its worst form is inevitable if our national life brings us nothing better than swollen fortunes for the few and the triumph in both politics and business of a sordid and selfish materialism.

If our political institutions were perfect, they would absolutely prevent the political domination of money in any part of our affairs. We need to make our political representatives more quickly and sensitively responsive to the people whose servants they are. More direct action by the people in their own affairs under proper safeguards is vitally necessary. The direct primary is a step in this direction, if it is associated with a corrupt practices act effective to prevent the advantage of the man willing recklessly and unscrupulously to spend money over his more honest competitor. It is particularly important that all moneys received or expended for campaign purposes should be publicly accounted for, not only after election, but before election as well. Political action must be made simpler, easier, and freer from confusion for every citizen. I believe that the prompt removal of unfaithful or incompetent public servants should be made easy and sure in whatever way experience shall show to be most expedient in any given class of cases.

One of the fundamental necessities in a representative government such as ours is to make certain that the men to whom the people delegate their power shall serve the people by whom they are elected, and not the special interests. I believe that every national officer, elected or appointed, should be forbidden to perform any service or receive any compensation, directly or indirectly, from interstate corporations; and a similar provision could not fail to be useful within the states.

The object of government is the welfare of the people. The material progress and prosperity of a nation are desirable chiefly so far as they lead to the moral and material welfare of all good citizens. Just in proportion as the average man and woman are honest, capable of sound judgment and high ideals, active in public affairs,—but, first of all, sound in their home life, and the father and mother of healthy children whom they bring up well,—just so far, and no farther, we may count our civilization a success. We must have—I believe we have already—a genuine and permanent moral awakening, without which no wisdom of legislation or administration really means anything; and, on the other hand, we must try to secure the social and economic legislation without which any improvement due to purely moral agitation is necessarily evanescent. Let me again illustrate by a reference to the Grand Army. You could not have won simply as a disorderly and disorganized mob. You needed generals; you needed careful administration of the most advanced type; and a good commissary—the cracker line. You well remember that success was necessary in many different lines in order to bring about general success. You had to have the administration at Washington good, just as you had to have the administration in the field; and you had to have the work of the generals good. You could not have triumphed without that administration and leadership; but it would all have been worthless if the average soldier had not had the right stuff in him. He had to have the right stuff in him, or you could not get it out of him. In the last analysis, therefore, vitally necessary though it was to have the right kind of organization and the right kind of generalship, it was even more vitally necessary that the average soldier should have the fighting edge, the right character. So it is in our civil life. No matter how honest and decent we are in our private lives, if we do not have the right kind of law and the right kind of administration of the law, we cannot go forward as a nation. That is imperative; but it must be an addition to, and not a substitution for, the qualities that make us good citizens. In the last analysis, the most important elements in any man's career must be the sum of those qualities which, in the aggregate, we speak of as character. If he has not got it, then no law that the wit of man can devise, no administration of the law by the boldest and strongest executive, will avail to help him. We must have the right kind of character—character that makes a man, first of all, a good man in the home, a good father, a good husband—that makes a man a good neighbor. You must have that, and, then, in addition, you must have the kind of law and the kind of administration of the law which will give to those qualities in the private citizen the best possible chance for development. The prime problem of our nation is to get the right type of good citizenship, and, to get it, we must have progress, and our public men must be genuinely progressive.

SELECTION **13**

What They Stood for at Armageddon: The Platform of the Progressive Party, 1912

The night before the Republican national convention opened in Chicago in June, 1912, Theodore Roosevelt addressed a large meeting of his followers in the convention city in a manner intended to intensify the enthusiasm of his convention delegates and to identify his forces with all that was just, noble, and true. His final sentence was, "We fight in honorable fashion for the good of mankind; unheeding of our individual fates; with unflinching hearts and undimmed eyes; we stand at Armageddon, and we battle for the Lord." Although the Roosevelt forces thought themselves on the Lord's side and the Lord on theirs, the standpatters had the votes and nominated Taft. Immediately after their defeat, TR and his followers split from the GOP and announced a convention of a new party to meet in Chicago in August. The new party, officially called the Progressive party and frequently called the Bull Moose party, nominated Roosevelt and Governor Hiram Johnson of California. Its platform had been largely spelled out in Roosevelt's opening speech to its convention.

The Progressive platform was notable for its advanced position, the most radical that had been adopted by a major party or a splinter group from a major party unless one counts the Populists, and for the number of its planks that subsequently were implemented by national legislation enacted by other parties. But the Progressive platform was notable as well for what it did not say. The Bull Moosers, unlike the Republicans and Democrats in 1912, said nothing in their platform about the Sherman Antitrust Act, a major omission which indicated a sharp difference of opinion within the new party; and their platform said nothing about the Negro, a rather minor omission in the politics of that era.

The Negro matter first. Hoping to attract the more progressive Southern whites, the Bull Moose party adopted a lily-white policy for its units in the South. There were no Southern Negro delegates seated at the Progressive convention, although Negro hopefuls appeared to contest seats. Considering the Progressive intention to make inroads into Democratic strength in Dixie, the absence of a reference to the Negro in the platform was not surprising even though the Republican platform had condemned lynching. The Democratic platform was, as usual, silent on the matter.

The absence of an antitrust plank involved a dispute of major dimensions. A central figure in the story was the party's chief financial supporter, George W. Perkins, a Morgan partner and a director of International Harvester and United States Steel. Perkins opposed antitrust suits but supported governmental regulation of a special sort. Roosevelt concurred with Perkins, and in his opening speech to the convention he criticized the Democratic plank that called for strengthening of the Sherman Act. Nevertheless, the platform committee adopted a plank that endorsed the Sherman Act and spelled out how it should be strengthened. After the platform passed the committee, it went to Roosevelt, Perkins, and Senator Albert Beveridge. They struck out the antitrust plank and returned the platform to the committee. Accounts of what then happened in the committee conflict, but the committee probably adopted the platform as originally written, with the antitrust plank restored. The next day the platform that was presented to the convention included the antitrust statement that had offended Perkins and Roosevelt. When it was read to the convention Perkins shouted, "That does not belong in the platform. We cut it out last night." At a hurriedly called meeting of party leaders Roosevelt instructed the convention secretary to delete the antitrust paragraph, and the platform copy the press received had no mention of the Sherman Act. After the election, when the Progressives wrangled bitterly among themselves, much of the criticism directed against Perkins had to do with the antitrust plank that had failed to survive the party machinery.

The version of the platform reprinted here without abridgment is the one the Progressive National Committee published during the campaign as a pamphlet entitled A Contract with the People: Platform of the Progressive Party Adopted at Its First National Convention, Chicago, August 7th, 1912. *The platform is more readily available in Kirk H. Porter and Donald Johnson, compilers,* National Party Platforms, 1840–1960 *(Urbana, Ill.: University of Illinois Press, 1961), pages 175–182. The best account of the platform controversy as well as the Progressive party generally is George E. Mowry,* Theodore Roosevelt and the Progressive Movement *(Madison, Wis.: University of Wisconsin Press, 1946); for an interesting interpretation which sees the Progressives' "basic problem" as "how to appear radical while really remaining conservative,"* see Gabriel Kolko, The Triumph of Conservatism: A Reinterpretation of American History, 1900–1916 *(New York: The Free Press, 1963).*

The conscience of the people, in a time of grave national problems, has called into being a new party, born of the nation's awakened sense of justice. We of the Progressive party here dedicate ourselves to the fulfillment of the duty laid upon us by our fathers to maintain that government of the people, by the people and for the people whose foundations they laid.

We hold with Thomas Jefferson and Abraham Lincoln that the people are the masters of their constitution, to fulfill its purposes and to safeguard it from those who, by perversion of its intent, would convert it into an instrument of injustice. In accordance with the needs of each generation the people must use their sovereign powers to establish and maintain equal opportunity and industrial justice, to secure which this government was founded and without which no republic can endure.

This country belongs to the people who inhabit it. Its resources, its business, its institutions and its laws should be utilized, maintained or altered in whatever manner will best promote the general interest.

It is time to set the public welfare in the first place.

The Old Parties

Political parties exist to secure responsible government and to execute the will of the people.

From these great tasks both of the old parties have turned aside. Instead of instruments to promote the general welfare, they have become the tools of corrupt interests which use them impartially to serve their selfish purposes. *Behind the ostensible government sits enthroned an invisible government, owing no allegiance and acknowledging no responsibility to the people.*

To destroy this invisible government, to dissolve the unholy alliance between corrupt business and corrupt politics is the first task of the statesmanship of the day.

The deliberate betrayal of its trust by the Republican party, and the fatal incapacity of the Democratic party to deal with the new issues of the new time, have compelled the people to forge a new instrument of government through which to give effect to their will in laws and institutions.

Unhampered by tradition, uncorrupted by power, undismayed by the magnitude of the task, the new party offers itself as the instrument of the people to sweep away old abuses, to build a new and nobler commonwealth.

A Covenant with the People

This declaration is our covenant with the people, and we hereby bind the party and its candidates in state and nation to the pledges made herein.

The Rule of the People

The Progressive party, committed to the principle of government by a self-controlled democracy expressing its will through representatives of the people, pledges itself to secure such alterations in the fundamental law of the several states and of the United States as shall insure the representative character of the government.

In particular, the party declares for direct primaries for the nomination of state and national officers, for nation-wide preferential primaries for candidates for the presidency, for the direct election of United States senators by the people; and we urge on the states the policy of the short ballot, with responsibility to the people secured by the initiative, referendum and recall.

Amendment of Constitution

The Progressive party, believing that a free people should have the power from time to time to amend their fundamental law so as to adapt it progressively to the changing needs of the people, pledges itself to provide a more easy and expeditious method of amending the federal constitution.

Nation and State

Up to the limit of the constitution, and later by amendment of the constitution, if found necessary, we advocate bringing under effective national jurisdiction those problems which have expanded beyond reach of the individual states.

It is as grotesque as it is intolerable that the several states should by unequal laws in matter of common concern become competing commercial agencies, barter the lives of their children, the health of their women and the safety and well-being of their working people for the profit of their financial interests.

The extreme insistence on states' rights by the Democratic party in the Baltimore platform demonstrates anew its inability to understand the world into which it has survived or to administer the affairs of a union of states which have in all essential respects become one people.

Social and Industrial Justice

The supreme duty of the nation is the conservation of human resources through an enlightened measure of social and industrial justice. We pledge ourselves to work unceasingly in state and nation for:—

Effective legislation looking to the prevention of industrial accidents, occupational diseases, overwork, involuntary unemployment, and other injurious effects incident to modern industry;

The fixing of minimum safety and health standards for the various occupations, and the exercise of the public authority of state and nation, including the federal control over interstate commerce and the taxing power, to maintain such standards;

The prohibition of child labor;

Minimum wage standards for working women, to provide a living scale in all industrial occupations;

The prohibition of night work for women and the establishment of an eight-hour day for women and young persons;

One day's rest in seven for all wage-workers;

The eight-hour day in continuous twenty-four-hour industries;

The abolition of the convict contract labor system; substituting a system of prison production for governmental consumption only; and the application of prisoners' earnings to the support of their dependent families;

Publicity as to wages, hours and conditions of labor; full reports upon industrial accidents and diseases, and the opening to public inspection of all tallies, weights, measures and check systems on labor products;

Standards of compensation for death by industrial accident and injury and trade diseases which will transfer the burden of lost earnings from the families of working people to the industry, and thus to the community;

The protection of home life against the hazards of sickness, irregular employment and old age through the adoption of a system of social insurance adapted to American use;

The development of the creative labor power of America by lifting the last load of illiteracy from American youth and establishing continuation schools for industrial education under public control and encouraging agricultural education and demonstration in rural schools;

The establishment of industrial research laboratories to put the methods and discoveries of science at the service of American producers.

We favor the organization of the workers, men and women, as a means of protecting their interests and of promoting their progress.

Business

We believe that true popular government, justice and prosperity go hand in hand, and, so believing, it is our purpose to secure that large measure of general prosperity which is the fruit of legitimate and honest business, fostered by equal justice and by sound progressive laws.

We demand that the test of true prosperity shall be the benefits conferred thereby on all the citizens not confined to individuals or classes and that the test of corporate efficiency shall be the ability better to serve the public; that those who profit by control of business affairs shall justify that profit and that control by sharing with the public the fruits thereof.

We therefore demand a strong national regulation of interstate corporations. The corporation is an essential part of modern business. The concentration of modern business, in some degree, is both inevitable and necessary for national and international business efficiency. But the existing concentration of vast wealth under a corporate system, unguarded and uncontrolled by the nation, has placed in the hands of a few men enormous, secret, irresponsible power over the daily life of the citizen—a power insufferable in a free government and certain of abuse.

This power has been abused, in monopoly of national resources, in stock watering, in unfair competition and unfair privileges, and finally in sinister influences on the public agencies of state and nation. We do not fear commercial power, but we insist that it shall be exercised openly, under publicity, supervision and regulation of the most efficient sort, which will preserve its good while eradicating and preventing its evils.

To that end we urge the establishment of a strong federal administrative commission of high standing, which shall maintain permanent active supervision over industrial corporations engaged in interstate commerce, or such of them as are of public importance, doing for them what the government now does for the national banks, and what is now done for the railroads by the Interstate Commerce Commission.

Such a commission must enforce the complete publicity of those corporation transactions which are of public interest; must attack unfair competition, false capitalization and special privilege, and by continuous trained watchfulness guard and keep open equally to all the highways of American commerce.

Thus the business man will have certain knowledge of the law, and will be able to conduct his business easily in conformity therewith; the investor will find security for his capital; dividends will be rendered more certain, and the savings of the people will be drawn naturally and safely into the channels of trade.

Under such a system of constructive regulation, legitimate business, freed from confusion, uncertainty and fruitless litigation, will develop normally in response to the energy and enterprise of the American business man.

Commercial Development

The time has come when the federal government should co-operate with manufacturers and producers in extending our foreign commerce. To this end we demand adequate appropriations by Congress, and the appointment of diplomatic and consular officers solely with a view to their special fitness and worth, and not in consideration of political expediency.

It is imperative to the welfare of our people that we enlarge and extend our foreign commerce. We are pre-eminently fitted to do this because as a people we have developed high skill in the art of manufacturing; our business men are strong executives, strong organizers. In every way possible our Federal Government should co-operate in this important matter. Anyone who has had opportunity to study and observe first-hand Germany's course in this respect must realize that their policy of co-operation between Government and business has in comparatively few years made them a leading competitor for the commerce of the world. It should be remembered that they are doing this on a national scale and with large units of business, while the Democrats would have us believe that we should do it with small units of business, which would be controlled not by the National Government but by forty-nine conflicting sovereignties. Such a policy is utterly out of keeping with the progress of the times and gives our great commercial rivals in Europe—hungry for international markets—golden opportunities of which they are rapidly taking advantage.

Tariff

We believe in a protective tariff which shall equalize conditions of competition between the United States and foreign countries, both for the farmer and the manufacturer and which shall maintain for labor an adequate standard of living.

Primarily the benefit of any tariff should be disclosed in the pay envelope of the laborer. We declare that no industry deserves protection which is unfair to labor or which is operating in violation of federal law. We believe that the presumption is always in favor of the consuming public.

We demand tariff revision because the present tariff is unjust to the people of the United States. Fair-dealing toward the people requires an immediate downward revision of those schedules wherein duties are shown to be unjust or excessive.

We pledge ourselves to the establishment of a nonpartisan scientific tariff commission, reporting both to the President and to either branch of Congress, which shall report, first, as to the costs of production, efficiency of labor, capitalization, industrial organization and efficiency and the general competitive position in this country and abroad of industries seeking protection from Congress; second, as to the revenue-producing power of the tariff and its relation to the resources of government; and, third, as to the effect of the tariff on prices, operations of middlemen, and on the purchasing power of the consumer.

We believe that this commission should have plenary power to elicit information, and for this purpose to prescribe a uniform system of accounting for the great protected industries. The work of the commission should not prevent the immediate adoption of acts reducing those schedules generally recognized as excessive.

We condemn the Payne-Aldrich bill as unjust to the people. The Republican organization is in the hands of those who have broken, and cannot again be trusted to keep, the promise of necessary downward revision. The Democratic party is committed to the destruction of the protective system through a tariff for revenue only—a policy which would inevitably produce widespread industrial and commercial disaster.

We demand the immediate repeal of the Canadian reciprocity act.

High Cost of Living

The high cost of living is due partly to world-wide and partly to local causes; partly to natural and partly to artificial causes. The measures proposed in this platform on various subjects such as the tariff, the trusts and conservation, will of themselves tend to remove the artificial causes.

There will remain other elements such as the tendency to leave the country for the city, waste, extravagance, bad system of taxation, poor methods of raising crops and bad business methods in marketing crops.

To remedy these conditions requires the fullest information and based on this information, effective government supervision and control to remove all the artificial causes. We pledge ourselves to such full and immediate inquiry and to immediate action to deal with every need such inquiry discloses.

Currency

We believe there exists imperative need for prompt legislation for the improvement of our national currency system. We believe the present method of issuing notes through private agencies is harmful and unscientific.

The issue of currency is fundamentally a government function and the system should have as basic principles soundness and elasticity. The control should be lodged with the government and should be protected from domination or manipulation by Wall Street or any special interests.

We are opposed to the so-called Aldrich currency bill, because its provisions would place our currency and credit system in private hands, not subject to effective public control.

Conservation

The natural resources of the nation must be promptly developed and generously used to supply the people's needs, but we cannot safely allow them to be wasted, exploited, monopolized, or controlled against the general good. We heartily favor the policy of conservation, and we pledge our party to protect the national forests without hindering their legitimate use for the benefit of all the people.

Agricultural lands in the national forests are, and should remain, open to the genuine settler. Conservation will not retard legitimate development. The honest settler must receive his patent promptly, without needless restrictions or delays.

We believe that the remaining forests, coal and oil lands, water powers and other natural resources still in state or national control (except agricultural lands) are more likely to be wisely conserved and utilized for the general welfare if held in the public hands.

In order that consumers and producers, managers and workmen, now and hereafter, need not pay toll to private monopolies of power and raw material, we demand that such resources shall be retained by the state or nation, and opened to immediate use under laws which will encourage development and make to the people a moderate return for benefits conferred.

In particular we pledge our party to require reasonable compensation to the public for water-power rights hereafter granted by the public.

We pledge legislation to lease the public grazing lands under equitable provisions now pending which will increase the production of food for the people and thoroughly safeguard the rights of the actual homemaker. Natural resources, whose conservation is necessary for the national welfare, should be owned or controlled by the nation.

Waterways

The rivers of the United States are the natural arteries of this continent. We demand that they shall be opened to traffic as indispensable parts of a great nation-wide system of transportation in which the Panama canal will be the central link, thus enabling the whole interior of the United States to share with the Atlantic and Pacific seaboards in the benefit derived from the canal.

It is a national obligation to develop our rivers, and especially the Mississippi and its tributaries, without delay, under a comprehensive general plan covering each river system from its source to its mouth, designed to secure its highest usefulness for navigation, irrigation, domestic supply, water power and the prevention of floods.

We pledge our party to the immediate preparation of such a plan, which should be made and carried out in close and friendly co-operation between the nation, the states and the cities affected.

Under such a plan, the destructive floods of the Mississippi and other streams, which represent a vast and needless loss to the nation, would be controlled by forest conservation and water storage at the headwaters, and by levees below; land sufficient to support millions of people would be reclaimed from the deserts and the swamps, water power enough to transform the industrial standing of whole states would be developed, adequate water terminals would be provided, transportation by river would revive, and the railroads would be compelled to co-operate as freely with the boat lines as with each other.

The equipment, organization and experience acquired in constructing the Panama canal soon will be available for the Lakes-to-the-Gulf deep waterway and other portions of this great work, and should be utilized by the nation in co-operation with the various states, at the lowest net cost to the people.

Panama Canal

The Panama canal, built and paid for by the American people, must be used primarily for their benefit.

We demand that the canal shall be so operated as to break the transportation monopoly now held and misused by the trans-continental railroads by maintaining sea competition with them; that ships directly or indirectly owned or controlled by American railroad corporations shall not be permitted to use the canal, and that American ships engaged in coast wise trade shall pay no tolls.

The Progressive party will favor legislation having for its aim the development of friendship and commerce between the United States and Latin-American nations.

Alaska

The coal and other natural resources of Alaska should be opened to development at once. They are owned by the people of the United States, and are safe from monopoly, waste or destruction only while so owned.

We demand that they shall neither be sold nor given away, except under the homestead law, but while held in government ownership shall be opened to use promptly upon liberal terms requiring immediate development.

Thus the benefit of cheap fuel will accrue to the government of the United States and to the people of Alaska and the Pacific coast; the settlement of extensive agricultural lands will be hastened; the extermination of the salmon will be prevented, and the just and wise development of Alaskan resources will take the place of private extortion or monopoly.

We demand also that extortion or monopoly in transportation shall be prevented by the prompt acquisition, construction, or improvement by the government of such railroads, harbor and other facilities for transportation as the welfare of the people may demand.

We promise the people of the territory of Alaska the same measure of local self-government that was given to other American territories, and

that federal officials appointed there shall be qualified by previous bona-
fide residence in the territory.

Equal Suffrage

The Progressive party, believing that no people can justly claim to be a
true democracy which denies political rights on account of sex, pledges
itself to the task of securing equal suffrage to men and women alike.

Corrupt Practices

We pledge our party to legislation that will compel strict limitation on all
campaign contributions and expenditures, and detailed publicity of both
before as well as after primaries and elections.

Publicity and Public Service

We pledge our party to legislation compelling the registration of lobbyists;
publicity of committee hearings except on foreign affairs, and recording
of all votes in committee; and forbidding federal appointees from holding
office in state or national political organizations, or taking part as officers
or delegates in political conventions for the nomination of elective state
or national officials.

The Courts

The Progressive party demands such restriction of the power of the courts
as shall leave to the people the ultimate authority to determine fundamental questions of social welfare and public policy. To secure this end, it
pledges itself to provide:

1. That when an act, passed under the police power of the state, is held
unconstitutional under the state constitution, by the courts, the people, after
an ample interval for deliberation, shall have an opportunity to vote on the
question whether they desire the act to become a law, notwithstanding such
decision.
2. That every decision of the highest appellate court of a state declaring
an act of the legislature unconstitutional on the ground of its violation of the
federal constitution shall be subject to the same review by the Supreme Court
of the United States as is now accorded to decisions sustaining such legislation.

Administration of Justice

The Progressive party, in order to secure to the people a better administration of justice and by that means to bring about a more general respect
for the law and the courts, pledges itself to work unceasingly for the reform of legal procedure and judicial methods.

We believe that the issuance of injunctions in cases arising out of labor disputes should be prohibited when such injunctions would not apply when no labor disputes existed.

We also believe that a person cited for contempt in labor disputes, except when such contempt was committed in the actual presence of the court or so near thereto as to interfere with the proper administration of justice, should have a right to trial by jury.

Department of Labor

We pledge our party to establish a Department of Labor with a seat in the cabinet, and with wide jurisdiction over matters affecting the conditions of labor and living.

Country Life

The development and prosperity of country life are as important to the people who live in the cities as they are to the farmers. Increase of prosperity on the farm will favorably affect the cost of living and promote the interests of all who dwell in the country, and all who depend upon its products for clothing, shelter and food.

We pledge our party to foster the development of agricultural credit and co-operation, the teaching of agriculture in schools, agricultural college extension, the use of mechanical power on the farm, and to re-establish the Country Life Commission, thus directly promoting the welfare of the farmers, and bringing the benefits of better farming, better business and better living within their reach.

Health

We favor the union of all the existing agencies of the federal government dealing with the public health into a single national health service without discrimination against or for any one set of therapeutic methods, school of medicine, or school of healing with such additional powers as may be necessary to enable it to perform efficiently such duties in the protection of the public from preventable diseases as may be properly undertaken by the federal authorities; including the executing of existing laws regarding pure food; quarantine and cognate subjects; the promotion of appropriate action for the improvement of vital statistics and the extension of the registration area of such statistics, and co-operation with the health activities of the various states and cities of the nation.

Patents

We pledge ourselves to the enactment of a patent law which will make it impossible for patents to be suppressed or used against the public welfare in the interests of injurious monopolies.

Interstate Commerce Commission

We pledge our party to secure to the Interstate Commerce Commission the
the power to value the physical property of railroads. In order that the
power of the commission to protect the people may not be impaired or
destroyed, we demand the abolition of the Commerce Court.

Good Roads

We recognize the vital importance of good roads and we pledge our party
to foster their extension in every proper way, and we favor the early
construction of national highways. We also favor the extension of the rural
free delivery service.

Inheritance and Income Tax

We believe in a graduated inheritance tax as a national means of equalizing the obligations of holders of property to government, and we hereby
pledge our party to enact such a federal law as will tax large inheritances,
returning to the states an equitable percentage of all amounts collected.

We favor the ratification of the pending amendment to the constitution
giving the government power to levy an income tax.

Peace and National Defense

The Progressive party deplores the survival in our civilization of the
barbaric system of warfare among nations with its enormous waste of resources even in time of peace, and the consequent impoverishment of the
life of the toiling masses. We pledge the party to use its best endeavors to
substitute judicial and other peaceful means of settling international
differences.

We favor an international agreement for the limitation of naval forces.
Pending such an agreement, and as the best means of preserving peace,
we pledge ourselves to maintain for the present the policy of building two
battleships a year.

Treaty Rights

We pledge our party to protect the rights of American citizenship at home
and abroad. No treaty should receive the sanction of our government which
discriminates between American citizens because of birthplace, race, or
religion, or that does not recognize the absolute right of expatriation.

The Immigrant

Through the establishment of industrial standards we propose to secure
to the able-bodied immigrant and to his native fellow workers a larger share
of American opportunity.

We denounce the fatal policy of indifference and neglect which has left our enormous immigrant population to become the prey of chance and cupidity.

We favor governmental action to encourage the distribution of immigrants away from the congested cities, to rigidly supervise all private agencies dealing with them and to promote their assimilation, education and advancement.

Pensions

We pledge ourselves to a wise and just policy of pensioning American soldiers and sailors and their widows and children by the federal government. And we approve the policy of the southern states in granting pensions to the ex-Confederate soldiers and sailors and their widows and children.

Parcels Post

We pledge our party to the immediate creation of a parcels post, with rates proportionate to distance and service.

Civil Service

We condemn the violations of the civil service law under the present administration, including the coercion and assessment of subordinate employees, and the President's refusal to punish such violation after a finding of guilty by his own commission; his distribution of patronage among subservient congressmen, while withholding it from those who refuse support of administration measures; his withdrawal of nominations from the Senate until political support for himself was secured, and his open use of the offices to reward those who voted for his renomination.

To eradicate these abuses, we demand not only the enforcement of the civil service act in letter and spirit, but also legislation which will bring under the competitive system postmasters, collectors, marshals and all other nonpolitical officers, as well as the enactment of an equitable retirement law, and we also insist upon continuous service during good behavior and efficiency.

Government Business Organization

We pledge our party to readjustment of the business methods of the national government and a proper co-ordination of the federal bureaus, which will increase the economy and efficiency of the government service, prevent duplications and secure better results to the taxpayers for every dollar expended.

Government Supervision over Investments

The people of the United States are swindled out of many millions of dollars every year, through worthless investments. The plain people, the wage-earner and the men and women with small savings, have no way of knowing the merit of concerns sending out highly colored prospectuses offering stock for sale, prospectuses that make big returns seem certain and fortunes easily within grasp.

We hold it to be the duty of the government to protect its people from this kind of piracy. We, therefore, demand wise, carefully thought out legislation that will give us such governmental supervision over this matter as will furnish to the people of the United States this much-needed protection, and we pledge ourselves thereto.

Conclusion

On these principles and on the recognized desirability of uniting the Progressive forces of the nation into an organization which shall unequivocally represent the Progressive spirit and policy we appeal for the support of all American citizens, without regard to previous political affiliations.

SELECTION

Woodrow Wilson on Government, Liberty, and Business in the 1912 Campaign: Address to the New York Press Club, September 9, 1912

Roosevelt's and Wilson's differences about what should be the policy of the Federal government toward large and powerful corporations—loosely called trusts or monopolies although by this time they no longer used the trustee form of organization and rarely had a full monopoly of the market—was one of the fundamental issues of the 1912 election. In this speech to New York newspapermen Woodrow Wilson directed his main attention to this issue and the broader question of the proper role of government generally. Although, as many historians have noted, Wilson as President came around slowly to a position on government and business that was not far from Roosevelt's, the present document makes clear that he was sharply critical of this position in 1912. The Progressives proposed, said Wilson, "perpetuation of the existing alliance between the Government and big business" that the Republican party had welded. The Roosevelt platform proposed, as Wilson viewed it, to "legitimatize and regulate monopoly" when regulation of competition was actually in order.

To a generation accustomed to Republican criticisms of Democrats as "welfare statists" who improperly magnify the powers of government, particularly the Federal government, it may be surprising to read the 1912 Democratic nominee saying, "Liberty has never come from the Government. Liberty has always come from the subjects of it. The history of liberty is a history of resistance." Roosevelt, whose straying from the Republican flock proved to be only brief, attacked Wilson for this statement. Roosevelt was not truly representative of the traditional Republican position, but Wilson was quite representative of his party at that time. The Democratic party was historically the party of states' rights and limited Federal power. Wilson, a Virginian who had grown up in the Civil War and Reconstruction period (he was born in 1856), spoke words that came naturally to his lips.

The most comprehensive and perceptive biographer of Wilson is Arthur S. Link, who has written several volumes about the first Democratic President of the twentieth century. For a general work on Wilson and his first administration, see Link's Woodrow Wilson and the Progressive Era, 1910–1917 (New York: Harper & Row, 1954). For the volume in Link's multi-volume biography that relates to this campaign, see Wilson: The Road to the White House (Princeton, N.J.: Princeton, 1947). See also William Diamond, The Economic Thought of Woodrow Wilson (Baltimore: Johns Hopkins, 1943). This news story about the Wilson speech is from the World, the Pulitzer newspaper of New York City, September 10, 1912, page 4.

DEMOCRATS UNITED AND PROGRESSIVE; SHOULD WIN FIGHT—WOODROW WILSON

Woodrow Wilson in a speech at the New York Press Club last night made an attack upon the National Progressive Party's platform and Col. Roosevelt's "Confession of Faith." The 200 men present listened earnestly to every word of his address, which Acting Chairman William G. McAdoo of the Democratic National Committee declared was the greatest speech ever delivered by the Democratic Presidential nominee.

For nearly an hour the Governor reviewed the history of the three parties, but most of this time was given over to a careful analysis of the new party movement.

After a few brief remarks, Charles R. Macauley, President of the Press Club, introduced Joseph R. Wilson, city editor of the Nashville (Tenn.) Banner, with the request that he introduce his distinguished brother, Gov. Wilson, whom Macauley predicted would be "the next President of the United States." Other speakers of the evening were Representative William Sulzer, Ralph Pulitzer and Josephus Daniels of Raleigh, N.C., Chairman of the Publicity Committee of the Democratic National Committee.

Our Standard at the Start

"When we set up this Government," said Gov. Wilson, "we deliberately set ourselves at the front of the enterprises of civilization and of humanity. We said 'Governments hitherto have not been suited to the general interests; we are going to set up a government that is interested in the general advancement of the welfare of men of all classes and conditions.'"

He contended that it is wrong to look upon the Government as "if it were merely the instrument for party control."

"If we are to be free," he continued, "to serve civilization and humanity, what are we going to do in the present campaign?"

Then with a candor and frankness that surprised those who heard him, the Governor proceeded to give an analysis of the three political parties. He dismissed the Republican party in a few paragraphs, but he went deeply into the Progressive movement and led up to the birth of the Roosevelt movement in Orchestra Hall after the Colonel had been denied the nomination at the hands of the regular Republican party in Chicago.

After charging the leaders—not the rank and file—of the Republican party with the responsibility for the present conditions in the nation, the Governor asked this question:

"If you want to set the Government free can you employ the party that entangles it?"

"My implication in asking that question," he continued when the noise had subsided, "is not that any set of Republicans deliberately made partnerships which rendered it impossible for them to serve the people; simply I want, in every discussion, to discriminate between the great body of my fellow-citizens who have usually voted the Republican ticket and that small body of my fellow-citizens who have usually misled them into voting it."

Then in short, epigrammatic sentences, the Governor told how the rank and file of the Republican party had been betrayed by their chosen leaders. He confessed that, although born and bred a Democrat, he had always held in high esteem the historic traditions of the Republican party, and the cause which led to its formation.

"But the Republican party," he continued, "by reason of the tariff policy in particular, has tied the administration of this Government to certain great interests, chiefly by means of campaign contributions, so thoroughly and in such complicated fashion that it is unreasonable to suppose that the very next administration should seek to do what even this administration has not even attempted to do. Can you set the Government free and serve civilization through the regular Republican party? Well, if not to the Republican party to whom shall we turn?"

The Bull Moose Programme

Here the Governor began his analysis of the third party programme. While following the spirit of the text of his prepared speech his phraseology was much stronger.

"There is a new party," began the Governor, "which it is difficult to characterize, because it is made up of several elements. As I see it, it is made up of three elements in particular."

After a brief pause the Governor defined the three elements of the Bull Moose party in this manner.

"The first consists of those Republicans whose consciences and whose stomachs could not stand what the regular Republicans were doing. They were called at first in New Jersey 'New Idea Republicans,' when it was a new idea that a Republican could do wrong. Later in other States Republicans started an insurrection against the control of their own party, and now the insurrectors are outside.

"But added to this element is a second one that interests me very deeply. A great many men and women of noble character, of a most elevated purpose, have joined themselves to the new party because in the platform adopted most reforms which ought long ago to have been undertaken, but most of which have been absolutely ignored by political parties, have been embodied, and I venture to conjecture that these high-spirited men and women believed that this combination of forces may in the future bring them out on a plane where they can accomplish these things which their hearts have so long desired.

"I take off my hat to these people. I sympathize with their impulse. I haven't a word of criticism of them for joining with any force, any honorable force, which they think can accomplish these things.

"Then there is the third element in the new party, of which the less said the better. To discuss it would be interesting only if I could mention names, and I have forbidden myself that indulgence."

Thinks They Must Fail

With the three elements of the new party defined, the Governor continued his analysis. He questioned the ability of the new party leaders, even should the party succeed in November, to "carry out this programme of social betterment and reform."

"I do not know how to test that matter, how to answer that question, except by examination of the portion of the programme which seems to be distinctively political rather than social, because, let me remind you, the problem we start out with is that we want a free political instrument by which we can do these things. If we cannot get it it cannot be done by that instrument. You have in this new party two things—a political party and a body of social reformers."

Then, picking the political from the social reforms, Gov. Wilson endeavored to reason out for his audience how the Government is going to stand related to the central problems upon which, he said, its freedom depends.

"The freedom of the Government of the United States," he said, depends upon getting separated from, disentangled from, those interests which have chiefly enjoyed the patronage of that Government. The trouble with the tariff is not that it is protective, for, in recent years, it has been much more than protective, but because it has been one of the most colossal systems of deliberate patronage that has ever been conceived. The main trouble with it is that the protection stops where the patronage begins; if you could lop off the patronage, you would have taken away most of the objectionable features of the so-called protection. This patronage, this special privilege, these favors doled out to some persons and not to all, have been the basis of the control which has been set up over the industries and over the enterprises of this country by great combinations."

The Giants and the Pygmies

Illustrating the system built up by the protective tariff wall, the Governor likened the men who control the big business of the country to giants and the small group of independent manufacturers or dealers who have endeavored to compete with these monopolies to pygmies. Because free competition has been destroyed, he said, it was possible for the powerful to crush the weak.

"That," he continued, "is warfare; and because we did not check the free competition soon enough, because we did not check it at the point where pygmies entered the field against giants, we have created a condition of affairs in which the control of industry, and to a large extent the control of credit in this country, upon which industry feeds, and in which all new enterprises must be rooted, is in the hands of a comparatively small and very compact body of men.

"These are the gentlemen who have in some instances, perhaps in more than have been exhibited by legal proof, engaged in what we are expected to call 'unreasonable combinations in restraint of trade.' "

It was suggested by the Governor that the men who have most benefited by the protective tariff "have indulged themselves beyond reason in the exercise of that power which makes competition practically impossible."

"Are we going to take that power away from them, or are we going to leave it with them?" the Governor asked.

Answering his own question, he continued:

"You can take it away from them if you regulate competition and make it impossible for them to do some things that they have been doing. You leave it with them if you legitimatize and regulate monopoly. What the platform of the new party proposes to do is exactly that.

"It proposes to start where we are and without altering the established conditions of competition to say what these giants shall do and to what these pygmies shall submit. And we shall not do that by law, for if you will read the plank in its candid statement, for it is perfectly candid, you will find that it rejects regulation by law and proposes a commission which shall have the discretion to undertake what the plank calls 'constructive regulation.' As it handles these giants, so it shall shape its course.

"That, gentlemen, is nothing more than a legitimatized continuation of the present order of things with the alliance between the great interests and the Government open instead of covered. There will then be nothing wrong in the alliance. The alliance will be grafted into the policy of the nation and we shall simply say to one another, 'Big as these men are, the Federal Government is bigger than they are. We will depend upon the Federal Government to take care of them.' But, gentlemen, that depends on who takes care of the Federal Government."

Would Perpetuate Alliance

Adoption of the new party programme, the Governor asserted, would mean nothing less than consenting "to the perpetuation of the existing alliance between the Governor and big business."

Speaking of the union of power between the political and social reform forces in the new party, the Governor, referring to Col. Roosevelt, asked:

"Who will guarantee to us that this master will be just and pitiful? Has justice ever grown in the soil of absolute power? Has not justice always come from the press of the heart and the spirit of men who resist power?"

When the loud applause which greeted this query had subsided the Governor continued:

"Liberty has never come from the Government. Liberty has always come from the subjects of it. The history of liberty is a history of resistance. Do people dream that men are bred great enough now to be a Providence over the people over whom they preside?

"Great kings have been born in the world, men with big enough hearts to include their kingdom, men with big enough brains to comprehend anything that can come within the scope of their understanding. But there are only twenty-four hours in the day of a king as there are only twenty-four hours in the day of the humble workman. No brain in its twenty-four-hour day can comprehend the complex business of a nation."

Referring to Roosevelt's "Charter of Democracy" speech before the Ohio Constitutional Convention last spring, when his radical programme was first defined, the Government said:

"The sentiment of the speech, the sympathy of the speech in the first part was with radical ideas, but the programme of the speech was conceived for the purpose of showing that big business and the Government could live on amicable terms with one another."

At the conclusion of his speech Gov. Wilson gave an analysis of the Democratic party.

"Whether from virtue or necessity," he said, "the Democratic party has no entangling alliances." He pointed, however, to the fact that for sixteen years the party had suffered a voluntary exile because it had refused to trade. He reviewed the Baltimore Convention and told of the triumph of the progressive wing of the party. He predicted victory for the united Democracy in November.

"Here is a free party which can set up a free government," he said. "I can say, without even a touch of personal reference almost, that the Democratic party at least has a candidate who by no circumstances is not attached to any interests whatever."

At the conclusion of the dinner, Mr. Macauley, President of the Press Club, introduced Gov. Wilson to the 200 guests of the evening. The Governor will leave at 10 o'clock this morning for Atlantic City, where to-night he will address the Spanish-American war veterans at a dinner on the new steel pier. In the afternoon he will review the veterans.

SELECTION

Senator La Follette on the Trusts and Their Remedy: Speech to the Periodical Publishers' Association, Philadelphia, February 2, 1912

When he gave this speech, Senator Robert M. La Follette of Wisconsin was an active candidate for the Republican presidential nomination. His views of powerful corporations and what government should do about them differed from those of Roosevelt and those of Wilson and from those of the intellectuals Croly and Lippmann. Although certainly not a nationalist such as Roosevelt and Croly, La Follette did not share Wilson's view that governmental power must be kept limited in order to safeguard liberty. Indeed, it was the big corporation rather than big government that was the primary threat to liberty. Certain fields of business enterprise were necessarily monopolistic—he mentioned railroads and public utilities—but the monopolistic power of others depended upon "discriminatory practices and special privileges." The Sherman Antitrust Act of 1890 had given the President "the most perfect weapon which the ingenuity of man could forge for the protection of the people against the power of monopoly," but no administration had effectively used the instrument. The Supreme Court in the Standard Oil and American Tobacco Company cases had made it necessary for Congress to create an "interstate trade commission." Such a commission, however, should not merely regulate but should eliminate the practices and privileges that made monopoly possible.

Robert Marion La Follette was born in rural Wisconsin, near Madison, in 1855. He graduated from the University of Wisconsin, became county prosecuting attorney, and went to the House of Representatives for three terms. As Governor and, after 1906, as United States Senator, he led a strong political organization whose reform program attracted national attention. La Follette was the outstanding leader of the Republican insurgents in the upper Mississippi Valley. In 1911 he organized the National Progressive Republican League and began to work hard for the GOP nomination. However, Roosevelt captured the progressive wing of the party, and it was he rather than La Follette who challenged Taft at Chicago. When Taft won the struggle and TR bolted his party to form the Progressives, La Follette refused to follow him. In 1924, however, the aged Senator ran as an independent for the Presidency. He died in 1925.

This speech was a turning point in La Follette's bid for the presidential nomination. It was not well received, to put it mildly, and some of his followers who were restive under his leadership and eager to advance Roosevelt's candidacy, such as Gifford and Amos Pinchot, used the poor reception as an excuse to desert the La Follette cause. For further details see George E. Mowry, Theodore Roosevelt and the Progressive Movement *(Madison, Wis.: University of Wisconsin Press, 1946), and Belle Case La Follette and Fola La Follette, the Senator's widow and daughter, respectively,* Robert M. La Follette *(New York: Macmillan, 1953), two volumes.*

The speech is reproduced here as it appeared in the appendix of La Follette's Autobiography: A Personal Narrative of Political Experiences *(Madison, Wis.: La Follette Publishing Co., 1913), pages 762–771, 786–793. One of La Follette's weaknesses as a speaker was that his speeches were too long—John Sharp Williams of Mississippi once said on the floor of the Senate that "if immortality could be attained by verbal eternity, the Senator from Wisconsin would have approximated immortality"—and the selection here is about one-half the length of the published original.*

The great issue before the American people to-day is the control of their own government. In the midst of political struggle, it is not easy to see the historical relations of the present Progressive movement. But it represents a conflict as old as the history of man—the fight to maintain human liberty, the rights of all the people.

A mighty power has been builded up in this country in recent years, so strong, yet so insidious and far-reaching in its influence, that men are gravely inquiring whether its iron grip on government and business can ever be broken. Again and again it has proved strong enough to nominate the candidates of both political parties. It rules in the organization of legislative bodies, state and national, and of the committees which frame legislation. Its influence is felt in cabinets and in the policies of administrations, and is clearly seen in the appointment of prosecuting officers and the selection of judges upon the Bench.

In business it has crippled or destroyed competition. It has stifled individual initiative. It has fixed limitations in the field of production. It makes prices and imposes its burdens upon the consuming public at will.

In transportation, after a prolonged struggle for government control, it is, with only slight check upon its great power, still master of the highways of commerce.

In finance its power is unlimited. In large affairs it gives or withholds credit, and from time to time contracts or inflates the volume of the money required for the transaction of the business of the country, regardless of everything excepting its own profits.

It has acquired vast areas of the public domain, and is rapidly monopolizing the natural resources—timber, iron, coal, oil.

And this THING has grown up in a country where, under the Constitution and the law, the citizen is sovereign!

The related events which led to this centralized control are essential to a clear understanding of the real danger—the magnitude of this danger now menacing the very existence of every independent concern remaining in the field of business enterprise.

The First Period: The Individual and the Partnership

For nearly a century after Jefferson declared for a government of "equal rights for all, and special privileges for none," the business of the country was conducted by individuals and partnerships. During this first period business methods were simple, its proportions modest, and there was little call for larger capital than could be readily furnished by the individual or, in the most extreme cases, a partnership of fair size.

From the beginning, when men bartered their products in exchange, down through all the ages, the business of the world had been conducted under the natural laws of trade—demand, supply, competition. Like all natural laws, they were fair and impartial; they favored neither the producer nor the consumer. They had ruled the market and made the prices when the individual and the partnership conducted substantially all commercial enterprises during the first period of our business life.

But as the country developed, as the population poured over the Alleghenies, occupied the Mississippi Valley, pushed on to the Rocky Mountains and down the western slope to California, discovering the boundless wealth of our natural resources—the fields and forests, the mountains of iron and coal and precious metals, there was a pressing call on every hand for larger capital beyond the power of any individual or any partnership to supply. We had outgrown the simple methods; there was a demand for a new business device strong enough to unlock the treasure house of the new world.

The Second Period: The Private Corporation

The modern corporation was invented to meet that demand, and general statutes for incorporation were soon upon the statute books of every state. Their adoption marked the beginning of the second period of our business life. It was the best machine ever invented for the purpose; simple in organization, effective in operation.

A hundred, a thousand, any number of men could associate their capital, and employing the representative principle upon which our country was based, vote for and elect a president, a general manager, a board of directors, a body of men, no larger than an ordinary partnership, and clothe them with power to conduct the business to the success of which the aggregate capital was contributed.

Men no longer stood baffled by the magnitude of any undertaking, but promptly enlisted an army of contributors, large or small, massed together the required capital and under the direction of the officers and directors of the corporation, a small executive body, seized upon these waiting opportunities, and this second period marked a material development, surpassing anything in the world's history. It was not the era of greatest individual fortune building, but it was the period of greatest general prosperity. And why?

The natural laws of trade—demand, supply and competition—still ruled the market and made the prices in the second period of our business life.

The private corporation, in a large measure, supplanted the individual, and the partnership in mining, manufacturing and large commercial enterprises, but each corporation competed with every other in the same line of business. Production was larger, development more rapid, but, under the free play of competition, the resulting prosperity was fairly distributed between the producer and the consumer, the seller and the buyer, because profits and prices were reasonable.

Big capital behind the private corporations drove business at a pace and upon a scale never before witnessed. Competition was at once the spur to the highest efficiency and the check against waste and abuse of power.

In this period of our industrial and commercial progress, America amazed and alarmed our business rivals of the old world. We were soon foremost among the nations of the earth in agriculture, in mines and mining, in manufactures and in commerce as well.

The American market became the greatest thing in all the material world. Its control became the one thing coveted.

The Third Period: The Combination of Corporations

The evil hour was come upon us. Daring, unscrupulous men plotted in violation of the common law, the criminal statutes and against public right to become masters of that market and take what toll they pleased. To do this thing it was necessary to set aside, abrogate, nullify the natural laws of trade that had ruled in business for centuries. Production was to be limited, competition stifled and prices arbitrarily fixed by selfish decree. And thus we entered upon the third period of our business and commercial life—the period of a combination of the corporations under a single control in each line of business. It was not an evolution; it was a revolution.

And yet certain economists set it down in the literature of the day that the Supreme Ruler of the universe reserved in His great plan a divinely appointed place and time for a Rockefeller, a Morgan, a Carnegie, a Baer, to evolve this new law, which should enable them to appropriate the wealth of the country and Mexicanize its business and its people.

The combination became supreme in each important line, controlling the markets for the raw material and the finished product, largely dictating the price of everything we sell and the price of everything we buy—beef, sugar, woolens, cottons, coal, oil, copper, zinc, iron, steel, agricultural implements, hardware, gas, electric light, food supplies.

Monopoly acquired dominion everywhere.

It brought with it the inevitable results of monopoly—extortionate prices, inferior products. We soon found shoddy in everything we wear, and adulteration in everything we eat.

Did these masters of business stop there? By no means! "Increase of appetite had grown by what it fed on." The floodgates of fictitious capitalization were thrown wide open. These organizations of combinations overcapitalized for a double purpose. The issue of bonds and stocks in excess of investment covered up the exaction of their immense profits, and likewise offered an unlimited field for promotion and speculation.

The establishment of this third period was the beginning of rapidly advancing prices, increasing the cost of living upon people of average earning power until the burden is greater than they can bear.

The Fourth Period: The Combination of Combinations

The strife for more money, more power—more power, more money—swept everything before it.

It remained only to bring together into a community of interest or ownership the great combinations which controlled, each in its own field—in short, to combine these combinations.

One needs but to study the directory of directories of the great business concerns of the country to determine the extent to which this combination of combinations has been successfully accomplished, thus carrying us over into the fourth period of our industrial and commercial life—the period of complete industrial and commercial servitude in which we now unhappily find ourselves. And this supreme control of the business of the country is the triumph of men who have at every step defied public opinion, the common law and criminal statutes.

This condition is intolerable. It is hostile to every principle of democracy. If maintained it is the end of democracy. We may preserve the form of our representative government and lose the soul, the spirit of our free institutions.

John Sherman, the broadest, clearest visioned statesman of his time, saw this danger away in advance and wisely sought to fortify the government to meet and destroy it.

Of this mighty power he said:

> It is a kingly prerogative, inconsistent with our form of government. If anything is wrong, this is wrong. If we will not endure a king as a political power, we should not endure a king over the production, transportation, and sale of any of the necessities of life. If we would not submit to an emperor, we should not submit to an autocrat of trade with power to prevent competition and to fix the price of any commodity. . . . The remedy should be swift and sure.

Sherman well understood that this government could not exist as a free government with any man or group of men invested with the kingly prerogative over the production, transportation, and sale of any of the necessaries of life. No free people in history very long maintained their political freedom after having once surrendered their industrial and commercial freedom.

The Sherman law placed in the hands of the executive department of this government the most perfect weapon which the ingenuity of man could forge for the protection of the people against the power of monopoly.

It will be the impartial verdict of history that the executive department of government could have saved the people from the appalling conditions which confront us to-day, if all the power of this great government had been put forth to enforce the anti-trust law. Two or three score of prosecutions dragging along in the courts at a snail's pace, from administration to administration, was little more than notice to these business kings that they might proceed to set up their authority against the government and extend their dominion over trade and transportation; that here was no real danger of the law being so enforced as to do much more than to affect the political situation from time to time.

That this was accepted as the government's position by the interests can now be made very plain.

The organization of combinations began quite actively early in 1898. The high tariff rates of the Dingley law encouraged combination and aided in its ultimate purpose.

Between January 1, 1898, and January 1, 1900, 149 trusts were formed to suppress competition and control prices. These combinations were capitalized for $3,784,000,000. The next four years were years of enormous trust growth.

From January 1, 1900, to January 1, 1904, taking account of only the more important trusts, 8,664 great plants were combined, with a total capitalization of $20,379,162,511.

Prices were mounting higher and higher. The people were crying aloud in protest, but protest and denunciation caused no fear on the part of the trust makers, so long as the government was actually prosecuting less than an average of seven cases a year.

Mark what followed: From January 1, 1904, to January 1, 1908, trust consolidation made mighty strides, and the total capitalization reached the astounding sum of $31,672,160,754. In these four years the capitalization increased more than 55 per cent. . . .

This is but the barest outline of the upbuilding of the power which now controls.

Is there a way out? Let us consider.

By its decisions in the Standard Oil and Tobacco cases the Supreme Court has all at once created itself into a legislature, an interstate commerce commission and a supreme court, combined in one.

The "rule of reason" gives it legislative power, the power to determine according to its own opinion that some restraints of trade are lawful and other restraints unlawful. The power to carry out the dissolution and reorganization of the trusts and to work out the details is exactly the power that a legislature turns over to a commission. Punishment for contempt is the court's substitute for the criminal penalty that the legislature attaches to the violation of its statutes.

The supreme court has amended the antitrust act in exactly the way that Congress repeatedly refused to amend it, and has usurped both legislative and executive power in doing it. Whether we wish it or not, Congress is now compelled to create an interstate trade commission to control the trusts, or else leave the control to the federal courts, acting as a commission.

Such a commission should not fix prices. Price regulation assumes that we are dealing with a necessary monopoly, as in the case of railroads and public utilities. But the commercial monopolies are based on unfair and discriminatory practices and special privileges. These can be abolished in several ways.

Amend the Sherman law by enacting specific prohibitions against well-known practices that constitute unreasonable restraints of trade. One of these is the brutal method of the Standard Oil Company of cutting prices in any place where there is a competitor in order to kill him off, while keeping up prices in other places. Another is the club wielded by the tobacco trust, which put the jobbers in a position where, unless they refrained from buying of a competitor, they could not get from the trust the brands which were indispensable to the successful conduct of their business. These and several other obviously unreasonable restraints of trade are definitely prohibited in the bill which I have introduced in the Senate.

The bill also places the burden of proof on the trust to show that any restraint of trade which it practises is reasonable—that is, that it benefits the community.

It also provides that when the court has once entered its final decree and declared a trust illegal, any person who has suffered damages, may come in under that decree and simply petition that his damages be paid without proving anything except the amount of the damages. If this had been law when the Standard Oil and Tobacco decisions were rendered, those decisions would have meant something more than mere victories on paper.

In addition to these amendments to the antitrust law, there is need of a commission to stand between the people and the courts in order to investigate the facts and to prohibit all unreasonable restraints not specifically described in the law. This commission should have full power to ascertain the actual cost of reproduction, or physical value of the property; the reasonable value that the intangible property, such as good will, would have under conditions of fair competition, and to distinguish this from the illegal values that have been built up in violation of law. It should ascertain the values that depend on patents, monopoly of natural resources and all other forms of special privilege; the amount of property that has been paid for out of illegal profits taken from the public, distinguished from the property paid for out of legitimate profits and true investment. It should in this way ascertain the true cost of production and whether the prices charged are yielding extortionate profits or only the reasonable profits that competitors could earn. These are the facts that the people must know before they will consent to any legislation that treats illegal values as though they were legal.

With these facts ascertained and made *prima facie* evidence in court, these illegal values cannot be permanently fastened on the American people. It will take time to pull down this false structure of illegal capitalization of the trusts, but it is now the greatest menace to prosperity.

If these laws are adopted, then every business man, as well as the courts, will know definitely what is meant by the "rule of reason." Legitimate business will have its course laid out clear and certain before it, and every investor will know precisely what the law allows and what it prohibits.

The trust problem has become so interwoven in our legal and industrial system that no single measure or group of measures can reach all of it. It must be picked off at every point where it shows its head.

Every combination of a manufacturing business with the control of transportation, including pipe lines, should be prohibited, in order that competitors may have equal facilities for reaching markets.

The control of limited sources of raw material, like coal, iron ore, or timber, by a manufacturing corporation, should be broken up and these resources should be opened to all manufacturers on equal terms.

It is claimed on all sides that competition has failed. I deny it. Fair competition has not failed. It has been suppressed. When competitors are shut out from markets by discrimination, and denied either transportation, raw material or credit on equal terms, we do not have competition. We have the modern form of highway robbery. The great problem of legislation before us is first for the people to resume control of their government, and then to protect themselves against those who are throttling competition by the aid of government.

I do not say that competition does not have its evils. Labor organizations are the struggling protest against cut-throat competition. The anti-trust law was not intended or understood to apply to them. They should be exempt from its operation.

The tariff should be brought down to the difference in labor cost of the more efficient plants and the foreign competitor, and where there is no difference the tariff should be removed. Where the protective tariff is retained its advantages must be passed along to labor, for whose benefit the manufacturer contends it is necessary.

The patent laws should be so amended that the owners of patents will be compelled to develop them fully or permit their use on equal terms by others.

More vital and menacing than any other power that supports trusts is the control of credit through the control of the people's savings and deposits. When the Emergency Currency Bill was before Congress in 1908, Senator Aldrich slipped into the conference report certain provisions which he had withdrawn in the Senate, and withdrew provisions which he had first included. He eliminated protection against promotion schemes, excluded penalties for false reporting, dropped provisions for safeguarding reserves, inserted provisions for accepting railroad bonds as security. Now he comes with another plausible measure to remedy the admitted evils of our inelastic banking system.

When we realize that the control of credit and banking is the greatest power that the trusts possess to keep out competitors, we may well question their sincerity in offering a patriotic measure to dispossess themselves of that power. It is the people's money that is expected to give security to this plan and the people must and shall control it.

The proposed Aldrich Currency plan is the product of a commission composed of men who are or have been members of the committees of the two houses of Congress, which have controlled all legislation relating to currency and banking. With such a record it behooves the public to examine with the utmost care any plan which they recommend, however plausible it may appear upon its face. A critical study of the scheme of this commission will convince any student of government finance, that under the guise of providing elasticity to our currency system, it is in reality an adroit means of further concentration and control of the money and credits of the United States under a fifty-year franchise, augmenting the power of those who already dominate the banking and insurance resources of the country.

Our National Banking Law is a patchwork of legislation. It should be thoroughly revised. And all authorities agree that a comprehensive plan for an emergency currency is vitally important. When the basic principle of such a plan is once determined, when it is settled that government controlled banks are to be, *in fact,* controlled by the government *in the public interest,* the details can easily be worked out.

An emergency currency circulation should be backed by proper reserves, issued only against commercial paper that represents actual and legitimate business transactions. No plan should be adopted which admits of control by banking interests which, under existing conditions, means, in the end, control by the great speculative banking groups.

In all our plans for progressive legislation, it must not be forgotten that we are only just beginning to get control of the railroads. The present law is an improvement, but the Interstate Commerce Commission requires to be greatly strengthened. It should have a much larger appropriation, enabling it to prosecute investigations in all parts of the country. It should make physical valuations of the railroads, eliminating watered stock, monopoly values and the unwarranted inflation of railway terminals to conceal monopoly values. And the Commerce Court should be abolished as a mere subterfuge interposed to handicap the commission.

As a first necessary step for the regulation of interstate commerce, we *must* ascertain the reasonable value of the physical property of railroads, justly inventoried, upon a sound economic basis, distinguishing *actual* values from *monopoly* values derived from violations of law, and must make such discriminating values the *base line* for determining rates. The country should know how much of the eighteen billions of capitalization was contributed by those who own the railroads, and how much by the people themselves. We should also provide for the extension of the powers and the administrative control of the Interstate Commerce Commission. . . .

SELECTION

Lincoln Steffens on Civic Corruption: "The Shame of the Cities"

Lincoln Steffens thought of himself, not altogether justifiably, as the first muckraker, and many historians have agreed with his assessment. Whether he was the author of the first muckraking article or not, it is clear that the appearance of his exposé of civic corruption in St. Louis in the October, 1902, issue of McClure's Magazine *created a sensation and that other journalists and journals soon began to follow his lead. The publication of so many articles and books*

*revealing illegal and unethical practices in high places in both civic and busi-
ness affairs caused President Theodore Roosevelt some concern, and in a speech
in March, 1906, he disparagingly compared these writers with the character in
Bunyan's* Pilgrim's Progress *who fixed his attention only on muck and filth
to the exclusion of that which was noble and beautiful. But the writers took
TR's term of opprobrium and wore the badge of muckraker with pride. The
immediate and direct effect of muckraking upon reform accomplishments has
probably been exaggerated, but the fad for the literature of exposé both reflected and stimulated popular dissatisfaction with the* status quo.

In 1902 and 1903 Steffens wrote seven articles for McClure's *on municipal
corruption in St. Louis, Minneapolis, Chicago, New York, Philadelphia, and
Pittsburgh (spelled without the final letter in those days), and in December,
1903, he put the chapters together to make a book and added the following
selection as an introductory first chapter. The book appeared as* The Shame
of the Cities *in 1904, published in New York by McClure, Phillips, and Company, and the first chapter is reprinted here precisely as it was in this first
edition.*

*Steffens insisted near the beginning of this first chapter that his book was
journalism with "no further pretensions." Later, after a great deal of generali-
zation, he repeated the idea. "This is all very unscientific, but then, I am not
a scientist. I am a journalist." His protestations to the contrary, this chapter
of the book was not journalism as Steffens understood the term; it was not mere
reporting of the facts the author had discovered. The chapter was a collection
of generalizations, some explicit and some only implied, based upon the facts
reported in the later chapters. In his* Autobiography, *published in 1931, he
dropped this curious pretense. Writing of his experiences in researching the*
McClure's *articles, he declared, "I was on the track of a truth, a scientific basis
for a science of politics." Indeed he was. He made his career as a journalist,
and he was a superb reporter who dug out the facts carefully and resourcefully
and wrote them clearly and meaningfully, even dramatically. But he had had
a superior formal education at the Universities of California, Berlin, Heidelberg,
and Paris that had lifted his aspirations, at least, for lofty philosophic generali-
zation.*

*Superficially unconventional, Steffens enjoyed a tremendous prestige among
certain intellectuals and artists from the turn of the century until his death
in 1936. One could almost trace what was "in" in Greenwich Village intellectual
circles by following Steffens's enthusiasms. For further biographical material,
see, besides the* Autobiography, *the two volumes of his letters edited by Ella
Winter and Granville Hicks in 1938. For the muckraking movement, see C. C.
Regier,* The Era of the Muckrakers *(Chapel Hill, N.C.: University of North
Carolina Press, 1932) and Louis Filler,* Crusaders for American Liberalism
(New York: Harcourt, Brace & World, 1939).

This is not a book. It is a collection of articles reprinted from *McClure's
Magazine.* Done as journalism, they are journalism still, and no
further pretensions are set up for them in their new dress. This classification may seem pretentious enough; certainly it would if I should confess
what claims I make for my profession. But no matter about that; I insist

upon the journalism. And there is my justification for separating from the
bound volumes of the magazine and republishing, practically without re-
editing, my accounts as a reporter of the shame of American cities. They
were written with a purpose, they were published serially with a purpose,
and they are reprinted now together to further that same purpose, which
was and is—to sound for the civic pride of an apparently shameless
citizenship.

There must be such a thing, we reasoned. All our big boasting could not
be empty vanity, nor our pious pretensions hollow sham. American achievements in science, art, and business mean sound abilities at bottom, and our
hypocrisy a race sense of fundamental ethics. Even in government we have
given proofs of potential greatness, and our political failures are not complete; they are simply ridiculous. But they are ours. Not alone the
triumphs and the statesmen, the defeats and the grafters also represent us,
and just as truly. Why not see it so and say it?

Because, I heard, the American people won't "stand for" it. You may
blame the politicians, or, indeed, any one class, but not all classes, not
the people. Or you may put it on the ignorant foreign immigrant, or any
one nationality, but not on all nationalities, not on the American people.
But no one class is at fault, nor any one breed, nor any particular interest
or group of interests. The misgovernment of the American people is misgovernment by the American people.

When I set out on my travels, an honest New Yorker told me honestly
that I would find that the Irish, the Catholic Irish, were at the bottom of
it all everywhere. The first city I went to was St. Louis, a German city.
The next was Minneapolis, a Scandinavian city, with a leadership of New
Englanders. Then came Pittsburg, Scotch Presbyterian, and that was
what my New York friend was. "Ah, but they are all foreign populations,"
I heard. The next city was Philadelphia, the purest American community
of all, and the most hopeless. And after that came Chicago and New York,
both mongrel-bred, but the one a triumph of reform, the other the best
example of good government that I had seen. The "foreign element"
excuse is one of the hypocritical lies that save us from the clear sight of
ourselves.

Another such conceit of our egotism is that which deplores our politics
and lauds our business. This is the wail of the typical American citizen.
Now, the typical American citizen is the business man. The typical business man is a bad citizen; he is busy. If he is a "big business man" and
very busy, he does not neglect, he is busy with politics, oh, very busy and
very businesslike. I found him buying boodlers in St. Louis, defending
grafters in Minneapolis, originating corruption in Pittsburg, sharing with
bosses in Philadelphia, deploring reform in Chicago, and beating good
government with corruption funds in New York. He is a self-righteous
fraud, this big business man. He is the chief source of corruption, and it
were a boon if he would neglect politics. But he is not the business man
that neglects politics; that worthy is the good citizen, the typical business
man. He too is busy, he is the one that has no use and therefore no time
for politics. When his neglect has permitted bad government to go so
far that he can be stirred to action, he is unhappy, and he looks around
for a cure that shall be quick, so that he may hurry back to the shop.

Naturally, too, when he talks politics, he talks shop. His patent remedy is quack; it is business.

"Give us a business man," he says ("like me," he means). "Let him introduce business methods into politics and government; then I shall be left alone to attend to my business."

There is hardly an office from United States Senator down to Alderman in any part of the country to which the business man has not been elected; yet politics remains corrupt, government pretty bad, and the selfish citizen has to hold himself in readiness like the old volunteer firemen to rush forth at any hour, in any weather, to prevent the fire; and he goes out sometimes and he puts out the first (after the damage is done) and he goes back to the shop sighing for the business man in politics. The business man has failed in politics as he has in citizenship. Why?

Because politics is business. That's what's the matter with it. That's what's the matter with everything,—art, literature, religion, journalism, law, medicine,—they're all business, and all—as you see them. Make politics a sport, as they do in England, or a profession, as they do in Germany, and we'll have—well, something else than we have now,—if we want it, which is another question. But don't try to reform politics with the banker, the lawyer, and the dry-goods merchant, for these are business men and there are two great hindrances to their achievement of reform: one is that they are different from, but no better than, the politicians; the other is that politics is not "their line." There are exceptions both ways. Many politicians have gone out into business and done well (Tammany ex-mayors, and nearly all the old bosses of Philadelphia are prominent financiers in their cities), and business men have gone into politics and done well (Mark Hanna, for example). They haven't reformed their adopted trades, however, though they have sometimes sharpened them most pointedly. The politician is a business man with a specialty. When a business man of some other line learns the business of politics, he is a politician, and there is not much reform left in him. Consider the United States Senate, and believe me.

The commercial spirit is the spirit of profit, not patriotism; of credit, not honor; of individual gain, not national prosperity; of trade and dickering, not principle. "My business is sacred," says the business man in his heart. "Whatever prospers my business, is good; it must be. Whatever hinders it, is wrong; it must be. A bribe is bad, that is, it is a bad thing to take; but it is not so bad to give one, not if it is necessary to my business." "Business is business" is not a political sentiment, but our politician has caught it. He takes essentially the same view of the bribe, only he saves his self-respect by piling all his contempt upon the bribe-giver, and he has the great advantage of candor. "It is wrong, maybe," he says, "but if a rich merchant can afford to do business with me for the sake of a convenience or to increase his already great wealth, I can afford, for the sake of a living, to meet him half way. I make no pretensions to virtue, not even on Sunday." And as for giving bad government or good, how about the merchant who gives bad goods or good goods, according to the demand?

But there is hope, not alone despair, in the commercialism of our politics. If our political leaders are to be always a lot of political merchants, they will supply any demand we may create. All we have to do is to establish a steady demand for good government. The bosses have us split up into parties. To him parties are nothing but means to his corrupt ends. He "bolts" his party, but we must not; the bribe-giver changes his party, from one election to another, from one county to another, from one city to another, but the honest voter must not. Why? Because if the honest voter cared no more for his party than the politician and the grafter, then the honest vote would govern, and that would be bad—for graft. It is idiotic, this devotion to a machine that is used to take our sovereignty from us. If we would leave parties to the politicians, and would vote not for the party, not even for men, but for the city, and the State, and the nation, we should rule parties, and cities, and States, and nation. If we would vote in mass on the more promising ticket, or, if the two are equally bad, would throw out the party that is in, and wait till the next election and then throw out the other party that is in—then, I say, the commercial politician would feel a demand for good government and he would supply it. That process would take a generation or more to complete, for the politicians now really do not know what good government is. But it has taken as long to develop bad government, and the politicians know what that is. If it would not "go," they would offer something else, and, if the demand were steady, they, being so commercial, would "deliver the goods."

But do the people want good government? Tammany says they don't. Are the people honest? Are the people better than Tammany? Are they better than the merchant and the politician? Isn't our corrupt government, after all, representative?

President Roosevelt has been sneered at for going about the country preaching, as a cure for our American evils, good conduct in the individual, simple honesty, courage, and efficiency. "Platitudes!" the sophisticated say. Platitudes? If my observations have been true, the literal adoption of Mr. Roosevelt's reform scheme would result in a revolution, more radical and terrible to existing institutions, from the Congress to the Church, from the bank to the ward organization, than socialism or even than anarchy. Why, that would change all of us—not alone our neighbors, not alone the grafters, but you and me.

No, the contemned methods of our despised politics are the master methods of our braggart business, and the corruption that shocks us in public affairs we practice ourselves in our private concerns. There is no essential difference between the pull that gets your wife into society or for your book a favorable review, and that which gets a heeler into office, a thief out of jail, and a rich man's son on the board of directors of a corporation; none between the corruption of a labor union, a bank, and a political machine; none between a dummy director of a trust and the caucus-bound member of a legislature; none between a labor boss like Sam Parks, a boss of banks like John D. Rockefeller, a boss of railroads like J. P. Morgan, and a political boss like Matthew S. Quay. The boss is not a political, he is an American institution, the product of a freed people that have not the spirit to be free.

And it's all a moral weakness; a weakness right where we think we are strongest. Oh, we are good—on Sunday, and we are "fearfully patriotic" on the Fourth of July. But the bribe we pay to the janitor to prefer our interests to the landlord's, is the little brother of the bribe passed to the alderman to sell a city street, and the father of the air-brake stock assigned to the president of a railroad to have this life-saving invention adopted on his road. And as for graft, railroad passes, saloon and bawdy-house blackmail, and watered stock, all these belong to the same family. We are pathetically proud of our democratic institutions and our republican form of government, of our grand Constitution and our just laws. We are a free and sovereign people, we govern ourselves and the government is ours. But that is the point. We are responsible, not our leaders, since we follow them. We *let* them divert our loyalty from the United States to some "party"; we *let* them boss the party and turn our municipal democracies into autocracies and our republican nation into a plutocracy. We cheat our government and we let our leaders loot it, and we let them wheedle and bribe our sovereignty from us. True, they pass for us strict laws, but we are content to let them pass also bad laws, giving away public property in exchange; and our good, and often impossible, laws we allow to be used for oppression and blackmail. And what can we say? We break our own laws and rob our own government, the lady at the custom-house, the lyncher with his rope, and the captain of industry with his bribe and his rebate. The spirit of graft and of lawlessness is the American spirit.

And this shall not be said? Not plainly? William Travers Jerome, the fearless District Attorney of New York, says, "You can say anything you think to the American people. If you are honest with yourself you may be honest with them, and they will forgive not only your candor, but your mistakes." This is the opinion, and the experience too, of an honest man and a hopeful democrat. Who says the other things? Who says "Hush," and "What's the use?" and "ALL's well," when all is rotten? It is the grafter; the coward, too, but the grafter inspires the coward. The doctrine of "addition, division, and silence" is the doctrine of graft. "Don't hurt the party," "Spare the fair fame of the city," are boodle yells. The Fourth of July oration is the "front" of graft. There is no patriotism in it, but treason. It is part of the game. The grafters call for cheers for the flag, "prosperity," and "the party," just as a highwayman commands "hands up," and while we are waving and shouting, they float the flag from the nation to the party, turn both into graft factories, and prosperity into a speculative boom to make "weak hands," as the Wall Street phrase has it, hold the watered stock while the strong hands keep the property. "Blame us, blame anybody, but praise the people," this, the politician's advice, is not the counsel of respect for the people, but of contempt. By just such palavering as courtiers play upon the degenerate intellects of weak kings, the bosses, political, financial, and industrial, are befuddling and befooling our sovereign American citizenship; and—likewise—they are corrupting it.

And it is corruptible, this citizenship. "I know what Parks is doing," said a New York union workman, "but what do I care. He has raised my wages. Let him have his graft!" And the Philadelphia merchant says the same thing: "The party leaders may be getting more than they should out of the city, but that doesn't hurt me. It may raise taxes a little, but I can stand that. The party keeps up the protective tariff. If that were cut down, my business would be ruined. So long as the party stands pat on that, I stand pat on the party."

The people are not innocent. That is the only "news" in all the journalism of these articles, and no doubt that was not new to many observers. It was to me. When I set out to describe the corrupt systems of certain typical cities, I meant to show simply how the people were deceived and betrayed. But in the very first study—St. Louis—the startling truth lay bare that corruption was not merely political; it was financial, commercial, social; the ramifications of boodle were so complex, various, and far-reaching, that one mind could hardly grasp them, and not even Joseph W. Folk, the tireless prosecutor, could follow them all. This state of things was indicated in the first article which Claude H. Wetmore and I compiled together, but it was not shown plainly enough. Mr. Wetmore lived in St. Louis, and he had respect for names which meant little to me. But when I went next to Minneapolis alone, I could see more independently, without respect for persons, and there were traces of the same phenomenon. The first St. Louis article was called "Tweed Days in St. Louis," and though the "better citizen" received attention the Tweeds were the center of interest. In "The Shame of Minneapolis," the truth was put into the title; it was the Shame of Minneapolis; not of the Ames administration, not of the Tweeds, but of the city and its citizens. And yet Minneapolis was not nearly so bad as St. Louis; police graft is never so universal as boodle. It is more shocking, but it is so filthy that it cannot involve so large a part of society. So I returned to St. Louis, and I went over the whole ground again, with the people in mind, not alone the caught and convicted boodlers. And this time the true meaning of "Tweed days in St. Louis" was made plain. The article was called "The Shamelessness of St. Louis," and that was the burden of the story. In Pittsburg also the people was the subject, and though the civic spirit there was better, the extent of the corruption throughout the social organization of the community was indicated. But it was not till I got to Philadelphia that the possibilities of popular corruption were worked out to the limit of humiliating confession. That was the place for such a study. There is nothing like it in the country, except possibly, in Cincinnati. Philadelphia certainly is not merely corrupt, but corrupted, and this was made clear. Philadelphia was charged up to—the American citizen.

It was impossible in the space of a magazine article to cover in any one city all the phases of municipal government, so I chose cities that typified most strikingly some particular phase or phases. Thus as St. Louis exemplified boodle; Minneapolis, police graft; Pittsburg, a political and industrial machine; and Philadelphia, general civic corruption; so Chicago was an illustration of reform, and New York of good government. All these things occur in most of these places. There are, and long have been, reformers in St. Louis, and there is to-day police graft there. Minneapolis has had boodling and council reform, and boodling is breaking out there again. Pittsburg has general corruption, and Philadelphia a very perfect political machine. Chicago has police graft and a low order of administrative and general corruption which permeates business, labor, and society generally. As for New York, the metropolis might exemplify almost anything that occurs anywhere in American cities, but no city has had for many years such a good administration as was that of Mayor Seth Low.

That which I have made each city stand for, is that which it had most highly developed. It would be absurd to seek for organized reform in St. Louis, for example, with Chicago next door; or for graft in Chicago with Minneapolis so near. After Minneapolis, a description of administrative corruption in Chicago would have seemed like a repetition. Perhaps it was not just to treat only the conspicuous element in each situation. But why should I be just? I was not judging; I arrogated to myself no such function. I was not writing about Chicago for Chicago, but for the other cities, so I picked out what light each had for the instruction of the others. But, if I was never complete, I never exaggerated. Every one of those articles was an understatement, especially where the conditions were bad, and the proof thereof is that while each article seemed to astonish other cities, it disappointed the city which was its subject. Thus my friends in Philadelphia, who knew what there was to know, and those especially who knew what I knew, expressed surprise that I reported so little. And one St. Louis newspaper said that "the facts were thrown at me and I fell down over them." There was truth in these flings. I cut twenty thousand words out of the Philadelphia article and then had not written half my facts. I know a man who is making a history of the corrupt construction of the Philadelphia City Hall, in three volumes, and he grieves because he lacks space. You can't put all the known incidents of the corruption of an American city into a book.

This is all very unscientific, but then, I am not a scientist. I am a journalist. I did not gather with indifference all the facts and arrange them patiently for permanent preservation and laboratory analysis. I did not want to preserve, I wanted to destroy the facts. My purpose was no more scientific than the spirit of my investigation and reports; it was, as I said above, to see if the shameful facts, spread out in all their shame, would not burn through our civic shamelessness and set fire to American pride. That was the journalism of it. I wanted to move and to convince. That is why I was not interested in all the facts, sought none that was new, and rejected half those that were old. I often was asked to expose something suspected. I couldn't: and why should I? Exposure of the unknown was not my purpose. The people: what they will put up with, how they are fooled, how cheaply they are bought, how dearly sold, how easily intimidated, and how led, for good or for evil—that was the inquiry, and so the significant facts were those only which everybody in each city knew, and of these, only those which everybody in every other town would recognize, from their common knowledge of such things, to be probable. But these, understated, were charged always to the guilty persons when individuals were to blame, and finally brought home to the people themselves, who, having the power, have also the responsibility, they and those they respect, and those that guide them.

This was against all the warnings and rules of demagogy. What was the result?

After Joseph W. Folk had explored and exposed, with convictions, the boodling of St. Louis, the rings carried an election. "Tweed Days in St. Louis" is said to have formed some public sentiment against the boodlers, but the local newspapers had more to do with that than *McClure's Magazine*. After the Minneapolis grand jury had exposed and the courts had tried and the common juries had convicted the grafters there, an election showed that public opinion was formed. But that one election was regarded as final. When I went there the men who had led the reform movement were "all through." After they had read the "Shame of Minneapolis," however, they went back to work, and they have perfected a plan to keep the citizens informed and to continue the fight for good government. They saw, these unambitious, busy citizens, that it was "up to them," and they resumed the unwelcome duties of their citizenship. Of resentment there was very little. At a meeting of leading citizens there were honest speeches suggesting that something should be said to "clear the name of Minneapolis," but one man rose and said very pleasantly, but firmly, that the article was true; it was pretty hard on them, but it was true and they all knew it. That ended that.

When I returned to St. Louis and rewrote the facts, and, in rewriting, made them just as insulting as the truth would permit, my friends there expressed dismay over the manuscript. The article would hurt Mr. Folk; it would hurt the cause; it would arouse popular wrath.

"That was what I hoped it would do," I said.

"But the indignation would break upon Folk and reform, not on the boodlers," they said.

"Wasn't it obvious," I asked, "that this very title, 'Shamelessness,' was aimed at pride; that it implied a faith that there was self-respect to be touched and shame to be moved?"

That was too subtle. So I answered that if they had no faith in the town, I had, and anyway, if I was wrong and the people should resent, not the crime, but the exposure of it, then they would punish, not Mr. Folk, who had nothing to do with the article, but the magazine and me. Newspaper men warned me that they would not "stand for" the article, but would attack it. I answered that I would let the St. Louisans decide between us. It was true, it was just; the people of St. Louis had shown no shame. Here was a good chance to see whether they had any. I was a fool, they said. "All right," I replied. "All kings had fools in the olden days, and the fools were allowed to tell them the truth. I would play the fool to the American people."

The article, published, was attacked by the newspapers; friends of Mr. Folk repudiated it; Mr. Folk himself spoke up for the people. Leading citizens raised money for a mass meeting to "set the city right before the world." The mayor of the city, a most excellent man, who had helped me, denounced the article. The boodle party platform appealed for votes on the strength of the attacks in "Eastern magazines." The people themselves contradicted me; after the publication, two hundred thousand buttons for "Folk and Reform" were worn on the streets of St. Louis.

But those buttons were for "Folk and Reform." They did go to prove that the article was wrong, that there was pride in St. Louis, but they proved also that that pride had been touched. Up to that time nobody knew exactly how St. Louis felt about it all. There had been one election, another was pending, and the boodlers, caught or to be caught, were in control. The citizens had made no move to dislodge them. Mr. Folk's splendid labors were a spectacle without a chorus, and, though I had met men who told me the people were with Folk, I had met also the grafters, who cursed only Folk and were building all their hopes on the assumption that "after Folk's term" all would be well again. Between these two local views no outsider could choose. How could I read a strange people's hearts? I took the outside view, stated the facts both ways,—the right verdicts of the juries and the confident plans of the boodlers,—and the result was, indeed, a shameless state of affairs for which St. Louis, the people of St. Louis, were to blame.

And they saw it so, both in the city and in the State, and they ceased to be spectators. That article simply got down to the self-respect of this people. And who was hurt? Not St. Louis. From that moment the city has been determined and active, and boodle seems to be doomed. Not Mr. Folk. After that, his nomination for Governor of the State was declared for by the people, who formed Folk clubs all over the State to force him upon his party and theirs, and thus insure the pursuit of the boodlers in St. Louis and in Missouri too. Nor was the magazine hurt, or myself. The next time I went to St. Louis, the very men who had raised money for the mass meeting to denounce the article went out of their way to say to me that I had been right, the article was true, and they asked me to "do it again." And there may be a chance to do it again. Mr. Folk lifted the lid off Missouri for a moment after that, and the State also appeared ripe for the gathering. Moreover, the boodlers of State and city have joined to beat the people and keep them down. The decisive election is not till the fall of 1904, and the boodlers count much on the fickleness of public opinion. But I believe that Missouri and St. Louis together will prove then, once for all, that the people can rule—when they are aroused.

The Pittsburg article had no effect in Pittsburg, nor had that on Philadelphia any results in Philadelphia. Nor was any expected there. Pittsburg, as I said in the article, knew itself, and may pull out of its disgrace, but Philadelphia is contented and seems hopeless. The accounts of them, however, and indeed, as I have said, all of the series, were written, not for the cities described, but for all our cities; and the most immediate response came from places not mentioned, but where similar evils existed or similar action was needed. Thus Chicago, intent on its troubles, found useless to it the study of its reform, which seems to have been suggestive elsewhere, and Philadelphia, "Corrupt and Contented," was taken home in other cities and seems to have made the most lasting impression everywhere.

But of course the tangible results are few. The real triumph of the year's work was the complete demonstration it has given, in a thousand little ways, that our shamelessness is superficial, that beneath it lies a pride which, being real, may save us yet. And it is real. The grafters who said you may put the blame anywhere but on the people, where it belongs, and that Americans can be moved only by flattery,—they lied. They lied about themselves. They, too, are American citizens; they too, are of the people; and some of them also were reached by shame. The great truth I tried to make plain was that which Mr. Folk insists so constantly upon: that bribery is no ordinary felony, but treason, that the "corruption which breaks out here and there and now and then" is not an occasional offense, but a common practice, and that the effect of it is literally to change the form of our government from one that is representative of the people to an oligarchy, representative of special interests. Some politicians have seen that this is so, and it bothers them. I think I prize more highly than any other of my experiences the half-dozen times when grafting politicians I had "roasted," as they put it, called on me afterwards to say, in the words of one who spoke with a wonderful solemnity:

"You are right. I never thought of it that way, but it's right. I don't know whether you can do anything, but you're right, dead right. And I'm all wrong. We're all, all wrong. I don't see how we can stop it now; I don't see how I can change. I can't, I guess. No, I can't, not now. But, say, I may be able to help you, and I will if I can. You can have anything I've got."

So you see, they are not such bad fellows, these practical politicians. I wish I could tell more about them: how they have helped me; how candidly and unselfishly they have assisted me to facts and an understanding of the facts, which, as I warned them, as they knew well, were to be used against them. If I could—and I will some day—I should show that one of the surest hopes we have is the politician himself. Ask him for good politics; punish him when he gives bad, and reward him when he gives good; make politics pay. Now, he says, you don't know and you don't care, and that you must be flattered and fooled—and there, I say, he is wrong. I did not flatter anybody; I told the truth as near as I could get it, and instead of resentment there was encouragement. After "The Shame of Minneapolis," and "The Shamelessness of St. Louis," not only did citizens of these cities approve, but citizens of other cities, individuals, groups, and organizations, sent in invitations, hundreds of them, "to come and show us up; we're worse than they are."

We Americans may have failed. We may be mercenary and selfish. Democracy with us may be impossible and corruption inevitable, but these articles, if they have proved nothing else, have demonstrated beyond doubt that we can stand the truth; that there is pride in the character of American citizenship; and that this pride may be a power in the land. So this little volume, a record of shame and yet of self-respect, a disgraceful confession, yet a declaration of honor, is dedicated, in all good faith, to the accused—to all the citizens of all the cities in the United States.

SELECTION

The Changing Law: The Fourteenth Amendment, Justice Holmes, and the Brandeis Brief

The law, based as it is upon precedent and tradition, is slower to change than most institutions, but so pervasive was progressivism at the beginning of the century that it affected even the law, which modified itself in its own way and following its own logic. In the United States Supreme Court decisions repro-

duced here we see, first, in Lochner v. New York, *198 U.S. 45 (1905), judicial orthodoxy represented in the opinion of Justice Rufus W. Peckham and vigorous dissent from that orthodoxy by Justice Oliver Wendell Holmes, and second, in* Muller v. Oregon, *208 U.S. 412 (1908), a court yielding to change by considering the social implications of legislation as well as legalistic or constitutional implications.*

A little background is necessary for understanding these opinions. The Fourteenth Amendment to the Constitution, ratified in 1868 as one of the Reconstruction amendments, provided, among other things, that a state could not "deprive any person of life, liberty, or property, without due process of law." The Court subsequently interpreted this constitutional clause in such a way as to protect corporations from state regulation. The Court's reasoning, worked out over the course of several decisions, was: A corporation legally is a person, the amendment prohibits a state from depriving a person of liberty or property without due process of law, this particular state law does deprive this person of liberty or property contrary to the amendment, and therefore this state law is void. The states had certain police powers, to be sure, and it was for the Federal courts to decide whether or not a state law was justified under the police powers or unjustified as contrary to the Fourteenth Amendment. This was the question Justice Peckham dealt with in his long, rambling, and rather opinionated majority decision in Lochner v. New York, *reproduced here in abridged form. Justice Peckham ruled that an 1897 New York law that limited the working hours of bakers to ten a day and sixty a week was not a proper exercise of New York's police power and was a violation of the Fourteenth Amendment. It was a 5-to-4 decision. Justices John M. Harlan, Edward D. White, and William R. Day joined in one dissenting opinion, not here reprinted, and Justice Holmes wrote his own dissent, here reproduced in its entirety except for legal citations. (Legal citations in these opinions are eliminated without indication of an omission.) Holmes put his argument for judicial restraint in strong and memorable though dispassionate language, and he may have been intentionally irritating Justice Peckham as well as exhorting his colleagues.*

Muller v. Oregon is notable for a brief filed with the Court by Louis D. Brandeis, later to be a Justice of the Court himself, and for the Court's acceptance of the ideas of the brief. In 1903 Oregon had enacted a law limiting the hours of women employees in factories and laundries to not more than ten a day. A laundry owner had challenged the validity of the law, lost in the state supreme court, and carried the case to the United States Supreme Court. In his brief arguing the constitutionality of the Oregon law Brandeis spent little time with the legal argument and concentrated on a great deal of evidence intended to show that regulating the hours of work for women was necessary for the public health and safety as well as the health and safety of the women employees. Thus the Oregon law, he argued, was justified by the police power of the states. Justice David J. Brewer, speaking for the Court, accepted the Brandeis line of reasoning. As the reader of his opinion, here reproduced in abridged form, will note, he accepted it only quite gingerly and self-consciously. Nevertheless, he did accept it, and in subsequent years the Court approved other state laws that it would have had to reject if it had followed Justice Peckham's argument in the Lochner case. Perhaps most important was the acceptance of the Brandeis brief approach—a willingness to consider sociological, medical, or statistical evidence, a recognition that the Court's decisions were important in the lives of real people and not just applications of abstract logic and precedent to legal situations. Approval of the Brandeis approach was more important than approval of the Brandeis conclusions. The Brewer opinion did not, one should note, contradict any of the legal reasoning in Peckham's Lochner decision; nor, for that matter, did Brandeis in his brief.

LOCHNER V. NEW YORK

Mr. Justice Peckham. . . . The statute necessarily interferes with the right of contract between the employer and employés, concerning the number of hours in which the latter may labor in the bakery of the employer. The general right to make a contract in relation to his business is part of the liberty of the individual protected by the Fourteenth Amendment of the Federal Constitution. Under that provision no State can deprive any person of life, liberty or property without due process of law. The right to purchase or to sell labor is part of the liberty protected by this amendment, unless there are circumstances which exclude the right. There are, however, certain powers, existing in the sovereignty of each State in the Union, somewhat vaguely termed police powers, the exact description and limitation of which have not been attempted by the courts. Those powers, broadly stated and without, at present, any attempt at a more specific limitation, relate to the safety, health, morals and general welfare of the public. Both property and liberty are held on such reasonable conditions as may be imposed by the governing power of the State in the exercise of those powers, and with such conditions the Fourteenth Amendment was not designed to interfere.

The State, therefore, has power to prevent the individual from making certain kinds of contracts, and in regard to them the Federal Constitution offers no protection. If the contract be one which the State, in the legitimate exercise of its police power, has the right to prohibit, it is not prevented from prohibiting it by the Fourteenth Amendment. Contracts in violation of a statute, either of the Federal or state government, or a contract to let one's property for immoral purposes, or to do any other unlawful act, could obtain no protection from the Federal Constitution, as coming under the liberty of person or of free contract. Therefore, when the State, by its legislature, in the assumed exercise of its police powers, has passed an act which seriously limits the right to labor or the right of contract in regard to their means of livelihood between persons who are *sui juris* (both employer and employé), it becomes of great importance to determine which shall prevail—the right of the individual to labor for such time as he may choose, or the right of the State to prevent the individual from laboring or from entering into any contract to labor, beyond a certain time prescribed by the State.

This court has recognized the existence and upheld the exercise of the police powers of the States in many cases which might fairly be considered as border ones, and it has, in the course of its determination of questions regarding the asserted invalidity of such statutes, on the ground of their violation of the rights secured by the Federal Constitution, been guided by rules of a very liberal nature, the application of which has resulted, in numerous instances, in upholding the validity of state statutes thus assailed. . . .

It must, of course, be conceded that there is a limit to the valid exercise of the police power by the State. There is no dispute concerning this general proposition. Otherwise the Fourteenth Amendment would have no efficacy and the legislatures of the States would have unbounded power, and it would be enough to say that any piece of legislation was enacted to conserve the morals, the health or the safety of the people; such legislation would be valid, no matter how absolutely without foundation the claim might be. The claim of the police power would be a mere pretext—become another and delusive name for the supreme sovereignty of the State to be exercised free from constitutional restraint. This is not contended for. In every case that comes before this court, therefore, where legislation of this character is concerned and where the protection of the Federal Constitution is sought, the question necessarily arises: Is this a fair, reasonable and appropriate exercise of the police power of the State, or is it an unreasonable, unnecessary and arbitrary interference with the right of the individual to his personal liberty or to enter into those contracts in relation to labor which may seem to him appropriate or necessary for the support of himself and his family? Of course the liberty of contract relating to labor includes both parties to it. The one has as much right to purchase as the other to sell labor.

This is not a question of substituting the judgment of the court for that of the legislature. If the act be within the power of the State it is valid, although the judgment of the court might be totally opposed to the enactment of such a law. But the question would still remain: Is it within the police power of the State? and that question must be answered by the court.

The question whether this act is valid as a labor law, pure and simple, may be dismissed in a few words. There is no reasonable ground for interfering with the liberty of person or the right of free contract, by determining the hours of labor, in the occupation of a baker. There is no contention that bakers as a class are not equal in intelligence and capacity to men in other trades or manual occupations, or that they are not able to assert their rights and care for themselves without the protecting arm of the State, interfering with their independence of judgment and of action. They are in no sense wards of the State. Viewed in the light of a purely labor law, with no reference whatever to the question of health, we think that a law like the one before us involves neither the safety, the morals nor the welfare of the public, and that the interest of the public is not in the slightest degree affected by such an act. The law must be upheld, if at all, as a law pertaining to the health of the individual engaged in the occupation of a baker. It does not affect any other portion of the public than those who are engaged in that occupation. Clean and wholesome bread does not depend upon whether the baker works but ten hours per day or only sixty hours a week. The limitation of the hours of labor does not come within the police power on that ground.

It is a question of which of two powers or rights shall prevail—the power of the State to legislate or the right of the individual to liberty of person and freedom of contract. The mere assertion that the subject relates though but in a remote degree to the public health does not necessarily render the enactment valid. The act must have a more direct relation, as a means to an end, and the end itself must be appropriate and legitimate, before an act can be held to be valid which interferes with the general right of an individual to be free in his person and in his power to contract in relation to his own labor. . . .

We think the limit of the police power has been reached and passed in this case. There is, in our judgment, no reasonable foundation for holding this to be necessary or appropriate as a health law to safeguard the public health or the health of the individuals who are following the trade of a baker. If this statute be valid, and if, therefore, a proper case is made out in which to deny the right of an individual, *sui juris,* as employer or employé, to make contracts for the labor of the latter under the protection of the provisions of the Federal Constitution, there would seem to be no length to which legislation of this nature might not go. The case differs widely, as we have already stated, from the expressions of this court in regard to laws of this nature, as stated in *Holden* v. *Hardy* and *Jacobson* v. *Massachusetts.*

We think that there can be no fair doubt that the trade of a baker, in and of itself, is not an unhealthy one to that degree which would authorize the legislature to interfere with the right to labor, and with the right of free contract on the part of the individual, either as employer or employé. In looking through statistics regarding all trades and occupations, it may be true that the trade of a baker does not appear to be as healthy as some other trades, and is also vastly more healthy than still others. To the common understanding the trade of a baker has never been regarded as an unhealthy one. Very likely physicians would not recommend the exercise of that or of any other trade as a remedy for ill health. Some occupations are more healthy than others, but we think there are none which might not come under the power of the legislature to supervise and control the hours of working therein, if the mere fact that the occupation is not absolutely and perfectly healthy is to confer that right upon the legislative department of the Government. It might be safely affirmed that almost all occupations more or less affect the health. There must be more than the mere fact of the possible existence of some small amount of unhealthiness to warrant legislative interference with liberty. It is unfortunately true that labor, even in any department, may possibly carry with it the seeds of unhealthiness. But are we all, on that account, at the mercy of legislative majorities? A printer, a tinsmith, a locksmith, a carpenter, a cabinetmaker, a dry goods clerk, a bank's, a lawyer's or a physician's clerk, or a clerk in almost any kind of business, would all come under the power of the legislature, on this assumption. No trade, no occupation, no mode of earning one's living, could escape this all-pervading power, and the acts of the legislature in limiting the hours of labor in all employments would be valid, although such limitation might seriously cripple the ability of the laborer to support himself and his family. . . . The act is not, within any fair meaning of the term, a health law, but is an illegal interference with the rights of individuals, both employers and employés, to make contracts regarding labor upon such terms as they may think best, or which they may agree upon with the other parties to such contracts. Statutes of the nature of that under review, limiting the hours in which grown and intelligent men may labor to earn their living, are mere meddlesome interferences with the rights of the individual, and they are not saved from condemnation by the claim that they are passed in the exercise of the police power and upon the subject of the health of the individual whose rights are interfered with, unless there be some fair ground, reasonable in and of itself, to say that there is material danger to the public health or to the health of the employés, if the hours of labor are not curtailed. . . .

It was further urged on the argument that restricting the hours of labor in the case of bakers was valid because it tended to cleanliness on the part of the workers, as a man was more apt to be cleanly when not overworked, and if cleanly then his "output" was also more likely to be so. What has already been said applies with equal force to this contention. We do not admit the reasoning to be sufficient to justify the claimed right of such interference. The State in that case would assume the position of a supervisor, or *pater familias,* over every act of the individual, and its right of governmental interference with his hours of labor, his hours of exercise, the character thereof, and the extent to which it shall be carried would be recognized and upheld. In our judgment it is not possible in fact to discover the connection between the number of hours a baker may work in the bakery and the healthful quality of the bread made by the workman. The connection, if any exists, is too shadowy and thin to build any argument for the interference of the legislature. . . .

It is impossible for us to shut our eyes to the fact that many of the laws of this character, while passed under what is claimed to be the police power for the purpose of protecting the public health or welfare, are, in reality, passed from other motives. We are justified in saying so when, from the character of the law and the subject upon which it legislates, it is apparent that the public health or welfare bears but the most remote relation to the law. The purpose of a statute must be determined from the natural and legal effect of the language employed; and whether it is or is not repugnant to the Constitution of the United States must be determined from the natural effect of such statutes when put into operation, and not from their proclaimed purpose. The court looks beyond the mere letter of the law in such cases.

It is manifest to us that the limitation of the hours of labor as provided for in this section of the statute under which the indictment was found, and the plaintiff in error convicted, has no such direct relation to and no such substantial effect upon the health of the employé, as to justify us in regarding the section as really a health law. It seems to us that the real object and purpose were simply to regulate the hours of labor between the master and his employés (all being men, *sui juris*), in a private business, not dangerous in any degree to morals or in any real and substantial degree, to the health of the employés. Under such circumstances the freedom of master and employé to contract with each other in relation to their employment, and in defining the same, cannot be prohibited or interfered with, without violating the Federal Constitution.

The judgment of the Court of Appeals of New York as well as that of the Supreme Court and of the County Court of Oneida County must be reversed and the case remanded to the County Court for further proceedings not inconsistent with this opinion.

Reversed.

Mr. Justice Holmes Dissenting. I regret that I am unable to agree with the judgment in this case, and that I think it my duty to express my dissent.

This case is decided upon an economic theory which a large part of the country does not entertain. If it were a question whether I agree with that theory, I should desire to study it further and long before making up my mind. But I do not conceive that to be my duty, because I strongly believe that my agreement or disagreement has nothing to do with the right of a majority to embody their opinions in law. It is settled by various decisions of this court that state constitutions and state laws may regulate life in many ways which we as legislators might think as injudicious or if you like as tyrannical as this, and which equally with this interfere with the liberty to contract. Sunday laws and usury laws are ancient examples. A more modern one is the prohibition of lotteries. The liberty of the citizen to do as he likes so long as he does not interfere with the liberty of others to do the same, which has been a shibboleth for some well-known writers, is interfered with by school laws, by the Post Office, by every state or municipal institution which takes his money for purposes thought desirable, whether he likes it or not. The Fourteenth Amendment does not enact Mr. Herbert Spencer's Social Statics. The other day we sustained the Massachusetts vaccination law. United States and state statutes and decisions cutting down the liberty to contract by way of combination are familiar to this court. Two years ago we upheld the prohibition of sales of stock on margins or for future delivery in the constitution of California. The decision sustaining an eight hour law for miners is still recent. Some of these laws embody convictions or prejudices which judges are likely to share. Some may not. But a constitution is not intended to embody a particular economic theory, whether of paternalism and the organic relation of the citizen to the State or of *laissez faire*. It is made for people of fundamentally differing views, and the accident of our finding certain opinions natural and familiar or novel and even shocking ought not to conclude our judgment upon the question whether statutes embodying them conflict with the Constitution of the United States.

General propositions do not decide concrete cases. The decision will depend on a judgment or intuition more subtle than any articulate major premise. But I think that the proposition just stated, if it is accepted, will carry us far toward the end. Every opinion tends to become a law. I think that the word liberty in the Fourteenth Amendment is perverted when it is held to prevent the natural outcome of a dominant opinion, unless it can be said that a rational and fair man necessarily would admit that the statute proposed would infringe fundamental principles as they have been understood by the traditions of our people and our law. It does not need research to show that no such sweeping condemnation can be passed upon the statute before us. A reasonable man might think it a proper measure on the score of health. Men whom I certainly could not pronounce unreasonable would uphold it as a first instalment of a general regulation of the hours of work. Whether in the latter aspect it would be open to the charge of inequality I think it unnecessary to discuss.

MULLER V. OREGON

Mr. Justice Brewer. . . . The single question is the constitutionality of the statute under which the defendant was convicted so far as it affects the work of a female in a laundry. That it does not conflict with any provisions of the state constitution is settled by the decision of the Supreme Court of the State. . . .

It is the law of Oregon that women, whether married or single, have equal contractual and personal rights with men. . . .

It thus appears that, putting to one side the elective franchise, in the matter of personal and contractual rights they stand on the same plane as the other sex. Their rights in these respects can no more be infringed than the equal rights of their brothers. We held in *Lochner* v. *New York*, 198 U.S. 45, that a law providing that no laborer shall be required or permitted to work in a bakery more than sixty hours in a week or ten hours in a day was not as to men a legitimate exercise of the police power of the State, but an unreasonable, unnecessary and arbitrary interference with the right and liberty of the individual to contract in relation to his labor, and as such was in conflict with, and void under, the Federal Constitution. That decision is invoked by plaintiff in error as decisive of the question before us. But this assumes that the difference between the sexes does not justify a different rule respecting a restriction of the hours of labor.

In patent cases counsel are apt to open the argument with a discussion of the state of the art. It may not be amiss, in the present case, before examining the constitutional question, to notice the course of legislation as well as expressions of opinion from other than judicial sources. In the brief filed by Mr. Louis D. Brandeis, for the defendant in error, is a very copious collection of all these matters. . . .

The legislation and opinions referred to . . . may not be, technically speaking, authorities, and in them is little or no discussion of the constitutional question presented to us for determination, yet they are significant of a widespread belief that woman's physical structure, and the functions she performs in consequence thereof, justify special legislation restricting or qualifying the conditions under which she should be permitted to toil. Constitutional questions, it is true, are not settled by even a consensus of present public opinion, for it is the peculiar value of a written constitution that it places in unchanging form limitations upon legislative action, and thus gives a permanence and stability to popular government which otherwise would be lacking. At the same time, when a question of fact is debated and debatable, and the extent to which a special constitutional limitation goes is affected by the truth in respect to that fact, a widespread and long continued belief concerning it is worthy of consideration. We take judicial cognizance of all matters of general knowledge.

It is undoubtedly true, as more than once declared by this court, that the general right to contract in relation to one's business is part of the liberty of the individual, protected by the Fourteenth Amendment to the Federal Constitution; yet it is equally well settled that this liberty is not absolute and extending to all contracts, and that a State may, without conflicting with the provisions of the Fourteenth Amendment, restrict in many respects the individual's power of contract. Without stopping to discuss at length the extent to which a State may act in this respect, we refer to the following cases in which the question has been considered: *Allgeyer* v. *Louisiana*, 165 U.S. 578; *Holden* v. *Hardy*, 169 U.S. 366; *Lochner* v. *New York*, 198 U.S. 45.

That woman's physical structure and the performance of maternal functions place her at a disadvantage in the struggle for subsistence is obvious. This is especially true when the burdens of motherhood are upon her. Even when they are not, by abundant testimony of the medical fraternity continuance for a long time on her feet at work, repeating this from day to day, tends to injurious effects upon the body, and as healthy mothers are essential to vigorous offspring, the physical well-being of woman becomes an object of public interest and care in order to preserve the strength and vigor of the race.

Still again, history discloses the fact that woman has always been dependent upon man. He established his control at the outset by superior physical strength, and this control in various forms, with diminishing intensity, has continued to the present. As minors, though not to the same extent, she has been looked upon in the courts as needing especial care that her rights may be preserved. Education was long denied her, and while now the doors of the school room are opened and her opportunities for acquiring knowledge are great, yet even with that and the consequent increase of capacity for business affairs it is still true that in the struggle for subsistence she is not an equal competitor with her brother. Though limitations upon personal and contractual rights may be removed by legislation, there is that in her disposition and habits of life which will operate against a full assertion of those rights. She will still be where some legislation to protect her seems necessary to secure a real equality of right. Doubtless there are individual exceptions, and there are many respects in which she has an advantage over him; but looking at it from the viewpoint of the effort to maintain an independent position in life, she is not upon an equality. Differentiated by these matters from the other sex, she is properly placed in a class by herself, and legislation designed for her protection may be sustained, even when like legislation is not necessary for men and could not be sustained. It is impossible to close one's eyes to the fact that she still looks to her brother and depends upon him. Even though all restrictions on political, personal and contractual rights were taken away, and she stood, so far as statutes are concerned, upon an absolutely equal plane with him, it would still be true that she is so constituted that she will rest upon and look to him for protection; that her physical structure and a proper discharge of her maternal functions—having in view not merely her own health, but the well-being of the race—justify legislation to protect her from the greed as well as the passion of man. The limitations which this statute places upon her contractual powers, upon her right to agree with her employer as to the time she shall labor, are not imposed solely for her benefit, but also largely for the benefit of all. Many words cannot make this plainer. The two sexes differ in structure of body, in the functions to be performed by each, in the amount of physical strength, in the capacity for long-continued labor, particularly when done standing, the influence of vigorous health upon the future well-being of the race, the self-reliance which enables one to assert full rights, and in the capacity to maintain the struggle for subsistence. This difference justifies a difference in legislation and upholds that which is designed to compensate for some of the burdens which rest upon her.

We have not referred in this discussion to the denial of the elective franchise in the State of Oregon, for while it may disclose a lack of political equality in all things with her brother, that is not of itself decisive. The reason runs deeper, and rests in the inherent difference between the two sexes, and in the different functions in life which they perform.

For these reasons, and without questioning in any respect the decision in *Lochner* v. *New York*, we are of the opinion that it cannot be adjudged that the act in question is in conflict with the Federal Constitution, so far as it respects the work of a female in a laundry, and the judgment of the Supreme Court of Oregon is

Affirmed.

SELECTION

A Pioneer Social Worker Describes the Immigrants' Life: Jane Addams in "Twenty Years at Hull-House" (1910)

Americans like to think of their nation as classless, but the dreary fact in the late nineteenth and early twentieth centuries was that in the large industrial cities there was an enormous, poor working class of immigrants separated by a wide gulf of language and culture from Americans of earlier vintage. In some respects, the lines of demarcation between this urban industrial class of workers recently from abroad were clearer than the lines that delineated workers in London, Paris, or Berlin. The lines were so clearly drawn and so seldom crossed that millions of middle-class Americans knew only in the vaguest way how the immigrants lived in their parts of the city and how the leap from the traditional, agricultural, relatively stable peasant village of Europe to the antitraditional, industrial, dynamic metropolis of America wrenched the soul and left one unprepared to cope with his environment. Jane Addams was one of the first middle-class, old-stock Americans to cross the line and live among the immigrants. She was among the first of her background to write of immigrant life for the more comfortable Americans, to tell How the Other Half Lives, *to use the title of an 1890 book by Jacob Riis, a journalist who was himself an immigrant from Denmark.*

Miss Addams treated her immigrant neighbors with sympathy and respect and wrote of them with sympathy and respect. She recognized that some of their abilities and values were worthy of emulation. Instead of trying to force assimilation, the typical reaction of older-stock Americans to immigrants, she wrote that "immigrant colonies might yield to our American life something very valuable." She saw the mingling of cultures as something at least potentially desirable to those who had come to America's shores both recently and more remotely. Apparently, she did not question the melting-pot concept—as did Randolph Bourne in the next selection—but the culture which would eventually emerge, she thought, would be and should be one that had its origins among the recent immigrants as well as the older Americans.

Born in a northern Illinois village two months before Lincoln was elected President, Jane Addams graduated from Rockford College in 1881 and then studied medicine briefly until poor health forced her to quit. She and a friend traveled in Europe, where she became interested, for the first time apparently, in the condition of the poor. While in Europe, she resolved to establish in America a settlement house similar in concept to Toynbee Hall in the East End of London. In September, 1889, she opened Hull-House (named for the original owner of the building) at the corner of South Halsted and Polk Streets in Chicago, in the midst of one of the worst slums in the Western world. Hull-House was one of the first social settlements in the United States, and it and Miss Addams had a great influence on the settlement movement elsewhere. The effect Hull-House and Jane Addams had on Chicago and Chicagoans is impossible to measure, but none would deny it was great and pervading. Beatrice Webb, who was not given to generous appraisals of Americans or their institutions, found Hull-House to be "one continuous intellectual and emotional ferment" when she visited it in 1898. Her judgment of Jane Addams: "without doubt a remarkable woman, an interesting combination of the organiser, the enthusiast and the subtle observer of human characteristics . . . a charming personality, gentle and dignified, shrewdly observant. . . . She excels in persistency of purpose and unflinching courage." As well as a pioneer social worker, Jane Addams was a leader of the woman-suffrage movement and an indefatigable worker for world peace. In 1931 she became the first woman to receive the Nobel peace prize, which she was awarded jointly with Nicholas Murray Butler, president of Columbia University. A more bizarre bracketing of personalities would have been difficult. She died in 1935.

This selection, slightly abridged, is chapter XI of Twenty Years at Hull-House *(New York: Macmillan, 1910), pages 231–258.*

rom our very first months at Hull-House we found it much easier to deal with the first generation of crowded city life than with the second or third, because it is more natural and cast in a simpler mold. The Italian and Bohemian peasants who live in Chicago, still put on their bright holiday clothes on a Sunday and go to visit their cousins. They tramp along with at least a suggestion of having once walked over plowed fields and breathed country air. The second generation of city poor too often have no holiday clothes and consider their relations a "bad lot." I have heard a drunken man in a maudlin stage, babble of his good country mother and imagine he was driving the cows home, and I knew that his little son who laughed loud at him, would be drunk earlier in life and would have no such pastoral interlude to his ravings. Hospitality still survives among foreigners, although it is buried under false pride among the poorest Americans. One thing seemed clear in regard to entertaining immigrants; to preserve and keep whatever of value their past life contained and to bring them in contact with a better type of Americans. For several years, every Saturday evening the entire families of our Italian neighbors were our guests. These evenings were very popular during our first winters at Hull-House. Many educated Italians helped us, and the house became known as a place where Italians were welcome and where national holidays were observed. They come to us with their petty lawsuits, sad relics of the *vendetta,* with their incorrigible boys, with their hospital cases, with their aspirations for American clothes, and with their needs for an interpreter.

An editor of an Italian paper made a genuine connection between us and the Italian colony, not only with the Neapolitans and the Sicilians of the immediate neighborhood, but with the educated *connazionali* throughout the city, until he went south to start an agricultural colony in Alabama, in the establishment of which Hull-House heartily coöperated.

Possibly the South Italians more than any other immigrants represent the pathetic stupidity of agricultural people crowded into city tenements, and we were much gratified when thirty peasant families were induced to move upon the land which they knew so well how to cultivate. The starting of this colony, however, was a very expensive affair in spite of the fact that the colonists purchased the land at two dollars an acre; they needed much more than raw land, and although it was possible to collect the small sums necessary to sustain them during the hard time of the first two years, we were fully convinced that undertakings of this sort could be conducted properly only by colonization societies such as England has established, or, better still, by enlarging the functions of the Federal Department of Immigration.

An evening similar in purpose to the one devoted to the Italians was organized for the Germans, in our first year. Owing to the superior education of our Teutonic guests and the clever leading of a cultivated German woman, these evenings reflected something of that cozy social intercourse which is found in its perfection in the fatherland. Our guests sang a great deal in the tender minor of the German folksong or in the rousing spirit of the Rhine, and they slowly but persistently pursued a course in German history and literature, recovering something of that poetry and romance which they had long since resigned with other good things. We found strong family affection between them and their English-speaking children, but their pleasures were not in common, and they seldom went out together. Perhaps the greatest value of the Settlement to them was in placing large and pleasant rooms with musical facilities at their disposal, and in reviving their almost forgotten enthusiasms. I have seen sons and daughters stand in complete surprise as their mother's knitting needles softly beat time to the song she was singing, or her worn face turned rosy under the hand-clapping as she made an old-fashioned courtsey at the end of a German poem. It was easy to fancy a growing touch of respect in her children's manner to her, and a rising enthusiasm for German literature and reminiscence on the part of all the family, an effort to bring together the old life and the new, a respect for the older cultivation, and not quite so much assurance that the new was the best. . . .

An overmastering desire to reveal the humbler immigrant parents to their own children lay at the base of what has come to be called the Hull-House Labor Museum. This was first suggested to my mind one early spring day when I saw an old Italian woman, her distaff against her homesick face, patiently spinning a thread by the simple stick spindle so reminiscent of all southern Europe. I was walking down Polk Street, perturbed in spirit, because it seemed so difficult to come into genuine relations with the Italian women and because they themselves so often lost their hold upon their Americanized children. It seemed to me that Hull-House ought to be able to devise some educational enterprise, which should build a bridge between European and American experiences in such wise as to give them both more meaning and a sense of relation. I meditated that perhaps the power to see life as a whole, is more needed in the immigrant quarter of a large city than anywhere else, and that the lack of this power is the most fruitful source of misunderstanding between European immigrants and their children, as it is between them and their American neighbors; and why should that chasm between fathers and sons, yawning at the feet of each generation, be made so unnecessarily cruel and impassable to these bewildered immigrants? Suddenly I looked up and saw the old woman with her distaff, sitting in the sun on the steps of a tenement house. She might have served as a model for one of Michael Angelo's Fates, but her face brightened as I passed and, holding up her spindle for me to see, she called out that when she had spun a little more yarn, she would knit a pair of stockings for her goddaughter. The occupation of the old woman gave me the clew that was needed. Could we not interest the young people working in the neighboring factories, in these older forms of industry, so that, through their own parents and grandparents, they would find a dramatic representation of the inherited resources of their daily occupation. If these young people could actually see that the complicated machinery of the factory had been evolved from simple tools, they might at least make a beginning towards that education which Dr. Dewey defines as "a continuing reconstruction of experience." They might also lay a foundation for reverence of the past which Goethe declares to be the basis of all sound progress.

My exciting walk on Polk Street was followed by many talks with

Dr. Dewey and with one of the teachers in his school who was a resident at Hull-House. Within a month a room was fitted up to which we might invite those of our neighbors who were possessed of old crafts and who were eager to use them.

We found in the immediate neighborhood, at least four varieties of these most primitive methods of spinning and three distinct variations of the same spindle in connection with wheels. It was possible to put these seven into historic sequence and order and to connect the whole with the present method of factory spinning. The same thing was done for weaving, and on every Saturday evening a little exhibit was made of these various forms of labor in the textile industry. Within one room a Syrian woman, a Greek, an Italian, a Russian, and an Irishwoman enabled even the most casual observer to see that there is no break in orderly evolution if we look at history from the industrial standpoint; that industry develops similarly and peacefully year by year among the workers of each nation, heedless of differences in language, religion, and political experiences.

And then we grew ambitious and arranged lectures upon industrial history. I remember that after an interesting lecture upon the industrial revolution in England and a portrayal of the appalling conditions throughout the weaving districts of the north, which resulted from the hasty gathering of the weavers into the new towns, a Russian tailor in the audience was moved to make a speech. He suggested that whereas time had done much to alleviate the first difficulties in the transition of weaving from hand work to steam power, that in the application of steam to sewing we are still in the first stages, illustrated by the isolated woman who tries to support herself by hand needlework at home until driven out by starvation, as many of the hand weavers had been.

The historical analogy seemed to bring a certain comfort to the tailor as did a chart upon the wall, showing the infinitesimal amount of time that steam had been applied to manufacturing processes compared to the centuries of hand labor. Human progress is slow and perhaps never more cruel than in the advance of industry, but is not the worker comforted by knowing that other historical periods have existed similar to the one in which he finds himself, and that the readjustment may be shortened and alleviated by judicious action; and is he not entitled to the solace which an artistic portrayal of the situation might give him? I remember the evening of the tailor's speech that I felt reproached because no poet or artist has endeared the sweaters' victim to us as George Eliot has made us love the belated weaver, Silas Marner. The textile museum is connected directly with the basket weaving, sewing, millinery, embroidery, and dressmaking constantly being taught at Hull-House, and so far as possible with the other educational departments; we have also been able to make a collection of products, of early implements, and of photographs which are full of suggestion. Yet far beyond its direct educational value, we prize it because it so often puts the immigrants into the position of teachers, and we imagine that it affords them a pleasant change from the tutelage in which all Americans, including their own children, are so apt to hold them. I recall a number of Russian women working in a sewing-room near Hull-House, who heard one Christmas week that the House was going to give a party to which they might come. They arrived one afternoon when, unfortunately, there was no party on hand and, although the residents did their best to entertain them with impromptu music and refreshments, it was quite evident that they were greatly disappointed. Finally it was suggested that they be shown the Labor Museum—where gradually the thirty sodden, tired women were transformed. They knew how to use the spindles and were delighted to find the Russian spinning frame. Many of them had never seen the spinning wheel, which has not penetrated to certain parts of Russia, and they regarded it as a new and wonderful invention. They turned up their dresses to show their homespun petticoats; they tried the looms; they explained the difficulty of the old patterns; in short, from having been stupidly entertained, they themselves did the entertaining. Because of a direct appeal to former experiences, the immigrant visitors were able for the moment to instruct their American hostesses in an old and honored craft, as was indeed becoming to their age and experience. . . .

There has been some testimony that the Labor Museum has revealed the charm of woman's primitive activities. I recall a certain Italian girl who came every Saturday evening to a cooking class in the same building in which her mother spun in the Labor Museum exhibit; and yet Angelina always left her mother at the front door while she herself went around to a side door because she did not wish to be too closely identified in the eyes of the rest of the cooking class with an Italian woman who wore a kerchief over her head, uncouth boots, and short petticoats. One evening, however, Angelina saw her mother surrounded by a group of visitors from the School of Education, who much admired the spinning, and she concluded from their conversation that her mother was "the best stick-spindle spinner in America." When she inquired from me as to the truth of this deduction, I took occasion to describe the Italian village in which her mother had lived, something of her free life, and how, because of the opportunity she and the other women of the village had to drop their spindles over the edge of a precipice, they had developed a skill in spinning beyond that of the neighboring towns. I dilated somewhat on the freedom and beauty of that life—how hard it must be to exchange it all for a two-room tenement, and to give up a beautiful homespun kerchief for an ugly department store hat. I intimated it was most unfair to judge her by these things alone, and that while she must depend on her daughter to learn the new ways, she also had a right to expect her daughter to know something of the old ways.

That which I could not convey to the child but upon which my own mind persistently dwelt, was that her mother's whole life had been spent in a secluded spot under the rule of traditional and narrowly localized observances, until her very religion clung to local sanctities,—to the shrine before which she had always prayed, to the pavement and walls of the low vaulted church,—and then suddenly she was torn from it all and literally put out to sea, straight away from the solid habits of her religious and domestic life, and she now walked timidly but with poignant sensibility upon a new and strange shore.

It was easy to see that the thought of her mother with any other background than that of the tenement was new to Angelina and at least two things resulted; she allowed her mother to pull out of the big box under the bed the beautiful homespun garments which had been previously hidden away as uncouth; and she openly came into the Labor Museum by the same door as did her mother, proud at least of the mastery of the craft which had been so much admired.

A club of necktie workers formerly meeting at Hull-House, persistently resented any attempt on the part of their director to improve their minds. The president once said that she "wouldn't be caught dead at a lecture," that she came to the club "to get some fun out of it," and indeed it was most natural that she should crave recreation after a hard day's work. One evening I saw the entire club listening to quite a stiff lecture in the Labor Museum and to my rather wicked remark to the president that I was surprised to see her enjoying a lecture, she replied, that she did not call this a lecture, she called this "getting next to the stuff you work with all the time." It was perhaps the sincerest tribute we have ever received as to the success of the undertaking.

The Labor Museum continually demanded more space as it was enriched by a fine textile exhibit lent by the Field Museum, and later by carefully selected specimens of basketry from the Philippines. The shops have finally included a group of three or four women, Irish, Italian, Danish, who have become a permanent working force in the textile department which has developed into a self-supporting industry through the sale of its homespun products.

These women and a few men, who come to the museum to utilize their European skill in pottery, metal, and wood, demonstrate that immigrant colonies might yield to our American life something very valuable, if their resources were intelligently studied and developed. I recall an Italian, who had decorated the doorposts of his tenement with a beautiful pattern he had previously used in carving the reredos of a Neapolitan church, who was "fired" by his landlord on the ground of destroying property. His feelings were hurt, not so much that he had been put out of his house, as that his work had been so disregarded; and he said that when people traveled in Italy they liked to look at wood carvings but that in America "they only made money out of you."

Sometimes the suppression of the instinct of workmanship is followed by more disastrous results. A Bohemian whose little girl attended classes at Hull-House, in one of his periodic drunken spells had literally almost choked her to death, and later had committed suicide when in delirium tremens. His poor wife, who stayed a week at Hull-House after the disaster until a new tenement could be arranged for her, one day showed me a gold ring which her husband had made for their betrothal. It exhibited the most exquisite workmanship, and she said that although in the old country he had been a goldsmith, in America he had for twenty years shoveled coal in a furnace room of a large manufacturing plant; that whenever she saw one of his "restless fits," which preceded his drunken periods, "coming on," if she could provide him with a bit of metal and persuade him to stay at home and work at it, he was all right and the time passed without disaster, but that "nothing else would do it." This story threw a flood of light upon the dead man's struggle and on the stupid maladjustment which had broken him down. Why had we never been told? Why had our interest in the remarkable musical ability of his child, blinded us to the hidden artistic ability of the father? We had forgotten that a long-established occupation may form the very foundations of the moral life, that the art with which a man has solaced his toil may be the salvation of his uncertain temperament.

There are many examples of touching fidelity to immigrant parents on the part of their grown children; a young man, who day after day, attends ceremonies which no longer express his religious convictions and who makes his vain effort to interest his Russian Jewish father in social problems; a daughter who might earn much more money as a stenographer could she work from Monday morning till Saturday night, but who quietly and docilely makes neckties for low wages because she can thus abstain from work Saturdays to please her father; these young people, like poor Maggie Tulliver, through many painful experiences have reached the conclusion that pity, memory, and faithfulness are natural ties with paramount claims.

This faithfulness, however, is sometimes ruthlessly imposed upon by immigrant parents who, eager for money and accustomed to the patriarchal authority of peasant households, hold their children in a stern bondage which requires a surrender of all their wages and concedes no time or money for pleasures.

There are many convincing illustrations that this parental harshness often results in juvenile delinquency. A Polish boy of seventeen came to Hull-House one day to ask a contribution of fifty cents "towards a flower piece for the funeral of an old Hull-House club boy." A few questions made it clear that the object was fictitious, whereupon the boy broke down and half defiantly stated that he wanted to buy two twenty-five cent tickets, one for his girl and one for himself, to a dance of the Benevolent Social Twos; that he hadn't a penny of his own although he had worked in a brass foundry for three years and had been advanced twice, because he always had to give his pay envelope unopened to his father; "just look at the clothes he buys me" was his concluding remark. . . .

I know a Polish boy whose earnings were all given to his father who gruffly refused all requests for pocket money. One Christmas his little sisters, having been told by their mother that they were too poor to have any Christmas presents, appealed to the big brother as to one who was earning money of his own. Flattered by the implication, but at the same time quite impecunious, the night before Christmas he nonchalantly walked through a neighboring department store and stole a manicure set for one little sister and a string of beads for the other. He was caught at the door by the house detective as one of those children whom each local department store arrests in the weeks before Christmas at the daily rate of eight to twenty. The youngest of these offenders are seldom taken into court but are either sent home with a warning or turned over to the officers of the Juvenile Protective Association. Most of these premature law breakers are in search of Americanized clothing and others are only looking for playthings. They are all distracted by the profusion and variety of the display, and their moral sense is confused by the general air of openhandedness.

These disastrous efforts are not unlike those of many younger children who are constantly arrested for petty thieving because they are too eager to take home food or fuel which will relieve the distress and need they so constantly hear discussed. The coal on the wagons, the vegetables displayed in front of the grocery shops, the very wooden blocks in the loosened street paving are a challenge to their powers to help out at home. A Bohemian boy who was out on parole from the old detention home of the Juvenile Court itself, brought back five stolen chickens to the matron for Sunday dinner, saying that he knew the Committee were "having a hard time to fill up so many kids and perhaps these fowl would help out." The honest immigrant parents, totally ignorant of American laws and municipal regulations, often send a child to pick up coal on the railroad tracks or to stand at three o'clock in the morning before the side door of a restaurant which gives away broken food, or to collect grain for the chickens at the base of elevators and standing cars. The latter custom accounts for the large number of boys arrested for breaking the seals on grain freight cars. It is easy for a child thus trained to accept the proposition of a junk dealer to bring him bars of iron stored in freight yards. Four boys quite recently had thus carried away and sold to one man, two tons of iron.

Four fifths of the children brought into the Juvenile Court in Chicago are the children of foreigners. The Germans are the greatest offenders, Polish next. Do their children suffer from the excess of virtue in those parents so eager to own a house and lot? One often sees a grasping parent in the court, utterly broken down when the Americanized youth who has been brought to grief clings as piteously to his peasant father as if he were still a frightened little boy in the steerage.

Many of these children have come to grief through their premature fling into city life, having thrown off parental control as they have impatiently discarded foreign ways. Boys of ten and twelve will refuse to sleep at home, preferring the freedom of an old brewery vault or an empty warehouse to the obedience required by their parents, and for days these boys will live on the milk and bread which they steal from the back porches after the early morning delivery. Such children complain that there is "no fun" at home. One little chap who was given a vacant lot to cultivate by the City Garden Association, insisted upon raising only popcorn and tried to present the entire crop to Hull-House "to be used for the parties," with the stipulation that he would have "to be invited every single time." Then there are little groups of dissipated young men who pride themselves upon their ability to live without working, and who despise all the honest and sober ways of their immigrant parents. They are at once a menace and a center of demoralization. Certainly the bewildered parents, unable to speak English and ignorant of the city, whose children have disappeared for days or weeks, have often come to Hull-House, evincing that agony which fairly separates the marrow from the bone, as if they had discovered a new type of suffering, devoid of the healing in familiar sorrows. It is as if they did not know how to search for the children without the assistance of the children themselves. Perhaps the most pathetic aspect of such cases is their revelation of the premature dependence of the older and wiser upon the young and foolish, which is in itself often responsible for the situation because it has given the children an undue sense of their own importance and a false security that they can take care of themselves.

On the other hand, an Italian girl who has had lessons in cooking at the public school, will help her mother to connect the entire family with American food and household habits. That the mother has never baked bread in Italy—only mixed it in her own house and then taken it out to the village oven—makes all the more valuable her daughter's understanding of the complicated cooking stove. The same thing is true of the girl who learns to sew in the public school, and more than anything else, perhaps, of the girl who receives the first simple instruction in the care of little children,—that skillful care which every tenement-house baby requires if he is to be pulled through his second summer. As a result of this teaching I recall a young girl who carefully explained to her Italian mother that the reason the babies in Italy were so healthy and the babies in Chicago were so sickly, was not, as her mother had firmly insisted, because her babies in Italy had goat's milk and her babies in America had cow's milk, but because the milk in Italy was clean and the milk in Chicago was dirty. She said that when you milked your own goat before the door, you knew that the milk was clean, but when you bought milk from the grocery store after it had been carried for many miles in the country, you couldn't tell whether or not it was fit for the baby to drink until the men from the City Hall who had watched it all the way, said that it was all right.

Thus through civic instruction in the public schools, the Italian woman slowly became urbanized in the sense in which the word was used by her own Latin ancestors, and thus the habits of her entire family were modified. The public schools in the immigrant colonies deserve all the praise as Americanizing agencies which can be bestowed upon them, and there is little doubt that the fast-changing curriculum in the direction of the vacation-school experiments, will react still more directly upon such households.

It is difficult to write of the relation of the older and most foreign-looking immigrants to the children of other people,—the Italians whose fruit-carts are upset simply because they are "dagoes," or the Russian peddlers who are stoned and sometimes badly injured because it has become a code of honor in a gang of boys to thus express their derision. The members of a Protective Association of Jewish Peddlers organized at Hull-House, related daily experiences in which old age had been treated with such irreverence, cherished dignity with such disrespect, that a listener caught the passion of Lear in the old texts, as a platitude enunciated by a man who discovers in it his own experience, thrills us as no unfamiliar phrases can possibly do. The Greeks are filled with amazed rage when their very name is flung at them as an opprobrious epithet. Doubtless these difficulties would be much minimized in America, if we faced our own race problem with courage and intelligence, and these very Mediterranean immigrants might give us valuable help. Certainly they are less conscious than the Anglo-Saxon of color distinctions, perhaps because of their traditional familiarity with Carthage and Egypt. They listened with respect and enthusiasm to a scholarly address delivered by Professor Du Bois at Hull-House on a Lincoln's birthday, with apparently no consciousness of that race difference which color seems to accentuate so absurdly, and upon my return from various conferences held in the interest of "the advancement of colored people," I have had many illuminating conversations with my cosmopolitan neighbors.

The celebration of national events has always been a source of new understanding and companionship with the members of the contiguous foreign colonies not only between them and their American neighbors but between them and their own children. One of our earliest Italian events was a rousing commemoration of Garibaldi's birthday, and his imposing bust presented to Hull-House that evening, was long the chief ornament of our front hall. It called forth great enthusiasm from the *connazionali* whom Ruskin calls, not the "common people" of Italy, but the "companion people" because of their power for swift sympathy.

A huge Hellenic meeting held at Hull-House, in which the achievements of the classic period were set forth both in Greek and English by scholars of well-known repute, brought us into a new sense of fellowship with all our Greek neighbors. As the mayor of Chicago was seated upon the right hand of the dignified senior priest of the Greek Church and they were greeted alternately in the national hymns of America and Greece, one felt a curious sense of the possibility of transplanting to new and crude Chicago, some of the traditions of Athens itself, so deeply cherished in the hearts of this group of citizens. . . .

SELECTION

A Literary Radical on Immigrants and National Culture: Randolph Bourne, "Trans-national America" (1916)

The most striking thing about this article to one who has read many of the materials of American history is how remarkably ahead of its time it was. The values Bourne argued for in 1916 were not widely accepted until the 1930s and World War II, and there are thousands even today who regard as heretical such a concept of American culture as his.

The whole idea of the melting pot was a mistake, said Bourne. It was, first, a sham, because it did not really mean creating a new culture which would be an amalgam of the various immigrant cultures with the Anglo-Saxon civilization but actually meant a forcing of the immigrants into the Yankee mold. Second, the melting pot did not really bring full assimilation, which was on the whole fortunate. "The foreign cultures have not been melted down or run together, made into some homogeneous Americanism, and benefit, not only of themselves but of all the native 'Americanism' around them." And third, the degree to which there was a melting pot was unfortunate; melting created "insipidity," threatened to create "a tasteless, colorless fluid of uniformity." The goal actually should be cosmopolitanism, a "transnational America," or to use a more recent sociological term, "cultural pluralism." The results of narrow nationalism were disastrous, and Bourne pointed to the war in Europe to document his point. But to America there was given a great opportunity, an opportunity to build a cosmopolitan national culture. "In a world which has dreamed of internationalism, we find that we have all unawares been building up the first international nation."

Born in Bloomfield, New Jersey, in 1886 to a family whose origins went back to the English migration of the early seventeenth century, Bourne was a brilliant but tragic figure. He was a stunted hunchback with an unusually large head and twisted face. His family had been moderately well to do when he was a boy, but a change of luck required that he go to work when he finished high school and not attend Princeton, where he had been accepted. For six years he made a poor living as a piano teacher and operator of a machine that perforated player-piano rolls. In 1909, having won a scholarship, he began study at Columbia University. Columbia did a first-rate job of awakening and educating the young man. He worked with many great professors—Charles A. Beard, John Erskine, Frederick Woodbridge, and others—but it was John Dewey who had the greatest influence upon him. Through Dewey, Bourne became interested in the problems of education. His articles in The New Republic *on education, particularly on the Gary, Indiana, experimental schools that are mentioned in this selection, brought him national attention.*

Bourne opposed America's entry into World War I and refused to support the war. His opposition to the war was strongly anticipated at many points in this article. Many periodicals closed their columns to him during the war, and Bourne suffered economically as well as psychologically. He died of pneumonia only five weeks after the armistice.

For further information on Bourne see, besides his own writing, Louis Filler, Randolph Bourne *(Washington: Public Affairs Press, 1943). The full citation for this article: Randolph Silliman Bourne, "Trans-national America,"* The Atlantic Monthly, *volume 118, July, 1916, pages 86–97. The selection is reproduced here in slightly abridged form.*

No reverberatory effect of the great war has caused American public opinion more solicitude than the failure of the 'melting-pot.' The discovery of diverse nationalistic feelings among our great alien population has come to most people as an intense shock. It has brought out the unpleasant inconsistencies of our traditional beliefs. We have had to watch hard-hearted old Brahmins virtuously indignant at the spectacle of the immigrant refusing to be melted, while they jeer at patriots like Mary Antin who write about 'our forefathers.' We have had to listen to publicists who express themselves as stunned by the evidence of vigorous nationalistic and cultural movements in this country among Germans, Scandinavians, Bohemians, and Poles, while in the same breath they insist that the alien shall be forcibly assimilated to that Anglo-Saxon tradition which they unquestioningly label 'American.'

As the unpleasant truth has come upon us that assimilation in this country was proceeding on lines very different from those we had marked out for it, we found ourselves inclined to blame those who were thwarting our prophecies. The truth became culpable. We blamed the war, we blamed the Germans. And then we discovered with a moral shock that these movements had been making great headway before the war even began. We found that the tendency, reprehensible and paradoxical as it might be, has been for the national clusters of immigrants, as they became more and more firmly established and more and more prosperous, to cultivate more and more assiduously the literatures and cultural traditions of their homelands. Assimilation, in other words, instead of washing out the memories of Europe, made them more and more intensely real. Just as these clusters became more and more objectively American, did they become more and more German or Scandinavian or Bohemian or Polish.

To face the fact that our aliens are already strong enough to take a share in the direction of their own destiny, and that the strong cultural movements represented by the foreign press, schools, and colonies are a challenge to our facile attempts, is not, however, to admit the failure of Americanization. It is not to fear the failure of democracy. It is rather to urge us to an investigation of what Americanism may rightly mean. It is to ask ourselves whether our ideal has been broad or narrow—whether perhaps the time has not come to assert a higher ideal than the 'melting-pot.' Surely we cannot be certain of our spiritual democracy when, claiming to melt the nations within us to a comprehension of our free and democratic institutions, we fly into panic at the first sign of their own will and tendency. We act as if we wanted Americanization to take place only on our own terms, and not by the consent of the governed. All our elaborate machinery of settlement and school and union, of social and political naturalization, however, will move with friction just in so far as it neglects to take into account this strong and virile insistence that America shall be what the immigrant will have a hand in making it, and not what a ruling class, descendant of those British stocks which were the first permanent immigrants, decide that America shall be made. This is the condition which confronts us, and which demands a clear and general readjustment of our attitude and our ideal.

I

Mary Antin is right when she looks upon our foreign-born as the people who missed the Mayflower and came over on the first boat they could find. But she forgets that when they did come it was not upon other Mayflowers, but upon a 'Maiblume,' a 'Fleur de Mai,' a 'Fior di Maggio,' a 'Majblomst.' These people were not mere arrivals from the same family, to be welcomed as understood and long-loved, but strangers to the neighbor-hood, with whom a long process of settling down had to take place. For they brought with them their national and racial characters, and each new national quota had to wear slowly away the contempt with which its mere alienness got itself greeted. Each had to make its way slowly from the lowest strata of unskilled labor up to a level where it satisfied the ac-credited norms of social success.

We are all foreign-born or the descendants of foreign-born, and if dis-tinctions are to be made between us they should rightly be on some other ground than indigenousness. The early colonists came over with motives no less colonial than the later. They did not come to be assimilated in an American melting-pot. They did not come to adopt the culture of the American Indian. They had not the smallest intention of 'giving themselves without reservation' to the new country. They came to get freedom to live as they wanted to. They came to escape from the stifling air and chaos of the old world; they came to make their fortune in a new land. They in-vented no new social framework. Rather they brought over bodily the old ways to which they had been accustomed. Tightly concentrated on a hostile frontier, they were conservative beyond belief. Their pioneer daring was reserved for the objective conquest of material resources. In their folkways, in their social and political institutions, they were, like every colonial people, slavishly imitative of the mother-country. So that, in spite of the 'Revolution,' our whole legal and political system remained more English than the English, petrified and unchanging, while in England law devel-oped to meet the needs of the changing times.

It is just this English-American conservatism that has been our chief obstacle to social advance. We have needed the new peoples—the order of the German and Scandinavian, the turbulence of the Slav and Hun—to save us from our own stagnation. I do not mean that the illiterate Slav is now the equal of the New Englander of pure descent. He is raw material to be educated, not into a New Englander, but into a socialized American along such lines as those thirty nationalities are being educated in the amazing schools of Gary. I do not believe that this process is to be one of decades of evolution. The spectacle of Japan's sudden jump from mediævalism to post-modernism should have destroyed that superstition. We are not dealing with individuals who are to 'evolve.' We are dealing with their children, who, with that education we are about to have, will start level with all of us. Let us cease to think of ideals like democracy as magical qualities inherent in certain peoples. Let us speak, not of in-ferior races, but of inferior civilizations. We are all to educate and to be educated. These peoples in America are in a common enterprise. It is not what we are now that concerns us, but what this plastic next generation may become in the light of a new cosmopolitan ideal.

We are not dealing with static factors, but with fluid and dynamic gene-rations. To contrast the older and the newer immigrants and see the one class as democratically motivated by love of liberty, and the other by mere money-getting, is not to illuminate the future. To think of earlier nationali-ties as culturally assimilated to America, while we picture the later as a sodden and resistive mass, makes only for bitterness and misunderstanding. There may be a difference between these earlier and these later stocks, but it lies neither in motive for coming nor in strength of cultural allegiance to the homeland. The truth is that no more tenacious cultural allegiance to the mother country has been shown by any alien nation than by the ruling class of Anglo-Saxon descendants in these American States. English snobberies, English religion, English literary styles, English literary reverences and canons, English ethics, English superiorities, have been the cultural food that we have drunk in from our mothers' breasts. The distinctively American spirit—pioneer, as distinguished from the reminiscently English—that appears in Whitman and Emerson and James, has had to exist on sufferance alongside of this other cult, unconsciously belittled by our cultural makers of opinion. No country has perhaps had so great indigenous genius which had so little influence on the country's traditions and expressions. The unpopular and dreaded German-American of the present day is a beginning amateur in comparison with those foolish Anglophiles of Boston and New York and Philadelphia whose reversion to cultural types sees uncritically in England's cause the cause of Civilization, and, under the guise of ethical independence of thought, carries along European traditions which are no more 'American' than the German categories themselves.

It speaks well for German-American innocence of heart or else for its lack of imagination that it has not turned the hyphen stigma into a 'Tu quoque!' If there were to be any hyphens scattered about, clearly they should be affixed to those English descendants who had had centuries of time to be made American where the German had had only half a century. Most significantly has the war brought out of them this alien virus, showing them still loving English things, owing allegiance to the English Kultur, moved by English shibboleths and prejudice. It is only because it has been the ruling class in this country that bestowed the epithets that we have not heard copiously and scornfully of 'hyphenated English-Americans.' But even our quarrels with England have had the bad temper, the extravagance, of family quarrels. The Englishman of to-day nags us and dislikes us in that personal, peculiarly intimate way in which he dislikes the Australian, or as we may dislike our younger brothers. He still thinks of us incorrigibly as 'colonials.' America—official, controlling, literary, political America—is still, as a writer recently expressed it, 'culturally speaking, a self-governing dominion of the British Empire.'

The non-English American can scarcely be blamed if he sometimes thinks of the Anglo-Saxon predominance in America as little more than a predominance of priority. The Anglo-Saxon was merely the first immigrant, the first to found a colony. He has never really ceased to be the descendant of immigrants, nor has he ever succeeded in transforming that colony into a real nation, with a tenacious, richly woven fabric of native culture. Colonials from the other nations have come and settled down beside him. They found no definite native culture which should startle them out of their colonialism, and consequently they looked back to their mother-country, as the earlier Anglo-Saxon immigrant was looking back to his. What has been offered the newcomer has been the chance to learn English, to become a citizen, to salute the flag. And those elements of our ruling classes who are responsible for the public schools, the settlements, all the organizations for amelioration in the cities, have every reason to be proud of the care and labor which they have devoted to absorbing the immigrant. His opportunities the immigrant has taken to gladly, with almost a pathetic eagerness to make his way in the new land without friction or disturbance. The common language has made not only for the necessary communication, but for all the amenities of life.

If freedom means the right to do pretty much as one pleases, so long as one does not interfere with others, the immigrant has found freedom, and the ruling element has been singularly liberal in its treatment of the invading hordes. But if freedom means a democratic coöperation in determining the ideals and purposes and industrial and social institutions of a country, then the immigrant has not been free, and the Anglo-Saxon element is guilty of just what every dominant race is guilty of in every European country: the imposition of its own culture upon the minority peoples. The fact that this imposition has been so mild and, indeed, semi-conscious does not alter its quality. And the war has brought out just the degree to which that purpose of 'Americanizing,' that is, 'Anglo-Saxonizing,' the immigrant has failed.

For the Anglo-Saxon now in his bitterness to turn upon the other peoples, talk about their 'arrogance,' scold them for not being melted in a pot which never existed, is to betray the unconscious purpose which lay at the bottom of his heart. It betrays too the possession of a racial jealousy similar to that of which he is now accusing the so-called 'hypenates.' Let the Anglo-Saxon be proud enough of the heroic toil and heroic sacrifices which moulded the nation. But let him ask himself, if he had had to depend on the English descendants, where he would have been living to-day. To those of us who see in the exploitation of unskilled labor the strident red *leit-motif* of our civilization, the settling of the country presents a great social drama as the waves of immigration broke over it.

Let the Anglo-Saxon ask himself where he would have been if these races had not come? Let those who feel the inferiority of the non-Anglo-Saxon immigrant contemplate that region of the States which has remained the most distinctively 'American,' the South. Let him ask himself whether he would really like to see the foreign hordes Americanized into such an Americanization. Let him ask himself how superior this native civilization is to the great 'alien' states of Wisconsin and Minnesota, where Scandinavians, Poles, and Germans have self-consciously labored to preserve their traditional culture, while being outwardly and satisfactorily American. Let him ask himself how much more wisdom, intelligence, industry and social leadership has come out of these alien states than out of all the truly American ones. The South, in fact, while this vast Northern development has gone on, still remains an English colony, stagnant and complacent, having progressed culturally scarcely beyond the early Victorian era. It is culturally sterile because it has had no advantage of cross-fertilization like the Northern states. What has happened in states such as Wisconsin and Minnesota is that strong foreign cultures have struck root in a new and fertile soil. America has meant liberation, and German and Scandinavian political ideas and social energies have expanded to a new potency. The process has not been at all the fancied 'assimilation' of the Scandinavian or Teuton. Rather has it been a process of their assimilation of us—I speak as an Anglo-Saxon. The foreign cultures have not been melted down or run together, made into some homogeneous Americanism, but have remained distinct but coöperating to the greater glory and benefit, not only of themselves but of all the native 'Americanism' around them.

What we emphatically do not want is that these distinctive qualities should be washed out into a tasteless, colorless fluid of uniformity. Already we have far too much of this insipidity,—masses of people who are cultural half-breeds, neither assimilated Anglo-Saxons nor nationals of another culture. Each national colony in this country seems to retain in its foreign press, its vernacular literature, its schools, its intellectual and patriotic leaders, a central cultural nucleus. From this nucleus the colony extends out by imperceptible gradations to a fringe where national characteristics are all but lost. Our cities are filled with these half-breeds who retain their foreign names but have lost the foreign savor. This does not mean that they have actually been changed into New Englanders or Middle Westerners. It does not mean that they have been really Americanized. It means that, letting slip from them whatever native culture they had, they have substituted for it only the most rudimentary American— the American culture of the cheap newspaper, the 'movies,' the popular song, the ubiquitous automobile. The unthinking who survey this class call them assimilated, Americanized. The great American public school has done its work. With these people our institutions are safe. We may thrill with dread at the aggressive hyphenate, but this tame flabbiness is accepted as Americanization. The same moulders of opinion whose ideal is to melt the different races into Anglo-Saxon gold hail this poor product as the satisfying result of their alchemy. . . .

II

If we come to find this point of view plausible, we shall have to give up the search for our native 'American' culture. With the exception of the South and that New England which, like the Red Indian, seems to be passing into solemn oblivion, there is no distinctively American culture. It is apparently our lot rather to be a federation of cultures. This we have been for half a century, and the war has made it ever more evident that this is what we are destined to remain. This will not mean, however, that there are not expressions of indigenous genius that could not have sprung from any other soil. Music, poetry, philosophy, have been singularly fertile and new. Strangely enough, American genius has flared forth just in those directions which are least understood of the people. If the American note is bigness, action, the objective as contrasted with the reflective life, where is the epic expression of this spirit? Our drama and our fiction, the peculiar fields for the expression of action and objectivity, are somehow exactly the fields of the spirit which remain poor and mediocre. American materialism is in some way inhibited from getting into impressive artistic form its own energy with which it bursts. Nor is it any better in architecture, the least romantic and subjective of all the arts. We are inarticulate of the very values which we profess to idealize. But in the finer forms —music, verse, the essay, philosophy—the American genius puts forth work equal to any of its contemporaries. Just in so far as our American genius has expressed the pioneer spirit, the adventurous, forward-looking drive of a colonial empire, is it representative of that whole America of the many races and peoples, and not of any partial or traditional enthusiasm. And only as that pioneer note is sounded can we really speak of the American culture. As long as we thought of Americanism in terms of the 'melting-pot,' our American cultural tradition lay in the past. It was something to which the new Americans were to be moulded. In the light of our changing ideal of Americanism, we must perpetrate the paradox that our American cultural tradition lies in the future. It will be what we all together make out of this incomparable opportunity of attacking the future with a new key.

Whatever American nationalism turns out to be, it is certain to become something utterly different from the nationalisms of twentieth-century Europe. This wave of reactionary enthusiasm to play the orthodox nationalistic game which is passing over the country is scarcely vital enough to last. We cannot swagger and thrill to the same national self-feeling. We must give new edges to our pride. We must be content to avoid the unnumbered woes that national patriotism has brought in Europe, and that fiercely heightened pride and self-consciousness. Alluring as this is, we must allow our imaginations to transcend this scarcely veiled belligerency. We can be serenely too proud to fight if our pride embraces the creative forces of civilization which armed contest nullifies. We can be too proud to fight if our code of honor transcends that of the schoolboy on the playground surrounded by his jeering mates. Our honor must be positive and creative, and not the mere jealous and negative protectiveness against metaphysical violations of our technical rights. When the doctrine is put forth that in one American flows the mystic blood of all our country's sacred honor, freedom, and prosperity, so that an injury to him is to be the signal for turning our whole nation into that clan-feud of horror and reprisal which would be war, then we find ourselves back among the musty schoolmen of the Middle Ages, and not in any pragmatic and realistic America of the twentieth century.

We should hold our gaze to what America has done, not what mediæval codes of dueling she has failed to observe. We have transplanted European modernity to our soil, without the spirit that inflames it and turns all its energy into mutual destruction. Out of these foreign peoples there has somehow been squeezed the poison. An America, 'hyphenated' to bitterness, is somehow non-explosive. For, even if we all hark back in sympathy to a European nation, even if the war has set every one vibrating to some emotional string twanged on the other side of the Atlantic, the effect has been one of almost dramatic harmlessness.

What we have really been witnessing, however unappreciatively, in this country has been a thrilling and bloodless battle of Kulturs. In that arena of friction which has been the most dramatic—between the hyphenated German-American and the hyphenated English-American—there have emerged rivalries of philosophies which show up deep traditional attitudes, points of view which accurately reflect the gigantic issues of the war. America has mirrored the spiritual issues. The vicarious struggle has been played out peacefully here in the mind. We have seen the stout resistiveness of the old moral interpretation of history on which Victorian England thrived and made itself great in its own esteem. The clean and immensely satisfying vision of the war as a contest between right and wrong; the the enthusiastic support of the Allies as the incarnation of virtue-on-a-rampage; the fierce envisaging of their selfish national purposes as the ideals of justice, freedom and democracy—all this has been thrown with intensest force against the German realistic interpretations in terms of the struggle for power and the virility of the integrated State. America has been the intellectual battleground of the nations.

III

The failure of the melting-pot, far from closing the great American democratic experiment, means that it has only just begun. Whatever American nationalism turns out to be, we see already that it will have a color richer and more exciting than our ideal has hitherto encompassed. In a world which has dreamed of internationalism, we find that we have all unawares been building up the first international nation. The voices which have cried for a tight and jealous nationalism of the European pattern are failing. From that ideal, however valiantly and disinterestedly it has been set for us, time and tendency have moved us further and further away. What we have achieved has been rather a cosmopolitan federation of national colonies, of foreign cultures, from whom the sting of devastating competition has been removed. America is already the world-federation in miniature, the continent where for the first time in history has been achieved that miracle of hope, the peaceful living side by side, with character substantially preserved, of the most heterogeneous peoples under the sun. Nowhere else has such contiguity been anything but the breeder of misery. Here, notwithstanding our tragic failures of adjustment, the outlines are already too clear not to give us a new vision and a new orientation of the American mind in the world.

It is for the American of the younger generation to accept this cosmopolitanism, and carry it along with self-conscious and fruitful purpose. In his colleges, he is already getting, with the study of modern history and politics, the modern literatures, economic geography, the privilege of a cosmopolitan outlook such as the people of no other nation of to-day in Europe can possibly secure. If he is still a colonial, he is no longer the colonial of one partial culture, but of many. He is a colonial of the world. Colonialism has grown into cosmopolitanism, and his motherland is no one nation, but all who have anything life-enhancing to offer to the spirit. That vague sympathy which the France of ten years ago was feeling for the world—a sympathy which was drowned in the terrible reality of war—may be the modern American's, and that in a positive and aggressive sense. If the American is parochial, it is in sheer wantonness or cowardice. His provincialism is the measure of his fear of bogies or the defect of his imagination.

Indeed, it is not uncommon for the eager Anglo-Saxon who goes to a vivid American university to-day to find his true friends not among his own race but among the acclimatized German or Austrian, the acclimatized Jew, the acclimatized Scandinavian or Italian. In them he finds the cosmopolitan note. In these youths, foreign-born or the children of foreign-born parents, he is likely to find many of his old inbred morbid problems washed away. These friends are oblivious to the repressions of that tight little society in which he so provincially grew up. He has a pleasurable sense of liberation from the stale and familiar attitudes of those whose ingrowing culture has scarcely created anything vital for his America of to-day. He breathes a larger air. In his new enthusiasms for continental literature, for unplumbed Russian depths, for French clarity of thought, for Teuton philosophies of power, he feels himself citizen of a larger world. He may be absurdly superficial, his outward-reaching wonder may ignore all the stiller and homelier virtues of his Anglo-Saxon home, but he has at least found the clue to that international mind which will be essential to all men and women of good-will if they are ever to save this Western world of ours from suicide. His new friends have gone through a similar evolution. America has burned most of the baser metal also from them. Meeting now with this common American background, all of them may yet retain that distinctiveness of their native cultures and their national spiritual slants. They are more valuable and interesting to each other for being different, yet that difference could not be creative were it not for this new cosmopolitan outlook which America has given them and which they all equally possess.

A college where such a spirit is possible even to the smallest degree, has within itself already the seeds of this international intellectual world of the future. It suggests that the contribution of America will be an intellectual internationalism which goes far beyond the mere exchange of scientific ideas and discoveries and the cold recording of facts. It will be an intellectual sympathy which is not satisfied until it has got at the heart of the different cultural expressions, and felt as they feel. It may have immense preferences, but it will make understanding and not indignation its end. Such a sympathy will unite and not divide.

Against the thinly disguised panic which calls itself 'patriotism' and the thinly disguised militarism which calls itself 'preparedness' the cosmopolitan ideal is set. This does not mean that those who hold it are for a policy of drift. They, too, long passionately for an integrated and disciplined America. But they do not want one which is integrated only for domestic economic exploitation of the workers or for predatory economic imperialism among the weaker peoples. They do not want one that is integrated by coercion or militarism, or for the truculent assertion of a mediæval code of honor and of doubtful rights. They believe that the most effective integration will be one which coördinates the diverse elements and turns them consciously toward working out together the place of America in the world-situation. They demand for integration a genuine integrity, a wholeness and soundness of enthusiasm and purpose which can only come when no national colony within our America feels that it is being discriminated against or that its cultural case is being prejudged. This strength of coöperation, this feeling that all who are here may have a hand in the destiny of America, will make for a finer spirit of integration than any narrow 'Americanism' or forced chauvinism.

In this effort we may have to accept some form of that dual citizenship which meets with so much articulate horror among us. Dual citizenship we may have to recognize as the rudimentary form of that international citizenship to which, if our words mean anything, we aspire. We have assumed unquestioningly that mere participation in the political life of the United States must cut the new citizen off from all sympathy with his old allegiance. Anything but a bodily transfer of devotion from one sovereignty to another has been viewed as a sort of moral treason against the Republic. We have insisted that the immigrant whom we welcomed escaping from the very exclusive nationalism of his European home shall forthwith adopt a nationalism just as exclusive, just as narrow, and even less legitimate because it is founded on no warm traditions of his own. Yet a nation like France is said to permit a formal and legal dual citizenship even at the present time. Though a citizen of hers may pretend to cast off his allegiance in favor of some other sovereignty, he is still subject to her laws when he returns. Once a citizen, always a citizen, no matter how many new citizenships he may embrace. And such a dual citizenship seems to us sound and right. For it recognizes that, although the Frenchman may accept the formal institutional framework of his new country and indeed become intensely loyal to it, yet his Frenchness he will never lose. What makes up the fabric of his soul will always be of this Frenchness, so that unless he becomes utterly degenerate he will always to some degree dwell still in his native environment.

Indeed, does not the cultivated American who goes to Europe practice a dual citizenship, which, if not formal, is no less real? The American who lives abroad may be the least expatriate of men. If he falls in love with French ways and French thinking and French democracy and seeks to saturate himself with the new spirit, he is guilty of at least a dual spiritual citizenship. He may be still American, yet he feels himself through sympathy also a Frenchman. And he finds that this expansion involves no shameful conflict within him, no surrender of his native attitude. He has rather for the first time caught a glimpse of the cosmopolitan spirit. And after wandering about through many races and civilizations he may return to America to find them all here living vividly and crudely, seeking the same adjustment that he made. He sees the new peoples here with a new vision. They are no longer masses of aliens, waiting to be 'assimilated,' waiting to be melted down into the indistinguishable dough of Anglo-Saxonism. They are rather threads of living and potent cultures, blindly striving to weave themselves into a novel international nation, the first the world has seen. In an Austria-Hungary or a Prussia the stronger of these cultures would be moving almost instinctively to subjugate the weaker. But in America those wills-to-power are turned in a different direction into learning how to live together.

Along with dual citizenship we shall have to accept, I think, that free and mobile passage of the immigrant between America and his native land again which now arouses so much prejudice among us. We shall have to accept the immigrant's return for the same reason that we consider justified our own flitting about the earth. To stigmatize the alien who works in America for a few years and returns to his own land, only perhaps to seek American fortune again, is to think in narrow nationalistic terms. It is to ignore the cosmopolitan significance of this migration. It is to ignore the fact that the returning immigrant is often a missionary to an inferior civilization.

This migratory habit has been especially common with the unskilled laborers who have been pouring into the United States in the last dozen years from every country in southeastern Europe. Many of them return to spend their earnings in their own country or to serve their country in war. But they return with an entirely new critical outlook, and a sense of the superiority of American organization to the primitive living around them. This continued passage to and fro has already raised the material standard of living in many regions of these backward countries. For these regions are thus endowed with exactly what they need, the capital for the exploitation of their natural resources, and the spirit of enterprise. America is thus educating these laggard peoples from the very bottom of society up, awakening vast masses to a new-born hope for the future. In the migratory Greek, therefore, we have not the parasitic alien, the doubtful American asset, but a symbol of that cosmopolitan interchange which is coming, in spite of all war and national exclusiveness.

Only America, by reason of the unique liberty of opportunity and traditional isolation for which she seems to stand, can lead in this cosmopolitan enterprise. Only the American—and in this category I include the migratory alien who has lived with us and caught the pioneer spirit and a sense of new social vistas—has the chance to become that citizen of the world. America is coming to be, not a nationality but a trans-nationality, a weaving back and forth, with the other lands, of many threads of all sizes and colors. Any movement which attempts to thwart this weaving, or to dye the fabric any one color, or disentangle the threads of the strands, is false to this cosmopolitan vision. I do not mean that we shall necessarily glut ourselves with the raw product of humanity. It would be folly to absorb the nations faster than we could weave them. We have no duty either to admit or reject. It is purely a question of expediency. What concerns us is the fact that the strands are here. We must have a policy and an ideal for an actual situation. Our question is, What shall we do with our America? How are we likely to get the more creative America—by confining our imaginations to the ideal of the melting-pot, or broadening them to some such cosmopolitan conception as I have been vaguely sketching?

The war has shown America to be unable, though isolated geographically and politically from a European world-situation, to remain aloof and irresponsible. She is a wandering star in a sky dominated by two colossal constellations of states. Can she not work out some position of her own, some life of being in, yet not quite of, this seething and embroiled European world? This is her only hope and promise. A trans-nationality of all the nations, it is spiritually impossible for her to pass into the orbit of any one. It will be folly to hurry herself into a premature and sentimental nationalism, or to emulate Europe and play fast and loose with the forces that drag into war. No Americanization will fulfill this vision which does not recognize the uniqueness of this trans-nationalism of ours. The Anglo-Saxon attempt to fuse will only create enmity and distrust. The crusade against 'hyphenates' will only inflame the partial patriotism of trans-nationals, and cause them to assert their European traditions in strident and unwholesome ways. But the attempt to weave a wholly novel international nation out of our chaotic America will liberate and harmonize the creative power of all these peoples and give them the new spiritual citizenship, as so many individuals have already been given, of a world.

Is it a wild hope that the undertow of opposition to metaphysics in international relations, opposition to militarism, is less a cowardly provincialism than a groping for this higher cosmopolitan ideal? One can understand the irritated restlessness with which our proud pro-British colonists contemplate a heroic conflict across the seas in which they have no part. It was inevitable that our necessary inaction should evolve in their minds into the bogey of national shame and dishonor. But let us be careful about accepting their sensitiveness as final arbiter. Let us look at our reluctance rather as the first crude beginnings of assertion on the part of certain strands in our nationality that they have a right to a voice in the construction of the American ideal. Let us face realistically the America we have around us. Let us work with the forces that are at work. Let us make something of this trans-national spirit instead of outlawing it. Already we are living this cosmopolitan America. What we need is everywhere a vivid consciousness of the new ideal. Deliberate headway must be made against the survivals of the melting-pot ideal for the promise of American life.

We cannot Americanize America worthily by sentimentalizing and moralizing history. When the best schools are expressly renouncing the questionable duty of teaching patriotism by means of history, it is not the time to force shibboleth upon the immigrant. This form of Americanization has been heard because it appealed to the vestiges of our old sentimentalized and moralized patriotism. This has so far held the field as the expression of the new American's new devotion. The inflections of other voices have been drowned. They must be heard. We must see if the lesson of the war has not been for hundreds of these later Americans a vivid realization of their trans-nationality, a new consciousness of what America meant to them as a citizenship in the world. It is the vague historic idealisms which have provided the fuel for the European flame. Our American ideal can make no progress until we do away with this romantic gilding of the past.

All our idealisms must be those of future social goals in which all can participate, the good life of personality lived in the environment of the Beloved Community. No mere doubtful triumphs of the past, which redound to the glory of only one of our trans-nationalities, can satisfy us. It must be a future America, on which all can unite, which pulls us irresistibly toward it, as we understand each other more warmly.

To make real this striving amid dangers and apathies is work for a younger *intelligentsia* of America. Here is an enterprise of integration into which we can all pour ourselves, of a spiritual welding which should make us, if the final menace ever came, not weaker, but infinitely strong.

PART **THREE**

War and Peace

One of the most important watersheds in American history—European history, too—was the half decade between 1914 and 1919. One could argue that the Serbian nationalist who assassinated the crown prince of the Austro-Hungarian Empire at Sarajevo killed the nineteenth century and its relatively stable way of life as well. The war brought unprecedentedly rapid change to America; and when the shooting and shouting were over and the dust settled again, the old prewar America and the prewar world were gone.

We usually think of America's experience during the war years in terms of a swing from isolation to international participation and back again to isolation. There is much to be said for this way of looking at the period, but we miss an important dimension of the war if we concentrate on the isolation-internationalism aspect to the exclusion of consideration of the war as a stimulus to mass society. Mass organization, mass markets, mass finance, mass destruction, mass production, and mass manipulation of social attitudes and values—all of them aspects of the twentieth-century world—became part of American life during these years, particularly in 1917 and 1918, as never they had before.

The documents in this part illustrate both these ways of looking at the war. Selections 20 through 22, which have to do with the nation's involvement in the war, and Selections 26 through 28 are basically related to the isolation-internationalism aspect, although the Wilson and Norris speeches are certainly not irrelevant to the subject of mass suasion. The same double framework can be used to view Selection 29. Selections 23 through 25 are concerned with various aspects of mass warfare.

Submarines and Loans during the Period of Neutrality

Soon after the war began in Europe in 1914, President Wilson issued a formal proclamation of neutrality in which he said this nation "must be neutral in fact as well as in name . . . impartial in thought as well as in action." Two and one-half years later, the United States declared war upon Germany. The reasons for this change are many and complex—all historical causation is as complicated as life itself because it is life—but most historians would agree that German submarine warfare and American loans to the Allies were important factors in the process of America's moving from neutrality to belligerency. These documents, the notes between Washington and Berlin over the torpedoing of the Sussex *and a letter from Secretary Lansing to President Wilson, have to do with these two factors.*

Great Britain effectively controlled the surface of the seas around Europe and prevented the shipment of goods to Germany; Germany tried to counter with a submarine barrier around Great Britain. German submarines brought a crisis in American-German relations only a few months after the war began, particularly after a German U-boat sank the English liner Lusitania *on May 7, 1915, with the loss of 128 American lives. The next turning point came after the* Sussex *affair in March, 1916. In the first of the documents reprinted here, Secretary Lansing warned Germany that unless it "should now immediately declare and effect an abandonment of its present methods of submarine warfare against passenger and freight-carrying vessels," the United States would "have no choice but to sever diplomatic relations." In the reply, the second document reprinted here, German Foreign Minister Gottlieb von Jagow said that merchant vessels "shall not be sunk without warning" but added a condition: that the United States demand that Great Britain observe prewar rules of international law. "Should the steps taken by the Government of the United States not attain the object it desires, to have the laws of humanity followed by all belligerent nations [that is, have Great Britain cease the blockade of Germany], the German Government would then be facing a new situation in which it must reserve itself complete liberty of decision." Wilson chose to accept the assurance and ignore the condition. The German note became known as the* Sussex *pledge. Until the end of January, 1917, Germany observed the pledge, tenuous as it was. Then it announced that effective February 1, it would resort to unrestricted submarine warfare. Immediately the United States broke diplomatic relations. Soon there were torpedoings of American ships, and in April Wilson asked Congress for a war declaration. Germany apparently gambled that submarines would deliver a knockout blow before American power would be felt on European battlefields. The* Sussex *notes reprinted here are from* Papers Relating to the Foreign Relations of the United States, 1916, *supplement,* The World War *(Washington: Government Printing Office, 1929), pages 232–234, 257–260.*

Critics of the Wilson administration have declared that its policy of allowing American bankers to extend credits and, later, ordinary loans through the sale of bonds had the effect of tying the American economy to the Allied war effort and required that the United States guarantee an Allied victory. The letter from Lansing to Wilson explains the economic background of these loans. Presi-

dent Wilson agreed with Secretaries Lansing and McAdoo, and soon bankers were privately and orally told that the government no longer objected to outright loans. J. P. Morgan and Company soon floated a 500-million-dollar issue of Allied bonds, a considerably larger sum than had been extended under the previous credit system. By the time the United States entered the war, Allied governments had borrowed about 2.3 billion dollars in America. Of this sum, England borrowed about 1.5 billion dollars. German borrowing in America was comparatively meager, about 27 million dollars.

This letter from the Secretary of State to the President is from Papers Relating to the Foreign Relations of the United States: The Lansing Papers, 1914–1920 *(Washington: Government Printing Office, 1939), volume 1, pages 144–147.*

The bibliography on American involvement in World War I is extensive. The best account from the point of view sympathetic to Wilson is Charles Seymour, American Neutrality, 1914–1917 *(New Haven, Conn.: Yale, 1935). The most comprehensive revisionist account is Charles C. Tansill,* America Goes to War *(Boston: Little, Brown, 1938), and the best written from that general viewpoint is Walter Millis,* Road to War: America, 1914–1917 *(Boston: Houghton Mifflin, 1935). Ernest R. May,* The World War and American Isolation, 1914–1917 *(Cambridge, Mass.: Harvard, 1959), is important because it is based on German and British as well as American sources.*

The Secretary of State to the Ambassador in Germany (Gerard)

[Telegram]

Washington, April 18, 1916, 6 p.m.

2913. You are instructed to deliver to the Secretary of Foreign Affairs a communication reading as follows:

I did not fail to transmit immediately, by telegraph, to my Government your excellency's note of the 10th instant in regard to certain attacks by German submarines, and particularly in regard to the disastrous explosion which, on March 24 last, wrecked the French S. S. *Sussex* in the English Channel. I have now the honor to deliver, under instructions from my Government, the following reply to your excellency:

Information now in the possession of the Government of the United States fully establishes the facts in the case of the *Sussex,* and the inferences which my Government has drawn from that information it regards as confirmed by the circumstances set forth in your excellency's note of the 10th instant. On the 24th of March 1916, at about 2.50 o'clock in the afternoon, the unarmed steamer *Sussex,* with 325 or more passengers on board, among whom were a number of American citizens, was torpedoed while crossing from

Folkstone to Dieppe. The *Sussex* had never been armed; was a vessel known to be habitually used only for the conveyance of passengers across the English Channel; and was not following the route taken by troopships or supply ships. About 80 of her passengers, non-combatants of all ages and sexes, including citizens of the United States, were killed or injured.

A careful, detailed, and scrupulously impartial investigation by naval and military officers of the United States has conclusively established the fact that the *Sussex* was torpedoed without warning or summons to surrender and that the torpedo by which she was struck was of German manufacture. In the view of the Government of the United States these facts from the first made the conclusion that the torpedo was fired by a German submarine unavoidable. It now considers that conclusion substantiated by the statements of your excellency's note. A full statement of the facts upon which the Government of the United States has based its conclusion is enclosed.

The Government of the United States, after having given careful consideration to the note of the Imperial Government of the 10th of April, regrets to state that the impression made upon it by the statements and proposals contained in that note is that the Imperial Government has failed to appreciate the gravity of the situation which has resulted, not alone from the attack on the *Sussex,* but from the whole method and character of submarine warfare as disclosed by the unrestrained practice of the commanders of German undersea craft during the past twelvemonth and more in the indiscriminate destruction of merchant vessels of all sorts, nationalities, and destinations. If the sinking of the *Sussex* had been an isolated case, the Government of the United States might find it possible to hope that the officer who was responsible for that act had wilfully violated his orders or had been criminally negligent in taking none of the precautions they prescribed, and that the ends of justice might be satisfied by imposing upon him an adequate punishment, coupled with a formal disavowal of the act and payment of a suitable indemnity by the Imperial Government. But, though the attack upon the *Sussex* was manifestly indefensible and caused a loss of life so tragical as to make it stand forth as one of the most terrible examples of the inhumanity of submarine warfare as the commanders of German vessels are conducting it, it unhappily does not stand alone.

On the contrary, the Government of the United States is forced by recent events to conclude that it is only one instance, even though one of the most extreme and most distressing instances, of the deliberate method and spirit of indiscriminate destruction of merchant vessels of all sorts, nationalities, and destinations which have become more and more unmistakable as the activity of German undersea vessels of war has in recent months been quickened and extended.

The Imperial Government will recall that when, in February 1915, it announced its intention of treating the waters surrounding Great Britain and Ireland as embraced within the seat of war and of destroying all merchant ships owned by its enemies that might be found within that zone of danger, and warned all vessels, neutral as well as belligerent, to keep out of the waters thus proscribed or to enter them at their peril, the Government of the United States earnestly protested. It took the position that such a policy could not be pursued without constant gross and palpable violations of the accepted law of nations, particularly if submarine craft were to be employed as its instruments, inasmuch as the rules prescribed by that law, rules founded on the principles of humanity and established for the protection of the lives of non-combatants at sea, could not in the nature of the case be observed by such vessels. It based its protest on the ground that persons of neutral nationality and vessels of neutral ownership would be exposed to extreme and intolerable risks; and that no right to close any part of the high seas could lawfully be asserted by the Imperial Government in the circumstances then existing. The law of nations in these matters, upon which the Government of the United States based that protest, is not of recent origin or founded upon merely arbitrary principles set up by convention. It is based, on the contrary, upon manifest principles of humanity and has long been established with the approval and by the express assent of all civilized nations.

The Imperial Government, notwithstanding, persisted in carrying out the policy announced, expressing the hope that the dangers involved, at any rate to neutral vessels, would be reduced to a minimum by the instructions which it had issued to the commanders of its submarines, and assuring the Government of the United States that it would take every possible precaution both to respect the rights of neutrals and to safeguard the lives of non-combatants.

In pursuance of this policy of submarine warfare against the commerce of its adversaries, thus announced and thus entered upon in despite of the solemn protest of the Government of the United States, the commanders of the Imperial Government's undersea vessels have carried on practices of such ruthless destruction which have made it more and more evident as the months have gone by that the Imperial Government has found it impracticable to put any such restraints upon them as it had hoped and promised to put. Again and again the Imperial Government has given its solemn assurances to the Government of the United States that at least passenger ships would not be thus dealt with, and yet it has repeatedly permitted its undersea commanders to disregard those assurances with entire impunity. As recently as February last it gave notice that it would regard all armed merchantmen owned by its enemies as part of the armed naval forces of its adversaries and deal with them as with men-of-war, thus, at least by implication, pledging itself to give warning to vessels which were not armed and to accord security of life to their passengers and crews; but even this limitation its submarine commanders have recklessly ignored.

Vessels of neutral ownership, even vessels of neutral ownership bound from neutral port to neutral port, have been destroyed along with vessels of belligerent ownership in constantly increasing numbers. Sometimes the merchantmen attacked have been warned and summoned to surrender before being fired on or torpedoed; sometimes their passengers and crews have been vouchsafed the poor security of being allowed to take to the ship's boats before the ship was sent to the bottom. But again and again no warning has been given, no escape even to the ship's boats allowed to those on board. Great liners like the *Lusitania* and *Arabic* and mere passenger boats like the *Sussex* have been attacked without a moment's warning, often before they have even become aware that they were in the presence of an armed ship of the enemy, and the lives of non-combatants, passengers, and crew have been destroyed wholesale and in a manner which the Government of the United States can not but regard as wanton and without the slightest color of justification. No limit of any kind has in fact been set to their indiscriminate pursuit and destruction of merchantmen of all kinds and nationalities within the waters which the Imperial Government has chosen to designate as lying within the seat of war. The roll of Americans who have lost their lives upon ships thus attacked and destroyed has grown month by month until the ominous toll has mounted into the hundreds.

The Government of the United States has been very patient. At every stage of this distressing experience of tragedy after tragedy it has sought to be governed by the most thoughtful consideration of the extraordinary circumstances of an unprecedented war and to be guided by sentiments of very genuine friendship for the people and Government of Germany. It has accepted the successive explanations and assurances of the Imperial Government as, of course, given in entire sincerity and good faith, and has hoped, even against hope, that it would prove to be possible for the Imperial Government so to order and control the acts of its naval commanders as to square its policy with the recognized principles of humanity as embodied in the law of nations. It has made every allowance for unprecedented conditions and has been willing to wait until the facts became unmistakable and were susceptible of only one interpretation.

It now owes it to a just regard for its own rights to say to the Imperial Government that that time has come. It has become painfully evident to it that the position which it took at the very outset is inevitable, namely, the use of submarines for the destruction of an enemy's commerce is, of necessity, because of the very character of the vessels employed and the very methods of attack which their employment of course involves, utterly incompatible with the principles of humanity, the long-established and incontrovertible rights of neutrals, and the sacred immunities of non-combatants.

If it is still the purpose of the Imperial Government to prosecute relentless and indiscriminate warfare against vessels of commerce by the use of submarines without regard to what the Government of the United States must consider the sacred and indisputable rules of international law and the universally recognized dictates of humanity, the Government of the United States is at last forced to the conclusion that there is but one course it can pursue. Unless the Imperial Government should now immediately declare and effect an abandonment of its present methods of submarine warfare against passenger and freight-carrying vessels, the Government of the United States can have no choice but to sever diplomatic relations with the German Empire altogether. This action the Government of the United States contemplates with the greatest reluctance but feels constrained to take in behalf of humanity and the rights of neutral nations.

LANSING

The Ambassador in Germany (Gerard) to the Secretary of State

[Telegram]

Berlin, May 4, 1916, 6 p.m.
[Received May 5. 7.30–10 p.m.]

3848. Following is the text of the note handed to me both in German and English at 5.30 this afternoon by Secretary of State for Foreign Affairs:

Foreign Office, Berlin, May 4, 1916.

The undersigned, on behalf of the Imperial Government, has the honor to present to his excellency the Ambassador of the United States, Mr. James W. Gerard, the following reply to the note of April 20 regarding the conduct of German submarine warfare:

The German Government has handed over to the proper naval authorities for further investigation the evidence concerning the *Sussex,* as communicated by the Government of the United States. Judging by results that this investigation has hitherto yielded, the German Government is alive to the possibility that the ship mentioned in the note of April 10 as torpedoed by a German submarine is actually identical with the *Sussex.* The German Government begs to reserve further communications on the matter until certain points are ascertained which are of decisive importance for establishing the facts of the case. Should it turn out that the commander was wrong in assuming the vessel to be a man-of-war, the German Government will not fail to draw the consequences resulting therefrom.

In connection with the case of the *Sussex,* the Government of the United States has made a series of statements, gist of which is the assertion that this incident is to be considered as one instance for [of] the deliberate method of indiscriminate destruction of vessels of all sorts, nationalities, and destinations by German submarine commanders. The German Government must emphatically repudiate this assertion. The German Government, however, thinks it of little avail to enter into details in the present stage of affairs, more particularly as the Government of the United States has omitted to substantiate this assertion by reference to concrete facts. The German Government will only state that it has imposed far-reaching restraints upon the use of the submarine weapon solely in consideration of the interests of neutrals, in spite of the fact that these restrictions are necessarily of advantage to Germany's enemies; no such consideration has ever been shown to the neutrals by Great Britain and her allies.

The German submarine forces have had, in fact, orders to conduct submarine warfare in accordance with the general principles of visit and search and destruction of merchant vessels as recognized by international law, the sole exception being the conduct of warfare against the enemy trade carried on enemy freight ships that are encountered in the war zone surrounding Great Britain; with regard to these no assurances have ever been given to the Government of the United States; no such assurance was contained in the declaration of February 8, 1916. The German Government can not admit any doubt that these orders have been given and are executed in good faith. Errors have actually occurred; they can in no kind of warfare be avoided altogether, and allowances must be made in the conduct of naval warfare against an enemy resorting to all kinds of ruses, whether permissible or illicit. But, apart from the possibility of errors, naval warfare, just like warfare on land, implies unavoidable dangers for neutral persons and goods entering the fighting zone. Even in cases where naval action was confined to their ordinary forms of cruiser warfare, neutral persons and goods have repeatedly come to grief. The German Government has repeatedly and explicitly pointed out the dangers from mines that have led to the loss of numerous ships. The German Government has made several proposals to the Government of the United States in order to reduce to a minimum for American travelers and goods the inherent dangers of naval warfare. Unfortunately the Government of the United States has decided not to accept these proposals; had it accepted, the Government of the United States would have been instrumental in preventing the greater part of the accidents that American citizens have met with in the meantime. The German Government still stands by its offer to come to an agreement along these lines.

As the German Government has repeatedly declared, it can not dispense with the use of the submarine weapon in the conduct of warfare against enemy trade. The German Government, however, has now decided to make a further concession in adopting the methods of submarine warfare to the interests of the neutrals; in reaching this decision the German Government has been actuated by considerations which are above the level of the disputed question.

The German Government attaches no less importance to the sacred principles of humanity than the Government of the United States. Again, it fully takes into account that both Governments have for many years cooperated in developing international law in conformity with these principles, the ultimate object of which has been always to confine warfare on sea and on land to the armed forces of the belligerents and to safeguard, as far as possible, non-combatants against the horrors of war.

But, although those considerations are of great weight, they alone would not, under the present circumstances, have determined the attitude of the German Government.

For, in answer to the appeal made by the United States Government on behalf of the sacred principles of humanity and international law, the German Government must repeat once more with all emphasis that it was not the German but the British Government which, ignoring all the accepted rules of international law, has extended this terrible war to the lives and property of non-combatants, having no regard whatever for the interests and rights of the neutrals and non-combatants that through this method of warfare have been severely injured.

In self-defense against the illegal conduct of British warfare, while fighting a bitter struggle for her national existence, Germany had to resort to the hard but effective weapon of submarine warfare. As matters stand, the German Government can not but reiterate its regret that the sentiments of humanity which the Government of the United States extends with such fervor to the unhappy victims of submarine warfare are not extended with the same warmth of feeling to the many millions of women and children who, according to the avowed intentions of the British Government, shall be starved and who, by their sufferings, shall force the victorious armies of the Central powers into ignominious capitulation. The German Government, in agreement with the German people, fails to understand this discrimination, all the more as it has repeatedly and explicitly declared itself ready to use the submarine weapon in strict conformity with the rules of international law as recognized before the outbreak of the war, if Great Britain were likewise ready to adapt her conduct of warfare to these rules. The several attempts made by the Government of the United States to prevail upon the British Government to act accordingly have failed because of the flat refusal on the part of the British Government. Moreover, Great Britain has ever since again and again violated international law, surpassing all bounds in outraging neutral rights. The latest measure adopted by Great Britain, declaring German bunker coal as contraband and establishing conditions under which alone English bunker coal shall be supplied to neutrals, is nothing but an unheard of attempt, by way of exaction, to force neutral tonnage into the service of the British trade war.

The German people knows that the Government of the United States has the power to confine this war to the armed forces of the belligerent countries in the interest of humanity and the maintenance of international law. The Government of the United States would have been certain of attaining this end had it been determined to insist against Great Britain on its incontestable rights to the freedom of the seas. But, as matters stand, the German people is under the impression that the Government of the United States, while demanding that Germany, struggling for her existence, shall restrain the use of an effective weapon, and while making the compliance with these demands a condition for the maintenance of relations with Germany, confines itself to protests against the illegal methods adopted by Germany's enemies. Moreover, the German people knows to what a considerable extent its enemies are supplied with all kinds of war material from the United States. It will therefore be understood that the appeal made by the Government of the United States to the sentiments of humanity and to the principles of international law can not, under the circumstances, meet with the same hearty response from the German people which such an appeal is otherwise always certain to find here. If the German Government, nevertheless, has resolved to go to the utmost limit of concessions, it has not alone been guided by the friendship connecting the two great nations for over a hundred years, but it also has thought of the great doom which threatens the entire civilized world should this cruel and sanguinary war be extended and prolonged.

The German Government, conscious of Germany's strength, has twice within the last few months announced before the world its readiness to make peace on a basis safeguarding Germany's vital interests, thus indicating that it is not Germany's fault if peace is still withheld from the nations of Europe.

The German Government feels all the more justified to declare that the responsibility could not be borne before the forum of mankind and history if, after 21 months' duration of the war, the submarine question under discussion between the German Government and the Government of the United States were to take a turn seriously threatening the maintenance of peace between the two nations.

As far as it lies with the German Government, it wishes to prevent things from taking such a course. The German Government, moreover, is prepared to do its utmost to confine the operations of war for the rest of its duration to the fighting forces of the belligerents, thereby also insuring the freedom of the seas, as principle upon which the German Government believes, now as before, to be in agreement with the Government of the United States.

The German Government, guided by this idea, notifies the Government of the United States that the German naval forces have received the following orders: In accordance with the general principles of visit and search and destruction of merchant vessels recognized by international law, such vessels, both within and without the area declared as naval war zone, shall not be sunk without warning and without saving human lives, unless these ships attempt to escape or offer resistance.

But neutrals can not expect that Germany, forced to fight for her existence, shall, for the sake of neutral interest, restrict the use of an effective weapon if her enemy is permitted to continue to apply at will methods of warfare violating the rules of international law. Such a demand would be incompatible with the character of neutrality, and the German Government is convinced that the Government of the United States does not think of making such a demand, knowing that the Government of the United States has repeatedly declared that it is determined to restore the principle of the freedom of the seas, from whatever quarter it has been violated.

Accordingly, the German Government is confident that, in consequence of the new orders issued to its naval forces, the Government of the United States will now also consider all impediments removed which may have been in the way of a mutual cooperation towards the restoration of the freedom of the seas during the war, as suggested in the note of July 23, 1915, and it does not doubt that the Government of the United States will now demand and insist that the British Government shall forthwith observe the rules of international law universally recognized before the war, as they are laid down in the notes presented by the Government of the United States to the

British Government on December 28, 1914, and November 5, 1915. Should the steps taken by the Government of the United States not attain the object it desires, to have the laws of humanity followed by all belligerent nations, the German Government would then be facing a new situation in which it must reserve itself complete liberty of decision.

The undersigned avails himself of this occasion to renew to the American Ambassador the assurances of his highest consideration.

[VON JAGOW]
Secretary of State

Foreign Office informs me note will be given out here to the German newspapers and American correspondents late to-morrow afternoon.

GERARD

The Secretary of State to President Wilson

Washington, September 6, 1915.

My Dear Mr. President:

Doubtless Secretary McAdoo has discussed with you the necessity of floating government loans for the belligerent nations, which are purchasing such great quantities of goods in this country, in order to avoid a serious financial situation which will not only affect them but this country as well.

Briefly the situation, as I understand it, is this: Since December 1st, 1914, to June 30, 1915, our exports have exceeded our imports by nearly a billion dollars, and it is estimated that the excess will be from July 1st to December 31, 1915, a billion and three quarters. Thus for the year 1915 the excess will be approximately two and [a] half billions of dollars.

It is estimated that the European banks have about three and [a] half billions of dollars in gold in their vaults. To withdraw any considerable amount would disastrously affect the credit of the European nations, and the consequence would be a general state of bankruptcy.

If the European countries cannot find means to pay for the excess of goods sold to them over those purchased from them, they will have to stop buying and our present export trade will shrink proportionately. The result would be restriction of outputs, industrial depression, idle capital and idle labor, numerous failures, financial demoralization, and general unrest and suffering among the laboring classes.

Probably a billion and three quarters of the excess of European purchases can be taken care of by the sale of American securities held in Europe and by the transfer of trade balances of oriental countries, but that will leave three quarters of a billion to be met in some other way. Furthermore, even if that is arranged, we will have to face a more serious situation in January, 1916, as the American securities held abroad will have been exhausted.

I believe that Secretary McAdoo is convinced and I agree with him that there is only one means of avoiding this situation which would so seriously affect economic conditions in this country, and that is the flotation of large bond issues by the belligerent governments. Our financial institutions have the money to loan and wish to do so. On account of the great balance of trade in our favor the proceeds of these loans would be expended here. The result would be a maintenance of the credit of the borrowing nations based on their gold reserve, a continuance of our commerce at its present volume and industrial activity with the consequent employment of capital and labor and national prosperity.

The difficulty is—and this is what Secretary McAdoo came to see me about—that the Government early in the war announced that it considered "war loans" to be contrary to "the true spirit of neutrality." A declaration to this effect was given to the press about August 15, 1914, by Secretary Bryan. The language is as follows: "In the judgment of this Government loans by American bankers to any foreign nation at war is inconsistent with the true spirit of neutrality."

In October, 1914, after a conference with you, I gave my "impressions" to certain New York bankers in reference to "credit loans," but the general statement remained unaffected. In drafting the letter of January 20, 1915, to Senator Stone I sought to leave out a broad statement and to explain merely the reasons for distinguishing between "general loans" and "credit loans." However, Mr. Bryan thought it well to repeat the August declaration and it appears in the first sentence of division 13 of the letter, a copy of which I enclose.

On March 31, 1915, another press statement was given out from the Department which reads as follows:

> The State Department has from time to time received information directly or indirectly to the effect that belligerent nations had arranged with Banks in the United States for credits in various sums. While loans to belligerents have been disapproved, this Government has not felt that it was justified in interposing objection to the credit arrangements which have been brought to its attention. It has neither approved these nor disapproved—it has simply taken no action in the premises and expressed no opinion.

Manifestly the Government has committed itself to the policy of discouraging general loans to belligerent governments. The practical reasons for the policy at the time we adopted it were sound, but basing it on the ground that loans are "inconsistent with the true spirit of neutrality" is now a source of embarrassment. This latter ground is as strong today as it was a year ago, while the practical reasons for discouraging loans have largely disappeared. We have more money than we can use. Popular sympathy has become crystallized in favor of one or another of the belligerents to such an extent that the purchase of bonds would in no way increase the bitterness of partisanship or cause a possibly serious situation.

Now, on the other hand, we are face to face with what appears to be a critical economic situation, which can only be relieved apparently by the investment of American capital in foreign loans to be used in liquidating the enormous balance of trade in favor of the United States.

Can we afford to let a declaration as to our conception of "the true spirit of neutrality" made in the first days of the war stand in the way of our national interests which seem to be seriously threatened?

If we cannot afford to do this, how are we to explain away the declaration and maintain a semblance of consistency?

My opinion is that we ought to allow the loans to be made for our own good, and I have been seeking some means of harmonizing our policy, so unconditionally announced, with the flotation of general loans. As yet I have found no solution to the problem.

Secretary McAdoo considers that the situation is becoming acute and that something should be done at once to avoid the disastrous results which will follow a continuance of the present policy.

Faithfully yours,

ROBERT LANSING

SELECTION

The President Calls for a Declaration of War: Wilson's Address to Congress, April 2, 1917

President Wilson apparently decided to request Congress to declare war on Germany about two weeks before he delivered the message reprinted here. At a meeting on March 19 the Cabinet urged war upon Wilson, but he did not commit himself. The next day, however, he called Congress into special session "to receive a communication concerning grave matters of national policy." During the nearly two weeks before Congress convened, Wilson's intention became known as he called the National Guard of most states into Federal service and directed the Navy to begin plans for coordination with the British. Yet Wilson apparently had misgivings even as he wrote his war message. The day before he delivered the message to a joint session of Congress he told his friend Frank Cobb, editor of the New York World, *that he saw no alternative to war but that war would have serious consequences. "Once lead this people into war and they'll forget there ever was such a thing as tolerance. To fight you must be brutal and ruthless, and the spirit of reckless brutality will enter into the very fibre of our national life, infecting Congress, the courts, the policeman on the beat, the man in the street."*

Wilson could have written a considerably different war message. He could have put his request for congressional action altogether in terms of national interest and security. At the Cabinet meeting of March 19 Secretary Lansing had urged war upon ideological grounds, to save democracy from German despotism, and Wilson had replied that he did not see how he could invoke democracy. But Wilson habitually saw issues in moral terms, as conflicts between high principles and base motives, and consciously or not he developed

*his war message so that it became an appeal for support of democracy, human-
ity, and justice against German autocracy and perfidy. "Our object . . . is to
vindicate the principles of peace and justice in the life of the world as against
selfish and autocratic power. . . ." Again, ". . . we act without animus, not in
emnity towards a people but only in armed opposition to an irresponsible
government which has thrown aside all considerations of humanity and of right
and is running amuck." And the most memorable sentence of the message:
"The world must be made safe for democracy."*

*Certain aspects of the message are interesting in view of subsequent develop-
ments. One gets an intimation of the League of Nations in the "concert of
purpose and of action" of the "really free and self-governed peoples of the
world." And Russia, which had only a few days before overthrown the Czar,
had become "a fit partner for a League of Honour." (The Bolshevik revolution
was to come in the autumn.) Although Wilson had expressed concern for
tolerance to Cobb, he included in his message some passages that foreshadowed
the hysteria about espionage and the repression of German-American culture
that were to come in the months ahead. One deeply concerned with discouraging
the excesses of war fever would not have been well advised to say that the
enemy "has filled our unsuspecting communities and even our offices of government with spies and set criminal intrigues everywhere afoot. . . ." And German-
Americans "are, most of them, . . . true and loyal Americans . . . prompt to
stand with us in rebuking and restraining the few who may be of a different
mind and purpose. If there should be disloyalty, it will be dealt with with a
firm hand of stern repression; but, if it lifts its head at all, it will lift it only
here and there and without countenance except from a lawless and malignant
few."*

The message is here reproduced in its entirety as it appears in the Congressional Record, *Sixty-fifth Congress, special session, volume 55, part 1, April 2,
1917, pages 102–104.*

Gentlemen of the Congress: I have called the Congress into extraordinary session because there are serious, very serious, choices of policy
to be made, and made immediately, which it was neither right nor con-
stitutionally permissible that I should assume the responsibility of making.

On the third of February last I officially laid before you the extraordinary announcement of the Imperial German Government that on and after
the first day of February it was its purpose to put aside all restraints of
law or of humanity and use its submarines to sink every vessel that sought
to approach either the ports of Great Britain and Ireland or the western
coasts of Europe or any of the ports controlled by the enemies of Germany within the Mediterranean. That had seemed to be the object of the
German submarine warfare earlier in the war, but since April of last year
the Imperial Government had somewhat restrained the commanders of its
undersea craft in conformity with its promise then given to us that passenger boats should not be sunk and that due warning would be given
to all other vessels which its submarines might seek to destroy, when
no resistance was offered or escape attempted, and care taken that their
crews were given at least a fair chance to save their lives in their open

boats. The precautions taken were meagre and haphazard enough, as was proved in distressing instance after instance in the progress of the cruel and unmanly business, but a certain degree of restraint was observed. The new policy has swept every restriction aside. Vessels of every kind, whatever their flag, their character, their cargo, their destination, their errand, have been ruthlessly sent to the bottom without warning and without thought of help or mercy for those on board, the vessels of friendly neutrals along with those of belligerents. Even hospital ships and ships carrying relief to the sorely bereaved and stricken people of Belgium, though the latter were provided with safe conduct through the proscribed areas by the German Government itself and were distinguished by unmistakable marks of identity, have been sunk with the same reckless lack of compassion or of principle.

I was for a little while unable to believe that such things would in fact be done by any government that had hitherto subscribed to the humane practices of civilized nations. International law had its origin in the attempt to set up some law which would be respected and observed upon the seas, where no nation had right of dominion and where lay the free highways of the world. By painful stage after stage has that law been built up, with meagre enough results, indeed, after all was accomplished that could be accomplished, but always with a clear view, at least, of what the heart and conscience of mankind demanded. This minimum of right the German Government has swept aside under the plea of retaliation and necessity and because it had no weapons which it could use at sea except these which it is impossible to employ as it is employing them without throwing to the winds all scruples of humanity or of respect for the understandings that were supposed to underlie the intercourse of the world. I am not now thinking of the loss of property involved, immense and serious as that is, but only of the wanton and wholesale destruction of the lives of non-combatants, men, women, and children, engaged in pursuits which have always, even in the darkest periods of modern history, been deemed innocent and legitimate. Property can be paid for; the lives of peaceful and innocent people cannot be. The present German submarine warfare against commerce is a warfare against mankind.

It is a war against all nations. American ships have been sunk, American lives taken, in ways which it has stirred us very deeply to learn of, but the ships and people of other neutral and friendly nations have been sunk and overwhelmed in the waters in the same way. There has been no discrimination. The challenge is to all mankind. Each nation must decide for itself how it will meet it. The choice we make for ourselves must be made with a moderation of counsel and a temperateness of judgment befitting our character and our motives as a nation. We must put excited feeling away. Our motive will not be revenge or the victorious assertion of the physical might of the nation, but only the vindication of right, of human right, of which we are only a single champion.

When I addressed the Congress on the twenty-sixth of February last I thought that it would suffice to assert our neutral rights with arms, our right to use the seas against unlawful interference, our right to keep our people safe against unlawful violence. But armed neutrality, it now appears, is impracticable. Because submarines are in effect outlaws when used as the German submarines have been used against merchant shipping, it is impossible to defend ships against their attacks as the law of nations has assumed that merchantmen would defend themselves against privateers or cruisers, visible craft giving chase upon the open sea. It is common prudence in such circumstances, grim necessity indeed, to endeavour to destroy them before they have shown their own intention. They must be dealt with upon sight, if dealt with at all. The German Government denies the right of neutrals to use arms at all within the areas of the sea which it has proscribed, even in the defense of rights which no modern publicist has ever before questioned their right to defend. The intimation is conveyed that the armed guards which we have placed on our merchant ships will be treated as beyond the pale of law and subject to be dealt with as pirates would be. Armed neutrality is ineffectual enough at best; in such circumstances and in the face of such pretensions it is worse than ineffectual: it is likely only to produce what it was meant to prevent; it is practically certain to draw us into the war without either the rights or the effectiveness of belligerents. There is one choice we cannot make, we are incapable of making: we will not choose the path of submission and suffer the most sacred rights of our nation and our people to be ignored or violated. The wrongs against which we now array ourselves are no common wrongs; they cut to the very roots of human life.

With a profound sense of the solemn and even tragical character of the step I am taking and of the grave responsibilities which it involves, but in unhesitating obedience to what I deem my constitutional duty, I advise that the Congress declare the recent course of the Imperial German Government to be in fact nothing less than war against the government and people of the United States; that it formally accept the status of belligerent which has thus been thrust upon it; and that it take immediate steps not only to put the country in a more thorough state of defense but also to exert all its power and employ all its resources to bring the Government of the German Empire to terms and end the war.

What this will involve is clear. It will involve the utmost practicable cooperation in counsel and action with the governments now at war with Germany, and, as incident to that, the extension to those governments of the most liberal financial credits, in order that our resources may so far as possible be added to theirs. It will involve the organization and mobilization of all the material resources of the country to supply the materials of war and serve the incidental needs of the nation in the most abundant and yet the most economical and efficient way possible. It will involve the immediate full equipment of the navy in all respects but particularly in supplying it with the best means of dealing with the enemy's submarines. It will involve the immediate addition to the armed forces of the United States already provided for by law in case of war at least five hundred thousand men, who should, in my opinion, be chosen upon the principle of universal liability to service, and also the authorization of subsequent additional increments of equal force so soon as they may be needed and can be handled in training. It will involve also, of course, the granting of adequate credits to the Government, sustained, I hope, so far as they can equitably be sustained by the present generation, by well conceived taxation.

I say sustained so far as may be equitable by taxation because it seems to me that it would be most unwise to base the credits which will now be necessary entirely on money borrowed. It is our duty, I most respectfully urge, to protect our people so far as we may against the very serious hardships and evils which would be likely to arise out of the inflation which would be produced by vast loans.

In carrying out the measures by which these things are to be accomplished we should keep constantly in mind the wisdom of interfering as little as possible in our own preparation and in the equipment of our own military forces with the duty,—for it will be a very practical duty,—of supplying the nations already at war with Germany with the materials which they can obtain only from us or by our assistance. They are in the field and we should help them in every way to be effective there.

I shall take the liberty of suggesting, through the several executive departments of the Government, for the consideration of your committees, measures for the accomplishment of the several objects I have mentioned. I hope that it will be your pleasure to deal with them as having been framed after very careful thought by the branch of the Government upon which the responsibility of conducting the war and safeguarding the nation will most directly fall.

While we do these things, these deeply momentous things, let us be very clear, and make very clear to all the world what our motives and our objects are. My own thought has not been driven from its habitual and normal course by the unhappy events of the last two months, and I do not believe that the thought of the nation has been altered or clouded by them. I have exactly the same things in mind now that I had in mind when I addressed the Senate on the twenty-second of January last; the same that I had in mind when I addressed the Congress on the third of February and on the twenty-sixth of February. Our object now, as then, is to vindicate the principles of peace and justice in the life of the world as against selfish and autocratic power and to set up amongst the really free and self-governed peoples of the world such a concert of purpose and of action as will henceforth ensure the observance of those principles. Neutrality is no longer feasible or desirable where the peace of the world is involved and the freedom of its peoples, and the menace to that peace and freedom lies in the existence of autocratic governments backed by organized force which is controlled wholly by their will, not by the will of their people. We have seen the last of neutrality in such circumstances. We are at the beginning of an age in which it will be insisted that the same standards of conduct and of responsibility for wrong done shall be observed among nations and their governments that are observed among the individual citizens of civilized states.

We have no quarrel with the German people. We have no feeling towards them but one of sympathy and friendship. It was not upon their impulse that their government acted in entering this war. It was not with their previous knowledge or approval. It was a war determined upon as wars used to be determined upon in the old, unhappy days when peoples were nowhere consulted by their rulers and wars were provoked and waged in the interest of dynasties or of little groups of ambitious men who were accustomed to use their fellow men as pawns and tools. Self-governed nations do not fill their neighbour states with spies or set the course of intrigue to bring about some critical posture of affairs which will give them an opportunity to strike and make conquest. Such designs can be successfully worked out only under cover and where no one has the right to ask questions. Cunningly contrived plans of deception or aggression, carried, it may be, from generation to generation, can be worked out and kept from the light only within the privacy of courts or behind the carefully guarded confidences of a narrow and privileged class. They are happily impossible where public opinion commands and insists upon full information concerning all the nation's affairs.

A steadfast concert for peace can never be maintained except by a partnership of democratic nations. No autocratic government could be trusted to keep faith within it or observe its covenants. It must be a league of honour, a partnership of opinion. Intrigue would eat its vitals away; the plottings of inner circles who could plan what they would and render account to no one would be a corruption seated at its very heart. Only free peoples can hold their purpose and their honour steady to a common end and prefer the interests of mankind to any narrow interest of their own.

Does not every American feel that assurance has been added to our hope for the future peace of the world by the wonderful and heartening things that have been happening within the last few weeks in Russia? Russia was known by those who knew it best to have been always in fact democratic at heart, in all the vital habits of her thought, in all the intimate relationships of her people that spoke their natural instinct, their habitual attitude towards life. The autocracy that crowned the summit of her political structure, long as it had stood and terrible as was the reality of its power, was not in fact Russian in origin, character, or purpose; and now it has been shaken off and the great, generous Russian people have been added in all their naive majesty and might to the forces that are fighting for freedom in the world, for justice, and for peace. Here is a fit partner for a League of Honour.

One of the things that has served to convince us that the Prussian autocracy was not and could never be our friend is that from the very outset of the present war it has filled our unsuspecting communities and even our offices of government with spies and set criminal intrigues everywhere afoot against our national unity of counsel, our peace within and without, our industries and our commerce. Indeed it is now evident that its spies were here even before the war began; and it is unhappily not a matter of conjecture but a fact proved in our courts of justice that the intrigues which have more than once come perilously near to disturbing the peace and dislocating the industries of the country have been carried on at the instigation, with the support, and even under the personal direction of official agents of the Imperial Government accredited to the Government of the United States. Even in checking these things and trying to extirpate them we have sought to put the most generous interpretation possible upon them because we knew that their source lay, not in any hostile feeling or purpose of the German people towards us (who were, no doubt as ignorant of them as we ourselves were), but only in the selfish designs of a Government that did what it pleased and told its people nothing. But they have played their part in serving to convince us at last that that Government entertains no real friendship for us and means to act against our peace and security at its convenience. That it means to stir up enemies against us at our very doors the intercepted note to the German Minister at Mexico City is eloquent evidence.

We are accepting this challenge of hostile purpose because we know that in such a government, following such methods, we can never have a friend; and that in the presence of its organized power, always lying in wait to accomplish we know not what purpose, there can be no assured security for the democratic governments of the world. We are now about to accept gauge of battle with this natural foe to liberty and shall, if necessary, spend the whole force of the nation to check and nullify its pretensions and its power. We are glad, now that we see the facts with no veil of false pretense about them, to fight thus for the ultimate peace of the world and for the liberation of its peoples, the German peoples included: for the rights of nations great and small and the privilege of men everywhere to choose their way of life and of obedience. The world must be made safe for democracy. Its peace must be planted upon the tested foundations of political liberty. We have no selfish ends to serve. We desire no conquest, no dominion. We seek no indemnities for ourselves, no material compensation for the sacrifices we shall freely make. We are but one of the champions of the rights of mankind. We shall be satisfied when those rights have been made as secure as the faith and the freedom of nations can make them.

Just because we fight without rancour and without selfish object, seeking nothing for ourselves but what we shall wish to share with all free peoples, we shall, I feel confident, conduct our operations as belligerents without passion and ourselves observe with proud punctilio the principles of right and of fair play we profess to be fighting for.

I have said nothing of the governments allied with the Imperial Government of Germany because they have not made war upon us or challenged us to defend our right and our honour. The Austro-Hungarian Government has, indeed, avowed its unqualified endorsement and acceptance of the reckless and lawless submarine warfare adopted now without disguise by the Imperial German Government, and it has therefore not been possible for this Government to receive Count Tarnowski, the Ambassador recently accredited to this Government by the Imperial and Royal Government of Austria-Hungary; but that Government has not actually engaged in warfare against citizens of the United States on the seas, and I take the liberty, for the present at least, of postponing a discussion of our relations with the authorities at Vienna. We enter this war only where we are clearly forced into it because there are no other means of defending our rights.

It will be all the easier for us to conduct ourselves as belligerents in a high spirit of right and fairness because we act without animus, not in enmity towards a people or with the desire to bring any injury or disadvantage upon them, but only in armed opposition to an irresponsible government which has thrown aside all considerations of humanity and of right and is running amuck. We are, let me say again, the sincere friends of the German people, and shall desire nothing so much as the early re-establishment of intimate relations of mutual advantage between us,—however hard it may be for them, for the time being, to believe that this is spoken from our hearts. We have borne with their present government through all these bitter months because of that friendship,—exercising a patience and forbearance which would otherwise have been impossible. We shall, happily, still have an opportunity to prove that friendship in our daily attitude and actions towards the millions of men and women of German birth and native sympathy who live amongst us and share our life, and we shall be proud to prove it towards all who are in fact loyal to their neighbours and to the Government in the hour of test. They are, most of them, as true and loyal Americans as if they had never known any other fealty or allegiance. They will be prompt to stand with us in rebuking and restraining the few who may be of a different mind and purpose. If there should be disloyalty, it will be dealt with with a firm hand of stern repression; but, if it lifts its head at all, it will lift it only here and there and without countenance except from a lawless and malignant few.

It is a distressing and oppressive duty, Gentlemen of the Congress, which I have performed in thus addressing you. There are, it may be, many months of fiery trial and sacrifice ahead of us. It is a fearful thing to lead this great peaceful people into war, into the most terrible and disastrous of all wars, civilization itself seeming to be in the balance. But the right is more precious than peace, and we shall fight for the things which we have always carried nearest our hearts,—for democracy, for the right of those who submit to authority to have a voice in their own governments, for the rights and liberties of small nations, for a universal dominion of right by such a concert of free peoples as shall bring peace and safety to all nations and make the world itself at last free. To such a task we can dedicate our lives and our fortunes, everything that we are and everything that we have, with the pride of those who know that the day has come when America is privileged to spend her blood and her might for the principles that gave her birth and happiness and the peace which she has treasured, God helping her, she can do no other.

SELECTION

Senator Norris Explains His Vote against War

Six senators and fifty representatives voted against the war resolution, which proclaimed that "the state of War between the United States and the Imperial German Government which has been thrust upon the United States is hereby formally declared." Senator Norris's explanation in Congress of why he was going to vote against the resolution struck the keynote of what became the most effective and most common criticism of the 1917 decision to go to war. Indeed.

in the 1930s, Norris's point of view was institutionalized in the neutrality laws.

There were two steps in the Senator's argument. First, the United States had not been truly neutral; it had taken a position that actually leaned in favor of the British. ". . . we finally acquiesced in the British war zone and kept our ships out of it, while in the German war zone we have refused to recognize its legality and have not kept either our ships or our citizens out of its area." Second, and more important, entrance into the war was a result of economic considerations rather than true national interest. ". . . there is no doubt in my mind but the enormous amount of money loaned to the allies in this country has been instrumental in bringing about a public sentiment in favor of our country taking a course that would make every bond worth a hundred cents on the dollar and making the payment of every debt certain and sure." Munitions manufacturers, too, "expect to make millions more if our country can be drawn into the catastrophe. . . ." In the vote for war, said Senator Norris, "I feel that we are about to put the dollar sign upon the American flag."

George W. Norris was born in rural Sandusky County, Ohio, in 1861. He went to college in Indiana and practiced law in Nebraska, where he became a district judge in 1895 and a member of the United States House of Representatives in 1903. He served in the House for ten years, the high tide of his career there coming in 1910 when he organized the rebellion against Speaker of the House Joseph G. Cannon and restricted the powers of that office. A Republican but a highly independent one, he served in the Senate from 1913 until his defeat in 1942. While in the Senate, he became best known for his championing of the Norris–La Guardia Act (1932), the Twentieth Amendment to the Constitution, and the Tennessee Valley Authority. He died in 1944. For further information, see his autobiography, Fighting Liberal *(New York: Macmillan, 1945); a two-volume life by Richard Lowitt, the first volume and only volume published at this time being* George W. Norris: The Making of a Progressive, 1861–1912 *(Syracuse, N.Y.: Syracuse University Press, 1963); and Alfred Lief,* Democracy's Norris: The Biography of a Lonely Crusade *(Harrisburg, Pa.: Stackpole Company, 1939).*

The Norris speech, here reproduced in its entirety, is from the Congressional Record, *Sixty-fifth Congress, special session, volume 55, part 1, April 4, 1917, pages 212–214. The material in the omission indicated near the end of the selection was an interruption by Senator Reed of Missouri.*

Mr. President, while I am most emphatically and sincerely opposed to taking any step that will force our country into the useless and senseless war now being waged in Europe, yet if this resolution passes I shall not permit my feeling of opposition to its passage to interfere in any way with my duty either as a Senator or as a citizen in bringing success and victory to American arms. I am bitterly opposed to my country entering the war, but if, notwithstanding my opposition, we do enter it, all of my energy and all of my power will be behind our flag in carrying it on to victory.

The resolution now before the Senate is a declaration of war. Before taking this momentous step, and while standing on the brink of this terrible vortex, we ought to pause and calmly and judiciously consider the terrible consequences of the step we are about to take. We ought to consider likewise the route we have recently traveled and ascertain whether we have reached our present position in a way that is compatible with the neutral position which we claimed to occupy at the beginning and through the various stages of this unholy and unrighteous war.

No close student of recent history will deny that both Great Britain and Germany have, on numerous occasions since the beginning of the war, flagrantly violated in the most serious manner the rights of neutral vessels and neutral nations under existing international law as recognized up to the beginning of this war by the civilized world.

The reason given by the President in asking Congress to declare war against Germany is that the German Government has declared certain war zones, within which, by the use of submarines, she sinks, without notice, American ships and destroys American lives.

Let us trace briefly the origin and history of these so-called war zones. The first war zone was declared by Great Britain. She gave us and the world notice of it on the 4th day of November, 1914. The zone became effective November 5, 1914, the next day after the notice was given. This zone so declared by Great Britain covered the whole of the North Sea. The order establishing it sought to close the north of Scotland route around the British Isles to Denmark, Holland, Norway, Sweden, and the Baltic Sea. The decree of establishment drew an arbitrary line from the Hebrides Islands along the Scottish coast to Iceland, and warned neutral shipping that it would cross those lines at its peril, and ordered that ships might go to Holland and other neutral nations by taking the English Channel route through the Strait of Dover.

The first German war zone was declared on the 4th day of February, 1915, just three months after the British war zone was declared. Germany gave 15 days' notice of the establishment of her zone, which became effective on the 18th day of February, 1915. The German war zone covered the English Channel and the high sea waters around the British Isles. It sought to close the English Channel route around the British Isles to Holland, Norway, Sweden, Denmark, and the Baltic Sea. The German war zone decreed that neutral vessels would be exposed to danger in the English Channel route, but that the route around the north of Scotland and in the eastern part of the North Sea, in a strip 30 miles wide along the Dutch coast, would be free from danger.

It will thus be seen that the British Government declared the north of Scotland route into the Baltic Sea as dangerous and the English Channel route into the Baltic Sea as safe.

The German Government in its order did exactly the reverse. It declared the north of Scotland route into the Baltic Sea as safe and the English Channel route into the Baltic Sea as dangerous.

The order of the British Government declaring the North Sea as a war zone used the following language:

> The British Admiralty gives notice that the waters of the North Sea must be considered a military area. Within this area merchant shipping of all kinds, traders of all countries, fishing craft, and other vessels will be exposed to the gravest danger from mines it has been necessary to lay.

The German Government, by its order declaring its war zone around the south of England, declared that the order would be made effective by the use of submarines.

Thus we have the two declarations of the two Governments, each declaring a military zone and warning neutral shipping from going into the prohibited area. England sought to make her order effective by the use of submerged mines. Germany sought to make her order effective by the use of submarines. Both of these orders were illegal and contrary to all international law as well as the principles of humanity. Under international law no belligerent Government has the right to place submerged mines in the high seas. Neither has it any right to take human life without notice by the use of submarines. If there is any difference on the ground of humanity between these two instrumentalities, it is certainly in favor of the submarines. The submarine can exercise some degree of discretion and judgment. The submerged mine always destroys without notice, friend and foe alike, guilty and innocent the same. In carrying out these two policies, both Great Britain and Germany have sunk American ships and destroyed American lives without provocation and without notice. There have been more ships sunk and more American lives lost from the action of submarines than from English mines in the North Sea; for the simple reason that we finally acquiesced in the British war zone and kept our ships out of it, while in the German war zone we have refused to recognize its legality and have not kept either our ships or our citizens out of its area. If American ships had gone into the British war zone in defiance of Great Britain's order, as they have gone into the German war zone in defiance of the German Government's order, there would have been many more American lives lost and many more American ships sunk by the instrumentality of the mines than the instrumentality of the submarines.

We have in the main complied with the demands made by Great Britain. Our ships have followed the instructions of the British Government in going not only to England but to the neutral nations of the world, and in thus complying with the British order American ships going to Holland, Denmark, Norway, and Sweden have been taken by British officials into British ports, and their cargoes inspected and examined. All the mails we have carried even to neutral countries have been opened and censored, and oftentimes the entire cargo confiscated by the Government. Nothing has been permitted to pass to even the most neutral nations except after examination and with the permission of the officials of the British Government.

I have outlined the beginning of the controversy. I have given in substance the orders of both of these great Governments that constituted the beginning of our controversy with each. There have been other orders made by both Governments subsequent to the ones I have given that interfered with our rights as a neutral Nation, but these two that I have outlined constitute the origin of practically the entire difficulty, and subsequent orders have only been modifications and reproductions of those I have already mentioned. It is unnecessary to cite authority to show that both of these orders declaring military zones were illegal and contrary to international law. It is sufficient to say that our Government has officially declared both of them to be illegal and has officially protested against both of them.

The only difference is that in the case of Germany we have persisted in our protest, while in the case of England we have submitted. What was our duty as a Government and what were our rights when we were confronted with these extraordinary orders declaring these military zones? First, we could have defied both of them and could have gone to war against both of these nations for this violation of international law and interference with our neutral rights. Second, we had the technical right to defy one and to acquiesce in the other. Third, we could, while denouncing them both as illegal, have acquiesced in them both and thus remained neutral with both sides, although not agreeing with either as to the righteousness of their respective orders. We could have said to American shipowners that, while these orders are both contrary to international law and are both unjust, we do not believe that the provocation is sufficient to cause us to go to war for the defense of our rights as a neutral nation, and, therefore, American ships and American citizens will go into these zones at their own peril and risk. Fourth, we might have declared an embargo against the shipping from American ports of any merchandise to either one of these Governments that persisted in maintaining its military zone. We might have refused to permit the sailing of any ship from any American port to either of these military zones. In my judgment, if we had pursued this course, the zones would have been of short duration. England would have been compelled to take her mines out of the North Sea in order to get any supplies from our country. When her mines were taken out of the North Sea then the German ports upon the North Sea would have been accessible to American shipping and Germany would have been compelled to cease her submarine warfare in order to get any supplies from our Nation into German North Sea ports.

There are a great many American citizens who feel that we owe it as a duty to humanity to take part in this war. Many instances of cruelty and inhumanity can be found on both sides. Men are often biased in their judgment on account of their sympathy and their interests. To my mind, what we ought to have maintained from the beginning was the strictest neutrality. If we had done this I do not believe we would have been on the verge of war at the present time. We had a right as a nation, if we desired, to cease at any time to be neutral. We had a technical right to respect the English war zone and to disregard the German war zone, but we could not do that and be neutral. I have no quarrel to find with the man who does not desire our country to remain neutral. While many such people are moved by selfish motives and hopes of gain, I have no doubt but that in a great many instances, through what I believe to be a misunderstanding of the real condition, there are many honest, patriotic citizens who think we ought to engage in this war and who are behind the President in his demand that we should declare war against Germany. I think such people err in judgment and to a great extent have been misled as to the real history and the true facts by the almost unanimous demand of the great combination of wealth that has a direct financial interest in our participation in the war. We have loaned many hundreds of millions of dollars to the allies in this controversy. While such action was legal and countenanced by international law, there is no doubt in my mind but the enormous amount of money loaned to the allies in this country has been instrumental in bringing about a public sentiment in favor of our country taking a course that would make every bond worth a hundred cents on the dollar and making the payment of every debt certain and sure. Through this instrumentality and also through the instrumentality of others who have not only made millions out of the war in the manufacture of munitions, etc., and who would expect to make millions more if our country can be drawn into the catastrophe, a large number of the great newspapers and news agencies of the country have been controlled and enlisted in the greatest propaganda that the world has ever known, to manufacture sentiment in favor of war. It is now demanded that the American citizens shall be used as insurance policies to guarantee the safe delivery of munitions of war to belligerent nations. The enormous profits of munition manufacturers, stockbrokers, and bond dealers must be still further increased by our entrance into the war. This has brought us to the present moment, when Congress, urged by the President and backed by the artificial sentiment, is about to declare war and engulf our country in the greatest holocaust that the world has ever known.

In showing the position of the bondholder and the stockbroker I desire to read an extract from a letter written by a member of the New York Stock Exchange to his customers. This writer says:

> Regarding the war as inevitable, Wall Street believes that it would be preferable to this uncertainty about the actual date of its commencement. Canada and Japan are at war, and are more prosperous than ever before. The popular view is that stocks would have a quick, clear, sharp reaction immediately upon outbreak of hostilities, and that then they would enjoy an old-fashioned bull market such as followed the outbreak of war with Spain in 1898. The advent of peace would force a readjustment of commodity prices and would probably mean a postponement of new enterprises. As peace negotiations would be long drawn out, the period of waiting and uncertainty for business would be long. If the United States does not go to war it is nevertheless good opinion that the preparedness program will compensate in good measure for the loss of the stimulus of actual war.

Here we have the Wall Street view. Here we have the man representing the class of people who will be made prosperous should we become entangled in the present war, who have already made millions of dollars, and who will make many hundreds of millions more if we get into the war. Here we have the cold-blooded proposition that war brings prosperity to that class of people who are within the view point of this writer. He expresses the view, undoubtedly, of Wall Street, and of thousands of men elsewhere, who see only dollars coming to them through the handling of stocks and bonds that will be necessary in case of war. "Canada and Japan," he says, "are at war, and are more prosperous than ever before."

To whom does war bring prosperity? Not to the soldier who for the munificent compensation of $16 per month shoulders his musket and goes into the trench, there to shed his blood and to die if necessary; not to the broken-hearted widow who waits for the return of the mangled body of her husband; not to the mother who weeps at the death of her brave boy; not to the little children who shiver with cold; not to the babe who suffers from hunger; nor to the millions of mothers and daughters who carry broken hearts to their graves. War brings no prosperity to the great mass of common and patriotic citizens. It increases the cost of living of those who toil and those who already must strain every effort to keep soul and body together. War brings prosperity to the stock gambler on Wall Street—to those who are already in possession of more wealth than can be realized or enjoyed. Again this writer says that if we can not get war, "it is nevertheless good opinion that the preparedness program will compensate in good measure for the loss of the stimulus of actual war." That is, if we can not get war, let us go as far in that direction as possible. If we can not get war, let us cry for additional ships, additional guns, additional munitions, and everything else that will have a tendency to bring us as near as possible to the verge of war. And if war comes do such men as these shoulder the musket and go into the trenches?

Their object in having war and in preparing for war is to make money. Human suffering and the sacrifice of human life are necessary, but Wall Street considers only the dollars and the cents. The men who do the fighting, the people who make the sacrifices, are the ones who will not be counted in the measure of this great prosperity that he depicts. The stock brokers would not, of course, go to war, because the very object they have in bringing on the war is profit, and therefore they must remain in their Wall Street offices in order to share in that great prosperity which they say war will bring. The volunteer officer, even the drafting officer, will not find them. They will be concealed in their palatial offices on Wall Street, sitting behind mahogany desks, covered up with clipped coupons— coupons soiled with the sweat of honest toil, coupons stained with mothers' tears, coupons dyed in the lifeblood of their fellow men.

We are taking a step to-day that is fraught with untold danger. We are going into war upon the command of gold. We are going to run the risk of sacrificing millions of our countrymen's lives in order that other countrymen may coin their lifeblood into money. And even if we do not cross the Atlantic and go into the trenches, we are going to pile up a debt that the toiling masses that shall come many generations after us will have to pay. Unborn millions will bend their backs in toil in order to pay for the terrible step we are now about to take. We are about to do the bidding of wealth's terrible mandate. By our act we will make millions of our countrymen suffer, and the consequences of it may well be that millions of our brethren must shed their lifeblood, millions of broken-hearted women must weep, millions of children must suffer with cold, and millions of babes must die from hunger, and all because we want to preserve the commercial right of American citizens to deliver munitions of war to belligerent nations. . . .

I know that I am powerless to stop it. I know that this war madness has taken possession of the financial and political powers of our country. I know that nothing I can say will stay the blow that is soon to fall. I feel that we are committing a sin against humanity and against our countrymen. I would like to say to this war god, You shall not coin into gold the lifeblood of my brethren. I would like to prevent this terrible catastrophe from falling upon my people. I would be willing to surrender my own life if I could cause this awful cup to pass. I charge no man here with a wrong motive, but it seems to me that this war craze has robbed us of our judgment. I wish we might delay our action until reason could again be enthroned in the brain of man. I feel that we are about to put the dollar sign upon the American flag.

I have no sympathy with the military spirit that dominates the Kaiser and his advisers. I do not believe that they represent the heart of the great German people. I have no more sympathy with the submarine policy of Germany than I have with the mine-laying policy of England. I have heard with rejoicing of the overthrow of the Czar of Russia and the movement in that great country toward the establishment of a government where the common people will have their rights, liberty, and freedom respected. I hope and pray that a similar revolution may take place in Germany, that the Kaiser may be overthrown, and that on the ruins of his military despotism may be established a German republic, where the great German people may work out their world destiny. The working out of that problem is not an American burden. We ought to remember the advice of the Father of our Country and keep out of entangling alliances. Let Europe solve her problems as we have solved ours. Let Europe bear her burdens as we have borne ours. In the greatest war of our history and at the time it occurred, the greatest war in the world's history, we were engaged in solving an American problem. We settled the question of human slavery and washed our flag clean by the sacrifice of human blood. It was a great problem and a great burden, but we solved it ourselves. Never once did we think of asking Europe to take part in its solution. Never once did any European nation undertake to settle the great question. We solved it, and history has rendered a unanimous verdict that we solved it right. The troubles of Europe ought to be settled by Europe, and wherever our sympathies may lie, disagreeing as we do, we ought to remain absolutely neutral and permit them to settle their questions without our interference. We are now the greatest neutral nation. Upon the passage of this resolution we will have joined Europe in the great catastrophe and taken America into entanglements that will not end with this war, but will live and bring their evil influences upon many generations yet unborn.

SELECTION

The Committee on Public Information and the War Fever

President Wilson created the Committee on Public Information (CPI) by executive action only days after the declaration of war, even before the establishment of selective service and the organization of Liberty bond drives. Headed by George Creel, a Denver journalist, the CPI was responsible for uniting public opinion behind the war. As Creel put it, his job was "to sell the war to America," and he worked at his task with an evangelical fervor and an efficiency expert's sense of organization. The CPI turned out scores of pamphlets, translated them into most of the languages Americans spoke, and distributed them by the millions. The CPI arranged for over 7 million speeches during the eighteen months of its existence.

If toleration is a part of democracy, few would dispute that in the war to make the world safe for democracy the United States set back the cause of democracy at home. In the name of democracy, democracy was diminished. There was no room for voices of dissent. Critics either remained silent or suffered the consequences, often severe. For a generation which saw most problems in simple terms and therefore susceptible of easy solutions, a generation with an excess of moral or moralistic energy, and a generation already acutely self-conscious about its identity and faced with serious division in the face of national emergency, it was perhaps inevitable that the war spirit would become feverish and repressive. Certainly, however, the Committee on Public Information stimulated the war fever with statements such as appear in the pamphlet reprinted here. "Our danger is from within. Our enemies have representatives everywhere; they tell lies; they misrepresent the truth; they deceive our own people; they are a real menace to our country." Trust not your neighbor, for he may be a spy.

This sixteen-page pamphlet, reprinted wholly except for a letter from Creel on the first page, appeared in late 1917. The main purpose of it, obviously, was to develop the Boy Scout organization as a distributor of CPI publications. The pamphlet requires little explanation. The Mr. Livingstone referred to near the beginning was Colin H. Livingstone, a Washington banker who was president of the National Council, Boy Scouts of America, from 1910 to 1925. James E. West, over whose name the direct exhortation to Scouts appeared, was an attorney and professional Boy Scout executive. Editor of the magazine Boys' Life for many years, he included in a Who's Who in America sketch of himself that he had been awarded a silver buffalo "for distinguished service to boyhood."

The title page of the pamphlet: "Every Scout to Boost America" as a Government Dispatch Bearer. Manual for Boy Scouts of America Government Messenger Service. To be Kept for Reference by Scouts during Period of War. The standard work on the Creel committee is James R. Mock and Cedric Larsen, Words That Won the War: The Story of the Committee on Public Information, 1917–1919 (Princeton, N.J.: Princeton, 1939).

To the Members of the Boy Scouts of America!
        Attention, Scouts! We are again called upon to do active service for our country! Every one of the 285,661 Scouts and 76,957 Scout Officials has been summoned by President Woodrow Wilson, Commander-in-Chief of the Army and Navy, to serve as a dispatch bearer from the Government at Washington to the American people all over the country. The prompt, enthusiastic, and hearty response of every one of us has been pledged by our President, Mr. Livingstone. Our splended record of accomplishments in war activities promises full success in this new job.

This patriotic service will be rendered under the slogan

"EVERY SCOUT TO BOOST AMERICA"
AS A GOVERNMENT DISPATCH BEARER

The World War is for liberty and democracy.

America has long been recognized as the leader among nations standing for liberty and democracy.

America entered the war as a sacred duty to uphold the principles of liberty and democracy.

As a democracy, our country faces great danger—not so much from submarines, battleships and armies, because, thanks to our allies, our enemies have apparently little chance of reaching our shores.

Our danger is from within.

Our enemies have representatives everywhere; they tell lies; they misrepresent the truth; they deceive our own people; they are a real menace to our country.

Already we have seen how poor Russia has been made to suffer because her people do not know the truth. Representatives of the enemy have been very effective in their deceitful efforts to make trouble for the Government.

Fortunately here in America our people are better educated—they want the truth. Our President recognized the justice and wisdom of this demand when in the early stages of the war he created the Committee on Public Information. He knew that the Government would need the confidence, enthusiasm and willing service of every man and woman, every boy and girl in the nation. He knew that the only possible way to create a genuine feeling of partnership between the people and its representatives in Washington was to take the people into his confidence by full, frank statements concerning the reasons for our entering the war, the various steps taken during the war and the ultimate aims of the war.

Neither the President as Commander-in-Chief, nor our army and navy by land and sea, can alone win the war.

At this moment the best defense that America has is an enlightened and loyal citizenship. Therefore, we as scouts are going to have the opportunity of rendering real patriotic service under our slogan

"EVERY SCOUT TO BOOST AMERICA"
AS A GOVERNMENT DISPATCH BEARER

Here is where our service begins.

We are to help spread the facts about America and America's part in the World War.

We are to fight lies with truth.

We are to help create public opinion "just as effective in helping to bring victory as ships and guns," to stir patriotism, the great force behind the ships and guns. Isn't that a challenge for every loyal Scout?

Special Word to Scouts

A Scout Is Clean.   Again you are the messenger of the Government to the people. *Look the part.* See that your face and hands are clean, shoes polished, badge on your hat, uniform correct and spotless. What you have to say will count more if you make a good impression.

A Scout Is Courteous.   Again you are the President's messenger, with a big message to carry. *Act the part.* Remember that politeness pays every time.

A Scout Is Prepared.   Know what the Committee on Public Information stands for and what it is working for. Know what that Committee wants you to do. Know what is in the series of pamphlets yourself as listed on pages 12–15, so you can tell other people what is in them. Know how the pamphlets are obtained, so as to explain to other people how to get them. Remember, the public wants just the information you have to give.

Know whom you are to interview. Your Scoutmaster will arrange your territory. Get your instructions from him. Cover your territory. Get people interested, if they aren't interested. Give them the information they want, not something they don't want. Get everybody to read the Flag Day Speech. The chances are they won't be willing to stop there, but will want to know more about how war came to America.

It is for you to keep your eyes and ears open. Find out what the public wants to know. The Government may later ask you just this question. Be prepared to answer.

"Every Scout to Boost America" as a Government Dispatch Bearer: How?

As Mr. George Creel, the Chairman of the Committee on Public Information, says in his letter, scouts are to serve as direct special representatives of the Committee on Public Information to keep the people informed about the War and its causes and progress. The Committee has already prepared a number of special pamphlets and others will be prepared. It places upon the members of the Boy Scouts of America the responsibility of putting the information in these pamphlets in the homes of the American people. Every Scout will be furnished a credential card by his Scoutmaster. Under the direction of our leaders, the Boy Scouts of America are to serve as an intelligence division of the citizen's army, always prepared and alert to respond to any call which may come from the President of the United States and the Committee on Public Information at Washington.

Every Home to Be Reached.   The Boy Scouts of America as now organized, have troops of scouts in practically every part of this great country of ours. Over a third of our troops are in rural communities. In such places the Scoutmasters will work out a definite plan so that all of the homes of the community will be reached. In our larger cities where there are two or more troops, and therefore local council organizations, Scout Commissioners and Scout Executives will assign to each troop definite territory to cover. All scouts will be expected to work in full harmony with such arrangements.

Scouts to Get 15 Adult "Boosters."   It will be the duty of every scout official and every scout to know his territory well. Each scout should discover at least fifteen people who will be influential in boosting the cause of America. Friendly relationship should be established with these people as soon as possible. From time to time as official bulletins or pamphlets are sent out from Washington by the Committee on Public Information for distribution by scouts as dispatch bearers of the government, the scouts will deliver such pamphlets to the list of people whom they have selected as being good boosters for America in the community. The pamphlets will be delivered whenever possible upon the condition that the person receiving the same will not only read the publication himself, but agrees to place each copy in the hands of some other person where it is most likely to do practical good in boosting the cause of America. In all cases where possible have the person receiving the pamphlet sign his or her name on your record sheet. In some cases the pamphlets may well be passed on to more than one person—the more the better, naturally.

Other Free Pamphlets Available.   Each scout is to be furnished with a list of all of the publications available without charge from the Committee on Public Information at Washington, D. C., through the Scoutmasters. These reports will give the scouts and scout officials an opportunity to make available to the Committee on Public Information from time to time, not only facts about their work, but suggestions as to additional publications which might be helpful.

A Scout Is Thrifty.   Avoid waste. A scout is thrifty, he wastes nothing, and in this special responsibility all scouts will be particularly careful to avoid the wasting of any printed matter.

"Every Scout to Boost America" Results

If each of the 285,661 scouts does his job well and reaches on an average of fifteen persons, who will join with him in working under the slogan "EVERY SCOUT TO BOOST AMERICA," and if each of these fifteen in turn places important printed matter in the hands of at least one other person, it will mean that through the Boy Scouts of America the Committee on Public Information will have an audience of over eight million people. Worth working for? We should say so!

General Information

A supply of franked postal cards is to be given to each Scoutmaster so that the persons who have been selected for the honor list of influential persons may have the opportunity of selecting from the available government publications any or all of these publications that they wish to read, provided they will agree after reading the same to pass them on where they will serve the purpose of public enlightenment.

Each Scoutmaster is to be furnished with a complete set of all of the government publications, in order that all of the members of his troop may be completely informed. Each scout and scout official is expected to seize every opportunity to serve the Committee on Public Information by making available authoritative information. It is up to the Boy Scouts to see that as many people as possible have an intelligent understanding of any and all facts incident to our present national crisis and the World War.

Reports

Each scout is to be furnished with a blank report on which he will write the name and address of the persons to whom he distributes any of the government publications. These reports are to be sent to the Committee on Public Information, through the Scoutmasters or scout officials.

Points to Remember

A Brief Review.

1. Get your district assigned by Scoutmaster.
2. Make up your list of influential persons with the aid of your Scoutmaster.
3. Read this book of instructions and study the list of other pamphlets available for free distribution, as shown on pages 12–15.
4. Go to the person or persons whom you have agreed to interview. Ask directly for such person or persons.
5. Tell them, simply and courteously, why you are there. Show them President Wilson's letter on the back of your credential card.
6. Tell them what the Committee on Public Information is for.
7. Tell them what the Committee on Public Information has to give them. Explain what is in the pamphlets.
8. Tell them where and how they can get the pamphlets. Show them the post cards which will order the pamphlets. Offer to mail the post cards.
9. Tell them you will, if desired, get any of the free publications for them.
10. When you deliver any of the pamphlets, get the persons to whom you deliver them, to promise not only to read the pamphlets but to place them in the hands of some person where they will likely do good.
11. If anybody asks you questions you cannot answer, find out the answer and go back with it.

12. Go to your Scoutmaster for information. If he wants more particulars he will be able to get them from National Headquarters, Boy Scouts of America.

13. Don't waste pamphlets. They keep alive the spirit of the Declaration of Independence.

14. Be proud of your job. Enthusiasm catches like fire. "Boost America."

> Sincerely yours,
> JAMES E. WEST,
> *Chief Scout Executive.*

PAMPHLETS NOW READY FOR CIRCULATION

NOTE.—A set will be sent every Scoutmaster. You will need to know what is in these pamphlets so as to act as a serviceable bureau of information and be able to give each person the particular intelligence he seeks.

Series I. (Red, White and Blue Covers.)

No. 1. How the War Came to America. This is what a good many people want to know. They realize that war is here, knocking at the gates, but how it came to be here—as to that they are a little hazy in their minds. They know it has something to do with the Monroe Doctrine and the freedom of the seas and a meeting held at the Hague, but just what—well, that is what the pamphlet can tell them. Then there are the people who wish they had saved the President's speech to the Senate last January and his great war message to Congress, last April, which fired another shot "heard round the world," and his almost equally significant Flag Day speech last June. And here they are gathered together in this pamphlet in convenient form. The pamphlet has been also translated into German, Polish, Bohemian, Italian, Spanish, Swedish, Yiddish and Portuguese and stands the Melting Pot process very well too.

No. 4. The President's Flag Day Speech with Evidence of Germany's Plans. In this address, with the accompanying notes, are marshalled forth an impressive array of facts as to how Germany—or rather, "Germany's military masters" forced us into the war. By their own mouths they are condemned. Why they wanted war, what price they were willing to pay for it, the scope and treachery of the scheme involved is all here for him to read who will and many will be interested to read the record.

NOTE.—This is the pamphlet Scouts are asked to deliver in person to those interested.

No. 5. Conquest and Kultur. This pamphlet, too, deals searchingly with Germany's war aims and dreams of a "Deutschland uber Alles" with a vengeance. It contains a statement of Germany's attitude toward America and a considerable body of quotations from the pens and lips of some of the German war lords, given without comment. No comment is necessary. The evidence of Kultur is all in. Germany meant to swallow the world as its oyster. Her benevolent intention is disclosed in this pamphlet.

No. 6. German War Practices. A calm statement of facts for those who really want to know just how the German military machine worked in Belgium and Northern France, based solely upon American and German evidence. The pamphlet is cool, but does not leave the reader in that condition.

Series II. (Plain Black Covers.)

No. 101. The War Message and the Facts behind It. The President's War Message, with the explanatory notes, makes a brief document—only 32 pages—but it contains the Bed Rock Facts every citizen of these United States ought to know.

No. 102. The Nation in Arms. Addresses by Secretaries Lane and Baker, showing simply and forcefully why we are at war.

No. 103. The Government of Germany. We hear often that Germany is liberal and democratic. This study of the German Constitution and the actual workings of government under the Prussian rule of thumb is likely to upset that theory.

No. 104. The Great War. It is not precisely the same thing to be watching a "scrap" from outside the ring as it is to be in the scrimmage. A good many Americans went through this change of mind and temper in their relations to the great war. This pamphlet makes a study of that change. It will interest those who have passed through it.

No. 105. The War of Self Defense. Another expression of how war was thrust upon us, containing addresses by Lansing, Secretary of State, and Post, the Assistant Secretary of Labor.

No. 106. American Loyalty. An interesting pamphlet for and by the open minded, written by Americans of German descent who, having found their ideal of political liberty in this country, believe with President Wilson—and don't mind saying so—that we are fighting for and not against the German people in this war.

No. 107. A German Translation of the Above.

No. 108. American Interest in Popular Government Abroad. A pamphlet of particular appeal to historians and others interested in proof from historic utterances and government records that America is only living true to her destiny and the ideals of her great leaders in helping to make the "world safe for Democracy."

No. 109. Home Reading Course for Citizen Soldiers. Thirty daily lessons with practical hints for men selected for service in the National Army— an introductory course to the various manuals and regulations of the United States Army.

No. 110. First Session of the War Congress.   A reference volume containing a complete summary of all legislation passed by the first session of the 65th Congress with dates, notes and brief extracts from important debates.

How to Secure the Pamphlets

Address:
Committee on Public Information,
10 Jackson Place,
Washington, D. C.
Give the titles of the two books you desire. Do not order by catalogue number.
Give your name, street number, city and state. Write plainly. Typewriter preferred.
Use Official Request blanks when available.

SELECTION **24**

The Yanks Who Went "Over There": Report of General John J. Pershing, November 20, 1918

John J. Pershing had the kind of military background that might have made him, under different circumstances, a popular hero comparable to General Grant or Admiral Dewey. But very few boys were to be named Pershing, as many had been named Grant and Dewey—or, for that matter, as many would be named Woodrow or Wilson. Born and reared in Missouri, Pershing had fought against Geronimo just after graduating from West Point in 1886. He later led a campaign against the Sioux and fought in the Philippines during the insurrection. He first came to national attention in 1916 as commander of the Punitive Expedition in Mexico. Indian fighter, bandit chaser, dashing, and tall in the saddle, Pershing, superficially at least, should have been a natural as a military hero. But the scope and complexity of World War I required that a commanding general be essentially a military administrator rather than a charismatic man on horseback. People tried hard but unsuccessfully to make Black Jack—his nickname that never really caught on—into the traditional kind of hero gen-

eral. He remained a somewhat distant and impersonal but efficient and effective military executive in an olive-drab suit. His no-nonsense, matter-of-fact manner, as well as his confident command, revealed itself in crisp if cliché-ridden military prose.

The reader should bear in mind as he reads this report by General Pershing that the doughboy, as the American foot soldier of World War I was popularly called, hardly saw the war the way his commanding general saw it. After the first weeks of war in 1914, the war on the western front settled down to four years of particularly unpleasant and dangerous nastiness. Each side was dug in well in labyrinthine trenches and had heavy artillery support. The front remained relatively static, and each side threw thousands of lives into sporadic efforts to push the enemy back a few hundred yards. (The total casualties suffered by American forces during the war do not compare too badly with casualties in other American wars, but the ratio of battle casualties to men engaged in battle was unusually high.) The doughboy lived in the cold mud, ever vulnerable to enemy action he could do little about, and this persistent suffering and danger were to him the reality of the war, rather than the bird's-eye view of a general concerned with maps and organization charts.

General Pershing's report on casualties near the end of this selection needs elaboration. His figures applied only to the American Expeditionary Force and were preliminary. This report was prepared only nine days after the armistice. The subsequent official statistics, as reported in U.S. Bureau of the Census. Historical Statistics of the United States: Colonial Times to 1957 *(Washington: Government Printing Office, 1960) page 735, were as follows: battle deaths, 53,402; other deaths, 63,114; wounds not mortal, 204,002. Comparison with other wars is interesting. Total battle deaths for the Union forces in the Civil War were 140,414; the figures for World War II and the Korean War were 291,557 and 33,629, respectively.*

This report, cut by about one-fourth by eliminating some of the details of army organization, may be found in War Department Annual Reports, 1918 *(Washington: Government Printing Office, 1919), volume I, pages 69, 73–83, 85.*

November 20, 1918.

My Dear Mr. Secretary:

In response to your request, I have the honor to submit this brief summary of the organization and operations of the American Expeditionary Force from May 26, 1917, until the signing of the armistice November 11, 1918. Pursuant to your instructions, immediately upon receiving my orders I selected a small staff and proceeded to Europe in order to become familiar with conditions at the earliest possible moment.

The warmth of our reception in England and France was only equaled by the readiness of the commanders in chief of the veteran armies of the Allies and their staffs to place their experience at our disposal. In consultation with them the most effective means of cooperation of effort was considered. With French and British armies at their maximum strength, and all efforts to dispossess the enemy from his firmly intrenched positions in Belgium and France failed, it was necessary to plan for an American force adequate to turn the scale in favor of the Allies. Taking account of the strength of the central powers at that time, the immensity of the problem which confronted us could hardly be overestimated. The first requisite being an organization that could give intelligent direction to effort, the formation of a General Staff occupied my early attention. . . .

Artillery, Airplanes, and Tanks

Our entry into the war found us with few of the auxiliaries necessary for its conduct in the modern sense. Among our most important deficiencies in material were artillery, aviation, and tanks. In order to meet our requirements as rapidly as possible, we accepted the offer of the French Government to provide us with the necessary artillery equipment of seventy-fives, one fifty-five millimeter howitzers, and one fifty-five G. P. F. guns from their own factories for thirty divisions. The wisdom of this course is fully demonstrated by the fact that, although we soon began the manufacture of these classes of guns at home, there were no guns of the calibers mentioned manufactured in America on our front at the date the armistice was signed. The only guns of these types produced at home thus far received in France are 109 seventy-five millimeter guns.

In aviation we were in the same situation, and here again the French Government came to our aid until our own aviation program should be under way. We obtained from the French the necessary planes for training our personnel, and they have provided us with a total of 2,676 pursuit, observation, and bombing planes. The first airplanes received from home arrived in May, and altogether we have received 1,379. The first American squadron completely equipped by American production, including airplanes, crossed the German lines on August 7, 1918. As to tanks, we were also compelled to rely upon the French. Here, however, we were less fortunate, for the reason that the French production could barely meet the requirements of their own armies.

It should be fully realized that the French Government has always taken a most liberal attitude and has been most anxious to give us every possible assistance in meeting our deficiencies in these as well as in other respects. Our dependence upon France for artillery, aviation, and tanks was, of course, due to the fact that our industries had not been exclusively devoted to military production. All credit is due our own manufacturers for their efforts to meet our requirements, as at the time the armistice was signed we were able to look forward to the early supply of practically all our necessities from our own factories.

The welfare of the troops touches my responsibility as Commander in Chief to the mothers and fathers and kindred of the men who came to France in the impressionable period of youth. They could not have the privilege accorded European soldiers during their periods of leave of visiting their families and renewing their home ties. Fully realizing that the standard of conduct that should be established for them must have a permanent influence in their lives and on the character of their future citizenship, the Red Cross, the Young Men's Christian Association, Knights of Columbus, the Salvation Army, and the Jewish Welfare Board, as auxiliaries in this work, were encouraged in every possible way. The fact that our soldiers, in a land of different customs and language, have borne themselves in a manner in keeping with the cause for which they fought, is due not only to the efforts in their behalf but much more to other high ideals, their discipline, and their innate sense of self-respect. It should be recorded, however, that the members of these welfare societies have been untiring in their desire to be of real service to our officers and men. The patriotic devotion of these representative men and women has given a new significance to the Golden Rule, and we owe to them a debt of gratitude that can never be repaid.

Combat Operations

During our periods of training in the trenches some of our divisions had engaged the enemy in local combats, the most important of which was Seicheprey by the Twenty-sixth on April 20, in the Toul sector, but none had participated in action as a unit. The First division, which had passed through the preliminary stages of training, had gone to the trenches for its first period of instruction at the end of October and by March 21, when the German offensive in Picardy began, we had four divisions with experience in the trenches, all of which were equal to any demands of battle action. The crisis which this offensive developed was such that our occupation of an American sector must be postponed.

On March 28 I placed at the disposal of Marshal Foch who had been agreed upon as Commander in Chief of the Allied Armies, all of our forces to be used as he might decide. At his request the first division was transferred from the Toul sector to a position in reserve at Chaumont en Vexin. As German superiority in numbers required prompt action, an agreement was reached at the Albeville conference of the Allied premiers and commanders and myself on May 2 by which British shipping was to transport 10 American divisions to the British Army area, where they were to be trained and equipped, and additional British shipping was to be provided for as many divisions as possible for use elsewhere.

On April 26 the First Division had gone into the line in the Montdidier salient on the Picardy battle front. Tactics had been suddenly revolutionized to those of open warfare, and our men, confident of the results of their training, were eager for the test. On the morning of May 28 this division attacked the commanding German position in its front, taking with splendid dash the town of Cantigny and all other objectives, which were organized and held steadfastly against vicious counterattacks and galling artillery fire. Although local, this brilliant action had an electrical effect, as it demonstrated our fighting qualities under extreme battle conditions, and also that the enemy's troops were not altogether invincible.

The Germans' Aisne offensive, which began on May 27 had advanced rapidly toward the River Marne and Paris, and the Allies faced a crisis equally as grave as that of the Picardy offensive in March. Again every available man was placed at Marshal Foch's disposal, and the Third Division, which had just come from its preliminary training in the trenches, was hurried to the Marne. Its motorized machine-gun battalion preceded the other units and successfully held the bridgehead at the Marne, opposite Chateau Thierry. The Second Division, in reserve near Montdidier, was sent by motor trucks and other available transport to check the progress of the enemy toward Paris. The Division attacked and retook the town and railroad station at Bouresches and sturdily held its ground against the enemy's best guard divisions. In the battle of Belleau Wood, which followed, our men proved their superiority and gained a strong tactical position, with far greater loss to the enemy than to ourselves. On July 1, before the Second was relieved, it captured the village of Vaux with most splendid precision.

Meanwhile our Second Corps, under Maj. Gen. George W. Read, had been organized for the command of our divisions with the British, which were held back in training areas or assigned to second-line defenses. Five of the ten divisions were withdrawn from the British area in June, three to relieve divisions in Lorraine and the Vosges and two to the Paris area to join the group of American divisions which stood between the city and any farther advance of the enemy in that direction.

The great June-July troop movement from the States was well under way, and, although these troops were to be given some preliminary training before being put into action, their very presence warranted the use of all the older divisions in the confidence that we did not lack reserves. Elements of the Forty-second Division were in the line east of Rheims against the German offensive of July 15, and held their ground unflinchingly. On the right flank of this offensive four companies of the Twenty-eighth Division were in position in face of the advancing waves of the German infantry. The Third Division was holding the bank of the Marne from the bend east of the mouth of the Surmelin to the west of Mézy, opposite Chateau Thierry, where a large force of German infantry sought to force a passage under support of powerful artillery concentrations and under cover of smoke screens. A single regiment of the Third wrote one of the most brilliant pages in our military annals on this occasion. It prevented the crossing at certain points on its front while, on either flank, the Germans, who had gained a footing, pressed forward. Our men, firing in three directions, met the German attacks with counterattacks at critical points and succeeded in throwing two German divisions into complete confusion, capturing 600 prisoners.

The great force of the German Chateau Thierry offensive established the deep Marne salient, but the enemy was taking chances, and the vulnerability of this pocket to attack might be turned to his disadvantage. Seizing this opportunity to support my conviction, every division with any sort of training was made available for use in a counter-offensive. The place of honor in the thrust toward Soissons on July 18 was given to our First and Second Divisions in company with chosen French divisions. Without the usual brief warning of a preliminary bombardment, the massed French and American artillery, firing by the map, laid down its rolling barrage at dawn while the infantry began its charge. The tactical

handling of our troops under these trying conditions was excellent throughout the action. The enemy brought up large numbers of reserves and made
a stubborn defense both with machine guns and artillery, but through five
days' fighting the First Division continued to advance until it had gained
the heights above Soissons and captured the village of Berzy-le-sec. The
Second Division took Beau Repaire farm and Vierzy in a very rapid
advance and reached a position in front of Tigny at the end of its second
day. These two divisions captured 7,000 prisoners and over 100 pieces of
artillery.

The Twenty-sixth Division, which, with a French division, was under
command of our First Corps, acted as a pivot of the movement toward
Soissons. On the 18th it took the village of Torcy while the Third Division
was crossing the Marne in pursuit of the retiring enemy. The Twenty-sixth
attacked again on the 21st, and the enemy withdrew past the Chateau
Thierry-Soissons road. The Third Division, continuing its progress, took
the heights of Mont St. Père and the villages of Chartèves and Jaulgonne
in the fact of both machine-gun and artillery fire.

On the 24th, after the Germans had fallen back from Trugny and
Epieds, our Forty-second Division, which had been brought over from
the Champagne, relieved the Twenty-sixth and, fighting its way through
the Forêt de Fère, overwhelmed the nest of machine guns in its path. By
the 27th it had reached the Oureq, whence the Third and Fourth Divisions
were already advancing while the French divisions with which we were
cooperating were moving forward at other points.

The Third Division had made its advance into Roncheres Wood on the
29th and was relieved for rest by a brigade of the Thirty-second. The
Forty-second and Thirty-second undertook the task of conquering the
heights beyond Cierges, the Forty-second capturing Sergy and the Thirty-
second capturing Hill 230, both American divisions joining in the pursuit
of the enemy to the Vesle, and thus the operation of reducing the salient
was finished. Meanwhile the Forty-second was relieved by the Fourth at
Chéry-Chartreuve, and the Thirty-second by the Twenty-eighth, while
the Seventy-seventh Division took up a position on the Vesle. The operations of these divisions on the Vesle were under the Third Corps, Maj.
Gen. Robert L. Bullard, commanding.

Battle of St. Mihiel

With the reduction of the Marne salient we could look forward to the
concentration of our divisions in our own zone. In view of the forthcoming
operation against the St. Mihiel salient, which had long been planned
as our first offensive action on a large scale, the First Army was organized
on August 10 under my personal command. While American units had
held different divisional and corps sectors along the western front, there
had not been up to this time, for obvious reasons, a distinct American
sector; but, in view of the important parts the American forces were now
to play, it was necessary to take over a permanent portion of the line.
Accordingly, on August 30, the line beginning at Port sur Seille, east of

the Moselle and extending to the west through St. Mihiel, thence north to a point opposite Verdun, was placed under my command. The American sector was afterwards extended across the Meuse to the western edge of the Argonne Forest, and included the Second Colonial French, which held the point of the salient, and the Seventeenth French Corps, which occupied the heights above Verdun.

The preparation for a complicated operation against the formidable defenses in front of us included the assembling of divisions and of corps and army artillery, transport, aircraft, tanks, ambulances, the location of hospitals, and the molding together of all of the elements of a great modern army with its own railheads, supplied directly by our own Service of Supply. The concentration for this operation, which was to be a surprise, involved the movement, mostly at night, of approximately 600,000 troops, and required for its success the most careful attention to every detail.

The French were generous in giving us assistance in corps and army artillery, with its personnel, and we were confident from the start of our superiority over the enemy in guns of all calibers. Our heavy guns were able to reach Metz and to interfere seriously with German rail movements. The French Independent Air Force was placed under my command which, together with the British bombing squadrons and our air forces, gave us the largest assembly of aviation that had ever been engaged in one operation on the western front.

From Les Eparges around the nose of the salient at St. Mihiel to the Moselle River the line was roughly 40 miles long and situated on commanding ground greatly strengthened by artificial defenses. Our First Corps (Eighty-second, Ninetieth, Fifth, and Second Divisions) under command of Maj. Gen. Hunter Liggett, restrung its right on Pont-a-Mousson, with its left joining our Third Corps (the Eighty-ninth, Forty-second, and First Divisions), under Maj. Gen. Joseph T. Dickman, in line to Xivray, were to swing in toward Vigneulles on the pivot of the Moselle River for the initial assault. From Xivray to Mouilly the Second Colonial French Corps was in line in the center and our Fifth Corps, under command of Maj. Gen. George H. Cameron, with our Twenty-sixth Division and a French division at the western base of the salient, were to attack three difficult hills—Les Eparges, Combres, and Amaramthe. Our First Corps had in reserve the Seventy-eighth Division, our Fourth Corps the Third Division, and our First Army the Thirty-fifth and Ninety-first Divisions with the Eightieth and Thirty-third available. It should be understood that our corps organizations are very elastic, and that we have at no time had permanent assignments of divisions to corps.

After four hours artillery preparation, the seven American divisions in the front line advanced at 5 a. m., on September 12, assisted by a limited number of tanks manned partly by Americans and partly by the French. These divisions, accompanied by groups of wire cutters and others armed with bangalore torpedoes, went through the successive bands of barbed wire that protected the enemy's front line and support trenches, in irresistible waves on schedule time, breaking down all defense of an enemy demoralized by the great volume of our artillery fire and our sudden approach out of the fog.

Our First Corps advanced to Thiaucourt, while our Fourth Corps curved back to the southwest through Nonsard. The Second Colonial French Corps made the slight advance required of it on very difficult ground, and the Fifth Corps took its three ridges and repulsed a counter attack. A rapid march brought reserve regiments of a Division of the Fifth Corps into Vigneulles in the early morning, where it linked up with patrols of our Fourth Corps, closing the salient and forming a new line west of Thiaucourt to Vigneulles and beyond Fresnes-en-Woevre. At the cost of only 7,000 casualties, mostly light, we had taken 16,000 prisoners and 443 guns, a great quantity of material, released the inhabitants of many villages from enemy domination, and established our lines in a position to threaten Metz. This signal success of the American First Army in its first offensive was of prime importance. The Allies found they had a formidable army to aid them, and the enemy learned finally that he had one to reckon with.

Meuse-Argonne Offensive: First Phase

On the day after we had taken the St. Mihiel salient, much of our Corps and Army artillery which had operated at St. Mihiel, and our Divisions in reserve at other points, were already on the move toward the area back of the line between the Meuse River and the western edge of the forest of Argonne. With the exception of St. Mihiel, the old German front line from Switzerland to the east of Rheims was still intact. In the general attack all along the line, the operation assigned the American Army as the hinge of this Allied offensive was directed toward the important railroad communications of the German armies through Méziéres and Sedan. The enemy must hold fast to this part of his lines or the withdrawal of his forces with four years' accumulation of plants and material would be dangerously imperiled.

The German Army had as yet shown no demoralization and, while the mass of its troops had suffered in morale, its first-class divisions and notably its machine-gun defense were exhibiting remarkable tactical efficiency as well as courage. The German General Staff was fully aware of the consequences of a success on the Meuse-Argonne line. Certain that he would do everything in his power to oppose us, the action was planned with as much secrecy as possible and was undertaken with the determination to use all our Divisions in forcing decision. We expected to draw the best German divisions to our front and to consume them while the enemy was held under grave apprehension lest our attack should break his line, which it was our firm purpose to do.

Our right flank was protected by the Meuse, while our left embraced the Argonne Forest whose ravines, hills, and elaborate defense screened by dense thickets had been generally considered impregnable. Our order of battle from right to left was the Third Corps from the Meuse to Malancourt, with the Thirty-third. Eightieth, and Fourth Divisions in line, and the Third Division as corps reserve; the Fifth Corps from Malancourt to Vauquois, with Seventy-ninth, Eighty-seventh, and Ninety-first Divisions in line, and the Thirty-second in corps reserve; and the First

Corps, from Vauquois to Vienne le Chateau, with Thirty-fifth, Twenty-eighth, and Seventy-seventh Divisions in line, and the Ninety-second in corps reserve. The Army reserve consisted of the First, Twenty-ninth, and Eighty-second Divisions.

On the night of September 25 our troops quietly took the place of the French who thinly held the line in this sector which had long been inactive. In the attack which began on the 26th we drove through the barbed wire entanglements and the sea of shell craters across No Man's Land, mastering all the first-line defenses. Continuing on the 27th and 28th, against machine guns and artillery of an increasing number of enemy reserve divisions, we penetrated to a depth of from 3 to 7 miles, and took the village of Montfaucon and its commanding hill and Exermont, Gercourt, Cuisy, Septsarges, Malancourt, Ivoiry, Epinonville, Charpentry, Very, and other villages. East of the Meuse one of our Divisions, which was with the Second Colonial French Corps, captured Marcheville and Rieville, giving further protection to the flank of our main body. We had taken 10,000 prisoners, we had gained our point of forcing the battle into the open and were prepared for the enemy's reaction, which was bound to come as he had good roads and ample railroad facilities for bringing up his artillery and reserves.

In the chill rain of dark nights our engineers had to build new roads across spongy, shell-torn areas, repair broken roads beyond No Man's Land, and build bridges. Our gunners, with no thought of sleep, put their shoulders to wheels and dragropes to bring their guns through the mire in support of the infantry, now under the increasing fire of the enemy's artillery. Our attack had taken the enemy by surprise, but, quickly recovering himself, he began to fire counter attacks in strong force, supported by heavy bombardments, with large quantities of gas. From September 28 until October 4 we maintained the offensive against patches of woods defended by snipers and continuous lines of machine guns, and pushed forward our guns and transport, seizing strategical points in preparation for further attacks.

Other Units with Allies

Other Divisions attached to the Allied armies were doing their part. It was the fortune of our Second Corps, composed of the Twenty-seventh and Thirtieth Divisions, which had remained with the British, to have a place of honor in cooperation with the Australian Corps on September 29 and October 1 in the assault on the Hindenburg line where the St. Quentin Canal passes through a tunnel under a ridge. The Thirtieth Division speedily broke through the main line of defense for all its objectives, while the Twenty-seventh pushed on impetuously through the main line until some of its elements reached Gouy. In the midst of the maze of trenches and shell craters and under cross fire from machine guns the other elements fought desperately against odds. In this and in later actions, from October 6 to October 19, our Second Corps captured over 6,000 prisoners and advanced over 13 miles. The spirit and aggressiveness of these Divisions have been highly praised by the British Army commander under whom they served.

On October 2–9 our Second and Thirty-sixth Divisions were sent to assist the French in an important attack against the old German positions before Rheims. The Second conquered the complicated defense works on their front against a persistent defense worthy of the grimmest period of trench warfare and attacked the strongly held wooded hill of Blanc Mont, which they captured in a second assault, sweeping over it with consummate dash and skill. This Division then repulsed strong counter attacks before the village and cemetery of Ste. Etienne and took the town, forcing the Germans to fall back from before Rheims and yield positions they had held since September, 1914. On October 9 the Thirty-sixth Division relieved the Second and, in its first experience under fire, withstood very severe artillery bombardment and rapidly took up the pursuit of the enemy, now retiring behind the Aisne.

Meuse-Argonne Offensive; Second Phase

The Allied progress elsewhere cheered the efforts of our men in this crucial contest as the German command threw in more and more first-class troops to stop our advance. We made steady headway in the almost impenetrable and strongly held Argonne Forest, for, despite this reinforcement, it was our Army that was doing the driving. Our aircraft was increasing in skill and numbers and forcing the issue, and our Infantry and Artillery were improving rapidly with each new experience. The replacements fresh from home were put into exhausted divisions with little time for training, but they had the advantage of serving beside men who knew their business and who had almost become veterans overnight. The enemy had taken every advantage of the terrain, which especially favored the defense by a prodigal use of machine guns manned by highly trained veterans and by using his artillery at short ranges. In the face of such strong frontal positions we should have been unable to accomplish any progress according to previously accepted standards, but I had every confidence in our aggressive tactics and the courage of our troops.

On October 4 the attack was renewed all along our front. The Third Corps tilting to the left followed the Brieulles-Cunel road; our Fifth Corps took Gesnes while the First Corps advanced for over 2 miles along the irregular valley of the Aire River and in the wooded hills of the Argonne that bordered the river, used by the enemy with all his art and weapons of defense. This sort of fighting continued against an enemy striving to hold every foot of ground and whose very strong counter-attacks challenged us at every point. On the 7th the First Corps captured Chatel-Chéhéry and continued along the river to Cornay. On the east of Meuse sector one of the two Divisions cooperating with the French captured Consenvoye and the Haumont Woods. On the 9th the Fifth Corps, in its progress up the Aire, took Fléville, and the Third Corps which had continuous fighting against odds was working its way through Brieulles and Cunel. On the 10th we had cleared the Argonne Forest of the enemy.

It was now necessary to constitute a second army, and on October 9 the immediate command of the First Army was turned over to Lieut. Gen. Hunter Liggett. The command of the Second Army, whose divisions occupied a sector in the Woevre, was given to Lieut. Gen. Robert L. Bullard, who had been commander of the First Division and then of the Third Corps. Maj. Gen. Dickman was transferred to the command of the First Corps, while the Fifth Corps was placed under Maj. Gen. Charles P. Summerall, who had recently commanded the First Division. Maj. Gen. John L. Hines, who had gone rapidly up from regimental to division commander, was assigned to the Third Corps. These four officers had been in France from the early days of the expedition and had learned their lessons in the school of practical warfare.

Our constant pressure against the enemy brought day by day more prisoners, mostly survivors from machine-gun nests captured in fighting at close quarters. On October 18 there was very fierce fighting in the Caures Woods east of the Meuse and in the Ormont Woods. On the 14th the First Corps took St. Juvin, and the Fifth Corps, in hand-to-hand encounters, entered the formidable Kriemhilde line, where the enemy had hoped to check us indefinitely. Later the Fifth Corps penetrated further the Kriemhilde line, and the First Corps took Champigneulles and the important town of Grandpre. Our dogged offensive was wearing down the enemy, who continued desperately to throw his best troops against us, thus weakening his line in front of our Allies and making their advance less difficult.

Divisions in Belgium

Meanwhile we were not only able to continue the battle, but our Thirty-seventh and Ninety-first Divisions were hastily withdrawn from our front and dispatched to help the French Army in Belgium. Detraining in the neighborhood of Ypres, these Divisions advanced by rapid stages to the fighting line and were assigned to adjacent French corps. On October 31, in continuation of the Flanders offensive, they attacked and methodically broke down all enemy resistance. On November 3 the Thirty-seventh had completed its mission in dividing the enemy across the Escaut River and firmly established itself along the east bank included in the division zone of action. By a clever flanking movement troops of the Ninety-first Division captured Spitaals Bosschen, a difficult wood extending across the central part of the division sector, reached the Escaut, and penetrated into the town of Audenarde. These divisions received high commendation from their corps commanders for their dash and energy.

Meuse-Argonne: Last Phase

On the 23d the Third and Fifth Corps pushed northward to the level of Bantheville. While we continued to press forward and throw back the enemy's violent counter-attacks with great loss to him, a regrouping of our forces was under way for the final assault. Evidences of loss of morale by the enemy gave our men more confidence in attack and more fortitude in enduring the fatigue of incessant effort and the hardships of very inclement weather.

With comparatively well-rested divisions, the final advance in the Meuse-Argonne front was begun on November 1. Our increased artillery force acquitted itself magnificently in support of the advance, and the enemy broke before the determined infantry, which, by its presistent fighting of the past weeks and the dash of this attack, had overcome his will to resist. The Third Corps took Aincreville, Doulcon, and Andevanne, and the Fifth Corps took Landres et St. Georges and pressed through successive lines of resistance to Bayonville and Chennery. On the 2d the First Corps joined in the movement, which now became an impetuous onslaught that could not be stayed.

On the 3d advance troops surged forward in pursuit, some by motor trucks, while the artillery pressed along the country roads close behind. The First Corps reached Authe and Châtillon-Sur-Bar, the Fifth Corps, Fosse and Nouart, and the Third Corps Halles, penetrating the enemy's line to a depth of 12 miles. Our large caliber guns had advanced and were skillfully brought into position to fire upon the important lines at Montmedy, Longuyon, and Conflans. Our Third Corps crossed the Meuse on the 5th and the other corps, in the full confidence that the day was theirs, eagerly cleared the way of machine guns as they swept northward, maintaining complete coordination throughout. On the 6th, a division of the First Corps reached a point on the Meuse opposite Sedan, 25 miles from our line of departure. The strategical goal which was our highest hope was gained. We had cut the enemy's main line of communications, and nothing but surrender or an armistice could save his army from complete disaster.

In all 40 enemy divisions had been used against us in the Meuse-Argonne battle. Between September 26 and November 6 we took 26,059 prisoners and 468 guns on this front. Our Divisions engaged were the First, Second, Third, Fourth, Fifth, Twenty-sixth, Twenty-eighth, Twenty-ninth, Thirty-second, Thirty-third, Thirty-fifth, Thirty-seventh, Forty-second, Seventy-seventh, Seventy-eighth, Seventy-ninth, Eightieth, Eighty-second, Eighty-ninth, Ninetieth, and Ninety-first. Many of our divisions remained in line for a length of time that required nerves of steel, while others were sent in again after only a few days of rest. The First, Fifth, Twenty-sixth, Forty-second, Seventh-seventh, Eightieth, Eighty-ninth, and Ninetieth were in the line twice. Although some of the divisions were fighting their first battle, they soon became equal to the best.

Operations East of the Meuse

On the three days preceding November 10, the Third, the Second Colonial, and the Seventeeth French Corps fought a difficult struggle through the Meuse Hills south of Stenay and forced the enemy into the plain. Meanwhile, my plans for further use of the American forces contemplated an advance between the Meuse and the Moselle in the direction of Longwy by the First Army, while, at the same time, the Second Army should assure the offensive toward the rich iron fields of Briey. These operations were to be followed by an offensive toward Chateau-Salins east of the Moselle, thus isolating Metz. Accordingly, attacks on the American front had been ordered and that of the Second Army was in progress on the morning of November 11, when instructions were received that hostilities should cease at 11 o'clock a. m.

At this moment the line of the American sector, from right to left, began at Port-Sur-Seille, thence across the Moselle to Vandieres and through the Woevre to Bezonvaux in the foothills of the Meuse, thence along to the foothills and through the northern edge of the Woevre forests to the Meuse at Mouzay, thence along the Meuse connecting with the French under Sedan.

Relations with the Allies

Cooperation among the Allies has at all times been most cordial. A far greater effort has been put forth by the Allied armies and staffs to assist us than could have been expected. The French Government and Army have always stood ready to furnish us with supplies, equipment, and transportation and to aid us in every way. In the towns and hamlets wherever our troops have been stationed or billeted the French people have everywhere received them more as relatives and intimate friends than as soldiers of a foreign army. For these things words are quite inadequate to express our gratitude. There can be no doubt that the relations growing out of our associations here assure a permanent friendship between the two peoples. Although we have not been so intimately associated with the people of Great Britain, yet their troops and ours when thrown together have always warmly fraternized. The reception of those of our forces who have passed through England and of those who have been stationed there has always been enthusiastic. Altogether it has been deeply impressed upon us that the ties of language and blood bring the British and ourselves together completely and inseparably.

Strength

There are in Europe altogether including a regiment and some sanitary units with the Italian Army and the organizations at Murmansk, also including those en route from the States, approximately 2,053,347 men, less our losses. Of this total there are in France 1,338,169 combatant troops. Forty divisions have arrived, of which the Infantry personnel of 10 have been used as replacements, leaving 30 divisions now in France organized into three armies of three corps each.

The losses of the Americans up to November 18 are: Killed and wounded, 36,145; died of disease, 14,811; deaths unclassified, 2,204; wounded, 179,625; prisoners, 2,163; missing, 1,160. We have captured about 44,000 prisoners and 1,400 guns, howitzers and trench mortars. . . .

Finally, I pay the supreme tribute to our officers and soldiers of the line. When I think of their heroism, their patience under hardships, their unflinching spirit of offensive action, I am filled with emotion which I am unable to express. Their deeds are immortal, and they have earned the eternal gratitude of our country.

I am, Mr. Secretary, very respectfully,
JOHN J. PERSHING,
General, Commander in Chief
American Expeditionary Forces.

To the Secretary of War.

SELECTION

Rationalizing Industrial Production for the War: Bernard Baruch and the War Industries Board

The concept of rationalization—that is, of economic organization for maximum efficiency—is as basic to the development of a technologically advanced society as harnessing steam or electric power. Rationalization of production began first at the level of the individual firm, which made its operations efficient to compete advantageously with other firms in its industry. In the late nineteenth century some industries in the United States began to become rationalized, either through the domination of one giant firm in the field or through the cooperation of several corporations. Not until World War I, however, had it ever appeared important to rationalize all of American industry, to reorganize manufacturing and distribution generally; the purpose then, of course, was to win the war as quickly as possible. Operating at forced draft, American industry performed what only a few months before would have been thought miracles of production. The chief organizing, coordinating, planning, regulating agency of the wondrously complex national industrial machine was the War Industries Board (WIB).

Early in the war the Federal government only groped and stumbled along the way to industrial adequacy. At first the government concerned itself only with expediting the production of munitions, but the experience of the General Munitions Board soon made clear that far more was involved. In late July, 1917, the WIB came into being, but the powers granted it were too limited to perform the task that the situation demanded. The next winter saw fantastic industrial chaos. A Senate committee revealed the confusion and recommended abolition of all government controls, the introduction of thorough laissez faire, as a solution. President Wilson and his advisers believed that the difficulty lay with too little rather than too much governmental direction, and in March, 1918, the Federal government reorganized the WIB, increased its powers, and made Bernard Baruch its Chairman. In the next eight months the WIB made a great number of innovations. This selection, from Baruch's report on its operations, describes some of these innovations in the area of reducing irrational waste.

Baruch's comments near the end of this selection on the applicability of WIB principles to the peacetime economy pose some critical questions as to the role of the Federal government in the modern technologically advanced economy and are interesting in view of the subsequent activities of Secretary of Commerce Herbert C. Hoover and, in the early Franklin D. Roosevelt administration, of the National Recovery Administration, or NRA. (Many WIB officials, incidentally, were later important in similar work for Presidents Hoover and Roosevelt. Among them, besides Baruch himself, were Alexander Legge and General Hugh S. Johnson.) One of these critical questions, one that obviously caused Hoover and Baruch a great deal of worry, was how far government's powers should go in forcing rationalization upon what Baruch called "recalcitrants." In peacetime at least, thought Baruch, government's approach should be "in a friendly spirit, with a view to help and not to hinder." Even in wartime Baruch preferred government-business cooperation to regulation. "Most men will observe a pledge when once given and they need not be vigilated." (We may give thanks that this particular verb did not come into general use, even in bureaucratic language.)

Bernard Mannes Baruch was born in 1870 in Camden, South Carolina. He graduated from the College of the City of New York in 1889 and in the next ten years became a wealthy man through stock market speculation. An active Democrat but not deeply engaged in public life, Baruch in 1915, during the preparedness campaign, proposed to the administration the rationalization and synchronization idea that the WIB later was to attempt. He was an economic adviser to Wilson at the Paris Peace Conference, was again active as a wartime industrial mobilizer during World War II, and after 1945 was the United States representative on the United Nations Atomic Energy Commission. For further biographical information see the life by Margaret Coit, Mr. Baruch *(Boston: Houghton Mifflin, 1957) and his two autobiographical volumes,* Baruch: My Own Story *(New York: Holt, 1957) and* Baruch: The Public Years *(New York: Holt, 1960). For additional material on the WIB see Grosvenor B. Clarkson,* Industrial America in the World War: The Strategy behind the Line, 1917–1918 *(Boston: Houghton Mifflin, 1923).*

This selection is from the fifth and ninth chapters of American Industry in the War: A Report of the War Industries Board *(Washington: Government Printing Office. 1921). pages 61. 63–67. 69, 98–100.*

The work of the Priorities Division was intimately related to that of another very important and very energetic division of the Board— the Conservation Division. The President's letter of March 4, 1918, charged the War Industries Board with the duty of promoting "the conservation of resources and facilities by means of scientific, industrial, and commercial economies." But the work was at that time already well under way, and the establishment of the Conservation Division under the Board on May 8, 1918, represented only a transfer from the council, and a reorganization of the Commercial Economy Board, which had been created as early as March 24, 1917. . . .

The plan of conservation laid down by the division for the guidance of the commodity sections and of its own agents was to undertake studies of industries, particularly those in which there were shortages of materials, facilities, or labor, with a view to formulating sets of regulations to accomplish one or more of the following purposes:

1. To secure all feasible reductions in the number of styles, varieties, sizes, colors, finishes, etc., of the several products of the industry in question. This would accomplish economies in manufacture by reducing the number of operations, and the amount of reserve stock, raw and finished, which had to be carried; it would speed up the turn-over, reduce the labor and expense of selling, and decrease the loss due to depreciation.

2. To eliminate styles and varieties of articles which violated the principle of economy in the use of constituent materials; for example, garments requiring unusual yardage could be eliminated.

3. To eliminate features of adornment which added nothing to the usefulness of articles.

4. To reduce the production and sale of such articles as were of lesser importance for the comfort and satisfaction of the population.

5. To foster the substitution of articles and materials which were plentiful for those which were scarce and difficult to produce.

6. To discourage the use for unimportant purposes of articles which were needed for more important purposes.

7. To standardize sizes, lengths, widths, thicknesses, weights, gauges, etc., in such a way as to preserve sufficient strength and durability, but to effect economies in materials and labor.

8. To reduce the waste of materials in manufacturing processes generally.

9. To secure economies in the use of samples for selling purposes.

10. To secure economy in containers by eliminating the smaller and odd sizes.

11. To secure economy in packing by increasing the number of units per package.

12. To secure economy in shipping space and packing materials by baling instead of boxing wherever this was practicable.

The process of drawing up tentative schedules of regulations, based on the recommendations of the trade organizations themselves, and sending them out to all parties directly interested for criticism and comment, that they might be revised before being issued as binding regulations, was designed to safeguard so far as possible against unfairness and injustice to any industry or firm. By canvassing conditions in their industries, by furnishing technical information and advice, by their loyal readiness to cooperate with the Government in carrying out the plans, often for drastic changes in trade practices, the business men in industry made these conservation projects possible. When the need was explained, they were always found ready to take the necessary steps, often at heavy sacrifices. The thoughts of the men at the helms of their own industrial enterprises were linked with the thoughts of the men at the seat of government in the common purpose of winning the war.

But there was an additional sanction for these regulations which gave confidence to each business man that all his fellows in trade would observe like practices with himself, and this last means of enforcement would have been of increasing importance had the war lasted over a long period. Whenever a schedule of conservation was issued, each manufacturer and dealer was required to give a pledge that he would observe it and do all in his power to see it observed on the part of those with whom he dealt. Most American business men will observe a pledge when once given and they need not be vigilated.

But there was a further power to encourage the good will of those who were tempted to waver. By the summer of 1918, the priorities commissioner was in a position to exercise control not only over the distribution of iron and steel, copper, and numerous other elemental constituents of manufacture, but, through the cooperation of the Fuel and Railroad Administrations, he could also withhold, for the purpose of bringing recalcitrants into line, supplies of coal, coke, and oil, or the use of freight cars for transportation. With this sanction at the foundation of its efforts, the Conservation Division developed in rapid succession during the summer and fall of 1918 a series of "agreements," issued in the form of schedules of regulations to nearly a hundred different groups of producers—regulations which were already showing their effect in reducing the industrial activities of the country to a more efficient basis—when the end of the war made such undertaking no longer necessary.

Curtailment plans were carried out not by agreement among the concerns of an industry but by agreement between the industry as a group, on the one hand, and the Government, on the other. Many new trade practices were inaugurated in the same way. . . . Reference, by way of illustration, to some of these will be of general interest.

The conservation schedules for makers of men's and youths' clothing limited the length of sack coats and the length and sweep of overcoats, reduced the size of samples, and restricted each manufacturer to not more than 10 models of suits per season, resulting in a saving of 12 to 15 per cent in yardage. The number of trunks carried by traveling salesmen of dry goods houses underwent an average reduction of 44 per cent. The schedule for the women's garment industry was calculated as capable of saving 20 to 25 per cent in yardage.

The standardization of colors together with certain restrictions in styles of sweaters and analogous knitted articles released 33 per cent of the wool ordinarily used in that industry. A schedule providing that hosiery, underwear, and other knit goods, with certain small exceptions, should be packed for shipment in paper covered bales instead of pasteboard boxes resulted in a large saving in shipping space, while at the same time it released pasteboard to be used as a substitute for tin plate in the manufacture of containers for articles for which tin plate had been forbidden. It was estimated that this schedule would have effected an annual saving of 17,312 carloads of freight space, 141,000,000 cartons, and nearly a half million wooden packing cases. . . .

The manufacturers of automobile tires agreed to a reduction from 287 styles and sizes of tires to 32, with a further reduction to 9 within two years. This had a tendency to release a large amount of rubber and capital tied up in stocks everywhere. A schedule was issued also to the rubber clothing and the rubber footwear industries, the former eliminating 272 styles and types and agreeing to bale their product instead of shipping it in cartons. Even bathing caps were restricted to one style and one color for each manufacturer.

Savings in the agricultural implement industry are among the most important effected. Implement manufacturers were able to simplify manufacturing operations and reduce their stocks of raw materials; manufacturers, dealers, and jobbers found it possible to do business with smaller stocks of finished products; the steel mills saved, because every variation in size or shape had required a different set of rolls, and so on. Schedules were issued to manufacturers of portable grain elevators, plows and tillage implements, grain drills and seeders, harvesters, mowers, hay rakes, ensilage machinery, springtooth harrows, farm wagons and trucks, land rollers and pulverizers, and cream separators. The number of sizes and types of steel plows was reduced from 312 to 76; planters and drills from 784 to 29; disk harrows from 589 to 38; buggy wheels from 232 to 4; spring-wagon wheels from 32 to 4; buggy axles from over 100 to 1; buggy springs from over 120 to 1; spring wagons from over 25 to 2; buggy shafts from 36 to 1; buggy bodies from over 20 to 1 style, two widths; spring-wagon bodies from 6 to 2.

By making his line of farm wagons conform to this schedule, one manufacturer reduced his variety of front and rear gears from 1,736 to 16. Yet the farmers were as well taken care of in the growing, harvesting, and marketing of their crops with this smaller variety of agricultural implements to draw upon as they had been with the wide variety previously manufactured. The habits and prejudices of localities and individual farmers had made it necessary for manufacturers to make many more sizes and types of equipment than were essential, for all of which parts had to be carried, and the number of finished implements in the hands of manufacturers, jobbers, and retailers were unnecessarily large because of this multiplicity. . . .

The experience of the Conservation Division has clearly demonstrated that there are many practices in American industry which cost the ultimate consumers in the aggregate enormous sums without enriching the producers. These are often due to competitive demands, real or assumed. Many salesmen, in order to please the whims of particular customers, will insist upon the manufacture of new styles or new shapes of articles, requiring increased expense to the manufacturers and increased expense to both wholesalers and retailers in carrying more lines of stock; these in turn causing increased expense in maintaining salesmen and providing them with samples as well as in advertising. The consumer, the general public, is no better served by the satisfaction of these unreasonable demands, but the public ultimately pays the bill. We may well draw from this war experience a lesson to be applied to peace, by providing some simple machinery for eliminating wasteful trade practices which increase prices without in the remotest degree contributing to the well-being of the people. There is enough natural wealth in this country, and there is enough labor and technical skill for converting that wealth into objects of human satisfaction to provide abundantly for the elemental comforts of every person in the land. The problem before our Nation to-day is to bring about such adjustments of the industrial processes as lead toward that long-sought condition of life. . . .

The experience of the Board in exercising control over American industry leads it to make a further suggestion, which has less to do with war than with the normal practices of business.

During the past few decades, while the American business man, uniting his talents with those of the technical expert, has, through the control of great masses of capital, made such extraordinary strides in converting the natural wealth of this country into means for human comfort and satisfaction; the processes of trade have so changed their nature that the older and simpler relations of Government to business have been gradually forced to give way before certain new principles of supervision. We have been gradually compelled to drift away from the old doctrine of Anglo-American law, that the sphere of Government should be limited to preventing breach of contract, fraud, physical injury and injury to property, and that the Government should exercise protection only over non-competent persons. The modern industrial processes have been rendering it increasingly necessary for the Government to reach out its arm to protect competent individuals against the discriminating practices of mass industrial power. We have already evolved a system of Government control of no mean significance over our railroads and over our merchant fleet, but we continue to argue, and in a measure believe, that the principles of competition can be preserved in sufficient power in respect to all other industries to protect the interests of the public and insure efficiency and wholesome growth in the development of natural wealth. With this in view, the Sherman and Clayton Acts have forbidden combinations in restraint of trade, monopolies, and many other vices attendant upon group action by individuals controlling great masses of capital. This legislation, while valuable for immediate purposes, represents little more than a moderately ambitious effort to reduce by Government interference the processes of business so as to make them conform to the simpler principles sufficient for the conditions of a bygone day.

The war has introduced a new element into this situation. The individual units of corporations which had been dissolved under the Sherman Act have, in many cases, grown during the war into corporations many fold larger than the parent organization which before the war the law construed as a menace. The conditions of war made this sort of thing necessary and in all respects desirable. The war gave rise to a kind of demand unknown in time of peace—an absolute demand, which was halted neither by prices nor difficulty of procurement. There followed an absolute shortage in some trades, and a time shortage in most of them. Group action, industry by industry, accompanied by Government control of prices and distribution, was the natural and, so far as we know, the only solution which could be devised.

In line with the principle of united action and cooperation, hundreds of trades were organized for the first time into national associations, each responsible in a real sense for its multitude of component companies, and they were organized on the suggestion and under the supervision of the Government. Practices looking to efficiency in production, price control, conservation, control in quantity of production, etc., were inaugurated everywhere. Many business men have experienced during the war, for the first time in their careers, the tremendous advantages, both to themselves and to the general public, of combination, of cooperation and common action, with their natural competitors. To drive them back through new legislation, or through the more rigid and rapid enforcement of present legislation, to the situation which immediately preceded the war will be very difficult in many cases, though in a few it is already occurring spontaneously. To leave these combinations without further supervision and attention by the Government than can be given by the Attorney General's Department, or by the Federal Trade Commission in its present form, will subject business men to such temptations as many of them will be unable to resist—temptations to conduct their businesses for private gain with little reference to general public welfare.

These associations, as they stand, are capable of carrying out purposes of greatest public benefit. They can increase the amount of wealth available for the comfort of the people by inaugurating rules designed to eliminate wasteful practices attendant upon multiplicity of styles and types of articles in the various trades; they can assist in cultivating the public taste for rational types of commodities; by exchange of trade information, extravagant methods of production and distribution can be avoided through them, and production will tend to be localized in places best suited economically for it. By acting as centers of information, furnishing lists of sources to purchasers and lists of purchasers to producers, supply and demand can be more economically balanced. From the point of vantage which competent men have at the central bureau of an association, not only can new demands be cultivated, but new sources of unexploited wealth can be indicated. In case of a national emergency, the existence of these associations at the beginning would be of incalculable aid to the supply organizations. Many of these considerations apply to large individual companies as well as to associations.

These combinations are capable also—and very easily capable—of carrying out purposes of greatest public disadvantage. They can so subtly influence production as to keep it always just short of current demand and thus keep prices ever high and going higher. They can encourage a common understanding on prices, and, without great difficulty, can hold price levels at abnormal positions. They can influence the favoring of one type of buyer over another. Nearly every business man in the country has learned by the war that a shortage in his product, if it be not too great, is distinctly to his advantage. Trade associations with real power can, in respect to most of the staples, so influence production as to keep the margin of shortage at a point most favorable to high prices and rapid turnovers.

The question, then, is what kind of Government organization can be devised to safeguard the public interest while these associations are preserved to carry on the good work of which they are capable. The country will quite properly demand the vigorous enforcement of all proper measures for the suppression of unfair competition and unreasonable restraint of trade. But this essentially negative policy of curbing vicious practices should, in the public interest, be supplemented by a positive program, and to this end the experience of the War Industries Board points to the desirability of investing some Government agency, perhaps the Department of Commerce or the Federal Trade Commission, with constructive as well as inquisitorial powers—an agency whose duty it should be to encourage, under strict Government supervision, such cooperation and coordination in industry as should tend to increase production, eliminate waste, conserve natural resources, improve the quality of products, promote efficiency in operation, and thus reduce costs to the ultimate consumer.

Such a plan should provide a way of approaching industry, or rather of inviting industry to approach the Government, in a friendly spirit, with a view to help and not to hinder. The purpose contemplated is not that the Government should undertake any such far-reaching control over industry as was practiced during the war emergency by the War Industries Board; but that the experiences of the war should be capitalized; its heritage of dangerous practices should be fully realized that they might be avoided; and its heritage of wholesome and useful practices should be accepted and studied with a view to adapting them to the problems of peace. It is recommended that such practices of cooperation and coordination in industry as have been found to be clearly of public benefit should be stimulated and encouraged by a Government agency, which at the same time would be clothed with the power and charged with the responsibility of standing watch against and preventing abuses.

SELECTION

President Wilson Pronounces American War Aims: The Fourteen Points, January 8, 1918

In placing Wilson's Fourteen Points in historical perspective one must examine both the origins and context of this rather remarkable speech and the events that flowed from it subsequently.

President of a nation at war for almost nine months by New Year's Day of 1918, Woodrow Wilson had not been explicit about the kind of peace that the United States sought, beyond mouthing the usual patriotic wartime slogans. The world political situation in early 1918 demanded that leaders of the Allied and Associated Powers (the United States declined to be termed an Ally and insisted on this somewhat weasling language) declare their nations' purposes.

Recent events in Russia had brought the matter to a head. In November, 1917, the Bolsheviks overthrew the Mensheviks, and the new Russian leaders, V. I. Lenin and Leon Trotsky, brought about a truce with the Germans on December 15. Discussions looking forward to a peace treaty were under way at Brest Litovsk, and Wilson made clear in his Fourteen Points speech that he was acutely aware of the negotiations. Hope, which proved to be illusory, that the Bolshevik leaders might keep Russia in the war was one of Wilson's considerations in this speech. Another consideration grew from the Bolsheviks' publication of the secret war treaties they had discovered in government archives after they seized power. The selfish nature of the secret treaties, which provided for various territorial aggrandizements by the Allies, was hardly calculated to arouse a nation to valor and sacrifice. There had to be more noble purposes, and President Wilson, especially since the United States had not been a party to any of the treaties (although he had known of them since just after the nation declared war), was eager to state war aims to supplant the imperialistic aims revealed in the recently published agreements. The Prime Minister of Great Britain, David Lloyd George, was embarrassed by the publication of the treaties, and just three days before this speech of Wilson's made many of the points the President was to make. Still another consideration in Wilson's announcement of war aims was the possible effect on Germany. A promise of a just and liberal peace would appeal to many elements in Germany and might thereby hasten the war's end.

The Fourteen Points did play an important part in bringing about the armistice. Translated into German, printed as leaflets, and dropped over Germany by the hundreds of thousands, the Wilsonian points clearly affected German opinion, particularly after German military power began to wane significantly in the fall of 1918. Germany sued for a cease-fire based upon the Fourteen Points on October 6, 1918.

The Fourteen Points themselves require little explication. Their author was certainly capable of expressing his thoughts. It is only necessary to point out than when they were announced at a joint session of the two houses of Congress on January 8, 1918, they did not constitute an agreed-upon and official policy. The President had not consulted the Congress. It is difficult to imagine that body, which included many tariff protectionists, being strongly for Point III. And Wilson certainly did not speak for the Allies. Great Britain, for example, had no sympathy for the freedom-of-the-seas point.

The speech is here reprinted in its entirety as it appeared in the Congressional Record, *Sixty-fifth Congress, second session, volume 56, part 1, January 8, 1918, pages 680–681.*

entlemen of the Congress, once more, as repeatedly before, the spokesmen of the Central Empires have indicated their desire to discuss the objects of the war and the possible bases of a general peace. Parleys have been in progress at Brest-Litovsk between Russian representatives and representatives of the Central Powers, to which the attention of all the belligerents has been invited for the purpose of ascertaining whether it may be possible to extend these parleys into a general conference with regard to terms of peace and settlement. The Russian representatives presented not only a perfectly definite statement of the principles upon which they would be willing to conclude peace, but also an equally definite programme of the concrete application of those principles. The representatives of the Central Powers, on their part, presented an outline of settlement which, if much less definite, seemed susceptible of liberal interpretation until their specific programme of practical terms was added. That programme proposed no concessions at all either to the sovereignty of Russia or to the preferences of the populations with whose fortunes it dealt, but meant, in a word, that the Central Empires were to keep every foot of territory their armed forces had occupied,—every province, every city, every point of vantage,—as a permanent addition to their territories and their power. It is a reasonable conjecture that the general principles of settlement which they at first suggested originated with the more liberal statesmen of Germany and Austria, the men who have begun to feel the force of their own peoples' thought and purpose, while the concrete terms of actual settlement came from the military leaders who have no thought but to keep what they have got. The negotiations have been broken off. The Russian representatives were sincere and in earnest. They cannot entertain such proposals of conquest and domination.

The whole incident is full of significance. It is also full of perplexity. With whom are the Russian representatives dealing? For whom are the representatives of the Central Empires speaking? Are they speaking for the majorities of their respective parliaments or for the minority parties, that military and imperialistic minority which has so far dominated their whole policy and controlled the affairs of Turkey and of the Balkan states which have felt obliged to become their associates in the war? The Russian representatives have insisted, very justly, very wisely, and in the true spirit of modern democracy, that the conferences they have been holding with the Teutonic and Turkish statesmen should be held within open, not closed, doors, and all the world has been audience, as was desired. To whom have we been listening, then? To those who speak the spirit and intention of the Resolutions of the German Reichstag of the ninth of July last, the spirit and intention of the liberal leaders and parties of Germany, or to those who resist and defy that spirit and intention and insist upon conquest and subjugation? Or are we listening, in fact, to both, unreconciled and in open and hopeless contradiction? These are very serious and pregnant questions. Upon the answer to them depends the peace of the world.

But, whatever the results of the parleys at Brest-Litovsk, whatever the confusions of counsel and of purpose in the utterances of the spokesmen of the Central Empires, they have again attempted to acquaint the world with their objects in the war and have again challenged their adversaries to say what their objects are and what sort of settlement they would deem just and satisfactory. There is no good reason why that challenge should not be responded to, and responded to with the utmost candor. We did not wait for it. Not once, but again and again, we have laid our whole thought and purpose before the world, not in general terms only, but each time with sufficient definition to make it clear what sort of definitive terms of settlement must necessarily spring out of them. Within the last week Mr. Lloyd George has spoken with admirable candor and in admirable spirit for the people and Government of Great Britain. There is no confusion of counsel among the adversaries of the Central Powers, no uncertainty of principle, no vagueness of detail. The only secrecy of counsel, the only lack of fearless frankness, the only failure to make definite statement of the objects of the war, lies with Germany and her Allies. The issues of life and death hang upon these definitions. No statesman who has the least conception of his responsibility ought for a moment to permit himself to continue this tragical and appalling outpouring of blood and treasure unless he is sure beyond a peradventure that the objects of the vital sacrifice are part and parcel of the very life of Society, and that the people for whom he speaks think them right and imperative as he does.

There is, moreover, a voice calling for these definitions of principle and of purpose which is, it seems to me, more thrilling and more compelling than any of the many moving voices with which the troubled air of the world is filled. It is the voice of the Russian people. They are prostrate and all but helpless, it would seem, before the grim power of Germany, which has hitherto known no relenting and no pity. Their power, apparently, is shattered. And yet their soul is not subservient. They will not yield either in principle or in action. Their conception of what is right, of what it is humane and honorable for them to accept, has been stated with a frankness, a largeness of view, a generosity of spirit, and a universal human sympathy which must challenge the admiration of every friend of mankind; and they have refused to compound their ideals or desert others that they themselves may be safe. They call to us to say what it is that we desire, in what, if in anything, our purpose and our spirit differ from theirs; and I believe that the people of the United States would wish me to respond, with utter simplicity and frankness. Whether their present leaders believe it or not, it is our heartfelt desire and hope that some way may be opened whereby we may be privileged to assist the people of Russia to attain their utmost hope of liberty and ordered peace.

It will be our wish and purpose that the processes of peace, when they are begun, shall be absolutely open and that they shall involve and permit henceforth no secret understandings of any kind. The day of conquest and aggrandizement is gone by; so is also the day of secret covenants entered into in the interest of particular governments and likely at some unlooked-for moment to upset the peace of the world. It is this happy fact, now clear to the view of every public man whose thoughts do not still linger in an age that is dead and gone, which makes it possible for every nation whose purposes are consistent with justice and the peace of the world to avow now or at any other time the objects it has in view.

We entered this war because violations of right had occurred which touched us to the quick and made the life of our own people impossible unless they were corrected and the world secured once for all against their recurrence. What we demand in this war, therefore, is nothing peculiar to ourselves. It is that the world be made fit and safe to live in; and particularly that it be made safe for every peace-loving nation which, like our own, wishes to live its own life, determine its own institutions, be assured of justice and fair dealing by the other peoples of the world as against force and selfish aggression. All the peoples of the world are in effect partners in this interest, and for our own part we see very clearly that unless justice be done to others it will not be done to us. The programme of the world's peace, therefore, is our programme; and that programme, the only possible programme, as we see it, is this:

I. Open covenants of peace, openly arrived at, after which there shall be no private international understandings of any kind but diplomacy shall proceed always frankly and in the public view.

II. Absolute freedom of navigation upon the seas, outside territorial waters, alike in peace and in war, except as the seas may be closed in whole or in part by international action for the enforcement of international covenants.

III. The removal, so far as possible, of all economic barriers and the establishment of an equality of trade conditions among all the nations consenting to the peace and associating themselves for its maintenance.

IV. Adequate guarantees given and taken that national armaments will be reduced to the lowest point consistent with domestic safety.

V. A free, open-minded, and absolutely impartial adjustment of all colonial claims, based upon a strict observance of the principle that in determining all such questions of sovereignty the interests of the populations concerned must have equal weight with the equitable claims of the government whose title is to be determined.

VI. The evacuation of all Russian territory and such a settlement of all questions affecting Russia as will secure the best and freest cooperation of the other nations of the world in obtaining for her an unhampered and unembarrassed opportunity for the independent determination of her own political development and national policy and assure her a sincere welcome into the society of free nations under institutions of her own choosing; and, more than a welcome, assistance also of every kind that she may need and may herself desire. The treatment accorded Russia by her sister nations in the months to come will be the acid test of their good will, of their comprehension of her needs as distinguished from their own interests, and of their intelligent and unselfish sympathy.

VII. Belgium, the whole world will agree, must be evacuated and restored, without any attempt to limit the sovereignty which she enjoys in common with all other free nations. No other single act will serve as this will serve to restore confidence among the nations in the laws which they have themselves set and determined for the government of their relations with one another. Without this healing act the whole structure and validity of international law is forever impaired.

VIII. All French territory should be freed and the invaded portions restored, and the wrong done to France by Prussia in 1871 in the matter of Alsace-Lorraine, which has unsettled the peace of the world for nearly fifty years, should be righted, in order that peace may once more be made secure in the interest of all.

IX. A readjustment of the frontiers of Italy should be effected along clearly recognizable lines of nationality.

X. The peoples of Austria-Hungary, whose place among the nations we wish to see safeguarded and assured, should be accorded the freest opportunity of autonomous development.

XI. Rumania, Serbia, and Montenegro should be evacuated; occupied territories restored; Serbia accorded free and secure access to the sea; and the relations of the several Balkan states to one another determined by friendly counsel along historically established lines of allegiance and nationality; and international guarantees of the political and economic independence and territorial integrity of the several Balkan states should be entered into.

XII. The Turkish portions of the present Ottoman Empire should be assured a secure sovereignty, but the other nationalities which are now under Turkish rule should be assured an undoubted security of life and an absolutely unmolested opportunity of autonomous development, and the Dardanelles should be permanently opened as a free passage to the ships and commerce of all nations under international guarantees.

XIII. An independent Polish state should be erected which should include the territories inhabited by indisputably Polish populations, which should be assured a free and secure access to the sea, and whose political and economic independence and territorial integrity should be guaranteed by international covenant.

XIV. A general association of nations must be formed under specific covenants for the purpose of affording mutual guarantees of political independence and territorial integrity to great and small states alike.

In regard to these essential rectifications of wrong and assertions of right we feel ourselves to be intimate partners of all the governments and peoples associated together against the Imperialists. We cannot be separate in interest or divided in purpose. We stand together until the end.

For such arrangements and covenants we are willing to fight and to continue to fight until they are achieved; but only because we wish the right to prevail and desire a just and stable peace such as can be secured only by removing the chief provocations to war, which this programme does remove. We have no jealousy of German greatness, and there is nothing in this programme that impairs it. We grudge her no achievement or distinction of learning or of pacific enterprise such as have made her record very bright and very enviable. We do not wish to injure her or to block in any way her legitimate influence or power. We do not wish to fight her either with arms or with hostile arrangements of trade if she is willing to associate herself with us and the other peace-loving nations of the world in covenants of justice and law and fair dealing. We wish her only to accept a place of equality among the peoples of the world,— the new world in which we now live,—instead of a place of mastery.

Neither do we presume to suggest to her any alteration or modification of her institutions. But it is necessary, we must frankly say, and necessary as a preliminary to any intelligent dealings with her on our part, that we should know whom her spokesmen speak for when they speak to us, whether for the Reichstag majority or for the military party and the men whose creed is imperial domination.

We have spoken now, surely, in terms too concrete to admit of any further doubt or question. An evident principle runs through the whole programme I have outlined. It is the principle of justice to all peoples and nationalities, and their right to live on equal terms of liberty and safety with one another, whether they be strong or weak. Unless this principle be made its foundation no part of the structure of international justice can stand. The people of the United States could act upon no other principle; and to the vindication of this principle they are ready to devote their lives, their honor, and everything that they possess. The moral climax of this the culminating and final war for human liberty has come, and they are ready to put their own strength, their own highest purpose, their own integrity and devotion to the test.

SELECTION

President Wilson Defends the Treaty of Versailles: Speech at Des Moines, Iowa, September 6, 1919

President Wilson returned to the United States from France on July 8, 1919, only a few days after the signing of the Treaty of Versailles. Two days later he submitted the treaty to the Senate, which, under the Constitution, must ratify treaties by a two-thirds majority before they become effective so far as the United States is concerned. It soon became clear that the Senate divided into three groups on the treaty: those who favored quick ratification as submitted, most of whom were Wilson's fellow Democrats; those who demanded some modification of, or reservation to, the treaty before they would vote to ratify it, a group that was mostly Republican and that was headed by Henry Cabot Lodge, chairman of the Committee on Foreign Relations; and the so-called irreconcilables, who were predominantly Republican (many of them progressive Republicans), who would oppose the treaty even with modifications. The voters had not heeded Wilson's plea for a Democratic Congress in the 1918 elections, held a few days before the armistice, and the Republicans controlled the Senate. It became clear to Wilson that the treaty's advocates did not have the votes. He decided to carry his appeal directly to the people and, on September 4, embarked upon a tour of the West. He gave thirty-seven speeches in twenty-nine cities. On September 25 his health broke and he returned to Washington, where about a week later he suffered a stroke. How badly incapacitated he was and for how long are disputed matters, but clearly the Democrats and the treaty's friends in the Senate were at a bad disadvantage for want of leadership.

In this speech at Des Moines, as in others of the series, Wilson both made positive arguments for the treaty and countered those arguments of his opponents that he feared were proving the most effective. Of the positive arguments, Wilson in this particular speech concentrated upon the need for speed to prevent the spread of revolution and unrest, upon the theme that isolation was impossible, upon the economic advantages to America that would come with membership in the League of Nations, and upon the way he believed the League would operate to prevent war. Of the counterarguments, he maintained that the treaty provisions on Shantung were the best that could be made under unfortunate circumstances and that there was no conflict between American adherence to the League and the Monroe Doctrine.

Perhaps as important as the points made in the address is its tone or mood. It was a different Wilson at Des Moines from the Wilson who made the Fourteen Points speech, the war message of April, 1917, or even the campaign speech before the New York Press Club in 1912. He was more defensive, less confident, more prone to folksiness, a little irritable. The more confident and thoughtful Wilson would not likely have made these alarmed remarks about the Bolshevik "poison" having got "in the veins of this free people." The earlier Wilson showed, in general, more restraint than this 1919 Wilson. Certainly, the earlier Wilson would have been too embarrassed to utter the fulsome, cliché-ridden last sentence of this speech.

There are many solid and interesting books on the treaty and its reception. Among them are the companion volumes by Thomas A. Bailey, Woodrow Wilson and the Lost Peace *(New York: Macmillan, 1944) and* Woodrow Wilson and the Great Betrayal *(New York: Macmillan, 1945), and Denna F. Fleming,* The United States and the League of Nations, 1918–1920 *(New York: Putnam, 1932).*

The Democratic leader in the Senate, Gilbert M. Hitchcock of Nebraska, sought and received the Senate's unanimous consent to print Wilson's speeches on his Western trip in the Congressional Record. *This speech may be found in the* Congressional Record, *Sixty-sixth Congress, first session, volume 58, part 6, September 19, 1919, pages 5585–5588.*

Mr. Chairman and fellow countrymen, you make my heart very warm with your generous welcome, and I want to express my unaffected gratitude to your chairman for having so truly struck the note of an occasion like this. He has used almost the very words that were in my thought, that the world is inflamed and profoundly disturbed, and we are met to discuss the measures by which its spirit can be quieted and its affairs turned to the right courses of human life. My fellow countrymen, the world is desperately in need of the settled conditions of peace, and it can not wait much longer. It is waiting upon us. That is the thought, that is the burdensome thought, upon my heart to-night, that the world is waiting for the verdict of the Nation to which it looked for leadership and which it thought would be the last that would ask the world to wait.

My fellow citizens, the world is not at peace. I suppose that it is difficult for one who has not had some touch of the hot passion of the other side of the sea to realize how all the passions that have been slumbering for ages have been uncovered and released by the tragedy of this war. We speak of the tragedy of this war, but the tragedy that lay back of it was greater than the war itself, because back of it lay long ages in which the legitimate freedom of men was suppressed. Back of it lay long ages of recurrent war in which little groups of men, closeted in capitals, determined whether the sons of the land over which they ruled should go out upon the field and shed their blood. For what? For liberty? No; not for liberty, but for the aggrandizement of those who ruled them. And this had been slumbering in the hearts of men. They had felt the suppression of it. They had felt the mastery of those whom they had not chosen as their masters. They had felt the oppression of laws which did not admit them to the equal exercise of human rights. Now all of this is released and uncovered and men glare at one another and say, "Now we are free and what shall we do with our freedom?"

What happened in Russia was not a sudden and accidental thing. The people of Russia were maddened with the suppression of Czarism. When at last the chance came to throw off these chains, they threw them off, at first with hearts full of confidence and hope, and then they found out that they had been again deceived. There was no assembly chosen to frame a constitution for them, or, rather, there was an assembly chosen to choose a constitution for them and it was suppressed and dispersed, and a little group of men just as selfish, just as ruthless, just as pitiless, as the agents of the Czar himself, assumed control and exercised their power by terror and not by right. And in other parts of Europe the poison spread—the poison of disorder, the poison of revolt, the poison of chaos. And do you honestly think, my fellow citizens, that none of that poison has got in the veins of this free people? Do you not know that the world is all now one single whispering gallery? Those antennæ of the wireless telegraph are the symbols of our age. All the impulses of mankind are thrown out upon the air and reach to the ends of the earth; quietly upon steamships, silently under the cover of the Postal Service, with the tongue of the wireless and the tongue of the telegraph, all the suggestions of disorder are spread through the world. Money coming from nobody knows where is deposited by the millions in capitals like Stockholm, to be used for the propaganda of disorder and discontent and dissolution throughout the world, and men look you calmly in the face in America and say they are for that sort of revolution, when that sort of revolution means government by terror, government by force, not government by vote. It is negation of everything that is American; but it is spreading, and so long as disorder continues, so long as the world is kept waiting for the answer to the question, What kind of peace are we going to have and what kind of guaranties are there to be behind that peace? that poison will steadily spread more and more rapidly, spread until it may be that even this beloved land of ours will be distracted and distorted by it.

That is what is concerning me, my fellow countrymen. I know the splendid steadiness of the American people, but, my fellow citizens, the whole world needs that steadiness, and the American people are the make-weight in the fortunes of mankind. How long are we going to debate into which scale we will throw that magnificient equipoise that belongs to us? How long shall we be kept waiting for the answer whether the world may trust us or despise us? They have looked to us for leadership. They have looked to us for example. They have built their peace upon the basis of our suggestions. That great volume that contains the treaty of peace is drawn along the specifications laid down by the American Government, and now the world stands at amaze because an authority in America hesitates whether it will indorse an American document or not.

You know what the necessity of peace is. Political liberty can exist only when there is peace. Social reform can take place only when there is peace. The settlement of every question that concerns our daily life waits for peace. I have been receiving delegations in Washington of men engaged in the service of the Government temporarily in the administration of the railways, and I have had to say to them, "My friends, I can not tell what the railways can earn until commerce is restored to its normal courses. Until I can tell what the railroads can earn I can not tell what the wages that the railroads can pay will be. I can not suggest what the increase of freight and passenger rates will be to meet these increases in wages if the rates must be increased. I can not tell yet whether it will be necessary to increase the rates or not, and I must ask you to wait." But they are not the only people that have come to see me. There are all sorts of adjustments necessary in this country. I have asked representatives of capital and labor to come to Washington next month and confer—confer about the fundamental thing of our life at present; that is to say, the conditions of labor. Do you realize, my fellow citizens, that all through the world the one central question of civilization is, "What shall be the conditions of labor?" The profound unrest in Europe is due to the doubt prevailing as to what shall be the conditions of labor, and I need not tell you that that unrest is spreading to America.

In the midst of the treaty of peace is a Magna Charta, a great guaranty for labor. It provides that labor shall have the counsels of the world devoted to the discussion of its conditions and of its betterment, and labor all over the world is waiting to know whether America is going to take part in those conferences or not. The confidence of the men who sat at Paris was such that they put it in the document that the first meeting of the labor conference under that part of the treaty should take place in Washington upon the invitation of the President of the United States. I am going to issue that invitation, whether we can attend the conference or not. But think of the mortification! Think of standing by in Washington itself and seeing the world take counsel upon the fundamental matter of civilization without us. The thing is inconceivable, but it is true. The world is waiting, waiting to see, not whether we will take part but whether we will serve and lead, for it has expected us to lead. I want to testify that the most touching and thrilling thing that has ever happened to me was what happened almost every day when I was in Paris. Delegations from all over the world came to me to solicit the friendship of America. They frankly told us that they were not sure they could trust anybody else, but that they did absolutely trust us to do them justice and to see that justice was done them. Why, some of them came from countries which I have, to my shame, to admit that I never heard of before, and I had to ask as privately as possible what language they spoke. Fortunately they always had an interpreter, but I always wanted to know at least what family of languages they were speaking. The touching thing was that from the ends of the earth, from little pocketed valleys, where I did not know that a separate people lived, there came men—men of dignity, men of intellectual parts, men entertaining in their thought and in their memories a great tradition, some of the oldest people of the world—and they came and sat at the feet of the youngest nation of the world and said, "Teach us the way to liberty."

That is the attitude of the world, and reflect, my fellow countrymen, upon the reaction, the reaction of despair, that would come if America said, "We do not want to lead you. You must do without our advice. You must shift without us." Now, are we going to bring about a peace, for which everything waits? We can not bring it about by doing nothing. I have been very much amazed and very much amused, if I could be amused in such critical circumstances, to see that the statesmanship of some gentlemen consists in the very interesting proposition that we do nothing at all. I had heard of standing pat before, but I never had before heard of standpatism going to the length of saying it is none of our business and we do not care what happens to the rest of the world.

Your chairman made a profoundly true remark just now. The isolation of the United States is at an end, not because we chose to go into the politics of the world but because by the sheer genius of this people and the growth of our power we have become a determining factor in the history of mankind, and after you have become a determining factor you can not remain isolated, whether you want to or not. Isolation ended by the processes of history, not by the processes of our independent choice, and the processes of history merely fulfilled the prediction of the men who founded our Republic. Go back and read some of the immortal sentences of the men that assisted to frame this Government and see how they set up a standard to which they intended that the nations of the world should rally. They said to the people of the world, "Come to us; this is the home of liberty; this is the place where mankind can learn how to govern their own affairs and straighten out their own difficulties," and the world did come to us.

Look at your neighbor. Look at the statistics of the people of your State. Look at the statistics of the people of the United States. They have come, their hearts full of hope and confidence, from practically every nation in the world, to constitute a portion of our strength and of our hope and a contribution to our achievement. Sometimes I feel like taking off my hat to some of those immigrants. I was born an American. I could not help it, but they chose to be Americans. They were not born Americans. They saw this star in the west rising over the peoples of the world, and they said, "That is the star of hope and the star of salvation. We will set our footsteps toward the west and join that great body of men whom God has blessed with the vision of liberty." I honor those men. I say, "You made a deliberate choice which showed that you saw what the drift and history of mankind was." I am very grateful, I may say in parentheses, that I did not have to make that choice. I am grateful that ever since I can remember I have breathed this blessed air of freedom. I am grateful that every instinct in me, every drop of blood in me remembers and stands up and shouts at the traditions of the United States. But some gentlemen are not shouting now about that. They are saying, "Yes; we made a great promise to mankind, but it will cost too much to redeem it." My fellow citizens, that is not the spirit of America, and you can not have peace, you can not have even your legitimate part in the business of the world unless you are partners with the rest. If you are going to say to the world, "We will stand off and see what we can get out of this," the world will see to it that you do not get anything out of it. If it is your deliberate choice that instead of being friends you will be rivals and antagonists, then you will get exactly what rivals and antagonists always get, just as little as can be grudgingly vouchsafed you.

Yet you must keep the world on its feet. Is there any business man here who would be willing to see the world go bankrupt and the business of the world stop? Is there any man here who does not know that America is the only nation left by the war in a position to see that the world does go on with its business? And is it your idea that if we lend our money, as we must, to men whom we have bitterly disappointed, that money will bring back to us the largess to which we are entitled? I do not like to argue this thing on this basis, but if you want to talk business, I am ready to talk business. If it is a matter of how much you are going to get from your money, I say you will not get half as much as antagonists as you will get as partners. Think that over, if you have none of that thing that is so lightly spoken of, known as altruism. And, believe me, my fellow countrymen, the only people in the world who are going to reap the harvest of the future are the people who can entertain ideals, who can follow ideals to the death.

I was saying to another audience to-day that one of the most beautiful stories I know is the story that we heard in France about the first effect of the American soldiers when they got over there. The French did not believe at first, the British did not believe, that we could finally get 2,000,000 men over there. The most that they hoped at first was that a few American soldiers would restore their morale, for let me say that their morale was gone. The beautiful story to which I referred is this, the testimony that all of them rendered that they got their morale back the minute they saw the eyes of those boys. Here were not only soldiers. There was no curtain in front of the retina of those eyes. They were American eyes. They were eyes that had seen visions. They were eyes the possessors of which had brought with them a great ardor for a supreme cause, and the reason those boys never stopped was that their eyes were lifted to the horizon. They saw a city not built with hands. They saw a citadel toward which their steps were bent where dwelt the oracles of God himself. And on the battle field were found German orders to commanders here and there to see to it that the Americans did not get lodgment in particular places, because if they ever did you never could get them out. They had gone to Europe to go the whole way toward the realization of the teaching which their fathers had handed down to them. There never were crusaders that went to the Holy Land in the old ages that we read about that were more truly devoted to a holy cause than these gallant, incomparable sons of America.

My fellow citizens, you have got to make up your minds, because, after all, it is you who are going to make up the minds of this country. I do not owe a report or the slightest responsibility to anybody but you. I do not mean only you in this hall, though I am free to admit that this is just as good a sample of America as you can find anywhere, and the sample looks mighty good to me. I mean you and the millions besides you, thoughtful, responsible American men and women all over this country. They are my bosses, and I am mighty glad to be their servant. I have come out upon this journey not to fight anybody but to report to you, and I am free to predict that if you credit the report there will be no fighting. It is not only necessary that we should make peace with Germany and make peace with Austria, and see that a reasonable peace is made with Turkey and Bulgaria —that is not only not all of it, but it is a very dangerous beginning if you do not add something to it. I said just now that the peace with Germany, and the same is true of the pending peace with Austria, was made upon American specifications, not unwillingly. Do not let me leave the impression on your mind that the representatives of America in Paris had to insist and force their principles upon the rest. That is not true. Those principles were accepted before we got over there, and the men I dealt with carried them out in absolute good faith; but they were our principles, and at the heart of them lay this, that there must be a free Poland, for example.

I wonder if you realize what that means. We had to collect the pieces of Poland. For a long time one piece had belonged to Russia, and we can not get a clear title to that yet. Another part belonged to Austria. We got a title to that. Another part belonged to Germany, and we have settled the title to that. But we found Germany also in possession of other pieces of territory occupied predominately or exclusively by patriotic Poles, and we said to Germany, "You will have to give that up, too; that belongs to Poland." Not because it is ground, but because those people there are Poles and want to be parts of Poland, and it is not our business to force any sovereignty upon anybody who does not want to live under it. When we had determined the boundaries of Poland we set it up and recognized it as an independent Republic. There is a minister, a diplomatic representative, of the United States at Warsaw right now in virtue of our formal recognition of the Republic of Poland.

But upon Poland center some of the dangers of the future. South of Poland is Bohemia, which we cut away from the Austrian combination. Below Bohemia is Hungary, which can no longer rely upon the assistant strength of Austria, and below her is an enlarged Roumania. Alongside of Roumania is the new Slavic Kingdom, that never could have won its own independence, which had chafed under the chains of Austria-Hungary, but never could throw them off. We have said, "The fundamental wrongs of history center in these regions. These people have the right to govern their own Government and control their own fortunes." That is at the heart of the treaty, but, my fellow citizens, this is at the heart of the future: The business men of Germany did not want the war that we have passed through. The bankers and the manufacturers and the merchants knew that it was unspeakable folly. Why? Because Germany by her industrial genius was beginning to dominate the world economically, and all she had to do was to wait for about two more generations when her credit, her merchandise, her enterprise, would have covered all the parts of the world that the great fighting nations did not control. The formula of pan-Germanism, you remember, was Bremen to Bagdad—Bremen on the North

Sea to Bagdad in Persia. These countries that we have set up as the new home of liberty lie right along that road. If we leave them there without the guaranty that the combined force of the world will assure their independence and their territorial integrity, we have only to wait a short generation when our recent experience will be repeated. We did not let Germany dominate the world this time. Are we then? If Germany had known then that all the other fighting nations of the world would combine to prevent her action, she never would have dreamed of attempting it. If Germany had known—this is the common verdict of every man familiar with the politics of Europe—if Germany had known that England would go in, she never would have started it. If she had known that America would come in, she never would have dreamed of it. And now the only way to make it certain that there never will be another world war like that is that we should assist in guaranteeing the peace and its settlement.

It is a very interesting circumstance, my fellow countrymen, that the league of nations will contain all the nations of the world, great and small, except Germany, and Germany is merely put on probation. We have practically said to Germany, "If it turns out that you really have had a change of heart and have gotten nonsense out of your system; if it really does turn out that you have substituted a genuine self-governing Republic for a Kingdom where a few men on Wilhelmstrasse plotted the destiny of the world, then we will let you in as partners, because then you will be respectable." In the meantime, accepting the treaty, Germany's Army is reduced to 100,000 men, and she has promised to give up all the war material over and above what is necessary for 100,000 men. For a nation of 60,000,000! She has surrendered to the world. She has said, "Our fate is in your hands. We are ready to do what you tell us to do." The rest of the world is combined, and the interesting circumstance is that the rest of the world, excluding us, will continue combined if we do not go into it. Some gentlemen seem to think they can break up this treaty and prevent this league by not going into it. Not at all.

I can give you an interesting circumstance. There is the settlement, which you have heard so much discussed, about that rich and ancient Province of Shantung in China. I do not like that settlement any better than you do, but these were the circumstances: In order to induce Japan to cooperate in the war and clear the Pacific of the German power England, and subsequently France, bound themselves without any qualification to see to it that Japan got anything in China that Germany had, and that Japan would take it away from her, upon the strength of which promise Japan proceeded to take Kiaochow and occupy the portions of Shantung Province, which had been ceded by China for a term of years to Germany. The most that could be got out of it was that, in view of the fact that America had nothing to do with it, the Japanese were ready to promise that they would give up every item of sovereignty which Germany would otherwise have enjoyed in Shantung Province and return it without restriction to China, and that they would retain in the Province only the economic concessions such as other nations already had elsewhere in China—though you do not hear anything about that—concessions in the railway and the mines which had become attached to the railway for operative purposes. But suppose that you say that is not enough. Very well, then, stay out of the treaty, and how will that accomplish anything? England and France are bound and can not escape their obligation. Are you going to institute a war against Japan and France and England to get Shantung back for China? That is an enterprise which does not commend itself to the present generation.

I am putting it in brutal terms, my fellow citizens, but that is the fact. By disagreeing to that provision, we accomplish nothing for China. On the contrary, we stay out of the only combination of the counsels of nations in which we can be of service to China. With China as a member of the league of nations, and Japan as a member of the league of nations, and America as a member of the league of nations, there confronts every one of them that now famous article 10, by which every member of the league agrees to respect and preserve the territorial integrity and existing political independence of all the other member States. Do not let anybody persuade you that you can take that article out and have a peaceful world. That cuts at the root of the German war. That cuts at the root of the outrage against Belgium. That cuts at the root of the outrage against France. That pulls that vile, unwholesome Upas tree of Pan Germanism up by the roots, and it pulls all other "pans" up, too. Every land-grabbing nation is served notice, "Keep on your own territory. Mind your own business. That territory belongs to those people and they can do with it what they please, provided they do not invade other people's rights by the use they make of it." My fellow citizens, the thing is going to be done whether we are in it or not. If we are in it, then we are going to be the determining factor in the development of civilization. If we are out of it, we ourselves are going to watch every other nation with suspicion, and we will be justified, too; and we are going to be watched with suspicion. Every movement of trade, every relationship of manufacture, every question of raw materials, every matter that affects the intercourse of the world, will be impeded by the consciousness that America wants to hold off and get something which she is not willing to share with the rest of mankind. I am painting the picture for you, because I know that it is as intolerable to you as it is to me. But do not go away with the impression, I beg you, that I think there is any doubt about the issue. The only thing that can be accomplished is delay. The ultimate outcome will be the triumphant acceptance of the treaty and the league.

Let me pay the tribute which it is only just that I should pay to some of the men who have been, I believe, misunderstood in this business. It is only a handful of men, my fellow citizens, who are trying to defeat the treaty or to prevent the league. The great majority, in official bodies and out, are scrutinizing it, as it is perfectly legitimate that they should scrutinize it, to see if it is necessary that they should qualify it in any way, and my knowledge of their conscience, my knowledge of their public principle, makes me certain that they will sooner or later see that it is safest, since it is all expressed in the plainest English that the English dictionary affords, not to qualify it—to accept it as it is. I have been a student of the English language all my life and I do not see a single obscure sentence in the whole document. Some gentlemen either have not read it or do not understand the English language; but, fortunately, on the right-hand page it is printed in English and on the left-hand page it is printed in French. Now, if they do not understand English, I hope they will get a French dictionary and dig out the meaning on that side. The French is a very precise language, more precise than the English language, I am told. I am not on a speaking acquaintance with it, but I am told that it is the most precise language in Europe, and that any given phrase in French always means the same thing. That can not be said of English. In order to satisfy themselves, I hope these gentlemen will master the French version and then be reassured that there are no lurking monsters in that document; that there are no sinister purposes; that everything is said in the frankest way.

For example, they have been very much worried at the phrase that nothing in the document shall be taken as impairing in any way the validity of such regional understandings as the Monroe doctrine. They say, "Why put in 'such regional understandings as'? What other understandings are there? Have you got something up your sleeve? Is there going to be a Monroe doctrine in Asia? Is there going to be a Monroe doctrine in China?" Why, my fellow citizens, the phrase was written in perfect innocence. The men that I was associated with said, "It is not wise to put a specific thing that belongs only to one nation in a document like this. We do not know of any other regional understanding like it; we never heard of any other; we never expect to hear of any other, but there might some day be some other, and so we will say 'such regional understandings as the Monroe doctrine,' " and their phrase was intended to give right of way to the Monroe doctrine in the Western Hemisphere. I reminded the Committee on Foreign Relations of the Senate the other day that the conference I held with them was not the first conference I had held about the league of nations. When I came back to this our own dear country in March last I held a conference at the White House with the Senate Committee on Foreign Relations, and they made various suggestions as to how the covenant should be altered in phraseology. I carried those suggestions back to Paris, and every one of them was accepted. I think that is a sufficient guaranty that no mischief was intended. The whole document is of the same plain, practical, explicit sort, and it secures peace, my fellow citizens, in the only way in which peace can be secured.

I remember, if I may illustrate a very great thing with a very trivial thing, I had two acquaintances who were very much addicted to profanity. Their friends were distressed about it. It subordinated a rich vocabulary which they might otherwise have cultivated, and so we induced them to agree that they never would swear inside the corporate limits, that if they wanted to swear they would go out of town. The first time the passion of anger came upon them they rather sheepishly got in a street car and went out of town to swear, and by the time they got out of town they did not want to swear. That very homely illustration illustrates in my mind the value of discussion. Let me remind you that every fighting nation in the world is going to belong to this league, because we are going to belong to it, and they all make this solemn engagement with each other, that they will not resort to war in the case of any controversy until they have done one or other of two things, until they have either submitted the question at issue to arbitration, in which case they promise to abide by the verdict whatever it may be, or, if they do not want to submit it to arbitration, have submitted it to discussion by the council of the league.

They agree to give the council six months to discuss the matter, to supply the council with all the pertinent facts regarding it, and that, after the opinion of the council is rendered, they will not then go to war if they are dissatisfied with the opinion until three more months have elapsed. They give nine months in which to spread the whole matter before the judgment of mankind, and if they violate this promise, if any one of them violates it, the covenant prescribes that that violation shall in itself constitute an act of war against the other members of the league. It does not provide that there shall be war. On the contrary, it provides for something very much more effective than war. It provides that that nation, that covenant-breaking nation, shall be absolutely cut off from intercourse of every kind with the other nations of the world; that no merchandise shall be shipped out of it or into it; that no postal messages shall go into it or come out of it; that no telegraphic messages shall cross its borders; and that the citizens of the other member States shall not be permitted to have any intercourse or transactions whatever with its citizens or its citizens with them. There is not a single nation in Europe that can stand that boycott for six months. There is not a single nation in Europe that is self-sufficing in its resources of food or anything else that can stand that for six months. And in those circumstances we are told that this covenant is a covenant of war. It is the most drastic covenant of peace that was ever conceived, and its processes are the processes of peace. The nation that does not abide by its covenants is sent to coventry, is taboo, is put out of the society of covenant-respecting nations.

This is a covenant of compulsory arbitration or discussion, and just so soon as you discuss matters, my fellow citizens, peace looks in at the window. Did you ever really sit down and discuss matters with your neighbor when you had a difference and come away in the same temper that you went in? One of the difficulties in our labor situation is that there are some employers who will not meet their employees face to face and talk with them. I have never known an instance in which such a meeting and discussion took place that both sides did not come away in a softened temper and with an access of respect for the other side. The processes of frank discussion are the processes of peace not only, but the processes of settlement, and those are the processes which are set up for all the powerful nations of the world.

I want to say that this is an unparalleled achievement of thoughtful civilization. To my dying day I shall esteem it the crowning privilege of my life to have been permitted to put my name to a document like that; and in my judgment, my fellow citizens, when passion is cooled and men take a sober, second thought, they are all going to feel that the supreme thing that America did was to help bring this about and then put her shoulder to the great chariot of justice and of peace which was going to lead men along in that slow and toilsome march, toilsome and full of the kind of agony that brings bloody sweat, but nevertheless going up a slow incline to those distant heights upon which will shine at last the serene light of justice, suffusing a whole world in blissful peace.

SELECTION **28**

An Irreconcilable Criticizes the Versailles Treaty: Senator William E. Borah, November 19, 1919

Opponents of the Treaty of Versailles and of the League of Nations ran the gamut from left to right, from red to royal blue. The Nation *and* The New Republic, *generally considered left, opposed ratification of the treaty, as did the* Chicago Tribune, *seldom if ever considered leftward leaning. Marxists of various hues were critical of the treaty, as were such anti-Communist and non-Marxist progressives as Senators Norris and La Follette. Senators La Follette and Lodge, who normally had not much in common beyond a Republican label, began to call one another Bob and Cabot in the fall of 1919. Henry Clay Frick, Hiram Johnson, Philander C. Knox, Andrew Mellon, and Eugene V. Debs—certainly a mixed bag—all opposed ratification of the Treaty of Versailles.*

And then there was William Edgar Borah, who was sui generis. *His flight across the political skies was as unpredictable as a fly's. He could be left, center, and right in rapid succession, then turn and move in the reverse direction. First coming to national attention as a special prosecutor in 1907 in the trial of William D. Haywood for the murder of Frank Steunenberg, he soon became active as an insurgent against Taft. He worked for Roosevelt's nomination at the 1912 Republican convention but would not leave the GOP with him. He opposed most of Wilson's reforms. He was opposed to woman suffrage and quite vigorously for prohibition, which was an odd combination. As chairman of the Committee on Foreign Relations from 1925 to 1933, he worked for recognition of the Soviet Union and against intervention in Latin America. Almost elected to the Senate by the Idaho Legislature in 1903, he was successful four years later and was a Senator for the rest of his life, winning popular majorities even in such Democratic years as 1912, 1930, and 1936. He died in office in 1940. For further biographical information see Claudius O. Johnson,* Borah of Idaho *(New York: Longmans, 1936) and Marian McKenna,* Borah *(Ann Arbor, Mich.: University of Michigan Press, 1961).*

In this speech on the Senate floor on November 19, 1919, the day the Senate first voted down ratification of the treaty, Borah used mostly conservative and traditional arguments against ratification. The League would severely limit the role of the Congress in foreign relations; the treaty violated the historic Monroe Doctrine; it was counter to Washington's advice against "entangling alliances"; and it would restrict American sovereignty without really securing peace. But he also used an anti-imperialist argument against the treaty. The League will represent "the dominant people," who will "rule one-half of the inhabitants of the globe as subject peoples. . . ." The League and the treaty had to do with "the protection of real estate regardless of how it is obtained."

Borah's speech, here reprinted without abridgment, is from the Congressional Record, *Sixty-sixth Congress, first session. volume 58, part 9, November 19, 1919, pages 8781–8784.*

Mr. President, I am not misled by the debate across the aisle into the view that this treaty will not be ratified. I entertain little doubt that sooner or later—and entirely too soon—the treaty will be ratified with the league of nations in it, and I am of the opinion with the reservations in it as they are now written. There may possibly be some change in verbiage in order that there may be a common sharing of parentage, but our friends across the aisle will likely accept the league of nations with the reservations in substance as now written. I think, therefore, this moment is just as appropriate as any other for me to express my final views with reference to the treaty and the league of nations. It is perhaps the last opportunity I shall have to state, as briefly as I may, my reasons for opposing the treaty and the league.

Mr. President, after Mr. Lincoln had been elected President, before he assumed the duties of the office and at a time when all indications were to the effect that we would soon be in the midst of civil strife, a friend from the city of Washington wrote him for instructions. Mr. Lincoln wrote back in a single line, "Entertain no compromise; have none of it." That states the position I occupy at this time and which I have, in an humble way, occupied from the first contention in regard to this proposal.

My objections to the league have not been met by the reservations. I desire to state wherein my objections have not been met. Let us see what our attitude will be toward Europe and what our position will be with reference to the other nations of the world after we shall have entered the league with the present reservations written therein. With all due respect to those who think that they have accomplished a different thing and challenging no man's intellectual integrity or patriotism, I do not believe the reservations have met the fundamental propositions which are involved in this contest.

When the league shall have been formed, we shall be a member of what is known as the council of the league. Our accredited representative will sit in judgment with the accredited representatives of the other members of the league to pass upon the concerns not only of our country but of all Europe and all Asia and the entire world. Our accredited representatives will be members of the assembly. They will sit there to represent the judgment of these 110,000,000 people—more then—just as we are accredited here to represent our constituencies. We can not send our representatives to sit in council with the representatives of the other great nations of the world with mental reservations as to what we shall do in case their judgment shall not be satisfactory to us. If we go to the council or to the assembly with any other purpose than that of complying in good faith and in absolute integrity with all upon which the council or the assembly may pass, we shall soon return to our country with our self-respect forfeited and the public opinion of the world condemnatory.

Why need you gentlemen across the aisle worry about a reservation here or there when we are sitting in the council and in the assembly and bound by every obligation in morals, which the President said was supreme above that of law, to comply with the judgment which our representative and the other representatives finally form? Shall we go there, Mr. President, to sit in judgment, and in case that judgment works for peace join with our allies, but in case it works for war withdraw our cooperation? How long would we stand as we now stand, a great Republic commanding the respect and holding the leadership of the world, if we should adopt any such course?

So, sir, we not only sit in the council and in the assembly with our accredited representatives, but bear in mind that article 11 is untouched by any reservation which has been offered here; and with article 11 untouched and its integrity complete, article 10 is perfectly superfluous. If any war or threat of war shall be a matter of consideration for the league, and the league shall take such action as it deems wise to deal with it, what is the necessity of article 10? Will not external aggression be regarded as war or threat of war? If the political independence of some nation in Europe is assailed will it be regarded as a war or threat of war? Is there anything in article 10 that is not completely covered by article 11?

It remains complete, and with our representatives sitting in the council and the assembly, and with article 11 complete, and with the assembly and the council having jurisdiction of all matters touching the peace of the world, what more do you need to bind the United States if you assume that the United States is a Nation of honor?

We have said, Mr. President, that we would not send our troops abroad without the consent of Congress. Pass by now for a moment the legal proposition. If we create executive functions, the Executive will perform those functions without the authority of Congress. Pass that question by and go to the other question. Our members of the council are there. Our members of the assembly are there. Article 11 is complete, and it authorizes the league, a member of which is our representative, to deal with matters of peace and war, and the league through its council and its assembly deals with the matter, and our accredited representative joins with the others in deciding upon a certain course, which involves a question of sending troops. What will the Congress of the United States do? What right will it have left, except the bare technical right to refuse, which as a moral proposition it will not dare to exercise? Have we not been told day by day for the last nine months that the Senate of the United States, a coordinate part of the treaty-making power, should accept this league as it was written because the wise men sitting at Versailles had so written it, and has not every possible influence and every source of power in public opinion been organized and directed against the Senate to compel it to do that thing? How much stronger will be the moral compulsion upon the Congress of the United States when we ourselves have indorsed the proposition of sending our accredited representatives there to vote for us?

Ah, but you say that there must be unanimous consent, and that there is vast protection in unanimous consent.

I do not wish to speak disparagingly; but has not every division and dismemberment of every nation which has suffered dismemberment taken place by unanimous consent for the last 300 years? Did not Prussia and Austria and Russia by unanimous consent divide Poland? Did not the United States and Great Britain and Japan and Italy and France divide China and give Shantung to Japan? Was that not a unanimous decision? Close the doors upon the diplomats of Europe, let them sit in secret, give them the material to trade on, and there always will be unanimous consent.

How did Japan get unanimous consent? I want to say here, in my parting words upon this proposition, that I have no doubt the outrage upon China was quite as distasteful to the President of the United States as it is to me. But Japan said: "I will not sign your treaty unless you turn over to me Shantung, to be turned back at my discretion," and you know how Japan's discretion operates with reference to such things. And so, when we are in the league, and our accredited representatives are sitting at Geneva, and a question of great moment arises, Japan, or Russia, or Germany, or Great Britain will say, "Unless this matter is adjusted in this way I will depart from your league." It is the same thing, operating in the same way, only under a different date and under a little different circumstances.

Mr. President, if you have enough territory, if you have enough material, if you have enough subject peoples to trade upon and divide, there will no difficulty about unanimous consent.

Do our Democratic friends ever expect any man to sit as a member of the council or as a member of the assembly equal in intellectual power and in standing before the world with that of our representative at Versailles? Do you expect a man to sit in the council who will have made more pledges, and I shall assume made them in sincerity, for self-determination and for the rights of small peoples, than had been made by our accredited representative? And yet, what became of it? The unanimous consent was obtained nevertheless.

But take another view of it. We are sending to the council one man. That one man represents 110,000,000 people.

Here, sitting in the Senate, we have two from every State in the Union, and over in the other House we have Representatives in accordance with population, and the responsibility is spread out in accordance with our obligations to our constituency. But now we are transferring to one man the stupendous power of representing the sentiment and convictions of 110,000,000 people in tremendous questions which may involve the peace or may involve the war of the world.

However you view the question of unanimous consent, it does not protect us.

What is the result of all this? We are in the midst of all of the affairs of Europe. We have entangled ourselves with all European concerns. We have joined in alliance with all the European nations which have thus far joined the league, and all nations which may be admitted to the league. We are sitting there dabbling in their affairs and intermeddling in their concerns. In other words, Mr. President—and this comes to the question which is fundamental with me—we have forfeited and surrendered, once and for all, the great policy of "no entangling alliances" upon which the strength of this Republic has been founded for 150 years.

My friends of reservations, tell me where is the reservation in these articles which protects us against entangling alliances with Europe?

Those who are differing over reservations, tell me what one of them protects the doctrine laid down by the Father of his Country. That fundamental proposition is surrendered, and we are a part of the European turmoils and conflicts from the time we enter this league.

Let us not underestimate that. There has never been an hour since the

Venezuelan difficulty that there has not been operating in this country, fed by domestic and foreign sources, a powerful propaganda for the destruction of the doctrine of no entangling alliances.

Lloyd-George is reported to have said just a few days before the Conference met at Versailles that Great Britain could give up much, and would be willing to sacrifice much, to have America withdraw from that policy. That was one of the great objects of the entire conference at Versailles, so far as the foreign representatives were concerned. Clemenceau and Lloyd-George and others like them were willing to make any reasonable sacrifice which would draw America away from her isolation and into the internal affairs and concerns of Europe. This league of nations, with or without reservations, whatever else it does or does not do, does surrender and sacrifice that policy; and once having surrendered and become a part of the European concerns, where, my friends, are you going to stop?

You have put in here a reservation upon the Monroe doctrine. I think that, in so far as language could protect the Monroe doctrine, it has been protected. But as a practical proposition, as a working proposition, tell me candidly, as men familiar with the history of your country and of other countries, do you think that you can intermeddle in European affairs?

When Mr. Monroe wrote to Jefferson, he asked him his view upon the Monroe doctrine, and Mr. Jefferson said, in substance, our first and primary obligation should be never to interfere in European affairs; and, secondly, never to permit Europe to interfere in our affairs.

He understood, as every wise and practical man understands, that if we intermeddle in her affairs, if we help to adjust her conditions, inevitably and remorselessly Europe then will be carried into our affairs, in spite of anything you can write upon paper.

We can not protect the Monroe doctrine unless we protect the basic principle upon which it rests, and that is the Washington policy. I do not care how earnestly you may endeavor to do so, as a practical working proposition your league will come to the United States. Will you permit me to digress long enough to read a paragraph from a great French editor upon this particular phase of the matter, Mr. Stephen Lausanne, editor of Le Matin, of Paris?

> When the executive council of the league of nations fixes "the reasonable limits of the armament of Peru"; when it shall demand information concerning the naval program of Brazil; when it shall tell Argentina what shall be the measure of the "contribution to the armed forces to protect the signatures of the social covenant"; when it shall demand the immediate registration of the treaty between the United States and Canada at the seat of the league, it will control, whether it wills or no, the destinies of America. And when the American States shall be obliged to take a hand in every war or menace of war in Europe (art. 11), they will necessarily fall afoul of the fundamental principle laid down by Monroe, which was that Americans should never take part in a European war.
>
> If the league takes in the world, then Europe must mix in the affairs of America; if only Europe is included, then America will violate of necessity her own doctrine by intermixing in the affairs of Europe.

If the league includes the affairs of the world, does it not include the affairs of all the world? Is there any limitation of the jurisdiction of the council or of the assembly upon the question of peace or war? Does it not have now, under the reservations, the same as it had before, the power to deal with all matters of peace or war throughout the entire world? How shall you keep from meddling in the affairs of Europe or keep Europe from meddling in the affairs of America?

Mr. President, there is another and even a more commanding reason why I shall record my vote against this treaty. It imperils what I conceive to be the underlying, the very first principles of this Republic. It is in conflict with the right of our people to govern themselves free from all restraint, legal or moral, of foreign powers. It challenges every tenet of my political faith. If this faith were one of my own contriving, if I stood here to assert principles of government of my own evolving, I might well be charged with intolerable presumption, for we all recognize the ability of those who urge a different course. But I offer in justification of my course nothing of my own save the deep and abiding reverence I have for those whose policies I humbly but most ardently support. I claim no merit save fidelity to American principles and devotion to American ideals as they were wrought out from time to time by those who built the Republic and as they have been extended and maintained throughout these years. In opposing the treaty I do nothing more than decline to renounce and tear out of my life the sacred traditions which throughout 50 years have been translated into my whole intellectual and moral being. I will not, I can not, give up my belief that America must, not alone for the happiness of her own people, but for the moral guidance and greater contentment of the world, be permitted to live her own life. Next to the tie which binds a man to his God is the tie which binds a man to his country, and all schemes, all plans, however ambitious and fascinating they seem in their proposal, but which would embarrass or entangle and impede or shackle her sovereign will, which would compromise her freedom of action, I unhesitatingly put behind me.

Sir, since the debate opened months ago those of us who have stood against this proposition have been taunted many times with being little Americans. Leave us the word American, keep that in your presumptuous impeachment, and no taunt can disturb us, no gibe discompose our purposes. Call us little Americans if you will, but leave us the consolation and the pride which the term American, however modified, still imparts. Take away that term and though you should coin in telling phrase your highest eulogy we would hurl it back as common slander. We have been ridiculed because, forsooth, of our limited vision. Possibly that charge may be true. Who is there here that can read the future? Time, and time alone, unerring and remorseless, will give us each our proper place in the affections of our countrymen and in the esteem and commendation of those who are to come after us. We neither fear nor court her favor. But if our vision has been circumscribed it has at all times within its compass been clear and steady. We have sought nothing save the tranquillity of our own people and the honor and independence of our own Republic. No foreign flattery, no possible world glory and power have disturbed our poise or come between us and our devotion to the traditions which have made us a people or the policies which have made us a Nation, unselfish and commanding. If we have erred we have erred out of too much love for those things which from childhood you and we together have been taught to revere—yes, to defend even at the cost of limb and life. If we have erred it is because we have placed too high an estimate upon the wisdom of Washington and Jefferson, too exalted an opinion upon the patriotism of the sainted Lincoln. And blame us not therefore if we have, in our limited vision, seemed sometimes bitter and at all times uncompromising, for the things for which we have spoken, feebly spoken, the things which we have endeavored to defend, have been the things for which your fathers and our fathers were willing to die.

Senators, even in an hour so big with expectancy we should not close our eyes to the fact that democracy is something more, vastly more, than a mere form of government by which society is restrained into free and orderly life. It is a moral entity, a spiritual force, as well. And these are things which live only and alone in the atmosphere of liberty. The foundation upon which democracy rests is faith in the moral instincts of the people. Its ballot boxes, the franchise, its laws, and constitutions are but the outward manifestations of the deeper and more essential thing—a continuing trust in the moral purposes of the average man and woman. When this is lost or forfeited your outward forms, however democratic in terms, are a mockery. Force may find expression through institutions democratic in structure equal with the simple and more direct processes of a single supreme ruler. These distinguishing virtues of a real republic you can not commingle with the discordant and destructive forces of the Old World and still preserve them. You can not yoke a government whose fundamental maxim is that of liberty to a government whose first law is that of force and hope to preserve the former. These things are in eternal war, and one must ultimately destroy the other. You may still keep for a time the outward form, you may still delude yourself, as others have done in the past, with appearances and symbols, but when you shall have committed this Republic to a scheme of world control based upon force, upon the combined military force of the four great nations of the world, you will have soon destroyed the atmosphere of freedom, of confidence in the self-governing capacity of the masses, in which alone a democracy may thrive. We may become one of the four dictators of the world, but we shall no longer be master of our own spirit. And what shall it profit us as a Nation if we shall go forth to the dominion of the earth and share with others the glory of world control and lose that fine sense of confidence in the people, the soul of democracy?

Look upon the scene as it is now presented. Behold the task we are to assume, and then contemplate the method by which we are to deal with this task. Is the method such as to address itself to a Government "conceived in liberty and dedicated to the proposition that all men are created equal"? When this league, this combination, is formed four great powers representing the dominant people will rule one-half of the inhabitants of the globe as subject peoples—rule by force, and we shall be a party to the rule of force. There is no other way by which you can keep people in subjection. You must either give them independence, recognize their rights as nations to live their own life and to set up their own form of government, or you must deny them these things by force. That is the scheme, the method proposed by the league. It proposes no other. We will in time become inured to its inhuman precepts and its soulless methods, strange as this doctrine now seems to a free people. If we stay with our contract, we will come in time to declare with our associates that force—force, the creed of the Prussian military oligarchy—is after all the true foundation upon which must rest all stable governments. Korea, despoiled and bleeding at every pore; India, sweltering in ignorance and burdened with inhuman taxes after more than a hundred years of dominant rule; Egypt, trapped and robbed of her birthright; Ireland, with 700 years of sacrifice for independence—this is the task, this is the atmosphere, and this is the creed in and under which we are to keep alive our belief in the moral purposes and self-governing capacity of the people, a belief without which the Republic must disintegrate and die. The maxim of liberty will soon give way to the rule of blood and iron. We have been pleading here for our Constitution. Conform this league, it has been said, to the technical terms of our charter, and all will be well. But I declare to you that we must go further and conform to those sentiments and passions for justice and freedom which are essential to the existence of democracy. You must respect not territorial boundaries, not territorial integrity, but you must respect and preserve the sentiments and passions for justice and for freedom which God in His infinite wisdom has planted so deep in the human heart that no form of tyranny however brutal, no persecution however prolonged, can wholly uproot and kill. Respect nationality, respect justice, respect freedom, and you may have some hope of peace, but not so if you make your standard the standard of tyrants and despots, the protection of real estate regardless of how it is obtained.

Sir, we are told that this treaty means peace. Even so, I would not pay the price. Would you purchase peace at the cost of any part of our independence? We could have had peace in 1776—the price was high, but we could have had it. James Otis, Sam Adams, Hancock, and Warren were surrounded by those who urged peace and British rule. All through that long and trying struggle, particularly when the clouds of adversity lowered upon the cause, there was a cry of peace—let us have peace. We could have had peace in 1860; Lincoln was counseled by men of great influence and accredited wisdom to let our brothers—and, thank Heaven, they are brothers—depart in peace. But the tender, loving Lincoln, bending under the fearful weight of impending civil war, an apostle of peace, refused to pay the price, and a reunited country will praise his name forevermore—bless it because he refused peace at the price of national honor and national integrity. Peace upon any other basis than national independence, peace purchased at the cost of any part of our national integrity, is fit only for slaves, and even when purchased at such a price it is a delusion, for it can not last.

But your treaty does not mean peace—far, very far, from it. If we are to judge the future by the past it means war. Is there any guaranty of peace other than the guaranty which comes of the control of the war-making power by the people? Yet what great rule of democracy does the treaty leave unassailed? The people in whose keeping alone you can safely lodge the power of peace or war nowhere, at no time and in no place, have any voice in this scheme for world peace. Autocracy which has bathed the world in blood for centuries reigns supreme. Democracy is everywhere excluded. This, you say, means peace.

Can you hope for peace when love of country is disregarded in your scheme, when the spirit of nationality is rejected, even scoffed at? Yet what law of that moving and mysterious force does your treaty not deny? With a ruthlessness unparalleled your treaty in a dozen instances runs counter to the divine law of nationality. Peoples who speak the same language, kneel at the same ancestral tombs, moved by the same traditions, animated by a common hope, are torn asunder, broken in pieces, divided, and parceled out to antagonistic nations. And this you call justice. This, you cry, means peace. Peoples who have dreamed of independence, struggled and been patient, sacrified and been hopeful, peoples who were told that through this peace conference they should realize the aspirations of centuries, have again had their hopes dashed to earth. One of the most striking and commanding figures in this war, soldier and statesman, turned away from the peace table at Versailles declaring to the world, "The promise of the new life, the victory of the great humane ideals for which the peoples have shed their blood and their treasure without stint, the fulfillment of their aspirations toward a new international order and a fairer and better world, are not written into the treaty." No; your treaty means injustice. It means slavery. It means war. And to all this you ask this Republic to become a party. You ask it to abandon the creed under which it has grown to power and accept the creed of autocracy, the creed of repression and force.

Mr. President, I turn from this scheme based upon force to another scheme, planned 143 years ago in old Independence Hall, in the city of Philadelphia, based upon liberty. I like it better. I have become so accustomed to believe in it that it is difficult for me to reject it out of hand. I have difficulty in subscribing to the new creed of oppression, the creed of dominant and subject peoples. I feel a reluctance to give up the belief that all men are created equal—the eternal principle in government that all governments derive their just powers from the consent of the governed. I can not get my consent to exchange the doctrine of George Washington for the doctrine of Frederick the Great translated into mendacious phrases of peace. I go back to that serene and masterful soul who pointed the way to power and glory for the new and then weak Republic, and whose teachings and admonitions even in our majesty and dominance we dare not disregard.

I know well the answer to my contention. It has been piped about of late from a thousand sources—venal sources, disloyal sources, sinister sources—that Washington's wisdom was of his day only and that his teachings are out of fashion—things long since sent to the scrap heap of history —that while he was great in character and noble in soul he was untrained in the arts of statecraft and unlearned in the science of government. The puny demagogue, the barren editor, the sterile professor now vie with each other in apologizing for the temporary and commonplace expedients which the Father of his Country felt constrained to adopt in building a republic!

What is the test of statesmanship? Is it the formation of theories, the utterance of abstract and incontrovertible truths, or is it the capacity and the power to give to a people that concrete thing called liberty, that vital and indispensable thing in human happiness called free institutions, and to establish over all and above all the blessed and eternal reign of order and law? If this be the test, where shall we find another whose name is entitled to be written beside the name of Washington? His judgment and poise in the hour of turmoil and peril, his courage and vision in times of adversity, his firm grasp of fundamental principles, his almost inspired power to penetrate the future and read there the result, the effect of policies, have never been excelled, if equaled, by any of the world's commonwealth builders. Peter the Great, William the Silent, and Cromwell the Protector, these and these alone perhaps are to be associated with his name as the builders of States and the founders of governments. But in exaltation of moral purpose, in the unselfish character of his work, in the durability of his policies, in the permanency of the institutions which he more than anyone else called into effect, his service to mankind stands out separate and apart in a class by itself. The works of these other great builders, where are they now? But the work of Washington is still the most potent influence for the advancement of civilization and the freedom of the race.

Reflect for a moment over his achievements. He led the Revolutionary Army to victory. He was the very first to suggest a union instead of a confederacy. He presided over and counseled with great wisdom the convention which framed the Constitution. He guided the Government through its first perilous years. He gave dignity and stability and honor to that which was looked upon by the world as a passing experiment, and finally, my friends, as his own peculiar and particular contribution to the happiness of his countrymen and to the cause of the Republic, he gave us his great foreign policy under which we have lived and prospered and strengthened for nearly a century and a half. This policy is the most sublime confirmation of his genius as a statesman. It was then, and it now is, an indispensable part of our whole scheme of government. It is to-day a vital, indispensable element in our entire plan, purpose, and mission as a nation. To abandon it is nothing less than a betrayal of the American people. I say betrayal deliberately, in view of the suffering and the sacrifice which will follow in the wake of such a course.

But under the stress and strain of these extraordinary days, when strong men are being swept down by the onrushing forces of disorder and change, when the most sacred things of life, the most cherished hopes of a Christian world seem to yield to the mad forces of discontent—just such days as Washington passed through when the mobs of Paris, wild with new liberty and drunk with power, challenged the established institutions of all the world, but his steadfast soul was unshaken—under these conditions come again we are about to abandon this policy so essential to our happiness and tranquillity as a people and our stability as a Government. No leader with his commanding influence and his unquailing courage stands forth to stem the current. But what no leader can or will do experience, bitter experience, and the people of this country in whose keeping, after all, thank God, is the Republic, will ultimately do. If we abandon his leadership and teachings, we will go back. We will return to this policy. Americanism shall not, can not, die. We may go back in sackcloth and ashes, but we will return to the faith of the fathers. America will live her own life. The independence of this Republic will have its defenders. Thousands have suffered and died for it, and their sons and daughters are not of the breed who will be betrayed into the hands of foreigners. The noble face of the Father of his Country, so familiar to every boy and girl, looking out from the walls of the Capital in stern reproach, will call those who come here for public service to a reckoning. The people of our beloved country will finally speak, and we will return to the policy which we now abandon. America disenthralled and free in spite of all these things will continue her mission in the cause of peace, of freedom, and of civilization.

SELECTION

Fear and Intolerance, Reds and Aliens: "The Saturday Evening Post" during the Postwar Red Scare

Wartime passions and anxieties did not disappear with the armistice. Widespread hate and fear, directed at the "Hun" and the "slacker" during the war months, now were focused on the "Bolsheviks" and the "Reds." With the end of the war came a series of conflicts that seriously divided the country—in 1919 labor conflicts were more numerous than ever before, and the summer of 1919 saw race riots worse than any in the nation's previous history—and many people saw each conflict as the work of Reds and aliens. Solid, respectable, stable middle-class America, which had been on an emotional binge with a special kind of idealism (superpatriotism and prohibition, "Over There" and "Lips That Touch Liquor Shall Never Touch Mine"), required about another eighteen months to get back to what the next President of the United States called "normalcy."

Political figures both fed the hysteria and adapted their policies to it. The New York State Legislature refused to seat five properly elected Socialists from New York City solely because they were Socialists. Attorney General A. Mitchell Palmer in November, 1919, and again in January, 1920, swept up radicals all over the country in a series of raids and deported many of them who were aliens. (The reference to the Buford in the first of the two following editorials is to a ship that left New York Harbor soon before Christmas, 1919, with a load of alien radicals deported to Russia.) Many states adopted what were called criminal-syndicalism laws, acts which actually outlawed advocating revolution.

The Red Scare expired rather quickly in mid-1920. A. Mitchell Palmer, who hoped to ride the hysteria into the White House, found to his dismay that rather suddenly no one was much interested. It was by no means true, however, that the population quickly became tolerant of Reds and aliens. The trial and conviction of the Italian anarchists Nicola Sacco and Bartolomeo Vanzetti for murder and robbery in 1921 plainly indicated that antialien and antiradical prejudice continued to run high. But prejudice and irrationality did settle down to their customary level; people became less hysterical; solidity and prudence and circumspection again came to be counted as virtues.

The two following editorials appeared as the lead items in the editor's pages of The Saturday Evening Post, volume 192, February 7, 1920, pages 28–29, at the height of the Red Scare. George Horace Lorimer, the magazine's editor, never acquired a reputation as a political philosopher of the first magnitude, but he was normally more restrained and more consistent in thought than he was in these editorials. Note, for example, that aliens are portrayed at one and the same time as dangerously radical and as hopelessly traditional and conservative. They "want to take over our property and our country," but four sentences later, "They are serfs to tradition—narrow, suspicious, timid, brutal, rapacious—easily persuaded by their fears and blindly led through their ignorance." Later still, they are dangerously radical again, unable to distinguish between liberty and license.

The Saturday Evening Post was easily the most popular magazine in the nation at this time. It offered about 180 large pages of short stories, serialized novels, nonfiction, and many photographs and illustrations for 5 cents a copy or $2 a year. Many of the stories and articles were by the nation's top writers. Thousands, perhaps hundreds of thousands, of Americans read nothing but the weekly Post and their local newspaper. Fortunately, no journal in heterogeneous America could claim justifiably to represent American culture, but the Post came closer than most.

For the Red Scare, see Robert K. Murray, Red Scare: A Study in National Hysteria, 1919–1920 *(Minneapolis: University of Minnesota Press, 1955) and the pertinent chapters of Stanley Coben,* A. Mitchell Palmer: Politician *(New York: Columbia, 1963). For an excellent study of opposition to the immigrant, see John Higham,* Strangers in the Land: Patterns of American Nativism, 1860–1925 *(New Brunswick, N.J.: Rutgers, 1955).*

SANCTUARY

Two ships, the Mayflower and the Buford, mark epochs in the history of America. The Mayflower brought the first of the builders to this country; the Buford has taken away the first destroyers. In the wake of the Mayflower came many ships bringing desirables to these shores. Many ships must follow the Buford, taking back undesirables to the lands from which they came, there to stay. We have no room in America for a Society of Buford Descendants.

The men of the Mayflower came here to escape oppression and remained to build a great nation. The men of the Buford came here ostensibly to escape oppression and sought to destroy their protectors. The radical mind sees no difference between them and pronounces them both good—and red.

Loud cries are going up from both the out-and-out and the in-and-out Bolshevist papers. Knouts crack and chains rattle in their pages. They are making a martyr a minute. And they have succeeded in confusing a good many of the more simple-minded among their sitting-room and parlor readers, both street and college educated, in making them believe that in shipping back the reds to Utopia some awful thing has been done to them. They may be right at that, for it looks like work or starve in Russia this winter. But whatever befalls the comrades at the hands of their brothers we shall bear up bravely here in America.

Particularly in those curious periodicals devoted to governmental jazz and economic hokum that, together with spiritualism, have found a large following among our war psychopaths, the cry is being raised that America is no longer true to her old ideals; that she no longer offers asylum to those oppressed for conscience' sake and political beliefs.

Passing by as irrelevant the fact that a majority of these latter-day refugees show no signs of having a conscience and worship no god but the Revolution, it is probable that America will always offer asylum under proper conditions to the genuinely oppressed of the world. But it is highly improbable that she will continue to be the world lunatic asylum. In the past we have freely offered to these Russians, Germans and other aliens everything that we have—freedom to worship as they please; a chance to become citizens and to vote side by side with us; opportunity to make a living on equal terms with the native born. The law of self-preservation forbids this for the future. First we discover that one group of aliens is trying to impose the Kaiser on us as a master, and then that another is plotting to deliver us over to Lenine. And not only are these aliens seeking to destroy our country but they are progressively limiting opportunity for Americans.

We are in the position of a farmer who has granted shelter to a passing tramp, only to wake up from pleasant dreams to find him pouring kerosene on the kitchen floor, preparatory to looting and firing the house. And these pyromaniac editors, in pretty little pieces, bid us be perfectly calm and not throw out the poor tramp, who has been oppressed by a heartless brakeman on Number Three. Besides, the burning house will light up the surrounding landscape beautifully.

If these aliens for whom they bleed so freely and redly ever really needed asylum the occasion for it has passed. If they fear oppression at home it is at the hands of their comrades. If they linger on here it is not because Europe does not offer men of their expressed beliefs a congenial home. Their hopes have been wholly realized in Russia and partially realized elsewhere on the Continent. Their brothers are in the saddle, their ideals are in practical operation. Why then do they fight and kick and scratch against deportation to Utopia? Why do they conspire against the Government that has befriended them? Simply because the pickings are poor just now in Europe. Because over there the comrades must work or starve if they are not in on the ground floor. Because their real ideal is loot, and America is the richest country in the world, as it is the most careless, the most given to accepting men at their own valuations and professions. When a man proclaims that he is working for the brotherhood of man it seems to Americans like sacrilege to doubt and to investigate the holy one to see whether it is really for brotherhood or for his own pocket that he is working.

The average American is the easiest fellow in the world to con with professional uplift patter, because he is always an innocent bystander in the things that most concern him—politics, profiteering, labor-and-capital disputes, and now alien radicalism. He is only half awake to the extent and organization of this sinister red campaign against his Government, his prosperity and his liberties. "Let George do it" is the national motto where anything except the immediate dollar is concerned. And after George has done it the bystander is pretty apt to round on George and ask him why he kicked up all that fuss. The world is still wagging and business is as usual or a little better.

When it comes to public affairs and duties the average American leads a sheltered life that makes a convent-bred girl look unprotected. But there can be no innocent by-standers in this business, no hairsplitting, no passing the buck. It is not "just newspaper talk." It is a menacing fact, and sooner or later everyone must line up on one side or the other and take an active part in deciding whether this country shall remain America or become Russia.

Hand in hand with this demand that we keep our doors open to everyone is the demand that we open our mails to anything. In this instance the reds and their pink allies are pulling the strings that work the suppression-of-free-speech bogy, and under their manipulations it is making some terrifying faces.

Free speech, like the liberty to worship and to vote as one's conscience dictates, is one of the great rights of an American citizen, but a situation might easily arise where any or all of those rights would have to be abridged for the protection of the people. A group might conscientiously believe in human sacrifice or in its right to nominate a convicted murderer for President; but in either event its conscience would promptly be told to behave. The right of free speech that is being demanded is simply the right to incite listeners and readers to free love, free loot, free murder and a free field to overturn the Government by violence. Anyone who has studied the tons of red and pink pamphlets, newspapers and periodicals that are pouring from presses all over the country knows that this is being done boldly and directly by the reds, and timidly and indirectly by the pinkies.

This free-speech campaign has even deceived perfectly good American editors, who tremble lest their inherent right to print a corking scandal on the front page or to roast anything editorially is going to be taken away from them. They fear that an open season on skunks may in some way curtail their right to kill a frying chicken for supper. A country that has successfully distinguished between liberty and license in religion and voting can probably be depended on to show a little common sense in distinguishing between free speech and incitement to murder.

Any good citizen who will conscientiously attend a class in red rhetoric or take a course in Bolshevist literature will graduate with some pretty clear convictions on the proper limits to free speech.

People who demand free and unlimited speech for themselves are quite intolerant of it in others. There is no free speech, no free press in "free" Russia. A tendency to shut off all discussion of economic theories or criticism of government that is not in agreement with their views shows wherever radicals get the upper hand.

SELF-PRESERVATION

Deportation and immigration are the two great questions before us. We have made a good start at the first, but it will be useless to continue deportations unless we are prepared to take equally drastic action on immigration. Those aliens who deplore our individualistic, capitalistic system are preparing to come over here by the hundred thousand to enjoy its benefits and if possible to join with their fellows already here to short-cut to fortune by confiscating our capital.

We must rid our minds of the notion that America is some kind of a world institution for the care of nuts; that Americans have no rights that her guests are bound to respect; that her citizenship is open to anyone to accept or reject as his own whims and interests dictate; that men who cannot speak our language have a God-given right to tell us where to get off; that we can make a few passes over anyone regardless of race and presto! an American; or that we can keep on ceaselessly dividing with the whole world and have as much as we had before.

People talk of these immigrants from Russia, from Hungary, from the Balkans, as if all they need to become Americanized is to learn not to keep the coal in the bathtub and to be taught a little pushcart English. They see the negro problem; but they cannot grasp the Russian problem. They do not understand that many of these alien peoples are temperamentally and racially unfitted for easy assimilation; that they are living in an age two or three centuries behind ours. They are white, they can read a few lines, and they have a few dollars—so in they come. We need three generations to educate, to crossbreed with Western strains and to assimilate a large number of those that we have here now.

This matter of Americanization is only partly a question of education. Many second-generation Americans from Central and Eastern Europe, men with college degrees, are quite unassimilated to American ideals. Temperamentally and racially they are still Russian or Balkan or German. So further immigration must not only be rigidly limited in volume but we must analyze the possibilities and desirability of different races in a way that we have never done before. The matter of race, as well as the qualifications of individuals, must be given more attention.

Arguments for unrestricted immigration always go back to some petty selfish reason—never to the greatest good of the country. A woman wants a cook, a manufacturer wants cheap labor, a laborer wants his relatives to share in the big wages, a politician wants votes and aliens want to take over our property and our country. The rank and file of these unassimilated aliens still live mentally in the ghetto or as peasants on the great estates. In thought they are still stoned by the gentile; still ground down by the master—yoked in mind to the ox of the field. Freemen they walk among us, but they are not free. They are serfs to tradition—narrow, suspicious timid, brutal, rapacious—easily persuaded by their fears and blindly led through their ignorance.

It has been truly said that no man is under obligation to burn down his house even to warm the widow and the orphan. America is under no obligation to destroy herself in a hopeless effort to transform overnight the results of centuries of serfdom, ignorance and brutality into upstanding Americans. License is as close as the mass of these eastern Europeans can approximate to the idea of liberty.

No foreigner has any rights in or to America except those that we choose to give him, and we have been so free-handed in the past that we shall soon have very little left to give. Our great prosperity has been due to two factors—America and Americans—the country that was handed to us in trust and that because of its natural advantages bred a peculiarly happy and prosperous race. Increasing population beyond a certain point means decreasing opportunity and prosperity, and so a lowered standard of living. That is one great factor in Europe's troubles—overpopulation of the land, overcrowding in the cities, with fewer opportunities and less to go round. Many of the things on which we pride ourselves, that have made us strong, self-reliant and prosperous, are due to luck—our luck in having a big fertile country, rich in raw materials and with enough outdoors untouched and unspoiled so that we can get up against Nature in our work and our play. Conversely, many of Europe's troubles, many of the conditions over there that we decry, are due to over-population, insufficient natural resources and the lack of any real outdoors, except the sophisticated, dolled-up resorts of the tourist. Let us guard jealously what we have left and be in no hurry to hand it over to aliens, or we shall cheat our sons out of their rightful inheritance.

The supply of cooks may be increased, but only temporarily. Gone, too, is the day when labor can be regarded as a commodity, imported like raw material and treated like it. Relatively larger wages have been permanently secured by labor, with all that that means in the shape of better men and happier lives. We have been having a mad ride on the merry-go-round, bringing over more men to make more goods to sell to more immigrants to make bigger profits to build bigger factories to make more goods to sell. We are wasting and exploiting our resources to the limit, jazzing up production, jazzing up consumption, inflating population, inflating standards of living, inflating fortunes, living faster and faster, getting bigger and bigger, swelling up and up and up——

What's the hurry? What's the use? What's the finish? In the end, by some process, we must get back to sanity. It all works down to a question of short-sighted selfishness, the immediate dollar and the devil take our country; or far-sighted selfishness, conservation, and self-preservation, with the kind of an America that we found as a heritage for our children, with a chance for them to make good in the old American way.

A fair field and an unspoiled country is a start to which every American is entitled. The honest gains of his honest work, the reward of his brains, his efficiency and his industry, is a finish that no American will forgo because an alien wants to steal it from him.

PART FOUR

The New Era and
the Old Complacency

Public affairs during the 1920s, as compared with public affairs during the eras that sandwiched in the Harding-Coolidge-Hoover years from either side, were dull. Certainly the White House in these years was conspicuously less an object of public attention than it had been when Theodore Roosevelt and Woodrow Wilson occupied it and than it would be when Franklin D. and Eleanor Roosevelt resided behind the handsome iron gates on Pennsylvania Avenue. Perhaps it has been the relative pallor of Washington during the 1920s that has led many historians to seek drama elsewhere in American life and to emphasize the more bizarre aspects of society during the decade. To interpret these years as the Jazz Age or the Era of Wonderful Nonsense has dramatic value, but it ignores much that historians regard important when they deal with other epochs.

During the 1920s observers interpreted their times either as a retreat from the social consciousness of the Progressive Era to the old complacency of an earlier day or, to take the case of those who quite approved of, even gloried in, the status quo, as a New Era in which prosperity and harmony enveloped the land. In the 1928 elections Republicans used the term "New Era" to describe the results of their work of the previous eight years. Their candidate won the presidential election, but the term would acquire a special irony before he finished his term of office. Although the moment when one could refer with a straight face to the Republican achievement in the 1920s as a New Era was relatively brief, economic change during the decade was substantial and deserves the attention of students of history.

"After the Great Storm": Inaugural Address
of Warren Gamaliel Harding, March 4, 1921

The speeches that Presidents of the United States make immediately after they take the oath of office constitute a special category of political literature. Inaugural addresses rarely are disquisitions on political philosophy, although they usually reveal something of the new President's political views, and they seldom provide the nation with a preview of the speaker's subsequent program, although the nation listens to them and reads them carefully for the few foreshadowings that may appear. Perhaps the main value of an inaugural address as a historical document—as apart from the speech itself, which has an important ceremonial function—is the flavor of the man that it provides. Some inaugural addresses are memorable. One thinks of Jefferson's first, Lincoln's second, and Franklin Roosevelt's first two. But they are memorable because the men were great and their speeches—really, only a part of their speeches—revealed their greatness. President Harding's inaugural was less than memorable, but it too reveals much of the man.

H. L. Mencken, who had strong opinions about most things, commented upon Harding's style. It moved him to remark that if a man has mush in his head when he writes, ". . . the writing is mush too." Harding—Mencken delighted in calling him Dr. Harding—was "a highly self-conscious stylist. He practiced prose composition assiduously, and was regarded by the pedagogues of Marion, Ohio, and vicinity as a very talented fellow." But when he wrote a message to Congress, he was "so muddled in style that even the late Henry Cabot Lodge, a professional literary man, could not understand it." The reason was that Harding did not understand it either. When Harding understood what he wrote about, his style was strong. "I once heard him deliver a brief address upon the ideals of the Elks. It was a topic close to his heart, and he had thought about it at length and con amore. The result was an excellent speech—clear, logical, forceful, and with a touch of wild, romantic beauty."

Alas, there is no touch of wild, romantic beauty amid the flatulence and banality of this inaugural speech. Wariness is a common attribute of successful political figures, but few men have equaled Harding's ingenuity at devising variations on the theme of "on the one hand, and then on the other."

Note that the word "normalcy" does not appear in this speech, contrary to rather widespread belief. That word came from a speech Senator Harding gave at Boston in May of the year he was elected to the Presidency. What the country needed, he said, was "not heroism but healing, not nostrums but normalcy."

The speech appears here in full, as it was published in the Congressional Record, *Sixty-seventh Congress, special session, volume 61, part 1, March 4, 1921, pages 4–6. Harding's papers only recently became available, and as yet there is no satisfactory biography. However, see Samuel Hopkins Adams.* Incredible Era: The Life and Times of Warren Gamaliel Harding *(Boston: Houghton Mifflin, 1939). Adams also wrote a novel about Harding and his administration that only thinly disguised the real-life characters:* Revelry *(New York: Boni and Liveright, 1926).*

My Countrymen: When one surveys the world about him after the great storm, noting the marks of destruction and yet rejoicing in the ruggedness of the things which withstood it, if he is an American he breathes the clarified atmosphere with a strange mingling of regret and new hope. We have seen a world passion spend its fury, but we contemplate our Republic unshaken, and hold our civilization secure. Liberty— liberty within the law—and civilization are inseparable, and though both were threatened we find them now secure; and there comes to Americans the profound assurance that our representative government is the highest expression and surest guaranty of both.

Standing in this presence, mindful of the solemnity of this occasion, feeling the emotions which no one may know until he senses the great weight of responsibility for himself, I must utter my belief in the divine inspiration of the founding fathers. Surely there must have been God's intent in the making of this New World Republic. Ours is an organic law which had but one ambiguity, and we saw that effaced in a baptism of sacrifice and blood, with union maintained, the Nation supreme and its concord inspiring. We have seen the world rivet its hopeful gaze on the great truths on which the founders wrought. We have seen civil, human, and religious liberty verified and glorified. In the beginning the Old World scoffed at our experiment; to-day our foundations of political and social belief stand unshaken, a precious inheritance to ourselves, an inspiring example of freedom and civilization to all mankind. Let us express renewed and strengthened devotion in grateful reverence for the immortal beginning, and utter our confidence in the supreme fulfillment.

Progress Proves Wisdom

The recorded progress of our Republic, materially and spiritually, in itself proves the wisdom of the inherited policy of noninvolvement in Old World affairs. Confident of our ability to work out our own destiny, and jealously guarding our right to do so, we seek no part in directing the destinies of the Old World. We do not mean to be entangled. We will accept no responsibility except as our own conscience and judgment, in each instance, may determine.

Our eyes never will be blind to a developing menace, our ears never deaf to the call of civilization. We recognize the new order in the world, with the closer contacts which progress has wrought. We sense the call of the human heart for fellowship, fraternity, and cooperation. We crave friendship and harbor no hate. But America, our America, the America builded on the foundation laid by the inspired fathers, can be a party to no permanent military alliance. It can enter into no political commit-

ments, nor assume any economic obligations which will subject our decisions to any other than our own authority.

I am sure our own people will not misunderstand, nor will the world
misconstrue. We have no thought to impede the paths to closer relationship. We wish to promote understanding. We want to do our part in
making offensive warfare so hateful that governments and peoples who
resort to it must prove the righteousness of their cause or stand as outlaws
before the bar of civilization.

Association for Counsel

We are ready to associate ourselves with the nations of the world, great
and small, for conference, for counsel; to seek the expressed views of
world opinion; to recommend a way to approximate disarmament and
relieve the crushing burdens of military and naval establishments. We elect
to participate in suggesting plans for mediation, conciliation, and arbitration, and would gladly join in that expressed conscience of progress which
seeks to clarify and write the laws of international relationship, and establish a world court for the disposition of such justiciable questions as
nations are agreed to submit thereto. In expressing aspirations, in seeking
practical plans, in translating humanity's new concept of righteousness and
justice and its hatred of war into recommended action, we are ready most
heartily to unite, but every commitment must be made in the exercise of
our national sovereignty. Since freedom impelled, and independence inspired, and nationality exalted, a world supergovernment is contrary to
everything we cherish and can have no sanction by our Republic. This is
not selfishness; it is sanctity. It is not aloofness; it is security. It is not
suspicion of others; it is patriotic adherence to the things which made us
what we are.

To-day, better than ever before, we know the aspirations of humankind,
and share them. We have come to a new realization of our place in the
world, and a new appraisal of our Nation by the world. The unselfishness
of these United States is a thing proven, our devotion to peace for ourselves and for the world is well established, our concern for preserved
civilization has had its impassioned and heroic expression. There was no
American failure to resist the attempted reversion of civilization; there
will be no failure to-day or to-morrow.

Rests on Popular Will

The success of our popular government rests wholly upon the correct
interpretation of the deliberate, intelligent, dependable popular will of
America. In a deliberate questioning of a suggested change of national
policy, where internationality was to supersede nationality, we turned to
a referendum to the American people. There was ample discussion, and
there is a public mandate in manifest understanding.

America is ready to encourage, eager to initiate, anxious to participate in any seemly program likely to lessen the probability of war and promote that brotherhood of mankind which must be God's highest conception of human relationship. Because we cherish ideals of justice and peace, because we appraise international comity and helpful relationship no less highly than any people of the world, we aspire to a high place in the moral leadership of civilization, and we hold a maintained America, the proven Republic, the unshaken temple of representative democracy, to be not only an inspiration and example but the highest agency of strengthening good will and promoting accord on both continents.

Mankind needs a world-wide benediction of understanding. It is needed among individuals, among peoples, among governments, and it will inaugurate an era of good feeling to mark the birth of a new order. In such understanding men will strive confidently for the promotion of their better relationships, and nations will promote the comities so essential to peace.

Trade Ties Bind Closely

We must understand that ties of trade bind nations in closest intimacy, and none may receive except as he gives. We have not strengthened ours in accordance with our resources or our genius, notably on our continent, where a galaxy of republics reflect the glory of new-world democracy, but in the new order of finance and trade we mean to promote enlarged activities and seek expanded confidence.

Perhaps we can make no more helpful contribution by example than prove a Republic's capacity to emerge from the wreckage of war. While the world's embittered travail did not leave us devastated lands nor desolated cities, left no gaping wounds, no breast with hate, it did involve us in the delirium of expenditure, in expanded currency and credits, in unbalanced industry, in unspeakable waste and disturbed relationships. While it uncovered our portion of hateful selfishness at home, it also revealed the heart of America as sound and fearless, and beating in confidence unfailing.

Amid it all we have riveted the gaze of all civilization to the unselfishness and the righteousness of representative democracy, where our freedom never has made offensive warfare, never has sought territorial aggrandizement through force, never has turned to the arbitrament of arms until reason has been exhausted. When the Governments of the earth shall have established a freedom like our own and shall have sanctioned the pursuit of peace as we have practiced it, I believe the last sorrow and the final sacrifice of international warfare will have been written.

Let me speak to the maimed and wounded soldiers who are present to-day, and through them convey to their comrades the gratitude of the Republic for their sacrifices in its defense. A generous country will never forget the services you rendered, and you may hope for a policy under Government that will relieve any maimed successors from taking your places on another such occasion as this.

Our Supreme Task

Our supreme task is the resumption of our onward, normal way. Reconstruction, readjustment, restoration—all these must follow. I would like to hasten them. If it will lighten the spirit and add to the resolution with which we take up the task, let me repeat for our Nation we shall give no people just cause to make war upon us, we hold no national prejudices, we entertain no spirit of revenge, we do not hate, we do not covet, we dream of no conquest, nor boast of armed prowess.

If, despite this attitude, war is again forced upon us, I earnestly hope a way may be found which will unify our individual and collective strength and consecrate all America, materially and spiritually, body and soul, to national defense. I can vision the ideal republic, where every man and woman is called under the flag, for assignment to duty, for whatever service, military or civil, the individual is best fitted; where we may call to universal service every plant, agency, or facility, all in the sublime sacrifice for country, and not one penny of war profit shall inure to the benefit of private individual, corporation, or combination, but all above the normal shall flow into the defense chest of the Nation. There is something inherently wrong, something out of accord with the ideals of representative democracy, when one portion of our citizenship turns its activities to private gain amid defensive war while another is fighting, sacrificing, or dying for national preservation.

Unity of Spirit and Purpose

Out of such universal service will come a new unity of spirit and purpose, a new confidence and consecration, which would make our defense impregnable, our triumph assured. Then we should have little or no disorganization of our economic, industrial, and commercial systems at home, no staggering war debts, no swollen fortunes to flout the sacrifices of our soldiers, no excuse for sedition, no pitiable slackerism, no outrage of treason. Envy and jealousy would have no soil for their menacing development, and revolution would be without the passion which engenders it.

A regret for the mistakes of yesterday must not, however, blind us to the tasks of to-day. War never left such an aftermath. There has been staggering loss of life and measureless wastage of materials. Nations are still groping for return to stable ways. Discouraging indebtedness confronts us like all the war-torn nations, and these obligations must be provided for. No civilization can survive repudiation.

We can reduce the abnormal expenditures, and we will. We can strike at war taxation, and we must. We must face the grim necessity, with full knowledge that the task is to be solved, and we must proceed with a full realization that no statute enacted by man can repeal the inexorable laws of nature. Our most dangerous tendency is to expect too much of government, and at the same time do for it too little.

We contemplate the immediate task of putting our public household in order. We need a rigid and yet sane economy, combined with fiscal justice, and it must be attended by individual prudence and thrift, which are so essential to this trying hour and reassuring for the future.

Reflection of War's Reaction

The business world reflects the disturbance of war's reaction. Herein flows the lifeblood of material existence. The economic mechanism is intricate and its parts interdependent, and has suffered the shocks and jars incident to abnormal demands, credit inflations, and price upheavals. The normal balances have been impaired, the channels of distribution have been clogged, the relations of labor and management have been strained. We must seek the readjustment with care and courage. Our people must give and take. Prices must reflect the receding fever of war activities. Perhaps we never shall know the old levels of wage again, because war invariably readjusts compensations, and the necessaries of life will show their inseparable relationship, but we must strive for normalcy to reach stability. All the penalties will not be light nor evenly distributed. There is no way of making them so. There is no instant step from disorder to order. We must face a condition of grim reality, charge off our losses, and start afresh. It is the oldest lesson of civilization. I would like Government to do all it can to mitigate; then, in understanding, in mutuality of interest, in concern for the common good, our tasks will be solved. No altered system will work a miracle. Any wild experiment will only add to the confusion. Our best assurance lies in efficient administration of our proven system.

From Destruction to Production

The forward course of the business cycle is unmistakable. Peoples are turning from destruction to production. Industry has sensed the changed order and our own people are turning to resume their normal, onward way. The call is for productive America to go on. I know that Congress and the administration will favor every wise Government policy to aid the resumption and encourage continued progress.

I speak for administrative efficiency, for lightened tax burdens, for sound commercial practices, for adequate credit facilities, for sympathetic concern for all agricultural problems, for the omission of unnecessary interference of Government with business, for an end to Government's experiment in business, and for more efficient business in government administration. With all of this must attend a mindfulness of the human side of all activities, so that social, industrial, and economic justice will be squared with the purposes of a righteous people.

With the nation-wide induction of womanhood into our political life we may count upon her intuitions, her refinements, her intelligence, and her influence to exalt the social order. We count upon her exercise of the full privileges and the performance of the duties of citizenship to speed the attainment of the highest state.

Prayer for Industrial Peace

I wish for an America no less alert in guarding against dangers from within than it is watchful against enemies from without. Our fundamental law recognizes no class, no group, no section; there must be none in legislation or administration. The supreme inspiration is the common weal. Humanity hungers for international peace, and we crave it with all mankind. My most reverent prayer for America is for industrial peace, with its rewards, widely and generally distributed, amid the inspirations of equal opportunity. No one justly may deny the equality of opportunity which made us what we are. We have mistaken unpreparedness to embrace it to be a challenge of the reality, and due concern for making all citizens fit for participation will give added strength of citizenship and magnify our achievement.

If revolution insists upon overturning established order, let other peoples make the tragic experiment. There is no place for it in America. When world war threatened civilization we pledged our resources and our lives to its preservation, and when revolution threatens we unfurl the flag of law and order and renew our consecration. Ours is a constitutional freedom where the popular will is the law supreme and minorities are sacredly protected. Our revisions, reformations, and evolutions reflect a deliberate judgment and an orderly progress, and we mean to cure our ills, but never destroy or permit destruction by force.

I had rather submit our industrial controversies to the conference table in advance than to a settlement table after conflict and suffering. The earth is thirsting for the cup of good will; understanding is its fountain source. I would like to acclaim an era of good feeling amid dependable prosperity and all the blessings which attend.

Protection of Industries

It has been proved again and again that we can not, while throwing our markets open to the world, maintain American standards of living and opportunity, and hold our industrial eminence in such unequal competition. There is a luring fallacy in the theory of banished barriers of trade, but preserved American standards require our higher production costs to be reflected in our tariffs on imports. To-day, as never before, when peoples are seeking trade restoration and expansion, we must adjust our tariffs to the new order. We seek participation in the world's exchanges, because therein lies our way to widened influence and the triumphs of peace. We know full well we can not sell where we do not buy, and we can not sell successfully where we do not carry. Opportunity is calling not alone for the restoration but for a new era in production, transportation, and trade. We shall answer it best by meeting the demand of a surpassing home market, by promoting self-reliance in production, and by bidding enterprise, genius, and efficiency to carry our cargoes in American bottoms to the marts of the world.

An America of Homes

We would not have an America living within and for herself alone, but we would have her self-reliant, independent, and ever nobler, stronger, and richer. Believing in our higher standards, reared through constitutional liberty and maintained opportunity, we invite the world to the same heights. But pride in things wrought is no reflex of a completed task. Common welfare is the goal of our national endeavor. Wealth is not inimical to welfare; it ought to be its friendliest agency. There never can be equality of rewards or possessions so long as the human plan contains varied talents and differing degrees of industry and thrift, but ours ought to be a country free from great blotches of distressed poverty. We ought to find a way to guard against the perils and penalties of unemployment. We want an America of homes, illumined with hope and happiness, where mothers, freed from the necessity for long hours of toil beyond their own doors, may preside as befits the hearthstone of American citizenship. We want the cradle of American childhood rocked under conditions so wholesome and so hopeful that no blight may touch it in its development, and we want to provide that no selfish interest, no material necessity, no lack of opportunity, shall prevent the gaining of that education so essential to best citizenship.

There is no short cut to the making of these ideals into glad realities. The world has witnessed, again and again, the futility and the mischief of ill-considered remedies for social and economic disorders. But we are mindful to-day, as never before, of the friction of modern industrialism, and we must learn its causes and reduce its evil consequences by sober and tested methods. Where genius has made for great possibilities, justice and happiness must be reflected in a greater common welfare.

Service, the Supreme Commitment

Service is the supreme commitment of life. I would rejoice to acclaim the era of the golden rule and crown it with the autocracy of service. I pledge an administration wherein all the agencies of government are called to serve, and ever promote an understanding of government purely as an expression of the popular will.

One can not stand in this presence and be unmindful of the tremendous responsibility. The world upheaval has added heavily to our tasks. But with the realization comes the surge of high resolve, and there is reassurance in belief in the God-given destiny of our Republic. If I felt that there is to be sole responsibility in the Executive for the America of to-morrow I should shrink from the burden. But here are a hundred millions, with common concern and shared responsibility, answerable to God and country. The Republic summons them to their duty, and I invite cooperation.

I accept my part with single-mindedness of purpose and humility of spirit, and implore the favor and guidance of God in His heaven. With these I am unafraid, and confidently face the future.

I have taken the solemn oath of office on that passage of Holy Writ wherein it is asked: "What doth the Lord require of thee but to do justly, and to love mercy, and to walk humbly with thy God?" This I plight to God and country.

SELECTION

H. L. Mencken on the Age of Coolidge and on William Jennings Bryan

Henry Louis Mencken (1880–1956) was the most popular and most idolized, and in some quarters the most despised and feared, essayist in America between World War I and the Depression. Mencken began his writing career as a newspaperman in his native Baltimore, from which he never moved even when he had to spend a few days each week in New York City. From 1914 to 1923 he was coeditor, with George Jean Nathan, of Smart Set. *He and Nathan founded* The American Mercury *(first issue in January, 1924) with Alfred Knopf as publisher, and soon this dark-green-covered magazine was an intellectual institution. Mencken and the* Mercury—*he became sole editor in 1925— were devoted to good literature, but more than anything else they were dedicated to what the age called debunking. Exuberantly and often comically iconoclastic, Mencken made a career of pointing out that the emperor had no clothes. If, in retrospect, Mencken seems sometimes to have been unnecessarily brutal in his editorial attacks, sometimes a little silly in his enthusiasms, and rather often a verbal exhibitionist, like a small boy who has learned some bad words, he nevertheless had a healthy influence on his age. There was so much complacency in the United States in the 1920s, such a volume of hypocrisy and hot air, that his deflating arrows were badly needed.*

This selection is comprised of two typical Mencken essays, "Golden Age" and "In Memoriam: W. J. B." Although "Golden Age" is more benevolent in tone than the piece on Bryan, it is equally biting. Its last paragraph, a capsule political history of early-twentieth-century America, is especially pungent. "In Memoriam: W. J. B." truly was an obituary of Bryan, first appearing in the October, 1925, American Mercury, roughly two months after Bryan's death. This is perhaps the most widely quoted of Mencken's writings. It is clever and sometimes funny, but it lacks the light touch of the first selection. As a result of having only recently covered the Scopes trial at Dayton, Tennessee, for the Baltimore Sun *papers, Mencken was too deeply involved emotionally against Bryan and his fundamentalism to reach for his rapier rather than his club.*

"Golden Age," copyright 1926 by Alfred A. Knopf, Inc., renewed 1954 by

GOLDEN AGE

The rest of us, struggling onward painfully, must wait in patience for the booms and usufructs of Heaven; Judge Elbert Henry Gary, LL.D., chairman of the United States Steel Corporation, has them here and now. To few men in history, I believe, has it been given to live in a universe so nearly to their hearts' desire. Let the learned ex-jurist look East or West, he will find only scenes to content him. Let him look North or South, and his eye will be caressed and frankincense will spray his gills. The emperor and pope of all the Babbitts, he sits at the center of a Babbitts' paradise. For him and his like there dawns a Golden Age, and its hero is good Cal.

I hope I do not exaggerate. No doubt Judge Gary, in the privacy of his chamber, sweats and fumes against imperfections invisible to the rest of us. He is a man of imagination, and has, I daresay, a bold and soaring fancy. He can imagine a Republic even kinder and more osculatory than this one—that is, to Babbitts. He can even, perhaps, imagine a President more ineffable than Cal. But here we shoot into mere human weaknesses— the voluptuous, Freudian day-dreams of one who, like all of us, has his aberrant, goatish moods. Dr. John Roach Straton, I suppose, can imagine improvements in the Holy Scriptures—here a paragraph excised *pro bonos mores,* there a comma inserted to make sense. I myself have dreamed of a malt liquor better than Pilsner Bürgerbräu. But I do not sign my name to such inordinate speculations, and neither does Dr. Straton. Judge Gary, too, holds his tongue. The rest of us, contemplating him, can only envy him. A vast nation of 110,000,000 human beings, all of them alike, seems to be organized to the one end of making him happy. Whatever he wants it to do, it does. Its laws are framed to his precise taste; its public conscience approves his partisans and execrates his enemies; its high officers of state are his excellent friends, and humble and obedient servants. When he gives a feast, judges and ambassadors leap to grace it. When he would dine out, he is welcome at the White House. The newspapers fawn upon him. Labor licks his hand. His frown is dreaded in the Senate house and on the bench. Altogether, his life is happier than that of a Broadway actor, and if he is not content then it is only because contentment is physiologically impossible to *Homo sapiens.*

The United States, I believe, is the first great empire in the history of the world to ground its whole national philosophy upon business. There have been, of course, eminent trading nations in the past, but none ever went so far. Even in Carthage there was a *Junker* hierarchy that stood above the merchants; in Hannibal it actually had a Crown Prince. And even in England, the nation of shopkeepers of Napoleon's derision, there has always been an aristocracy (made up mainly of military freebooters, enterprising adulterers, the issue of the latter, and, in modern times, shyster lawyers, vaudeville magnates, and the proprietors of yellow newspapers) that has held its own against the men of trade, even at the cost of absorbing the more pugnacious of them. But here in this great Republic of the West the art of trafficking is king—and Judge Gary is its grand vizier, as Cal is its chief eunuch. No other human activity brings such great rewards in money and power, and none is more lavishly honored. The one aim of our jurisprudence is to safeguard business—to make its risks small and its profits sure. If the rights of the citizen get in the way, then the rights of the citizen must be sacrificed. Upon this point our higher courts have delivered themselves more than once, and in eloquent, ringing terms. Judge Gary and his friends prefer dry and dismal slaves to those who are stewed and happy. *Also,* to hell with the Bill of Rights! They prefer, when there is a strike, to win it rather than lose it. Out, then, with the pad of blank injunctions! They sweat under criticism, and shiver under attack. To the hoosegow, constable, with the Bolsheviks!

All this, of course, was not achieved without a struggle. For years the Constitution stood in the way—the Constitution and certain national superstitions—the latter sprung from the blather of the Revolutionary stump. But all those impediments are now surmounted. The bench gave Judge Gary to business, and business has reciprocated the favor by providing sound and sane men for the bench. To-day jurisprudence is unfettered. When, a year or so ago, the Supreme Court finally got rid of the Fourth Amendment, that delayed mopping up went almost unnoticed. As I say, Judge Gary, ought to be a happy man. The sun shines upon him from all four points of the compass. Congress, well rehearsed, plays soft jazz for him; bishops bring him his toddy; a straw issues from the White House and tickles him behind the ear. But never is his happiness greater, I believe, than when his thoughts turn idly upon the subject of labor, and he contemplates the state of the union movement in the Federal Union.

For this state, it is plain, he has the late Sam Gompers to thank—that great idealist and easy mark. If he sent less than ten hay-wagons of roses to Sam's funeral, then he is a niggard, indeed. For Sam got upon the back of the American labor movement when it was beginning to be dangerous, and rode it so magnificently that at the end of his life it was as tame as a tabby cat. It retains that character to-day, and will continue to do so as long as the Gompersian hierarchy lasts,—that is, so long as Judge Gary and his friends continue to appoint Sam's heirs and assigns to high-sounding committees, and to invite them to gaudy dinners. A plate of puddle duck and a chance to make a speech—that was always enough to fetch Sam. And when Sam was fetched, the 4,000,000 members of the American Federation of Labor were also fetched. Where else in the world is there a great union organization that has so long and honorable a record as a strike-breaker? Or that is so diligently devoted to keeping the lower ranks of labor in due subordination? If it had been conceived and hatched by Judge Gary himself, it could not have been more nearly perfect. Practically considered, it is not a labor organization at all; it is simply a balloon mattress interposed between capital and labor to protect the former from the latter. Gazing upon it, I daresay, Judge Gary feels a glow flickering along the periphery of his gizzard, and if he were not a Christian he would permit himself a guffaw.

I leave the sweetest to the last. The courts might be docile, Congress might be consecrated to right thought, labor might grovel and the bench of bishops might applaud, but if there were an anarchist in the White House it would all go for naught. Imagine, then, Judge Gary's joy in contemplating the incomparable Cal! It is almost as if, in New York, a bootlegger were made king. The man's merits, in the Babbitt view, are almost fabulous. He seems, indeed, scarcely like a man at all, but more like some miraculous visitation or act of God. He is the ideal made visible, if not audible—perfection put into a cutaway coat and trotted up and down like a mannequin in a cloak and suit atelier. Nor was there any long stress of training him—no season of doubt and misgiving. Nature heaved him forth full-blown, like a new star shot into the heavens. In him the philosophy of Babbitt comes to its perfect and transcendental form. Thrift, to him, is the queen of all the virtues. He respects money in each and every one of its beautiful forms—pennies, nickels, dimes, dollars, five-dollar bills, and so on *ad infinitum*. He venerates those who have it. He believes that they have wisdom. He craves the loan and use of that wisdom. He invites them to breakfast, and listens to them. The things they revere, he reveres. The things they long for, he longs to give them.

Judge Gary is an old man—just how old I do not know, for he withholds the date of his birth from "Who's Who in America," along with the principal suffragettes. He remembers the dreadful days of Roosevelt, with bombs going off every two hours. He remembers the turmoils of the Taft administration. He remembers how *difficile* Woodrow was—how he had to be wooed, flattered, led by the nose, drenched with goose-grease. He remembers the crude carnival under the martyr Harding—Broadway sports, pug managers, small-town Elks at the trough. And then he thinks of Washington to-day, and sees it bathed in pink sunshine. There he is ever welcome. There he is *imperator in imperio*. There is good *Geschäft*. There is the Athens of the new Golden Age.

IN MEMORIAM: W. J. B.

Has it been duly marked by historians that the late William Jennings Bryan's last secular act on this globe of sin was to catch flies? A curious detail, and not without its sardonic overtones. He was the most sedulous fly-catcher in American history, and in many ways the most successful. His quarry, of course, was not *Musca domestica* but *Homo neandertalensis*. For forty years he tracked it with coo and bellow, up and down the rustic backways of the Republic. Wherever the flambeaux of Chautauqua smoked and guttered, and the bilge of Idealism ran in the veins, and Baptist pastors dammed the brooks with the sanctified, and men gathered who were weary and heavy laden, and their wives who were full of Peruna and as fecund as the shad (*Alosa sapidissima*)—there the indefatigable Jennings set up his traps and spread his bait. He knew every country town in the South and West, and he could crowd the most remote of them to suffocation by simply winding his horn. The city proletariat, transiently flustered by him in 1896, quickly penetrated his buncombe and would have no more of him; the cockney gallery jeered him at every Democratic national convention for twenty-five years. But out where the grass grows high, and the horned cattle dream away the lazy afternoons, and men still fear the powers and principalities of the air—out there between the corn-rows he held his old puissance to the end. There was no need of beaters to drive in his game. The news that he was coming was enough. For miles the flivver dust would choke the roads. And when he rose at the end of the day to discharge his Message there would be such breathless attention, such a rapt and enchanted ecstasy, such a sweet rustle of amens as the world had not known since Johann fell to Herod's ax.

There was something peculiarly fitting in the fact that his last days were spent in a one-horse Tennessee village, and that death found him there. The man felt at home in such simple and Christian scenes. He liked people who sweated freely, and were not debauched by the refinements of the toilet. Making his progress up and down the Main street of little Dayton, surrounded by gaping primates from the upland valleys of the Cumberland Range, his coat laid aside, his bare arms and hairy chest shining damply, his bald head sprinkled with dust—so accoutred and on display he was obviously happy. He liked getting up early in the morning, to the tune of cocks crowing on the dunghill. He liked the heavy, greasy victuals of the farmhouse kitchen. He liked country lawyers, country pastors, all country people. He liked the country sounds and country smells. I believe that this liking was sincere—perhaps the only sincere thing in the man. His nose showed no uneasiness when a hillman in faded overalls and hickory shirt accosted him on the street, and besought him for light upon some mystery of Holy Writ. The simian gabble of the cross-roads was not gabble to him, but wisdom of an occult and superior sort. In the presence of city folks he was palpably uneasy. Their clothes, I suspect, annoyed him, and he was suspicious of their too delicate manners. He knew all the while that they were laughing at him—if not at his baroque theology, then at least at his alpaca pantaloons. But the yokels never laughed at him. To them he was not the huntsman but the prophet, and toward the end, as he gradually forsook mundane politics for more ghostly concerns, they began to elevate him in their hierarchy. When he died he was the peer of Abraham. His old enemy, Wilson, aspiring to the same white and shining robe, came down with a thump. But Bryan made the grade. His place in Tennessee hagiography is secure. If the village barber saved any of his hair, then it is curing gall-stones down there to-day.

But what label will he bear in more urbane regions? One, I fear, of a far less flattering kind. Bryan lived too long, and descended too deeply into the mud, to be taken seriously hereafter by fully literate men, even of the kind who write school-books. There was a scattering of sweet words in his funeral notices, but it was no more than a response to conventional sentimentality. The best verdict the most romantic editorial writer could dredge up, save in the humorless South, was to the general effect that his imbecilities were excused by his earnestness—that under his clowning, as under that of the juggler of Notre Dame, there was the zeal of a steadfast soul. But this was apology, not praise; precisely the same thing might be said of Mary Baker G. Eddy, the late Czar Nicholas, or Czolgosz. The truth is that even Bryan's sincerity will probably yield to what is called, in other fields, definitive criticism. Was he sincere when he opposed imperialism in the Philippines, or when he fed it with deserving Democrats in Santo Domingo? Was he sincere when he tried to shove the Prohibitionists under the table, or when he seized their banner and began to lead them with loud whoops? Was he sincere when he bellowed against war, or when he dreamed of himself as a tin-soldier in uniform, with a grave reserved among the generals? Was he sincere when he denounced the late John W. Davis, or when he swallowed Davis? Was he sincere when he fawned over Champ Clark, or when he betrayed Clark? Was he sincere when he pleaded for tolerance in New York, or when he bawled for the faggot and the stake in Tennessee?

This talk of sincerity, I confess, fatigues me. If the fellow was sincere, then so was P. T. Barnum. The word is disgraced and degraded by such uses. He was, in fact, a charlatan, a mountebank, a zany without shame or dignity. His career brought him into contact with the first men of his time; he preferred the company of rustic ignoramuses. It was hard to believe, watching him at Dayton, that he had traveled, that he had been received in civilized societies, that he had been a high officer of state. He seemed only a poor clod like those around him, deluded by a childish theology, full of an almost pathological hatred of all learning, all human dignity, all beauty, all fine and noble things. He was a peasant come home to the barnyard. Imagine a gentleman, and you have imagined everything that he was not. What animated him from end to end of his grotesque career was simply ambition—the ambition of a common man to get his hand upon the collar of his superiors, or, failing that, to get his thumb into their eyes. He was born with a roaring voice, and it had the trick of inflaming half-wits. His whole career was devoted to raising those half-wits against their betters, that he himself might shine. His last battle will be grossly misunderstood if it is thought of as a mere exercise in fanaticism—that is, if Bryan the Fundamentalist Pope is mistaken for one of the bucolic Fundamentalists. There was much more in it than that, as everyone knows who saw him on the field. What moved him, at bottom, was simply hatred of the city men who had laughed at him so long, and brought him at last to so tatterdemalion an estate. He lusted for revenge upon them. He yearned to lead the anthropoid rabble against them, to punish them for their execution upon him by attacking the very vitals of their civilization. He went far beyond the bounds of any merely religious frenzy, however inordinate. When he began denouncing the notion that man is a mammal even some of the hinds at Dayton were agape. And when, brought upon Darrow's cruel hook, he writhed and tossed in a very fury of malignancy, bawling against the baldest elements of sense and decency like a man frantic—when he came to that tragic climax of his striving there were snickers among the hinds as well as hosannas.

Upon that hook, in truth, Bryan committed suicide, as a legend as well as in the body. He staggered from the rustic court ready to die, and he staggered from it ready to be forgotten, save as a character in a third-rate farce, witless and in poor taste. It was plain to everyone who knew him, when he came to Dayton, that his great days were behind him—that, for all the fury of his hatred, he was now definitely an old man, and headed at last for silence. There was a vague, unpleasant manginess about his appearance; he somehow seemed dirty, though a close glance showed him as carefully shaven as an actor, and clad in immaculate linen. All the hair was gone from the dome of his head, and it had begun to fall out, too, behind his ears, in the obscene manner of the late Samuel Gompers. The resonance had departed from his voice; what was once a bugle blast had become reedy and quavering. Who knows that, like Demosthenes, he had a lisp? In the old days, under the magic of his eloquence, no one noticed it. But when he spoke at Dayton it was always audible.

When I first encountered him, on the sidewalk in front of the office of the rustic lawyers who were his associates in the Scopes case, the trial was yet to begin, and so he was still expansive and amiable. I had printed in the *Nation,* a week or so before, an article arguing that the Tennessee anti-evolution law, whatever its wisdom, was at least constitutional—that the rustics of the State had a clear right to have their progeny taught whatever they chose, and kept secure from whatever knowledge violated their superstitions. The old boy professed to be delighted with the argument, and gave the gaping bystanders to understand that I was a publicist of parts. Not to be outdone, I admired the preposterous country shirt that he wore—sleeveless and with the neck cut very low. We parted in the manner of two ambassadors. But that was the last touch of amiability that I was destined to see in Bryan. The next day the battle joined and his face became hard. By the end of the week he was simply a walking fever. Hour by hour he grew more bitter. What the Christian Scientists call malicious animal magnetism seemed to radiate from him like heat from a stove. From my place in the courtroom, standing upon a table, I looked directly down upon him, sweating horribly and pumping his palm-leaf fan. His eyes fascinated me; I watched them all day long. They were blazing points of hatred. They glittered like occult and sinister gems. Now and then they wandered to me, and I got my share, for my reports of the trial had come back to Dayton, and he had read them. It was like coming under fire.

Thus he fought his last fight, thirsting savagely for blood. All sense departed from him. He bit right and left, like a dog with rabies. He descended to demagogy so dreadful that his very associates at the trial table blushed. His one yearning was to keep his yokels heated up—to lead his forlorn mob of imbeciles against the foe. That foe, alas, refused to be alarmed. It insisted upon seeing the whole battle as a comedy. Even

Darrow, who knew better, occasionally yielded to the prevailing spirit. One day he lured poor Bryan into the folly I have mentioned: his astounding argument against the notion that man is a mammal. I am glad I heard it, for otherwise I'd never believe in it. There stood the man who had been thrice a candidate for the Presidency of the Republic—there he stood in the glare of the world, uttering stuff that a boy of eight would laugh at! The artful Darrow led him on: he repeated it, ranted for it, bellowed it in his cracked voice. So he was prepared for the final slaughter. He came into life a hero, a Galahad, in bright and shining armor. He was passing out a poor mountebank.

The chances are that history will put the peak of democracy in America in his time; it has been on the downward curve among us since the campaign of 1896. He will be remembered perhaps, as its supreme impostor, the *reductio ad absurdum* of its pretension. Bryan came very near being President. In 1896, it is possible, he was actually elected. He lived long enough to make patriots thank the inscrutable gods for Harding, even for Coolidge. Dullness has got into the White House, and the smell of cabbage boiling, but there is at least nothing to compare to the intolerable buffoonery that went on in Tennessee. The President of the United States may be an ass, but he at least doesn't believe that the earth is square, and that witches should be put to death, and that Jonah swallowed the whale. The Golden Text is not painted weekly on the White House wall, and there is no need to keep ambassadors waiting while Pastor Simpson, of Smithville, prays for rain in the Blue Room. We have escaped something —by a narrow margin, but still we have escaped.

That is, for far. The Fundamentalists, once apparently sweeping all before them, now face minorities prepared for battle even in the South— here and there with some assurance of success. But it is too early, it seems to me, to send the firemen home; the fire is still burning on many a far-flung hill, and it may begin to roar again at any moment. The evil that men do lives after them. Bryan, in his malice, started something that it will not be easy to stop. In ten thousand country towns his old heelers, the evangelical pastors, are propagating his gospel, and everywhere the yokels are ready for it. When he disappeared from the big cities, the big cities made the capital error of assuming that he was done for. If they heard of him at all, it was only as a crimp for real-estate speculators—the heroic foe of the unearned increment hauling it in with both hands. He seemed preposterous, and hence harmless. But all the while he was busy among his old lieges, preparing for a *jacquerie* that should floor all his enemies at one blow. He did his job competently. He had vast skill at such enterprises. Heave an egg out of a Pullman window, and you will hit a Fundamentalist almost everywhere in the United States to-day. They swarm in the country towns, inflamed by their *shamans*, and with a saint, now, to venerate. They are thick in the mean streets behind the gas-works. They are everywhere where learning is too heavy a burden for mortal minds to carry, even the vague, pathetic learning on tap in little red schoolhouses. They march with the Klan, with the Christian Endeavor Society, with the Junior Order of United American Mechanics, with the Epworth League, with all the rococo bands that poor and unhappy folk organize to bring some light of purpose into their lives. They have had a thrill, and they are ready for more.

Such is Bryan's legacy to his country. He couldn't be President, but he could at least help magnificently in the solemn business of shutting off the Presidency from every intelligent and self-respecting man. The storm, perhaps, won't last long, as time goes in history. It may help, indeed, to break up the democratic delusion, now already showing weakness, and so hasten its own end. But while it lasts it will blow off some roofs.

SELECTION **32**

Sinclair Lewis Coins a Word: "Babbitt" (1922)

People who subscribed to The American Mercury *were likely to be partisan readers of Sinclair Lewis's novels. Lewis (1885–1951) was as iconoclastic in his novels as Mencken was in his essays and reviews, and his portraits of businessmen, small-town life, and evangelists made a strong impression. Lewis had been a professional writer for over a decade without attracting much attention when suddenly in late 1920, his* Main Street *became a best seller and a topic of agitated comment. He followed his novel about a small town with* Babbitt, *a novel about a medium-sized American city. Lewis wrote much of* Babbitt *in Cincinnati, but that city was no more a real-life Zenith than many others. His characterization—indeed, caricature—of George F. Babbitt was so believable for all its excesses, so much like some businessmen that readers actually knew, that the name became a widely used noun. (Note that Mencken used the word near the beginning of "Golden Age.") Lewis wrote three other solid novels in the 1920s,* Arrowsmith *(1925) about a medical scientist,* Elmer Gantry *(1927) about a revivalist, and* Dodsworth *(1929) about a businessman, but his novels of the 1930s and later lacked the quality and did not win the popular reception of the earlier ones. Lewis rejected the Pulitzer prize for* Arrowsmith, *but in 1930 he became the first American to receive the Nobel prize for literature.*

One of Lewis's greatest strengths as a writer was a careful eye and ear for detail. In this selection the conversation between Babbitt and Howard Littlefield, Ph.D. (a fine Dickensian name), is a bit of detail that brings a jolt of recognition to the reader, just as is Babbitt's closing salutation in his mimeographed form letter, "Yours for service." These two passages also illustrate Lewis's capacity for caricature, his ability to exaggerate slightly and thereby make the truth more apparent. Lewis had to make George F. Babbitt more of a Babbitt than anyone ever was, but in doing so he pointed out a truth in American life.

Easily the most comprehensive and intelligent work on Sinclair Lewis despite the author's obvious and strong distate for his subject, is Mark Schorer, Sinclair Lewis: An American Life *(New York: McGraw-Hill, 1961). This selection is the third chapter of* Babbitt *(New York: Harcourt, Brace & World, 1922), pages 24–37.*

I

To George F. Babbitt, as to most prosperous citizens of Zenith, his motor car was poetry and tragedy, love and heroism. The office was his pirate ship but the car his perilous excursion ashore.

Among the tremendous crises of each day none was more dramatic than starting the engine. It was slow on cold mornings; there was the long, anxious whirr of the starter; and sometimes he had to drip ether into the cocks of the cylinders, which was so very interesting that at lunch he would chronicle it drop by drop, and orally calculate how much each drop had cost him.

This morning he was darkly prepared to find something wrong and he felt belittled when the mixture exploded sweet and strong, and the car didn't even brush the door-jamb, gouged and splintery with many bruisings by fenders, as he backed out of the garage. He was confused. He shouted "Morning!" to Sam Doppelbrau with more cordiality than he had intended.

Babbitt's green and white Dutch Colonial house was one of three in that block on Chatham Road. To the left of it was the residence of Mr. Samuel Doppelbrau, secretary of an excellent firm of bathroom-fixture jobbers. His was a comfortable house with no architectural manners whatever; a large wooden box with a squat tower, a broad porch, and glossy paint yellow as a yolk. Babbitt disapproved of Mr. and Mrs. Doppelbrau as "Bohemian." From their house came midnight music and obscene laughter; there were neighborhood rumors of bootlegged whisky and fast motor rides. They furnished Babbitt with many happy evenings of discussion, during which he announced firmly, "I'm not strait-laced, and I don't mind seeing a fellow throw in a drink once in a while, but when it comes to deliberately trying to get away with a lot of hell-raising all the while like the Doppelbraus do, it's too rich for my blood!"

On the other side of Babbitt lived Howard Littlefield, Ph.D., in a strictly modern house whereof the lower part was dark red tapestry brick, with a leaded oriel, the upper part of pale stucco like spattered clay, and the roof red-tiled. Littlefield was the Great Scholar of the neighborhood; the authority on everything in the world except babies, cooking, and motors. He was a Bachelor of Arts of Blodgett College, and a Doctor of Philosophy in economics of Yale. He was the employment-manager and publicity-counsel of the Zenith Street Traction Company. He could, on ten hours' notice, appear before the board of aldermen or the state legislature and prove, absolutely, with figures all in rows and with precedents from Poland and New Zealand, that the street-car company loved the Public and yearned over its employees; that all its stock was owned by Widows and

Orphans; and that whatever it desired to do would benefit property-owners by increasing rental values, and help the poor by lowering rents. All his acquaintances turned to Littlefield when they desired to know the date of the battle of Saragossa, the definition of the word "sabotage," the future of the German mark, the translation of *"hinc illæ lachrimæ,"* or the number of products of coal tar. He awed Babbitt by confessing that he often sat up till midnight reading the figures and footnotes in Government reports, or skimming (with amusement at the author's mistakes) the latest volumes of chemistry, archeology, and ichthyology.

But Littlefield's great value was as a spiritual example. Despite his strange learnings he was as strict a Presbyterian and as firm a Republican as George F. Babbitt. He confirmed the business men in the faith. Where they knew only by passionate instinct that their system of industry and manners was perfect, Dr. Howard Littlefield proved it to them, out of history, economics, and the confessions of reformed radicals.

Babbitt had a good deal of honest pride in being the neighbor of such a savant, and in Ted's intimacy with Eunice Littlefield. At sixteen Eunice was interested in no statistics save those regarding the ages and salaries of motion-picture stars, but—as Babbitt definitively put it—"she was her father's daughter."

The difference between a light man like Sam Doppelbrau and a really fine character like Littlefield was revealed in their appearances. Doppelbrau was disturbingly young for a man of forty-eight. He wore his derby on the back of his head, and his red face was wrinkled with meaningless laughter. But Littlefield was old for a man of forty-two. He was tall, broad, thick; his gold-rimmed spectacles were engulfed in the folds of his long face; his hair was a tossed mass of greasy blackness; he puffed and rumbled as he talked; his Phi Beta Kappa key shone against a spotty black vest; he smelled of old pipes; he was altogether funereal and archidiaconal; and to real-estate brokerage and the jobbing of bathroom-fixtures he added an aroma of sanctity.

This morning he was in front of his house, inspecting the grass parking between the curb and the broad cement sidewalk. Babbitt stopped his car and leaned out to shout "Mornin'!" Littlefield lumbered over and stood with one foot up on the running-board.

"Fine morning," said Babbitt, lighting—illegally early—his second cigar of the day.

"Yes, it's mighty fine morning," said Littlefield.

"Spring coming along fast now."

"Yes, it's real spring now, all right," said Littlefield.

"Still cold nights, though. Had to have a couple blankets, on the sleeping-porch last night."

"Yes, it wasn't any too warm last night," said Littlefield.

"But I don't anticipate we'll have any more real cold weather now."

"No, but still, there was snow at Tiflis, Montana, yesterday," said the Scholar, "and you remember the blizzard they had out West three days ago—thirty inches of snow at Greeley, Colorado—and two years ago we had a snow-squall right here in Zenith on the twenty-fifth of April."

"Is that a fact! Say, old man, what do you think about the Republican candidate? Who'll they nominate for president? Don't you think it's about time we had a real business administration?"

"In my opinion, what the country needs, first and foremost, is a good, sound, business-like conduct of its affairs. What we need is—a business administration!" said Littlefield.

"I'm glad to hear you say that! I certainly am glad to hear you say that! I didn't know how you'd feel about it, with all your associations with colleges and so on, and I'm glad you feel that way. What the country needs—just at this present juncture—is neither a college president nor a lot of monkeying with foreign affairs, but a good—sound—economical—business—administration, that will give us a chance to have something like a decent turnover."

"Yes. It isn't generally realized that even in China the schoolmen are giving way to more practical men, and of course you can see what that implies."

"Is that a fact! Well, well!" breathed Babbitt, feeling much calmer, and much happier about the way things were going in the world. "Well, it's been nice to stop and parleyvoo a second. Guess I'll have to get down to the office now and sting a few clients. Well, so long, old man. See you tonight. So long."

II

They had labored, these solid citizens. Twenty years before, the hill on which Floral Heights was spread, with its bright roofs and immaculate turf and amazing comfort, had been a wilderness of rank second-growth elms and oaks and maples. Along the precise streets were still a few wooded vacant lots, and the fragment of an old orchard. It was brilliant to-day; the apple boughs were lit with fresh leaves like torches of green fire. The first white of cherry blossoms flickered down a gully, and robbins clamored.

Babbitt sniffed the earth, chuckled at the hysteric robins as he would have chuckled at kittens or at a comic movie. He was, to the eye, the perfect office-going executive—a well-fed man in a correct brown soft hat and frameless spectacles, smoking a large cigar, driving a good motor along a semi-suburban parkway. But in him was some genius of authentic love for his neighborhood, his city, his clan. The winter was over; the time was come for the building, the visible growth, which to him was glory. He lost his dawn depression; he was ruddily cheerful when he stopped on Smith Street to leave the brown trousers, and to have the gasoline-tank filled.

The familiarity of the rite fortified him: the sight of the tall red iron gasoline-pump, the hollow-tile and terra-cotta garage, the window full of the most agreeable accessories—shiny casings, spark-plugs with immaculate porcelain jackets, tire-chains of gold and silver. He was flattered by the friendliness with which Sylvester Moon, dirtiest and most skilled of motor mechanics, came out to serve him. "Mornin,' Mr. Babbitt!" said Moon, and Babbitt felt himself a person of importance, one whose name even busy garagemen remembered—not one of these cheap-sports flying around in flivvers. He admired the ingenuity of the automatic dial, clicking off gallon by gallon; admired the smartness of the sign: "A fill in time saves getting stuck—gas to-day 31 cents"; admired the rhythmic gurgle of the gasoline as it flowed into the tank, and the mechanical regularity with which Moon turned the handle.

"How much we takin' to-day?" asked Moon, in a manner which combined the independence of the great specialist, the friendliness of a familiar gossip, and respect for a man of weight in the community, like George F. Babbitt.

"Fill 'er up."

"Who you rootin' for for Republican candidate, Mr. Babbitt?"

"It's too early to make any predictions yet. After all, there's still a good month and two weeks—no, three weeks—must be almost three weeks— well, there's more than six weeks in all before the Republican convention, and I feel a fellow ought to keep an open mind and give all the candidates a show—look 'em all over and size 'em up, and then decide carefully."

"That's a fact, Mr. Babbitt."

"But I'll tell you—and my stand on this is just the same as it was four years ago, and eight years ago, and it'll be my stand four years from now—yes, and eight years from now! What I tell everybody, and it can't be too generally understood, is that what we need first, last, and all the time is a good, sound business administration!"

"By golly, that's right!"

"How do those front tires look to you?"

"Fine! Fine! Wouldn't be much work for garages if everybody looked after their car the way you do."

"Well, I do try and have some sense about it." Babbitt paid his bill, said adequately, "Oh, keep the change," and drove off in an ecstasy of honest self-appreciation. It was with the manner of a Good Samaritan that he shouted at a respectable-looking man who was waiting for a trolley car, "Have a lift?" As the man climbed in Babbitt condescended, "Going clear down-town? Whenever I see a fellow waiting for a trolley, I always make it a practice to give him a lift—unless, of course, he looks like a bum."

"Wish there were more folks that were so generous with their machines," dutifully said the victim of benevolence.

"Oh, no, 'tain't a question of generosity, hardly. Fact, I always feel—I was saying to my son just the other night—it's a fellow's duty to share the good things of this world with his neighbors, and it gets my goat when a fellow gets stuck on himself and goes around tooting his horn merely because he's charitable."

The victim seemed unable to find the right answer. Babbitt boomed on:

"Pretty punk service the Company giving us on these carlines. Nonsense to only run the Portland Road cars once every seven minutes. Fellow gets mighty cold on a winter morning, waiting on a street corner with the wind nipping at his ankles."

"That's right. The Street Car company don't care a damn what kind of a deal they give us. Something ought to happen to 'em."

Babbitt was alarmed. "But still, of course it won't do to just keep knocking the Traction Company and not realize the difficulties they're operating under, like these cranks that want municipal ownership. The way these workmen hold up the Company for high wages is simply a crime, and of course the burden falls on you and me that have to pay a seven-cent fare! Fact, there's remarkable service on all their lines—considering."

"Well—" uneasily.

"Darn fine morning," Babbitt explained. "Spring coming along fast."

"Yes, it's real spring now."

The victim had no originality, no wit, and Babbitt fell into a great silence and devoted himself to the game of beating trolley cars to the corner: a spurt, a tail-chase, nervous speeding between the huge yellow side of the trolley and the jagged row of parked motors, shooting past just as the trolley stopped—a rare game and valiant.

And all the while he was conscious of the loveliness of Zenith. For weeks together he noticed nothing but clients and the vexing To Rent signs of rival brokers. To-day, in mysterious malaise, he raged or rejoiced with equal nervous swiftness, and to-day the light of spring was so winsome that he lifted his head and saw.

He admired each district along his familiar route to the office: The bungalows and shrubs and winding irregular driveways of Floral Heights. The one-story shops on Smith Street, a glare of plate-glass and new yellow brick; groceries and laundries and drug-stores to supply the more immediate needs of East Side housewives. The market gardens in Dutch Hollow, their shanties patched with corrugated iron and stolen doors. Billboards with crimson goddesses nine feet tall advertising cinema films, pipe tobacco, and talcum powder. The old "mansions" along Ninth Street, S.E., like aged dandies in filthy linen; wooden castles turned into boarding-houses, with muddy walks and rusty hedges, jostled by fast-intruding garages, cheap apartment-houses, and fruit-stands conducted by bland, sleek Athenians. Across the belt of railroad-tracks, factories with high-perched water-tanks and tall stacks—factories producing condensed milk, paper boxes, lighting-fixtures, motor cars. Then the business center, the thickening darting traffic, the crammed trolleys unloading, and high doorways of marble and polished granite.

It was big—and Babbitt respected bigness in anything; in mountains, jewels, muscles, wealth, or words. He was, for a spring-enchanted moment, the lyric and almost unselfish lover of Zenith. He thought of the outlying factory suburbs; of the Chaloosa River with its strangely eroded banks; of the orchard-dappled Tonawanda Hills to the North, and all the fat dairy land and big barns and comfortable herds. As he dropped his passenger he cried, "Gosh, I feel pretty good his morning!"

III

Epochal as starting the car was the drama of parking it before he entered his office. As he turned from Oberlin Avenue round the corner into Third Street, N.E., he peered ahead for a space in the line of parked cars. He angrily just missed a space as a rival driver slid into it. Ahead, another car was leaving the curb, and Babbitt slowed up, holding out his hand to the cars pressing on him from behind, agitatedly motioning an old woman to go ahead, avoiding a truck which bore down on him from one side. With front wheels nicking the wrought-steel bumper of the car in front, he stopped, feverishly cramped his steering-wheel, slid back into the vacant space and, with eighteen inches of room, manœuvered to bring the car level with the curb. It was a virile adventure masterfully executed. With satisfaction he locked a thief-proof steel wedge on the front wheel, and crossed the street to his real-estate office on the ground floor of the Reeves Building.

The Reeves Building was as fireproof as a rock and as efficient as a typewriter; fourteen stories of yellow pressed brick, with clean, upright, unornamented lines. It was filled with the offices of lawyers, doctors, agents for machinery, for emery wheels, for wire fencing, for mining-stock. Their gold signs shone on the windows. The entrance was too modern to be flamboyant with pillars; it was quiet, shrewd, neat. Along the Third Street side were a Western Union Telegraph Office, the Blue Delft Candy Shop, Shotwell's Stationery Shop, and the Babbitt-Thompson Realty Company.

Babbitt could have entered his office from the street, as customers did, but it made him feel an insider to go through the corridor of the building and enter by the back door. Thus he was greeted by the villagers.

The little unknown people who inhabited the Reeves Building corridors —elevator-runners, starter, engineers, superintendent, and the doubtful-looking lame man who conducted the news and cigar stand—were in no way city-dwellers. They were rustics, living in a constricted valley, interested only in one another and in The Building. Their Main Street was the entrance hall, with its stone floor, severe marble ceiling, and the inner windows of the shops. The liveliest place on the street was the Reeves Building Barber Shop, but this was also Babbitt's one embarrassment. Himself, he patronized the glittering Pompeian Barber Shop in the Hotel Thornleigh, and every time he passed the Reeves shop—ten times a day, a hundred times—he felt untrue to his own village.

Now, as one of the squirearchy, greeted with honorable salutations by the villagers, he marched into his office, and peace and dignity were upon him, and the morning's dissonances all unheard.

They were heard again, immediately.

Stanley Graff, the outside salesman, was talking on the telephone with tragic lack of that firm manner which disciplines clients: "Say, uh, I think I got just the house that would suit you—the Percival House, in Linton. . . . Oh, you've seen it. Well, how'd it strike you? . . . Huh? . . . Oh," irresolutely, "oh, I see."

As Babbitt marched into his private room, a coop with semi-partition of oak and frosted glass, at the back of the office, he reflected how hard it was to find employees who had his own faith that he was going to make sales.

There were nine members of the staff, besides Babbitt and his partner and father-in-law, Henry Thompson, who rarely came to the office. The nine were Stanley Graff, the outside salesman—a youngish man given to cigarettes and the playing of pool; old Mat Penniman, general utility man, collector of rents and salesman of insurance—broken, silent, gray; a mystery, reputed to have been a "crack" real-estate man with a firm of his own in haughty Brooklyn; Chester Kirby Laylock, resident salesman out at the Glen Oriole acreage development—an enthusiastic person with a silky mustache and much family; Miss Theresa McGoun, the swift and rather pretty stenographer; Miss Wilberta Bannigan, the thick, slow, laborious accountant and file-clerk; and four freelance part-time commission salesmen.

As he looked from his own cage into the main room Babbitt mourned, "McGoun's a good stenog., smart's a whip, but Stan Graff and all those bums—" The zest of the spring morning was smothered in the stale office air.

Normally he admired the office, with a pleased surprise that he should have created this sure lovely thing; normally he was stimulated by the clean newness of it and the air of bustle; but to-day it seemed flat—the tiled floor, like a bath-room, the ocher-colored metal ceiling, the faded maps on the hard plaster walls, the chairs of varnished pale oak, the desks and filing-cabinets of steel painted in olive drab. It was a vault, a steel chapel where loafing and laughter were raw sin.

He hadn't even any satisfaction in the new water-cooler! And it was the very best of water-coolers, up-to-date, scientific, and right-thinking. It had cost a great deal of money (in itself a virtue). It possessed a non-conducting fiber ice-container, a porcelain water-jar (guaranteed hygienic), a dripless non-clogging sanitary faucet, and machine-painted decorations in two tones of gold. He looked down the relentless stretch of tiled floor at the water-cooler, and assured himself that no tenant of the Reeves Building had a more expensive one, but he could not recapture the feeling of social superiority it had given him. He astoundingly grunted, "I'd like to beat it off to the woods right now. And loaf all day. And go to Gunch's again to-night, and play poker, and cuss as much as I feel like, and drink a hundred and nine-thousand bottles of beer."

He sighed; he read through his mail; he shouted "Msgoun," which meant "Miss McGoun"; and began to dictate.

This was his own version of his first letter:

"Omar Gribble, send it to his office, Miss McGoun, yours of twentieth to hand and in reply would say look here, Gribble, I'm awfully afraid if we go on shilly-shallying like this we'll just naturally lose the Allen sale, I had Allen up on carpet day before yesterday and got right down to cases and think I can assure you—uh, uh, no, change that: all my experience indicates he is all right, means to do business, looked into his financial record which is fine—that sentence seems to be a little balled up, Miss McGoun; make a couple sentences out of it if you have to, period, new paragraph.

"He is perfectly willing to pro rate the special assessment and strikes me, am dead sure there will be no difficulty in getting him to pay for title insurance, so now for heaven's sake let's get busy—no, make that: so now let's go to it and get down—no, that's enough—you can tie those sentences up a little better when you type 'em, Miss McGoun—yours sincerely, etcetera."

This is the version of his letter which he received, typed, from Miss McGoun that afternoon:

> Babbitt-Thompson Realty Co.
> Homes for Folks
> Reeves Bldg., Oberlin Avenue & 3d St., N.E.
> Zenith

Omar Gribble, Esq.,
576 North American Building,
Zenith.

Dear Mr. Gribble:
  Your letter of the twentieth to hand. I must say I'm awfully afraid that if we go on shilly-shallying like this we'll just naturally lose the Allen sale. I had Allen up on the carpet day before yesterday, and got right down to cases. All my experience indicates that he means to do business. I have also looked into his financial record, which is fine.
  He is perfectly willing to pro rate the special assessment and there will be no difficulty in getting him to pay for title insurance.
  So let's go!

> Yours sincerely,

As he read and signed it, in his correct flowing business-college hand, Babbitt reflected, "Now that's a good, strong letter, and clear's a bell. Now what the— I never told McGoun to make a third paragraph there! Wish she'd quit trying to improve on my dictation! But what I can't understand is: why can't Stan Graff or Chet Laylock write a letter like that? With punch! With a kick!"

The most important thing he dictated that morning was the fortnightly form-letter, to be mimeographed and sent out to a thousand "prospects." It was diligently imitative of the best literary models of the day; of heart-to-heart-talk advertisements, "sales-pulling" letters, discourses on the "development of Will-power," and hand-shaking house-organs, as richly poured forth by the new school of Poets of Business. He had painfully written out a first draft, and he intoned it now like a poet delicate and distrait!

Say, old man!
  I just want to know can I do you a whaleuva favor? Honest! No kidding! I know you're interested in getting a house, not merely a place where you hang up the old bonnet but a love-nest for the wife and kiddies—and maybe for the flivver out beyant (be sure and spell that b-e-y-a-n-t, Miss McGoun) the spud garden. Say, did you ever stop to think that we're here to save you trouble? That's how we make a living—folks don't pay us for our lovely beauty! Now take a look:
  Sit right down at the handsome carved mahogany escritoire and shoot us in a line telling us just what you want, and if we can find it we'll come hopping down your lane with the good tidings, and if we can't, we won't bother you. To save your time, just fill out the blank enclosed. On request will also send blank regarding store properties in Floral Heights, Silver Grove, Linton, Bellevue, and all East Side residential districts.

> Yours for service,

P.S.—Just a hint of some plums we can pick for you—some genuine bargains that came in to-day:

SILVER GROVE.—Cute four-room California bungalow, a.m.i., garage, dandy shade tree, swell neighborhood, handy car line. $3700, $780 down and balance liberal, Babbitt-Thompson terms, cheaper than rent.

DORCHESTER.—A corker! Artistic two-family house, all oak trim, parquet floors, lovely gas log, big porches, colonial, heated all-weather garage, a bargain at $11,250.

Dictation over, with its need of sitting and thinking instead of bustling around and making a noise and really doing something, Babbitt sat creakily back in his revolving desk-chair and beamed on Miss McGoun. He was conscious of her as a girl, of black bobbed hair against demure cheeks. A longing which was indistinguishable from loneliness enfeebled him. While she waited, tapping a long, precise pencil-point on the desk-tablet, he half identified her with the fairy girl of his dreams. He imagined their eyes meeting with terrifying recognition; imagined touching her lips with frightened reverence and— She was chirping "Any more, Mist' Babbitt?" He grunted, "That winds it up, I guess," and turned heavily away.

For all his wandering thoughts, they had never been more intimate than this. He often reflected, "Nev' forget how old Jake Offutt said a wise bird never goes love-making in his own office or his own home. Start trouble. Sure. But—"

In twenty-three years of married life he had peered uneasily at every graceful ankle, every soft shoulder; in thought he had treasured them; but not once had he hazarded respectability by adventuring. Now, as he calculated the cost of repapering the Styles house, he was restless again, discontented about nothing and everything, ashamed of his discontentment, and lonely for the fairy girl.

SELECTION

Keeping Cool with Complacent Calvin Coolidge: Extracts from His Messages on the State of the Union, 1925-1928

One of the Republican campaign slogans in 1924 was "Keep cool with Coolidge." After he walked away with the electorate's endorsement, the former Massachusetts Governor seemed to dedicate himself to furthering even more complacency and brightening the glow of the Golden Age. Referring to Judge Gary, Mencken had said, "The emperor and pope of all the Babbitts, he sits at the center of a Babbitts' paradise. For him and his like there dawns a Golden Age, and its hero is good Cal." As the opening remarks in his last four annual messages to Congress indicate, President Coolidge saw the period very much as Mencken had seen it through Gary's eyes.

Indeed, President Coolidge seemed to see America moving ever closer to the new El Dorado; each year's message was more confident, more glowing, more complacent than the last. In his 1925 message, the President surveyed the American scene, and, while finding the prospect satisfying, saw "here and there . . . comparatively small and apparently temporary difficulties." Flaws remained the next year: American diplomacy was "vexed," and "some occupations and areas" were not as prosperous as they should be, although ". . . in none does there remain any acute chronic depression." Things apparently improved in 1927, for at the end of that year all that the Chief Executive could find that merited concern was that some, presumably minor, ". . . parts of agriculture and industry have lagged." And, alas, there had been storms and floods, over which not even the Grand Old Party had control. But in 1928 the glow was untarnished. The United States had never before "met with a more pleasing prospect than that which appears at the present." Even foreign nations were behaving honorably and sensibly. Fifteen of them had signed the Kellogg-Briand Peace Pact, which did not supersede "our inalienable sovereign right and duty of national defense or . . . commit us . . . to any mode of action" and which promised "more for the peace of the world than any other agreement ever negotiated among the nations."

For a general political history of the 1920s see John D. Hicks, Republican Ascendancy, 1921–1933 *(New York: Harper, 1960). Claude M. Fuess,* Calvin Coolidge: The Man from Vermont *(Boston: Little, Brown, 1940) treats its subject kindly, certainly more kindly than did William Allen White in* A Puritan in Babylon: The Story of Calvin Coolidge *(New York: Macmillan, 1938).*

These selections are all from the Congressional Record: *Sixty-ninth Congress, first session, volume 67, part 1, December 8, 1925, pages 457–458; Sixty-ninth Congress, second session, volume 68, part 1, December 7, 1926, page 29; Seventieth Congress, first session, volume 69, part 1, December 6, 1927, page 103; and Seventieth Congress, second session, volume 70, part 1, December 4, 1928, pages 20–21.*

1925

Members of the Congress, in meeting the constitutional requirement of informing the Congress upon the state of the Union, it is exceedingly gratifying to report that the general condition is one of progress and prosperity. Here and there are comparatively small and apparently temporary difficulties needing adjustment and improved administrative methods, such as are always to be expected, but in the fundamentals of government and business the results demonstrate that we are going in the right direction. The country does not appear to require radical departures from the policies already adopted so much as it needs a further extension of these policies and the improvement of details. The age of perfection is still in the somewhat distant future, but it is more in danger of being retarded by mistaken Government activity than it is from lack of legislation. We are by far the most likely to accomplish permanent good if we proceed with moderation.

In our country the people are sovereign and independent, and must accept the resulting responsibilities. It is their duty to support themselves and support the Government. That is the business of the Nation, whatever the charity of the Nation may require. The functions which the Congress are to discharge are not those of local government but of National Government. The greatest solicitude should be exercised to prevent any encroachment upon the rights of the States or their various political subdivisions. Local self-government is one of our most precious possessions. It is the greatest contributing factor to the stability, strength, liberty, and progress of the Nation. It ought not to be infringed by assault or undermined by purchase. It ought not to abdicate its power through weakness or resign its authority through favor. It does not at all follow that because abuses exist it is the concern of the Federal Government to attempt their reform.

Society is in much more danger from encumbering the National Government beyond its wisdom to comprehend, or its ability to administer, than from leaving the local communities to bear their own burdens and remedy their own evils. Our local habit and custom is so strong, our variety of race and creed is so great, the Federal authority is so tenuous, that the area within which it can function successfully is very limited. The wiser policy is to leave the localities, so far as we can, possessed of their own sources of revenue and charged with their own obligations.

Government Economy

It is a fundamental principle of our country that the people are sovereign. While they recognize the undeniable authority of the state, they have established as its instrument a Government of limited powers. They hold inviolate in their own hands the jurisdiction over their own freedom and the ownership of their own property. Neither of these can be impaired except by due process of law. The wealth of our country is not public wealth, but private wealth. It does not belong to the Government, it belongs to the people. The Government has no justification in taking private property except for a public purpose. It is always necessary to keep these principles in mind in the laying of taxes and in the making of appropriations. No right exists to levy on a dollar, or to order the expenditure of a dollar, of the money of the people, except for a necessary public purpose duly authorized by the Constitution. The power over the purse is the power over liberty. . . .

1926

Members of the Congress, in reporting to the Congress the state of the Union, I find it impossible to characterize it other than one of general peace and prosperity. In some quarters our diplomacy is vexed with difficult and as yet unsolved problems, but nowhere are we met with armed conflict. If some occupations and areas are not flourishing, in none does there remain any acute chronic depression. What the country requires is not so much new policies as a steady continuation of those which are already being crowned with such abundant success. It can not be too often repeated that in common with all the world we are engaged in liquidating the war.

In the present short session no great amount of new legislation is possible, but in order to comprehend what is most desirable some survey of our general situation is necessary. A large amount of time is consumed in the passage of appropriation bills. If each Congress in its opening session would make appropriations to continue for two years, very much time would be saved which could either be devoted to a consideration of the general needs of the country or would result in decreasing the work of legislation.

Economy

Our present state of prosperity has been greatly promoted by three important causes, one of which is economy, resulting in reduction and reform in national taxation. Another is the elimination of many kinds of waste. The third is a general raising of the standards of efficiency. This combination has brought the perfectly astonishing result of a reduction in the index price of commodities and an increase in the index rate of wages. We have secured a lowering of the cost to produce and a raising of the ability to consume. Prosperity resulting from these causes rests on the securest of all foundations. It gathers strength from its own progress.

In promoting this progress the chief part which the National Government plays lies in the field of economy. Whatever doubts may have been entertained as to the necessity of this policy and the beneficial results which would accrue from it to all the people of the Nation, its wisdom must now be considered thoroughly demonstrated. It may not have appeared to be a novel or perhaps brilliant conception, but it has turned out to be preeminently sound. It has not failed to work. It has surely brought results. It does not have to be excused as a temporary expedient adopted as the lesser evil to remedy some abuse. It is not a palliative seeking to treat symptoms, but a major operation, for the eradication at the source of a large number of social diseases.

Nothing is easier than the expenditure of public money. It does not appear to belong to anybody. The temptation is overwhelming to bestow it on somebody. But the results of extravagance are ruinous. The property of the country, like the freedom of the country, belongs to the people of the country. They have not empowered their Government to take a dollar of it except for a necessary public purpose. But if the Constitution conferred such right, sound economics would forbid it. Nothing is more destructive of the progress of the Nation than Government extravagance. It means an increase in the burden of taxation, dissipation of the returns from enterprise, a decrease in the real value of wages, with ultimate stagnation and decay. The whole theory of our institutions is based on the liberty and independence of the individual. He is dependent on himself for support and therefore entitled to the rewards of his own industry. He is not to be deprived of what he earns that others may be benefited by what they do not earn. What he saves through his private effort is not to be wasted by Government extravagance.

Our national activities have become so vast that it is necessary to scrutinize each item of public expenditure if we are to apply the principle of economy. At the last session we made an immediate increase in the annual Budget of more than $100,000,000 in benefits conferred on the veterans of three wars, public buildings, and river and harbor improvement. Many projects are being broached requiring further large outlays. I am convinced that it would be greatly for the welfare of the country if we avoid at the present session all commitments except those of the most pressing nature. From a reduction of the debt and taxes will accrue a wider benefit to all the people of this country than from embarking on any new enterprise. When our war debt is decreased we shall have resources for expansion. Until that is accomplished we should confine ourselves to expenditures of the most urgent necessity. . . .

1927

Members of the Congress: It is gratifying to report that for the fourth consecutive year the state of the Union in general is good. We are at peace. The country as a whole has had a prosperity never exceeded. Wages are at their highest range, employment is plentiful. Some parts of agriculture and industry have lagged; some localities have suffered from storm and flood. But such losses have been absorbed without serious detriment to our great economic structure. Stocks of goods are moderate and a wholesome caution is prevalent. Rates of interest for industry, agriculture, and government have been reduced. Savers and investors are providing capital for new construction in industry and public works. The purchasing power of agriculture has increased. If the people maintain that confidence which they are entitled to have in themselves, in each other, and in America, a comfortable prosperity will continue.

Without constructive economy in Government expenditures we should not now be enjoying these results or these prospects. . . .

1928

No Congress of the United States ever assembled, on surveying the state of the Union, has met with a more pleasing prospect than that which appears at the present time. In the domestic field there is tranquillity and contentment, harmonious relations between management and wage earner, freedom from industrial strife, and the highest record of years of prosperity. In the foreign field there is peace, the good will which comes from mutual understanding, and the knowledge that the problems which a short time ago appeared so ominous are yielding to the touch of manifest friendship. The great wealth created by our enterprise and industry, and saved by our economy, has had the widest distribution among our own people, and has gone out in a steady stream to serve the charity and the business of the world. The requirements of existence have passed beyond the standard of necessity into the region of luxury. Enlarging production is consumed by an increasing demand at home and an expanding commerce abroad. The country can regard the present with satisfaction and anticipate the future with optimism.

The main source of these unexampled blessings lies in the integrity and character of the American people. They have had great faith, which they have supplemented with mighty works. They have been able to put trust in each other and trust in their Government. Their candor in dealing with foreign governments has commanded respect and confidence. Yet these remarkable powers would have been exerted almost in vain without the constant cooperation and careful administration of the Federal Government.

We have been coming into a period which may be fairly characterized as a conservation of our national resources. Wastefulness in public business and private enterprise has been displaced by constructive economy. This has been accomplished by bringing our domestic and foreign relations more and more under a reign of law. A rule of force has been giving way to a rule of reason. We have substituted for the vicious circle of increasing expenditures, increasing tax rates, and diminishing profits the charmed circle of diminishing expenditures, diminishing tax rates, and increasing profits.

Four times we have made a drastic revision of our internal revenue system, abolishing many taxes and substantially reducing almost all others. Each time the resulting stimulation to business has so increased taxable incomes and profits that a surplus has been produced. One-third of the national debt has been paid, while much of the other two-thirds has been refunded at lower rates, and these savings of interest and constant economies have enabled us to repeat the satisfying process of more tax reductions. Under this sound and healthful encouragement the national income has increased nearly 50 per cent, until it is estimated to stand well over $90,000,000,000. It has been a method which has performed the seeming miracle of leaving a much greater percentage of earnings in the hands of the taxpayers with scarcely any diminution of the Government revenue. That is constructive economy in the highest degree. It is the corner stone of prosperity. It should not fail to be continued.

This action began by the application of economy to public expenditure. If it is to be permanent, it must be made so by the repeated application of economy. There is no surplus on which to base further tax revision at this time. Last June the estimates showed a threatened deficit for the current fiscal year of $94,000,000. Under my direction the departments began saving all they could out of their present appropriations. The last tax reduction brought an encouraging improvement in business, beginning early in October, which will also increase our revenue. The combination of economy and good times now indicates a surplus of about $37,000,000. This is a margin of less than 1 per cent on our expenditures and makes it obvious that the Treasury is in no condition to undertake increases in expenditures to be made before June 30. It is necessary therefore during the present session to refrain from new appropriations for immediate outlay, or if such are absolutely required to provide for them by new revenue; otherwise we shall reach the end of the year with the unthinkable result of an unbalanced budget. For the first time during my term of office we face that contingency. I am certain that the Congress would not pass and I should not feel warranted in approving legislation which would involve us in that financial disgrace. . . .

One of the most important treaties ever laid before the Senate of the United States will be that which the 15 nations recently signed at Paris, and to which 44 other nations have declared their intention to adhere, renouncing war as a national policy and agreeing to resort only to peaceful means for the adjustment of international differences. It is the most solemn declaration against war, the most positive adherence to peace, that it is possible for sovereign nations to make. It does not supersede our inalienable sovereign right and duty of national defense or undertake to commit us before the event to any mode of action which the Congress might decide to be wise if ever the treaty should be broken. But it is a new standard in the world around which can rally the informed and enlightened opinion of nations to prevent their governments from being forced into hostile action by the temporary outbreak of international animosities. The observance of this covenant, so simple and so straightforward, promises more for the peace of the world than any other agreement ever negotiated among the nations.

National Defense

The first duty of our Government to its own citizens and foreigners within its borders is the preservation of order. Unless and until that duty is met a government is not even eligible for recognition among the family of nations. The advancement of world civilization likewise is dependent upon that order among the people of different countries which we term peace. To insure our citizens against the infringement of their legal rights at home and abroad, to preserve order, liberty, and peace by making the law supreme we have an Army and a Navy.

Both of these are organized for defensive purposes. Our Army could not be much reduced, but does not need to be increased. Such new housing and repairs as are necessary are under way and the 5-year program in aviation is being put into effect in both branches of our service.

Our Navy, according to generally accepted standards, is deficient in cruisers. We have 10 comparatively new vessels, 22 that are old, and 8 to be built. It is evident that renewals and replacements must be provided. This matter was thoroughly canvassed at the last session of the Congress and does not need restatement. The bill before the Senate with the elimination of the time clause should be passed. We have no intention of competing with any other country. This building program is for necessary replacements and to meet our needs for defense.

The cost of national defense is stupendous. It has increased $118,000,000 in the past four years. The estimated expenditure for 1930 is $668,000,000. While this is made up of many items it is, after all, mostly dependent upon numbers. Our defensive needs do not call for any increase in the number of men in the Army or the Navy. We have reached the limit of what we ought to expend for that purpose. . . .

SELECTION 34

"A New Era . . . an Economic Revolution of the Profoundest Character": John Moody in "The Atlantic Monthly," 1928

Economists are not often given to such extravagance of language as is often heard from politicians, even from so circumspect and inhibited a politico as Calvin Coolidge, but almost all the economists of the 1920s exuded confidence from at least most of their pores. Once termed "the dismal science" because of its gloomy prognosis for man rather than for the personality of its practitioners, economics now became a subject-matter area, if not precisely a discipline, of optimistic faith.

John Moody, the author of this article, "The New Era in Wall Street," The Atlantic Monthly, volume 142, August, 1928, pages 255–262, here abridged by about one-fifth, was no professional publicist hired to corral lambs into Wall Street. He was a respected writer on economic matters and an investment counselor whose advice was widely sought. He was president of Moody's Investors Service, which published the highly useful and reliable Moody's Manual. Some of his books on economic history even today remain on many professors' reading lists: The Truth about the Trusts (1904), The Railroad Builders (1919), and Masters of Capital (1919). When John Moody was confident about the stock exchange and about the American economy, skeptical indeed was the man who persisted in doubting.

This article not only sketches the economic history of the postwar decade but also indicates the mood that prosperity evoked. The fundamental causes of earlier depressions "have now been eliminated." In 1923, five years before the publication of this article, forecasts that indicated what actually happened on the stock exchange "would have been looked upon as fantastic by the average man." The next five years seemed at least as promising. "And, though the prices of investment securities of standard quality look high to us to-day, they easily may, by 1933, be quoted in many cases at far higher values." Indeed, "There is every indication that the steady growth in the wealth and savings of the American people . . . will continue through many years to come. . . ." After all, "Capital, credit, and confidence are practically interchangeable terms in our modern, mechanistic civilization. In the last analysis, their plenitude depends upon faith; that is, faith in the future." And of faith in the future there was plenty.

I

The trend of American security prices since 1922 presents a remarkable picture. Never before in the history of Wall Street has such a record been displayed. Before the Great War, so-called 'bull markets' sometimes ran two or three years without serious interruption. But now we have witnessed a bull market which had its inception nearly six years ago. And this market, instead of culminating in reaction, depression, or panic, as, according to all orthodox rules of the past, it should long ago have done, has this year been making such spectacular records for itself that the entire financial world has been amazed.

Nearly all of the accredited seers and economic experts have been at a loss to explain it. Most surprising of all, the incurable stock-market optimist and perennial 'bull,' as well as the great army of innocent 'lambs,' have for several years been led, not to the proverbial slaughter, but to a continuous feast of speculative profits. For the first time within the memory of man, 'tips' galore have made good. The Wall Street stock market, which, according to all rules of the old logic, should have 'petered out' two years ago and was then believed to be overdue for a wide-open crash, has this year displayed new and mysterious force. And even though the country has been going through a moderate business depression,—though credit conditions are beginning to display considerable strain, interest rates have long been rising, and brokers' loans have been soaring,—still the great bull market has gone on.

It is not in the stock-market field alone that a remarkable picture is presented of the six-year stretch from 1922. A chart of the investment-bond-market trend presents a similar though less startling exhibit; and if precise records could be produced showing the expansion in the volume and sale of 'outside' securities, with the broadening in the distribution of all types of investments throughout the country, equally dramatic comparisons with half a dozen years ago could now be made.

As a concrete illustration of what has happened in the Wall Street markets since 1923, certain exhibits of the price changes in standard, representative investment stocks and bonds have recently been compiled by the writer. In the field of railroad stocks, taking twenty-six representative dividend-paying issues, there has been an average advance in prices of about 100 per cent from the levels of 1923. Any investor who had in 1923 diversified a given sum, like $100,000, among these twenty-six railroad issues would recently have had a capital increase to about $200,000. In the public-utility field, an investor who had diversified a similar sum in twenty-seven representative stocks would recently have had a profit of over 200 per cent; his original $100,000 investment would be worth more than $300,000. In the industrial list, an investment in thirty representative issues (the sum being equally divided between all) recently showed a profit of over 230 per cent; that is, an investment of about $100,000 in 1923 recently had a value of about $330,000. In all of these exhibits no 'skyrockets' or purely speculative stocks were included; the selections were confined entirely to issues of standard character and to the investment classes.

But, as already stated, this continuous upward tendency in security prices since 1923 has not been confined to stocks alone. Investors in the highest-grade seasoned railroad bonds have reaped profits of 20 per cent or more during the period; purchasers of standard foreign dollar bonds in 1923 now find themselves with profits of from 20 per cent to 30 per cent on their original investments. In this general connection, the writer recently compiled a diversified list of American railroad bonds, foreign dollar bonds, railroad, public utility, and industrial stocks, and bank and trust-company stocks. Assuming that an investor had spread the specific sum of $100,000 in this list, in approximately equal amounts, he would now find himself with a capital value of nearly $400,000.

There has been strong emphasis laid for many months on what are called the dangers of the speculative situation and high market values by practically every public commentator. Dangers are present, it is true, and the thoughtless and venturesome speculator in these days runs great risk of having his fingers burned. But the average financial commentator or critic is too prone to hark back to the experiences of the years before the war and draw parallels with years like 1893, 1903, and 1907; years in which great bull movements culminated and were followed by depressions or panics. There is a similar tendency to ring the changes constantly on what happened immediately at the end of the wild post-war inflation period of 1919 and early 1920. It is confidently asserted that what happened in those years will presently happen again. And yet, notwithstanding the wide and persistent preaching of this orthodox doctrine, we have this year witnessed powerful financial interests and numerous shrewd, 'long-pull' investors purchasing vast blocks of high-priced standard shares and putting these shares in their strong boxes.

What is the correct explanation of it all? Is it entirely the commonplace one of unreasoned and excited speculation and manipulation, with nothing more tangible behind it than a dramatic manifestation of crowd psychology? Or are there more fundamental things behind it? A careful examination of all the facts seems to indicate that there are some fundamental factors of moment behind this extraordinary Wall Street situation; and it is the purpose of this article to attempt to bring some of these fundamental things to light.

II

It will be agreed by all thoughtful persons that to interpret the present intelligently one must first turn to a study of the past. But in turning to the past one should first give due weight to the fact that causes which greatly affected events in past years may no longer exist; that laws, customs, methods, perspectives, as well as the position and resources of the nation, may have materially changed. Let us examine for a moment the panic and depression periods of 1893, 1903, and 1907.

These years were all preceded by bull markets which, superficially at least, bore many of the earmarks of the present bull market. There was inflation then; there is inflation now. Standard stocks at the end of 1906 were selling, on the average, on a lower income basis than now; standard investment bonds were all higher than now. But the panics or depressions that followed closely on the heels of the booms of 1892, 1902, and 1906 were primarily caused, in all three cases, by certain outstanding factors which no longer exist in this country. The panic of 1893 was brought on almost entirely by the unsound currency legislation of the period; by the iniquitous workings of the Sherman Silver Purchase Law and the inadequacy of the National Banking System for coping with the situation. The depression of 1903 was caused primarily by the reckless, crude, and unscientific mania for industrial capitalizing and stockjobbing; by the overambitious railroad consolidation schemes; by the rise of radicalism in politics which largely resulted therefrom; and by the continued aggravation of a faulty banking and reserve system in a country which was growing by leaps and bounds and had far outgrown its credit machinery. The panic of 1907 was directly traceable to the same old panic-breeder, the National Banking Law, and to little else. It is true that the booms or bull markets which preceded these panics or depressions were overdone and were in many ways distinctly unhealthy; but they were unhealthy primarily because of the total absence of adequate banking and credit machinery.

Consequently, in comparing the pre-war past with the post-war present, we must first give due weight to the fact that the fundamental causes of the disasters mentioned have now been eliminated. Looking backward, as we now can, it is readily enough demonstrated that in the period of twenty years or more preceding the Great War there never was a time in which one could fairly count on a long period of sustained prosperity in this country. Banking conditions were always unsound; a large part of the period was checkered with radical antitrust legislation; socialistic ideas were rampant in all directions; the financing of this initial era of big business was in large part crude, unscientific, and ill considered. It was the period of the 'trust-buster,' the muckraker, and the 'undesirable citizen,' and, in its later years, the shadows of the Great War were dropping down over the world.

The saner method for attempting an analysis of the present is to seek for the background of the years which have gone by since the close of the war; especially those years which have intervened since the deflation collapse of 1920 and 1921. The background of these half-dozen years far more completely explains the present and indicates the probable future than any research, however exhaustive, into the generation which preceded the Great War.

In 1923, business in this country was just beginning definitely to recover from the deflation crash of more than two years before. Liabilities of business firms and corporations had been well liquidated, and acute deflation had done its work in the general fields of industry and finance. Political and labor conditions were becoming increasingly stable, and though Europe was still in the mire, and the German-French situation was acutely bad, there were not lacking signs that the reparation problem was definitely heading toward a solution. Based on these general facts, the belief that better times were ahead was justified; and even had there been nothing else of importance in the situation, it is probable that the following year would have been one of progress.

But, aside from all this, certain other fundamental facts should be brought to the front. The most important is that the position of the United States in relation to the rest of the world had completely changed. We had become a mighty creditor nation, whereas in the decades before the war we were still a borrowing nation. The sudden and dramatic events of the war period had increased the wealth and resources of this country to an extent which perhaps would not otherwise have been equaled within a generation or more; and, because of the exhaustion of Europe, the relative position of the United States had been made even stronger. An immense increase in our plant and producing capacity had also taken place as a result of abnormal war activities after 1914 and all through the war years. Thus, at the signing of the peace, this country was completely equipped for a vast new expansion in its wealth-producing activities.

Another vital fact which had gone far to stabilize fundamental financial and business conditions in America was the founding of the Federal Reserve Banking System. The new law, passed at the close of 1913, was the culmination of the agitation for sound banking which had been carried on with growing aggressiveness after the free-silver craze of the 1890's had spent itself. During the war period it saved the day for American war finance; it probably saved the day for the Allies. It carried the country through the disastrous deflation period of 1920 and 1921 by a process of orderly liquidation. Everyone who has full knowledge of the matter knows that if we had still been operating under the old banking system in 1920 we should then have experienced the worst financial and commercial panic of all history. By the opening of 1923, the Federal Reserve Law had demonstrated its thorough practicality and value, and thus had secured the general confidence of the business interests of the country. The old breeder of financial panics, the National Banking Law, which had been a menace to American progress for two decades, had now been replaced by a modern, scientific reserve system which embodied an elastic currency and an orderly control of the money market. . . .

After the war had closed and the wild speculative period of profiteering had collapsed, a declining tendency immediately set in in commodity prices. Margins of profit narrowed or entirely disappeared, and thus the old temptation for expanding inventories or buying goods or raw materials in anticipation of sharply rising prices was completely eliminated. A very direct and increasing impetus was thus given to the modern American effort toward the more scientific development of mass production and distribution, the speeding up of production, and the cutting out of waste and excess motion in all industrial activities. After the passage of the Railroad Transportation Act of 1920 and the restoration of the railroads to their owners, a remarkable increase in the speeding up of freight deliveries was developed, which in itself gave new facility to the hand-to-mouth policy among merchants and retailers. The new slogan, 'Keep your shelves as bare as you dare,' was taking the place of the old notion that an overstocked store was essential to prosperity.

Coincident with the growing efficiency in manufacturing and business methods, there was fully under way by 1923 a rapid development of new mechanical inventions in almost every business line. Old methods were being eliminated and new labor and time-saving devices installed as never before. Profits were being sought more and more through the elimination and cutting down of unnecessary costs rather than in mere attempts to increase volume and profit through possible advancing prices. This tendency was further accelerated by the continuous trend toward consolidation of small units into large; by the larger development of the chain-store and direct-delivery systems, with the resulting elimination of the middle man.

This general evolution in production and distribution was of course immensely stimulated by the perfecting of methods, going on all over the country, for the larger mobilization of investment capital; the gathering together, for the uses of industry and for direct investment in the big business and corporate enterprises of the times, of the surplus savings of the people. We were rapidly becoming a nation of investors—investors in our own industries from one end of the country to the other.

With the gradual disappearance of the war and post-war problems and the final adjustment of relations with our former Allies, and with the adjustment of our people to the habit of accepting the higher level of prices and cost of living as 'normal,' a new stabilization of political and labor interests took form. No longer were the people agitated by the pre-war political issues of tariff, antimonopoly, and 'trust-busting'; labor was no longer aggressively urging socialistic legislation; issues which had split the Republican Party in 1912, such as the recall of judges, initiative and referendum, direct election of senators, and woman suffrage, were either settled or forgotten; the League of Nations issue and the 'Wilson policies' had been pushed aside by the return of the Republicans to power in 1920. Labor was being quite uniformly employed on the new and higher wage scales and was beginning to share more and more in the profits of industry, while the general public were feeling the influences of growing stability and prosperity. As increasing numbers became investors in the rising corporate activities of the continent, the sentiment pervaded more and more widely that business enterprise and wealth production thrive best under political noninterference, though with proper and necessary regulation. This changing attitude of the people was well reflected in the national election of 1924, when the strongest argument which returned President Coolidge to office was the maintenance of business stability. . . .

No one can examine the panorama of business and finance in America during the past half-dozen years without realizing that we are living in a new era; that we have been going through an economic revolution of the profoundest character. America's world of to-day is not the world of twenty years ago.

In fact, a new age is taking form throughout the entire civilized world; civilization is taking on new aspects. We are only now beginning to realize, perhaps, that this modern, mechanistic civilization in which we live is now in the process of perfecting itself. Political problems nowadays are looming less large in the minds of men than are economic factors. The public more and more are thinking in terms of industry, wealth production, efficiency of method, income, and profits. What this portends for the longer future, no one can say; but it is a fact of great significance, nevertheless.

III

Naturally enough, forecasts made in 1923, which correctly foreshadowed what subsequently has happened in the security markets, would have been looked upon as fantastic by the average man, and any present forecast of the coming few years may also be looked upon as fantastic. Nevertheless, there seem to be many reasons for believing that the coming period may prove quite as stable and constructive in this country as have the five past years, if not more so. And, though the prices of investment securities of standard quality look high to us to-day, they easily may, by 1933, be quoted in many cases at far higher values. . . .

There is every indication that the steady growth in the wealth and savings of the American people which has been going on without material interruption for years, and is still persisting, will continue through many years to come, thus adding steadily to and maintaining a relative plethora of available capital and credit; a plethora which has by no means been offset thus far by the immense outpour of new securities or the heavy borrowings of foreign peoples. Capital, credit, and confidence are practically interchangeable terms in our modern, mechanistic civilization. In the last analysis, their plenitude depends on faith; that is, faith in the future. . . .

Not the least important fact of this new age in which we live is the profound change which has taken place within recent years in the public attitude toward corporate enterprise. To-day it is estimated that more than 15,000.000 Americans own stocks and bonds and governmental obligations, and the number is still growing by leaps and bounds. When it is realized that twenty years ago not more than 500,000 security investors existed in the United States, the significance of this fact will be recognized. And in this connection it should be noted that a rapidly increasing percentage of the genuine investment capital in America is going into 'equities'—that is, into preferred and common stocks of corporations as distinguished from bonds. To some extent, at least, does this account for the broad and stable condition, at high levels, of recent Wall Street markets. Not all of the 4,000,000-share days are the work of speculators and manipulators.

It is not for a moment intended to imply that in this new era the old-fashioned principles of cause and effect have lost their meaning. There is still as much truth as ever in the axiom that what is pushed up in speculative Wall Street is certain sooner or later to be pushed down. We have had demonstration enough, during the past five years, as values have been rising, that rash stock-market speculation is as dangerous as ever. The impressive thing, however, has been the gradual, though fluctuating, upward trend from year to year and the relative maintenance of values at the higher levels, regardless of business reactions, of temporary recessions in profits, money-market fluctuations, or such seemingly abnormal things as the heavy outflow of gold to Europe. Though the latter are all matters of importance, and are certain in the future, as in the past, to affect currently the speculative security markets, yet in the long run they are all relatively unimportant as compared with the broad fundamentals which have been discussed.

The mistake that many, no doubt, make is to assume that times have not fundamentally changed. They have changed. We are living in a new era, and Wall Street, in its present condition and activity, broadly stated, is simply reflecting this new era. It will continue to reflect it as the years go by, and if, as has been assumed, the present national and world trends continue without material change through the next decade, it is obvious enough that security values during future years will rise to higher levels.

But it should finally be emphasized that, though we are in the midst of a new and remarkable era, we have not reached the millennium. We should not assume that business reactions, periods of recession, and unsettlement, are to be abolished, or that Wall Street will enjoy an uninterrupted bull market indefinitely. Plenty of shocks will come in the months and years ahead to the speculator and gambler, and perhaps there will be more than one massacre of the innocents in Wall Street during the coming year or two. This seems likely enough, if only because of the vast increase in our 'lamb' population.

SELECTION

The Government Administrator as Efficiency Expert: Herbert Hoover's Annual Report as Secretary of Commerce, 1924

Born in 1874 and trained as a geologist and engineer at Stanford University, Herbert Clark Hoover became a mining expert whose work took him to Australia and several parts of Asia. As a mining engineer he was unusually competent, but his rarer excellence was in business organization and administration.

In 1902 he became a partner in a London-based mining firm, and with this company he soon became more of a reorganizer of poorly operated mining companies than a mining engineer as such. The young Hoover made a considerable fortune rather quickly. In 1914, when he was forty years old, his wealth was sufficient to enable him to stop his business career and devote the balance of his long life to government and other public service.

Coming to national attention first as organizer and chairman of the Commission for Relief in Belgium, a philanthropic activity consistent with his Quaker background, Hoover during World War I became Food Administrator, a position in agriculture similar to Baruch's in industry. Hoover brought to his task his wide organizational experience, and food production and distribution were as efficient as the somewhat defective legislation permitted. There was talk of Hoover as the Democratic presidential candidate in 1920 before he announced his Republican affiliation. Harding offered him the post of Secretary of Commerce, which he accepted with the understanding that he could expand the Department's activities and that he would have a voice in foreign policies that concerned business. Remaining as Secretary until he resigned in 1928 to run for the Presidency, Hoover attempted in a variety of ways to rationalize American business.

This selection, taken from the section on elimination of national waste in Twelfth Annual Report of the Secretary of Commerce, 1924 *(Washington: Government Printing Office, 1924), pages 10–16, 18–19, 22–24, describes many of these rationalizing activities. Because of the implications for traditional antitrust policy, Hoover's efforts to foster the development of trade associations encountered criticism. That he regarded some interpretations of antitrust law— particularly, ambiguous and hazy definitions of the boundaries between legality and illegality—as highly mischievous and socially harmful is clear from this report's comments on trade associations. Yet Hoover also made clear that he did not condone the trade association's being used as a device to stifle competition.*

There is no altogether satisfactory biography of Hoover, but see Eugene Lyons, Herbert Hoover, A Biography *(Garden City, N.Y.: Doubleday, 1964) and, for his Presidential years primarily, Harris Gaylord Warren,* Herbert Hoover and the Great Depression *(Fair Lawn, N.J.: Oxford University Press, 1959). No serious student should miss Hoover's* Memoirs, *of which volume 2,* The Cabinet and the Presidency, 1920–1933 *(New York: Macmillan, 1952) is the relevant one of the three.*

Outside of the very large functions of the department in the promotion of foreign trade, in aid to navigation, in provision of systematic economic information, and in cooperation with commerce and industry to advance productivity, a definite constructive national program has been developed for the elimination of waste in our economic system. The need is plain. The American standard of living is the product of high wages to producers and low prices to consumers. The road to national progress lies in increasing real wages through proportionately lower prices. The one and only way is to improve methods and processes and to eliminate waste. Just as 20 years ago we undertook nation-wide conservation of natural resources, so now we must undertake nation-wide elimination of waste. Regulation and laws are of but minor effect on these fundamental things. But by well-directed economic forces, by cooperation in the community we can not only maintain American standards of living—we can raise them.

We have the highest ingenuity and efficiency in the operation of our industry and commerce of any nation in the world. Yet our economic machine is far from perfect. Wastes are legion. There are wastes which arise from wide-spread unemployment during depressions, and from speculation and overproduction in booms; wastes attributable to labor turnover and the stress of labor conflicts; wastes due to intermittent and seasonal production, as in the coal and construction industries; vast wastes from strictures in commerce due to inadequate transportation, such as the lack of sufficient terminals; wastes caused by excessive variations in products; wastes in materials arising from lack of efficient processes; wastes by fire; and wastes in human life.

Against these and other wastes the department, acting always in cooperation with the industries themselves, has for the past three years developed an increasingly definite program. As these manifold activities of the department are based upon cooperation with industry and commerce, none of them leads to paternalistic ends. Many of the bureaus of the department have contributed to these activities, and the character of the work can be gleaned from the following short summary.

Unemployment and the Business Cycle

The greatest waste is periodic slackening of production and resultant unemployment. At the beginning of this administration there were 4,500,000 unemployed. To meet this situation, and acting under the direction of President Harding, I called in September, 1921, the First National Conference on Unemployment. This conference had as its primary purpose the promotion of temporary relief measures, but had in view a broader consideration of the whole problem of business slumps. The relief measures adopted by the conference proved so successful that we overcame unemployment in much less time than in any other depression in our history. While formulating emergency measures, however, the responsible business men, labor leaders, and economists of the conference agreed fully with the proposal that exhaustive investigations should be made of the whole problem, with a view to the abiding minimization of this waste.

In pursuance of this objective I appointed a committee on business cycles and unemployment, which brought in its report in April, 1923. The committee found that slumps in business are due fundamentally to the economic collapse from the wastes, extravagance, speculation, inflation, overexpansion, and relaxation of effort by labor developed during booms. Remedies were proposed in three directions: First, the better control of credit by the Federal reserve system and the individual bankers, so as to prevent rank speculation and overexpansion; second, the provision of more adequate information as to the tendencies in production, stocks, consumption of commodities, employment, etc., so as to enable business generally to judge better of the approach of dangerous periods; and third, the deferment of as much as possible of public construction work during periods of full private demand in the industry to those periods when the construction industries were not so much in demand.

There is no doubt that the appearance of the report, sponsored by such eminent business men, labor leaders, economists, and engineers, did much to curb the beginnings of a dangerous boom in the spring of 1923. Moreover, the report has enlisted remarkable public attention both in the United States and abroad. It has stimulated economic thought and has developed some very tangible results in application of the principles laid down for mitigating the high losses to the community through the waste of booms and their inevitable collapse into gigantic unemployment.

One of the important recommendations of the committee, as stated above, was the necessity for improved statistical services by the Department of Commerce. It was considered that no other agency could adequately provide such a service. In consonance with this recommendation the monthly Survey of Current Business was inaugurated in 1921 with the aim of bringing all of this type of information together and publishing it promptly. The publication has been steadily improved, until it now comprises 1,400 separate items collected from 55 Government departments, 116 voluntary agencies, and 35 technical and trade sources. Its paid subscription list has increased more than 50 per cent in the past year.

Wastes Due to Seasonal Construction

A second committee was named by me from the unemployment conference on seasonal operation in the construction industries, which carried on extensive research into this problem and made its report last July, just after the close of the fiscal year now under review. The report showed conclusively that custom, not climate, is mainly responsible for the seasonal ups and downs in building, and that these evils are largely unnecessary and can be eliminated. For most types of construction it is now possible to build the year round in all parts of the United States. The elimination of these wastes would strengthen the entire business structure, for construction is the balance wheel of American industry. The value of yearly construction in the United States is more than $5,000,000,000. If building falls off, there is always a slackening in many other lines of industry, resulting in unemployment, decreased purchasing power of employees, and further depression.

Neither of the reports of these two committees included any recommendation as to extension of governmental activities further than that there should be strengthening of the economic and physical research now being carried on by the department. It was felt that a stimulation of thought and organization in the local communities was more consonant with our national conception of individual and community initiative. Important action has now been taken in many communities in changing leasing dates and other devices to induce more regularity to construction.

Bituminous Coal Industry

Investigation made early in this administration, published in various departmental documents, revealed the high instability of the bituminous coal industry and the fact that it was functioning at great national loss. Committees of important men representing various phases of the problem were appointed and systematic cooperation has been set up in remedy. Due to the war and to periods of profiteering, far too many mines had been developed and placed in operation. Practically the whole of these mines had continued to operate on a basis of partial weekly employment. There were approximately 30 per cent too many mines engaged in the business and holding to themselves 30 per cent more labor than would be necessary to produce the nation's coal if they were continuously employed. One result of this intermittent employment is that a large proportion of the workers, although employed at a very high minimum daily wage, did not receive a sufficient annual employment to maintain a reasonable standard of living. Thus there grew out of this vicious cycle constant incitement to labor difficulties.

Investigation showed clearly that the primary remedies needed were (a) sufficient transportation facilities, because car shortages resulted in increase of prices, profiteering, and stimulus to the maintenance of high-cost mines; (b) the reduction of the seasonal character of the industry by the summer storage of coal by the larger commercial and industrial users; and (c) a period of industrial peace so that by avoiding strikes the subsequent profiteering would disappear and thus the fly-by-night and high-cost mines lose their support; in other words, the restoration of real competitive conditions. Through cooperation of trade associations of the principal industrial consumers, through chambers of commerce and public utilities a large amount of regular summer storage has been induced. Through the fine cooperation of the railways greater equipment and terminal facilities have been provided and car shortages have been largely eliminated. Through cooperation by the department with the unionized operators and with the leaders of the United Mine Workers a long term agreement has been entered upon, which insures industrial peace in the industry. These desired remedies have now in a great measure been attained. Here is a case where the saving of economic waste can be measured in the hundreds of millions of dollars.

It is true that during the past few months the industry has been somewhat demoralized by the large stocks of coal accumulated in anticipation of a possible strike last spring, and by the lessened demand during the summer. The broad result of gained stability, however, has been that the public has received its coal during the last fiscal year at the lowest price of any year since before the war. During the year under review prices averaged $2.23 per ton for run-of-mine coal at the mine. In 1920, chiefly because of car shortages, the price averaged $5.64. That was a year of wild speculation and profiteering, with no constructive effort by the Government to improve the position of the consumer. In the year 1922, before cooperation could effect a remedy, a strike of five months intervened, followed by a great car shortage. Nevertheless, owing to the restraint imposed on profiteering and to the cooperation of various industries in distribution, the average price for that year was $3.67.

The industry is now on the road to stabilization. The benefits lie not only in the provision of coal to the consumer at lower prices than have been attained at any time since the beginning of the war. The gradual elimination of the high-cost and fly-by-night mines is bringing about a greater degree of concentration of labor upon a smaller number of mines, the increase of days of employment per annum, and thus a larger annual return to the workers. The inherent risks in the industry will be decreased because the efficient and stable operator will no longer be subjected to the type of competition that comes from those mines that exist only to take advantage of profiteering periods. No better example of cooperation to secure the elimination of national waste can be presented. The past year, as compared to the year 1920, shows a saving to the consumer of about $1,000,000,000, which must be reflected in decreasing costs of production in every avenue of industry and commerce.

Interconnection of Electric Power and Lighting Systems

In October, 1923, with the approval of the President, I called a conference of the representatives of the State utility commissions of the 11 States from Maine to Maryland to consider what cooperative steps the Federal and State authorities could properly take to promote interconnection of power systems in those States. At this conference I outlined the problem in the following terms:

> This conference is not conceived as more Government in business. The public authorities are already deeply in the power business through many forms of regulation and a very large measure of control of power sources. The thought here is that coordination between public authorities and industries may secure further consummation of a great advance in the development of a great service to the public.
>
> The reason and need for this discussion are simply that engineering science has brought us to the threshold of a new era in the development of electric power. This era promises great reductions in power cost and wide expansion of its use. Fundamentally, this new stage in progress is due to the perfection of high voltage, longer transmission, and more perfect mechanical development in generation of power. We can now undertake the cheaper sources of power from water sources further afield, such as the St. Lawrence, and cheaper generation from coal through larger and more favorably placed coal generation plants. We can secure great economies in distribution through the interconnection of load between systems, for thus we secure a reduction of

the amount of reserve equipment, a better average load factor through pooling the effect of day and seasonal variations, together with wider diversification of use by increased industrial consumption. We can assure more security in the power supply from the effect of coal strikes and from transportation interruptions.

All this means the liquidity of power over whole groups of States. At once power distribution spreads across State lines and into diverse legal jurisdictions. We are, therefore, confronted not only with problems of the coordination in the industries of their engineering, financial, and ownership problems, but also with new legal problems in State rights and Federal relations to power distribution.

This superdevelopment of great areas of cheaper power has been dramatized by those less familiar with the problem as the construction of great power highways traversing several States into which we should pour great streams of high voltages from great giant water power or central steam stations to be distributed to the public utilities and other large users along the lines of these great power streams. This, indeed, serves perhaps to picture what is meant by superpower development. As a matter of practical fact, however, the natural development of this situation lies, first, in the interconnection of power supplies between the existing great utility systems, and second, in common action for the erection of large units of production at advantageous points for the mutual supply of two or more of the present systems, and in the development of such great water powers as the St. Lawrence. . . .

The savings in these 11 States resulting from a coordinated and fully developed electrical power system, would, by the time it could be erected, amount to a conservation of about 50,000,000 tons of coal per annum; an annual saving could be made of over $500,000,000 per annum at an additional capital outlay of about $1,250,000,000. In this area we are to-day producing something like 9,000,000 horsepower by direct steam and individual plant generation, a substantial part of which could be transferred to central generation with great economy.

With the crowding of our population in large areas we are faced with most difficult questions in the development of terminal facilities, the handling of traffic on our railways. There has been some electrification of transportation. The engineers who have made systematic superpower surveys are convinced that over 40 per cent of the mileage of the railways in this territory could be electrified at substantial economies in operation and with enlarged service if we should secure this greater and more economical power development.

The indirect results both human and material are even more important than these figures I have given would imply. They take no account of vast losses to industry and commerce by the actual interruption and threatened interruption of fuel supplies to our several hundred thousand independent power units; no account of the relief to shippers from our already overburdened transportation and terminal facilities; no account of the increased production of our factories from cheaper power; no account of the larger extension of power into farm and home; no account of the reduction of physical labor and increase of comfort.

To secure the rapid adoption of these demonstratedly possible results is of profound public importance. Every time we cheapen power and centralize its production we create new uses and we add security to production; we also increase the production; we eliminate waste; we decrease the burden of physical effort upon men. In sum, we increase the standards of living and comfort of all our people.

This conference recommended the formation of the Northeastern Super-power Committee under my chairmanship. The members of the committee have been designated by the governors of the various States representing their utilities commissions, together with representatives of the War Department, the Federal Power Commission, the United States Geological Survey, and the Department of Commerce. An engineering subcommittee, comprised of engineers of the various State utilities commissions and Federal engineers, brought in its report on April 14, 1924. This report deals comprehensively with the problems above outlined and with the major technical steps necessary to bring about the technical development required. Already a number of these steps have been undertaken by the various power systems throughout this area.

Studies as to the legal problems involved in interconnection over State lines, having in mind the involved and varying forms of regulation in different States, are being made by a legal subcommittee with a view to determining some basis of uniformity in such regulation.

It would be desirable to cover other areas of the country in the same fashion. . . .

Improvement in Technical Processes

As a result of the equipment built up during the war the Government possessed in the Bureau of Standards the greatest physics and research laboratory in the world. While the pre-war activities of the bureau were largely limited to the determination of physical standards and constants, it appeared to me that we should not lose in our industrial system the great values that could be obtained from the use of these laboratories in research into the elimination of waste in industrial processes where such research did not conflict with that normally carried on by the industries themselves. More particularly does this apply to industries comprised of great numbers of small manufacturers none of whom can afford to establish the laboratory and research staff necessary for consideration of broad problems. There has therefore been developed a large amount of research work of this character in cooperation with committees of the different industries.

The reports of the Bureau of Standards set out numbers of successful efforts of this character, resulting in the savings of enormous sums of money in the cost of production. Instances of such contributions to public interest may be enumerated in the successful development for methods of reducing the loss in the baking of Japan ware, in the installation of an optical-glass industry in the United States, in the progress made in the development of synthetic tanning material, in the development of use for cotton linters and other cotton wastes, and in the development of a method for reclamation of gasoline for the dry-cleaning industry. Many other activities of the Bureau of Standards result in savings of waste, such as the development of a standard test for determining the suitability of elevator interlocks which should reduce fatal elevator accidents; the substantial agreement reached on international temperature scales which will improve international industrial exchanges; the invention of instruments and methods for the determination of radiofrequency standards and measurements, etc.

Simplified Practice

A large field in the elimination of waste lies in the direction of simplified nomenclature, grades, and variations in dimensions of industrial products. The Division of Simplified Practice established early in 1921, serves as a centralizing agency in bringing together producers, distributors, and consumers, when so requested by any of these groups, for the purpose of assisting these interests in their mutual efforts to eliminate waste in production and distribution. Here the particular waste attacked was that caused by unnecessary diversification of practice or character resulting in the accumulation of excessive and consequently expensive, stocks of seldom-used varieties. Soon after the division was established the national brick manufacturers brought to its attention the need for simplifying the number of sizes of paving bricks. It developed that no less than 66 sizes were actually being manufactured and sold. This department promptly called a conference of all interested parties, with the result that varieties of paving brick were reduced by mutual consent from 66 to 11. Since then there has been a further reduction to 5 varieties.

This is but a sample of the accomplishments of this division. During the year under review varieties of files and rasps were simplified from 1,351 to 498; range boilers from 130 to 13; woven-wire fencing from 552 to 69; fencing package sizes from 2,072 to 138; sizes of bed blankets from 78 to 12; hollow building tile from 36 to 19; roofing slate sizes from 60 to 30; blackboard slate sizes from 141 to 14; forged tools from 665 to 351, and so on. Working along somewhat similar lines, the National Screw Thread Commission tackled the problem of making bolts and nuts of any make fit together and eliminating unnecessary variations.

Two national conferences of lumber manufacturers, dealers, consumers, and architects have been held and successfully established standard nomenclature, grades, and sizes for softwood lumber calling for a 60 per cent elimination of the present variety in yard lumber. Similar effort is under way in hardwood. The application of simplified practice to automotive parts, gas water heaters, steam boiler parts and fittings, hacksaw blades, pocket knives, shotgun shells, drills, and nearly a hundred other commodities, is being developed by those engaged in their manufacture, sale, and use, with the cooperation of the department.

The department has received the widest approval from the leaders in the industries affected that the simplified practice work is steadily decreasing the volume of retail stocks, production costs, and selling expenses, at the same time strengthening employment by allowing manufacture of standard articles for stock. Estimated annual savings by the industries as a result of this method of national waste elimination range from half a million dollars in one commodity field to a quarter of a billion dollars in another. These savings eventually find their way back to the consumer either in lower prices or better quality or both. All such efforts definitely advance competition. . . .

Trade Associations

One of the most important agencies through which the elimination of waste may be promoted is the trade association. It is true that a small minority of these associations have been in the past used as cloaks for restraint of trade by such activities as open-price associations and other attempts to control distribution or prices. It is equally true that the vast majority of trade associations have no such purpose and do no such things. The dividing line, however, between what activities are in the public interest and what are not in the public interest is not to-day clearly defined either by the law or by court decision. In consequence of recent decisions of the courts many associations are fearful of proceeding with work of vital public importance, and we are losing the value of much admirable activity. At the same time we are keeping alive the possibility of wrongful acts. It is imperative that some definition should be made by which an assurance of legality in proper conduct can be had, and by which illegality or improper conduct may be more vigorously attacked.

In the elimination of waste, trade associations have been among the most constructive agencies of the country, and will be far more so if the solution can be found to the above question. Their waste elimination activities extend in many directions, of which the following are but a part:

Collection and distribution of statistics as to actual production, capacity production, stocks on hand, shipments, orders on hand, cancellations, number of employees, and such other data as will enable the industry and its consumers intelligently to judge future demands and supply.

Elimination of waste and reductions in cost of production and distribution by standardizing sizes and types, eliminating excess varieties, and establishing grades and qualities, thus reducing the amount of stocks thrust upon the retailer and at the same time enabling factories to operate more regularly to stocks of standard requirements.

Elimination of misdirected credit and aid in the collection of accounts.

Provision for the settlement of trade disputes by arbitration.

Stamping out of unfair practices and misrepresentation in business or as to goods.

Promotion of the welfare of employees, by the improvement of working conditions, sanitation, safety appliances, accident prevention, housing conditions, and matters of like character.

Economy in insurance by handling that of all members, including fire, industrial, indemnity, or group insurance.

Economies in transportation through common agencies for settlement of rate matters, classification, car supply, auditing transportation bills, and the study of competitive transportation agencies.

Elimination of waste in processes by the establishment of laboratories for technical and scientific research.

Instances of the injury incurred because of lack of such activities could be recited in great numbers. Gigantic loss to the public and to the rubber and fertilizer trades in 1921 was in large measure due to the absence of statistical knowledge of stocks of raw material which had been imported into the country at that time. The instability of the bituminous coal industry, and the constant disintegration of its employers' associations through fear of the restraint-of-trade acts, contributed directly to their refusal to enter into negotiation with the unionized miners in 1922, and bears some share of responsibility for the long strike which then ensued.

Any collective activity can be used as a smoke screen to cover conspiracy against the public interest, but that is no reason for condemning all collective activities. Just because automobiles are sometimes used by bootleggers for the illegal transportation of liquor we do not prohibit their manufacture or their legitimate use. Probably the most compelling reason for maintaining proper trade associations lies in the fact that through them small business is given facilities more or less equivalent to those which big business can accumulate for itself.

Properly directed, this kind of activity is one of the strongest forces for the maintenance of competitive action. No one would advocate any amendment to the law that would sooner or later create monopoly, price fixing, domination or unfair practices, or any of the category of collective action detrimental to public interest. There is a vast difference between the whole social conception of capital combinations against public interest and cooperative organization profoundly in public interest. The former extinguishes individualism, legitimizes and fosters monopoly, dams up our economic channels, all of which penalize the consumer and make for less efficiency in production. The latter encourages individualism, fosters competition and initiative, resulting in efficient service and reasonable prices to the consumer.

Legislative definition of these matters has been given to the farmer and to labor, and I am convinced that the time has come when definition should be extended to those engaged in industry, trade, and commerce, particularly in the interest of maintaining the small business unit. The department has made definite proposals in this direction which it believes in no way open the door for illegal activities, and yet make ample provision for the maintenance of those activities which it is in the public interest to encourage.

SELECTION

President Coolidge on "the Spirit of Our Institutions": Veto of the McNary-Haugen Bill, May 23, 1928

In the decade before World War I American agriculture achieved relative prosperity and stability. Since 1914, however, it has been buffeted continuously by cyclical fluctuations—brief booms and extended depressions. Agriculture boomed during the war and immediately afterward, but it was as hard hit as industry, or worse, in the Depression of 1920–1921; and while industry revived and became quite prosperous in 1923 and thereafter, agriculture only slowly, fitfully, and painfully improved, without recovering its wartime or even its prewar prosperity. When the Great Depression began in the fall of 1929, it only extended an already existing agricultural depression.

Farm organizations resorted to political action in an attempt to raise farm prices. The problem, as farm leaders saw it, was that the world price of basic agricultural products was insufficient to meet production costs and bring a fair return in the United States; their proposed solution was to impose protection for agricultural production comparable to tariff protection for industry. But no tariff duty could be effective for products the United States produced in surplus and did not import, which was the situation with many basic farm products. The McNary-Haugen scheme (named for Senator Charles McNary of Oregon and Representative Gilbert Haugen of Iowa) was designed to create a domestic price higher than the world price through a rather complicated arrangement. President Coolidge briefly described this arrangement near the beginning of this selection, but a hypothetical example may be necessary to understand it. Let us assume that a wheat farmer had a crop of 2,000 bushels and that the world price was $1 a bushel. If the wheat was sold on the world market or on an unprotected home market, the farmer's receipts would be $2,000. Let us further assume the tariff on wheat amounted to 25 cents a bushel and that a fourth of the American wheat crop was exported. Under the McNary-Haugen plan, the hypothetical farmer would receive $1.25 for each bushel (the world price plus the tariff), or a total of $2,500. The farmer would have to pay an equalization fee, the same amount as the tariff, for each of the 500 bushels he exported. At 25 cents a bushel, the fees would total $125. His net receipts, then, would be $23.75, or $2,500 minus the $125 in equalization fees. So long as the domestic sales exceeded exports, farmers would come out ahead under the projected scheme.

McNary and Haugen introduced their proposal first in January, 1924. Congress failed to pass it, as it failed to pass another version in 1926, primarily because McNary and Haugen did not include protection for Southern farm products. Their third effort, however, passed Congress in February, 1927. Coolidge vetoed it. This was Senate Bill 4808, to which Coolidge referred in the first sentence of this selection. In May, 1928, Congress passed a similar bill, Senate Bill 3555, and Coolidge again vetoed it. This selection is his veto message, slightly abridged. Senate Bill 3555 had passed the Senate 58 to 23 and the House 204 to 121, and the effort to override the veto fell short, 51 to 30 in the Senate. Thus ended McNary-Haugenism. The system ultimately adopted to raise farm prices was to control supply by restricting production.

In his message Coolidge revealed many of his assumptions about economics and government. The law of supply and demand, Coolidge wrote, was immutable. The bill was guilty of "naively implying" that this immutable economic condition "can . . . be legislatively distorted" in the farmer's favor. "Economic history is filled with the evidences of the ghastly futility of such attempts. Fiat prices match the folly of fiat money." But the proposal, said the President, was worse than foolish. It was filled with "vicious devices," and the effort to use government to regulate prices was "repugnant . . . to the spirit of our institutions, both political and commercial." What annoyed advocates of McNary-Haugenism was that Coolidge's professions of laissez-faire economic theory did not apply to some of industry's requests. A protective tariff on industrial products did, quite obviously, legislatively distort the law of supply and demand by reducing the supply of foreign industrial products on the American market. What was sauce for the industrial goose did not seem to be sauce for the agricultural gander, and many farm leaders were seriously critical of the President.

For further discussion of agriculture during the 1920s and of McNary-Haugenism, see Theodore Saloutos and John D. Hicks, Agricultural Discontent in the Middle West, 1900–1939 *(Madison, Wis.: University of Wisconsin Press, 1951) and George Soule,* Prosperity Decade: From War to Depression, 1917–1929 *(New York: Rinehart, 1947). This veto message is to be found in the* Congressional Record, *Seventieth Congress, first session, volume 69, part 9, May 23, 1928, pages 9524–9527.*

S enate bill 3555, called the surplus control act, is in some respects an improvement over Senate bill 4808 of the last Congress. It includes several provisions, which, if unencumbered by objectionable features, would form a basis for a measure that should do much to develop stronger business organizations in agriculture. But the present bill contains not only the so-called equalization fee and other features of the old measure prejudicial, in my opinion, to sound public policy and to agriculture, but also new and highly objectionable provisions. In its entirety it is little less undesirable than the earlier measure. The bill still is unconstitutional. This position is supported by the opinion of the Attorney General, which is hereto attached.

In its essentials the objectionable plan proposed here is the stimulation of the price of agricultural commodities and products thereof by artificially controlling the surpluses so that there will be an apparent scarcity on the market. This is to be done by means of a board having supposedly adequate powers and adequate funds to accomplish such purpose through various agencies, governmental and private. The surpluses of the different selected commodities so accumulated by the board are then to be sold by export and otherwise directly or through such agencies at whatever loss is necessary in making the disposition. The fund to pay the losses and other costs while at first furnished by the Government is ultimately to be replaced and thereafter replenished from time to time by means of a tax or fee charged against the product. The theory is that the enhanced price of the commodity would enable the producer to pay the equalization fee and still reap a profit.

The recurring problem of surpluses in farm products has long been a subject of deep concern to the entire Nation, and any economically sound, workable solution of it would command not only the approval but the profound gratitude of our people. The present measure, however, falls far short of that most desirable objective; indeed, although it purports to provide farm relief by lessening the cares of our greatest industry, it not only fails to accomplish that purpose but actually heaps even higher its burdens of political control, of distribution costs, and of foreign competition. It embodies a formidable array of perils for agriculture which are all the more menacing because of their being obscured in a maze of ponderously futile bureaucratic paraphernalia. In fact, in spite of the inclusion in this measure of some constructive steps proposed by the administration, it renews most of the more vicious devices which appeared in the bill that was vetoed last year. This document is much altered from its previous form, but its substance, particularly as to its evident ultimate effect of tending to delude the farmer with a fantastic promise of unworkable governmental price regulation, is still as repugnant as ever to the spirit of our institutions, both political and commercial.

A detailed analysis of all the objections to the measure would involve a document of truly formidable proportions. However, its major weaknesses and perils may be summarized under six headings:

I. Its attempted price-fixing fallacy.
II. The tax characteristics of the equalization fee.
III. The widespread bureaucracy which it would set up.
IV. Its encouragement to profiteering and wasteful distribution by middlemen.
V. Its stimulation of overproduction.
VI. Its aid to our foreign agricultural competitors.

These topics by no means exhaust the list of fallacious and indeed dangerous aspects of the bill, but they afford ample ground for its emphatic rejection.

I. Price fixing: This measure is as cruelly deceptive in its disguise as governmental price-fixing legislation and involves quite as unmistakably the impossible scheme of attempted governmental control of buying and selling of agricultural products through political agencies as any of the other so-called surplus control bills. In fact, in certain respects it is much broader and more flagrant in its scope. The heights to which price lifting might be promised are freed from the limitations fixed in previous measures. The bill carefully avoids any direct allusion to such price-fixing functions, but there can be no doubt about its intentions and authorizations to the Federal farm board in this respect. There is apparently no change in the import of the bill in the resolution to impose upon the farmer and upon the consumers of farm produce a régime of futile, delusive experiments with price fixing, with indirect governmental buying and selling, and with a nation-wide system of regulatory policing, intolerable espionage, and tax collection on a vast scale.

These provisions would disappoint the farmer by naïvely implying that the law of supply and demand can thus be legislatively distorted in his favor. Economic history is filled with the evidences of the ghastly futility of such attempts. Fiat prices match the folly of fiat money.

The board would be compelled to arrive in some way at the premium on the domestic price which would be demanded from the consumer, and this figure would have to be fixed in the contracts which it would make with the millers, packers, canners, spinners, and other processors. Such prices and other terms fixed in the contracts would be used by the board to calculate the losses upon which it will base the size of the equalization fee. This procedure is the very essence of price fixing no matter how cumbersome and crudely camouflaged it may be. By throwing the very large resources of the Government into this operation the present bill gives the widest latitude for the most vicious temptations adherent in autocratic authority in complete command of vast industries and trades.

In previous bills definite yardsticks have been determined by which prices were to be established by the Government. They are omitted from this bill, which thereby leaves almost no restraint whatever upon the discretion of the board in this respect. The present measure, therefore, has even less merit than its predecessors in this regard since it carries no limitation as to the extent of price inflation which it can undertake.

II. The equalization fee, which is the kernel of this legislation, is a sales tax upon the entire community. It is in no sense a mere contribution to be made by the producers themselves, as has been represented by supporters of the measure. It can be assessed upon the commodities in transit to the consumer, and its burdens can often unmistakably be passed on to him.

Furthermore, such a procedure would certainly involve an extraordinary relinquishment of the taxing power on the part of Congress, because the tax would not only be levied without recourse to legislative authority but its proceeds would be expended entirely without the usual safeguards of congressional control of appropriations. This would be a most dangerous nullification of one of the essential checks and balances which lie at the very foundation of our Government.

Incidentally, this taxation or fee would not be for purposes of revenue in the accepted sense but would simply yield a subsidy for the special benefit of particular groups of processors and exporters. It would be a consumption or sales tax on the vital necessities of life, regulated not by the ability of the people to pay but only by the requirements and export losses of various trading intermediaries. It would be difficult indeed to conceive of a more flagrant case of the employment of all of the coercive powers of the Government for the profit of a small number of specially privileged groups.

It has been alleged that these operations would be inaugurated only as a last resort, but this would be scanty assurance indeed, since no board would be able to resist the pressure of the political forces which could be mustered in behalf of every staple commodity to demand that the Government should undertake the responsibility of attempting to legislate its prices above those fixed in the normal operations of the law of supply and demand.

III. Widespread bureaucracy: A bureaucratic tyranny of unprecedented proportions would be let down upon the backs of the farm industry and its distributors throughout the Nation in connection with the enforcement of this measure. Thousands of contracts involving scores of different grades, quantities, and varieties of products would have to be signed by the board with the 4,400 millers, the 1,200 meat-packing plants, the 3,000 or more cotton and woolen mills, and the 2,700 canners. If this bill had been in operation in 1925, it would have involved collections upon an aggregate of over 16,000,000,000 units of wheat, corn, and cotton.

The bill undertakes to provide insurance against loss, but presumably only against reasonable and unavoidable loss. Just what this might be would involve judgment on the part of Government employees upon tens of thousands of transactions running into billions of dollars. This is bureaucracy gone mad. Cooperative associations, flour mills, packing plants, and grain elevators will cease to be private and become public agencies. If there is any conclusion that we can announce as final with regard to governmental business operations, particularly after the bitter and excessively costly war-time experiences with such enterprises, it is that we can not maintain a bureaucracy of such vast proportions engaged in buying and selling without constant danger of corruption, mismanagement, and prodigious tax burdens. No private agency of so gigantic and complex a character attempting to juggle with profound economic principles in such fashion could survive under such circumstances, and the chances for a governmental trading organization would be even less.

Swarms of inspectors, auditors, disbursers, accountants, and regulatory officers would be let loose throughout the land to enforce the terms of these contracts and to curb the inevitable attempts at evasion of the equalization fee. This plague of petty officialdom would set up an intolerable tyranny over the daily lives and operations of farmers and of every individual and firm engaged in the distribution of farm products, intruding into every detail of their affairs, setting up thousands of prohibitory restrictions and obnoxious inspections.

Such autocratic domination over our major industry, its dependent trades, and the everyday activities of hundreds of thousands of our citizens would indeed be profoundly repugnant to every instinct of our institutions. It would undermine individual initiative, place a premium upon evasion and dishonesty, and poison the very wellsprings of our national spirit of providing abundant rewards for thrift and for open competitive effort.

The arbitrary powers in the hands of the 12 members of the board are almost incredible. But even more extraordinary would be the veto power over the board which this measure places in the hands of the commodity advisory councils.

Acting with the board, these men could throw the entire machinery of the Government into an attempt to raise or lower domestic prices at will. Even though such efforts would ultimately be doomed to certain failure, these men would meanwhile, during the course of costly experiment, hold in their hands the fate of vast industries using farm products employing millions of persons and of great cooperatives with thousands of farmer members. They could disrupt the settled channels of trade and commerce; they could alter at will the cost of living, influence wage levels in all lines of industry, and affect conditions of business in every part of the country. The mere enumeration of such powers is the complete answer to the proposal that they be granted.

IV. Encouragement to profiteering and wasteful distribution by middlemen: As was pointed out in the veto last year, it seems almost incredible that the farmers of this country are being offered this scheme of legislative relief in which the only persons who are guaranteed to benefit are the exporters, packers, millers, canners, spinners, and other processors. Their profits are definitely assured. They have, in other words, no particular incentive toward careful operation, since each of them holding a contract, no matter how unscrupulous, wasteful, or inefficient his operations may have been, would be fully reimbursed for all of his losses.

This would be bound to encourage wholesale profiteering at the expense of the farmer and of the consumer. Every one of these processors could charge what he chose to his domestic trade and recoup the loss incurred on any one of his products thus made unsalable at home through excessive prices by dumping it at reduced rates in foreign markets. With such a complete guaranty of profit these concerns would be entirely without restraint or limitation as to profiteering and as to slovenly and wasteful processing and selling operations.

Surely there could be no more direct means of destroying the very germ of American commercial genius which is so frankly envied by our foreign rivals—the tireless search for better and more efficient business methods, the competitive zeal for superior service, and for adequate returns through large sales of better merchandise at lower prices.

The packers could be commanded by the board to buy hogs enough to create a near shortage at home and then raise the prices to a fixed level. The unsalable surplus would then be dumped abroad at a loss, which would thereupon be made good out of the pockets of all taxpayers, including the farmers. The operations would involve an impenetrable maze of contracts between the board and hundreds of packers and provisioners. The result would be a bewildering snarl of entangled accounting problems, because packing houses buy one kind of product and sell a wide range of highly differentiated specialties. To "equalize" the losses on these would indeed be a task of overwhelming difficulty.

These objections were raised against the previous measure and apparently an attempt has been made to meet them by broadening the discretionary powers of the board so as to escape the necessity of describing its functions and limiting its authority. The result, however, has been entirely the reverse from that which was intended. The board is endowed with vast powers over our basic industry, but unlike every other agency in the Government, it would not be limited by congressional control over its appropriations, since it would have within itself the power to raise funds without limit by means of the compulsory equalization fee.

V. Stimulation of overproduction: The bill runs counter to an economic law as well settled as the law of gravitation. Increased prices decrease consumption; they also increase production. These two conditions are the very ones that spell disaster to the whole program. The vaguely drawn clause in the measure to meet this obvious danger merely amounts to moral suasion and, as a last resort, the withdrawal of the equalization fee. Thus, if 90 per cent of the growers of a given commodity heed the admonitions of the board and refrain from production, they will nevertheless be punished because of the evasions of the remaining 10 per cent who have ignored the board's requests. In other words, no farmer will be safe in directing his planning upon his individual judgment, for should the result be a stimulation of an increased yield, the board will be likely to withdraw the support which encouraged the surpluses and allow the prices to collapse under the weight of that artificially created excess. The annals of the industrial and agricultural world are replete with the catastrophes that have come in the wake of such attempted distortions of one of the most fundamental principles of commercial relations.

VI. Aid to our foreign agricultural competitors: This measure continues, as did its predecessor, to give substantial aid to the foreign competitors of American agriculture and industry. It continues the amazing proposal to supply foreign workers with cheaper food than those of the United States, and this at the expense of the American farm industry, thereby encouraging both the foreign peasant, whose produce is not burdened with the costs of any equalization fees, and also affording through reduced food prices the means of cutting the wage rates paid by foreign manufacturers. The latter step would promptly impair the prosperity of our manufacturing population, which is by far the leading and most profitable market for our farm produce. It is nonsense to say that our farmers are not interested in such a development, which can only result in unemployment and in consequent decreases in food consumption in the great industrial districts. It is surely poor business to transfer the farmer's market from an employed American workman to the latter's competitor in the low wage-scale countries across the seas, whose potential buying power and standards of living even at best are far below those of this country.

This is indeed an extraordinary process of economic reasoning, if such it could be called. Certainly it is a flagrant case of direct, insidious attack upon our whole agricultural and industrial strength. By the inevitable stimulation of production the bill can only mean an increase of exportable surplus to be dumped in the world market. This in turn will bring about a constantly decreasing world price, which will soon reach so low a figure that a wholesale curtailment of production in this country with its attendant demoralization and heavy losses would be certain. Where is the advantage of dragging our farmers into such folly?

Furthermore, as the board undertakes to dump the steadily mounting surplus into foreign countries at the low-cost figures, it will come into direct conflict with the dumping and similar trade laws of many foreign lands which are interested in the maintenance of their own agricultural industries. We might, therefore, expect immediately a series of drastic, retaliatory discriminations on the part of these consumer countries. This will drive our surplus into narrower market channels and force even further price reductions with consequent increases in the burdens of the equalization tax.

Lastly, and most important, in connection with this aspect of the bill as an aid to our foreign competitors, the measure will inevitably devastate many of our important farm areas. For instance, the board is expected to obtain higher prices for the American farmer for corn by removing the surplus from the home market and dumping it over our borders at a lower level of prices. In other words, the hog grower in Ontario, Canada, may buy American corn at a very much lower level than the hog grower in the State of Ohio. Both being situated equally as to the European market for their pork products, we shall see immediately the migration of the Ohio hog industries across the border into Canada with consequent losses to our pork industry by this Canadian competition.

Likewise the dumping of cheaper American feeds for Dutch and Scandinavian producers of dairy products further subsidizes them in direct competition with the American industry. In other words, the framers of this measure naïvely submit a proposal to save the American livestock grower and dairyman by supplying his overseas rivals with abundant feedstuffs at reduced rates. It would be difficult indeed to conceive of a more preposterous economic and commercial fallacy.

To take another illustration, our cotton-manufacturing industry, which now has some 18,400,000 spindles in the cotton-growing states and 16,400,-000 in the New England States, has been in a precarious condition for several years. Further handicaps imposed upon it by this bill might spell its ruin and the consequent serious crippling of our entire cotton-growing belt. Under this bill it would be quite conceivable that foreign mills could obtain American cotton for prices substantially less than those paid by domestic mills. Foreign mills could ship cotton goods to this country in spite of the tariff, since the equalization fee in this measure is not applied to cotton fabrics. Furthermore, foreign mills would undoubtedly capture our existing export markets for the 600,000,000 square yards which we ship abroad annually, valued at over $75,000,000. The very serious hardships thus inflicted upon the nearly 500,000 wage earners in the cotton-manufacturing industries and the consequent impairment of their consumption of farm produce, as well as of the raw cotton in the mills, would be indeed a tragic, if not disastrous episode. . . .

While agriculture has been distressed in many countries since the World War, the severity of the agricultural depression in the United States must not be underestimated. It is true there has been an increase in prices and purchasing power of agricultural products. Many important farm products have increased rapidly in price in recent months. Nor should we overlook the fact that our farmers have made noteworthy progress since 1921 both in the purchasing power of their products and in the output per worker in agriculture. The latter is the result of improved methods and equipment, and is in keeping with the fundamental cause of American prosperity—high productivity per worker. Moreover, we should avoid the error of seeking in laws the cause of the ills of agriculture. This mistake leads away from a permanent solution, and serves only to make political issues out of fundamental economic problems that can not be solved by political action.

In conclusion, if the measure is enacted one would be led to wonder how long it would be before producers in other lines would clamor for similar "equalizing" subsidies from the public coffers. The lobbies of Congress would be filled with emissaries from every momentarily distressed industry demanding similar relief of a burdensome surplus at the expense of the Treasury. Once we plunged into the futile sophistries of such a system of wholesale commercial doles for special groups of middlemen and distributors at the expense of farmers and other producers, it is difficult to see what the end might be.

I have believed at all times that the only sound basis for further Federal Government action in behalf of agriculture would be to encourage its adequate organization to assist in building up marketing agencies and facilities in the control of the farmers themselves. I want to see them undertake, under their own management, the marketing of their products under such conditions as will enable them to bring about greater stability in prices and less waste in marketing, but entirely within unalterable economic laws. Such a program, supported by a strong protective tariff on farm products, is the best method of effecting a permanent cure of existing agricultural ills. Such a program is in accordance with the American tradition and the American ideal of reliance on and maintenance of private initiative and individual responsibility, and the duty of the Government is discharged when it has provided conditions under which the individual can achieve success.

I am still hopeful that legislation along the lines suggested in my last annual message, with which many of the provisions of this bill are in harmony, may be enacted, but this bill embodies substantially all of the objectionable features which I said, in that message to the Congress, I could not indorse. I am therefore obliged to return Senate bill 3555, entitled "An act to establish a Federal farm board to aid in the orderly marketing and in the control and disposition of the surplus of agricultural commodities in interstate and foreign commerce" without my approval.

The White House, May 23, 1928.   CALVIN COOLIDGE.

SELECTION

The Secretary of State Proposes
to Scrap Battleships: Charles Evans Hughes
at the Washington Conference, November 12, 1921

Three years and a day after the end of what had been the world's worst war, diplomats from the major nations assembled at Washington for a Conference on the Limitation of Armament, to which the United States had invited them in August. President Harding welcomed the visitors with one of his cliché-packed ceremonial addresses, after which the delegates selected Secretary of State Charles Evan Hughes as permanent chairman of the conference. (It was to this honor that he referred in the opening sentence of his speech.) As Hughes began to speak, the delegates and the many visitors, including many senators and representatives, settled back for the expected second ceremonial speech of the morning. Few expected anything important in the speech; few really expected anything important and definite on naval disarmament from the conference. There had been general-disarmament conferences before, and they had never gone beyond acceptance of a resolution that declared reducing armaments desirable.

Hughes surprised the delegates and the world. After the usual sort of opening, the Secretary expressed a sense of urgency that was unexpected. "If there is to be economic rehabilitation, if the longings for reasonable progress are not to be denied, if we are to be spared the uprisings of peoples made desperate in the desire to shake off burdens no longer endurable, competition in armament must stop. . . . The time has come . . . not for general resolutions or mutual advice, but for action." He then proceeded, quite without precedent, to spell out just what action should be taken. The United States, Great Britain, and Japan should scrap a total of sixty-six capital ships, and he named them. In the words of a British reporter, Hughes sank more British battleships than "all the admirals of the world had destroyed in a cycle of centuries."

Hughes was vulnerable to the criticism that he had put the American cards on the table too fast, that he should have wrested concessions before saying bluntly what naval construction the nation would abandon, but it is likely that his stimulus gave the conference a spirit and momentum it otherwise would not have had. In any case, in February the three main naval powers plus France and Italy agreed to a naval-limitation treaty that was near the original proposal. Several other treaties were agreed upon at the conference. The Four-Power Treaty (United States, Japan, Great Britain, and France) abrogated the Anglo-Japanese alliance of 1911 and pledged each of the four nations to respect the others' positions in the Pacific and to confer in the event of a controversy involving any of the four. The Nine-Power Treaty (the five of the disarmament treaty plus Belgium, the Netherlands, Portugal, and China) constituted an international reaffirmation of the Open Door in China.

Charles Evans Hughes (1862–1948) was a man of unusual force, dignity, and acumen. He had been Governor of New York and an Associate Justice of the Supreme Court, from which he resigned in 1916 to accept the Republican presidential nomination. Wilson defeated Hughes by a hair. If Hughes had carried California, which he lost by less than four thousand votes, he would have been elected. He was Secretary of State from 1921 to 1925. Hoover appointed him Chief Justice of the Supreme Court in 1930, where he served until his retirement in 1941. For more on Hughes see Merlo J. Pusey, Charles Evans Hughes *(New York: Macmillan, 1952), two volumes. For his years in the Cabinet see the brief work by Charles Cheney Hyde in Samuel F. Bemis, editor,* The American Secretaries of State and Their Diplomacy, *volume X (New York: Knopf, 1929). Easily the most authoritative work on the Washington Conference, which is critical of the conference's work in some respects, is Harold H. and Margaret Sprout,* Toward a New Order of Sea Power: American Naval Policy and the World Scene, 1918–1922 *(Princeton, N.J.: Princeton, 1943).*

The selection is printed here in full as it appears in Conference on the Limitation of Armament, Washington, November 12, 1921–February 6, 1922 *(Washington: Government Printing Office, 1922), pages 50–66. In the original published proceedings of the conference the even-numbered pages are in English and the others in French.*

Gentlemen:
     It is with a deep sense of privilege and responsibility that I accept the honor you have conferred.

Permit me to express the most cordial appreciation of the assurances of friendly cooperation which have been generously expressed by the representatives of all the invited Governments. The earnest desire and purpose, manifested in every step in the approach to this meeting, that we should meet the reasonable expectation of a watching world by effective action suited to the opportunity, is the best augury for the success of the Conference.

The President invited the Governments of the British Empire, France, Italy and Japan to participate in a Conference on the subject of Limitation of Armament, in connection with which Pacific and Far Eastern questions would also be discussed. It would have been most agreeable to the President to have invited all the Powers to take part in this Conference, but it was thought to be a time when other considerations should yield to the practical requirements of the existing exigency, and in this view the invitation was extended to the group known as the Principal Allied and Associated Powers, which, by reason of the conditions produced by the war, control in the main the armament of the world. The opportunity to limit armament lies within their grasp.

It is recognized, however, that the interests of other Powers in the Far East made it appropriate that they should be invited to participate in the discussion of Pacific and Far Eastern problems, and, with the approval of the five Powers, an invitation to take part in the discussion of those questions has been extended to Belgium, China, the Netherlands and Portugal.

The inclusion of the proposal for the discussion of Pacific and Far Eastern questions was not for the purpose of embarrassing or delaying an agreement for limitation of armament, but rather to support that undertaking by availing ourselves of this meeting to endeavor to reach a common understanding as to the principles and policies to be followed in the Far East and thus greatly to diminish, and if possible wholly to remove, discernible sources of controversy. It is believed that by interchanges of views at this opportune time, the Governments represented here may find a basis of accord and thus give expression to their desire to assure enduring friendship.

In the public discussions which have preceded the Conference there have been apparently two competing views: one, that the consideration of armament should await the result of the discussion of Far Eastern questions, and another, that the latter discussion should be postponed until an agreement for limitation of armament has been reached. I am unable to find sufficient reason for adopting either of these extreme views. I think that it would be most unfortunate if we should disappoint the hopes which have attached to this meeting by a postponement of the consideration of the first subject. The world looks to this Conference to relieve humanity of the crushing burden created by competition in armament, and it is the view of the American Government that we should meet that expectation without any unnecessary delay. (*Applause.*) It is therefore proposed that the Conference should proceed at once to consider the question of the limitation of armament.

This, however, does not mean that we must postpone the examination of Far Eastern questions. These questions, of vast importance, press for solution. It is hoped that immediate provision may be made to deal with them adequately, and it is suggested that it may be found to be entirely practicable through the distribution of the work among designated Committees to make progress to the ends sought to be achieved without either subject being treated as a hindrance to the proper consideration and disposition of the other.

The proposal to limit armament by an agreement of the Powers is not a new one, and we are admonished by the futility of earlier efforts. It may be well to recall the noble aspirations which were voiced twenty-three years ago in the imperial rescript of His Majesty the Emperor of Russia. It was then pointed out with clarity and emphasis that "The intellectual and physical strength of the nations, labor and capital, are for the major part diverted from their natural application, and unproductively consumed. Hundreds of millions are devoted to acquiring terrible engines of destruction, which, though to-day regarded as the last word of science, are destined to-morrow to lose all value in consequence of some fresh discovery in the same field. National culture, economic progress, and the production of wealth are either paralyzed or checked in their development. Moreover, in proportion as the armaments of each Power increase, so do they less and less fulfill the object which the Governments have set before themselves. The economic crises, due in great part to the system of armaments *à outrance,* and the continual danger which lies in this massing of war material, are transforming the armed peace of our days into a crushing burden, which the peoples have more and more difficulty in bearing. It appears evident, then, that if this state of things were prolonged, it would inevitably lead to the very cataclysm which it is desired to avert, and the horrors of which make every thinking man shudder in advance. To put an end to these incessant armaments and to seek the means of warding off the calamities which are threatening the whole world—such is the supreme duty which is today imposed on all States."

It was with this sense of obligation that His Majesty the Emperor of Russia proposed the Conference, which was "to occupy itself with this grave problem" and which met at The Hague in the year 1899. Important as were the deliberations and conclusions of that Conference, especially with respect to the pacific settlement of international disputes, its result in the specific matter of limitation of armament went no further than the adoption of a final Resolution setting forth the opinion "that the restriction of military charges, which are at present a heavy burden on the world, is extremely desirable for the increase of the material and moral welfare of mankind," and the utterance of the wish that the Governments "may examine the possibility of an agreement as to the limitation of armed forces by land and sea, and of war budgets."

It was seven years later that the Secretary of State of the United States, Mr. Elihu Root, in answering a note of the Russian Ambassador suggesting in outline a program of the Second Peace Conference, said: "The Government of the United States, therefore, feels it to be its duty to reserve for itself the liberty to propose to the Second Peace Conference, as one of the subjects of consideration, the reduction or limitation of armaments, in the hope that, if nothing further can be accomplished, some slight advance may be made toward the realization of the lofty conception which actuated the Emperor of Russia in calling the First Conference." It is significant that the Imperial German Government expressed itself as absolutely opposed to the question of disarmament and that the Emperor of Germany threatened to decline to send Delegates if the subject of disarmament was to be discussed. In view, however, of the Resolution which had been adopted at the First Hague Conference, the Delegates of the United States were instructed that the subject of limitation of armament "should be regarded as unfinished business, and that the Second Conference should ascertain and give full consideration to the results of such examination as the Governments may have given to the possibility of an agreement pursuant to the wish expressed by the First Conference." But by reason of the obstacles which the subject had encountered, the Second Peace Conference at The Hague, although it made notable progress in provision for the peaceful settlement of controversies, was unable to deal with limitation of armament except by a Resolution in the following general terms: "The Conference confirms the Resolution adopted by the Conference of 1899 in regard to the limitation of military expenditure; and inasmuch as military expenditure has considerably increased in almost every country since that time, the Conference declares that it is eminently desirable that the Governments should resume the serious examination of this question."

This was the fruition of the efforts of eight years. Although the effect was clearly perceived, the race in preparation of armament, wholly unaffected by these futile suggestions, went on until it fittingly culminated in the greatest war of history; and we are now suffering from the unparalleled loss of life, the destruction of hopes, the economic dislocations and the widespread impoverishment which measure the cost of the victory over the brutal pretensions of military force.

But if we are warned by the inadequacy of earlier endeavors for limitation of armament, we can not fail to recognize the extraordinary opportunity now presented. We not only have the lessons of the past to guide us, not only do we have the reaction from the disillusioning experiences of war, but we must meet the challenge of imperative economic demands. What was convenient or highly desirable before is now a matter of vital necessity. If there is to be economic rehabilitation, if the longings for reasonable progress are not to be denied, if we are to be spared the uprisings of peoples made desperate in the desire to shake off burdens no longer endurable, competition in armament must stop. (*Great applause.*) The present opportunity not only derives its advantage from a general appreciation of this fact, but the power to deal with the exigency now rests with a small group of nations, represented here, who have every reason to desire peace and to promote amity. The astounding ambition which lay athwart the promise of the Second Hague Conference no longer menaces the world, and the great opportunity of liberty-loving and peace-preserving democracies has come. Is it not plain that the time has passed for mere resolutions, that the responsible Powers should examine the question of limitation of armament? We can no longer content ourselves with investigations, with statistics, with reports, with the circumlocution of inquiry. The essential facts are sufficiently known. The time has come, and this Conference has been called, not for general resolutions or mutual advice, but for action. (*Applause.*) We meet with full understanding that the aspirations of mankind are not to be defeated either by plausible suggestions of postponement or by impracticable counsels of perfection.

Power and responsibility are here and the world awaits a practicable program which shall at once be put into execution.

I am confident that I shall have your approval in suggesting that in this matter, as well as in others before the Conference, it is desirable to follow the course of procedure which has the best promise of achievement rather than one which would facilitate division; and thus, constantly aiming to agree so far as possible, we shall, with each point of agreement, make it easier to proceed to others.

The question, in relation to armament, which may be regarded as of primary importance at this time, and with which we can deal most promptly and effectively, is the limitation of naval armament. There are certain general considerations which may be deemed pertinent to this subject.

The first is that the core of the difficulty is to be found in the competition in naval programs, and that, in order appropriately to limit naval armament, competition in its production must be abandoned. Competition will not be remedied by resolves with respect to the method of its continuance. One program inevitably leads to another, and if competition continues, its regulation is impracticable. There is only one adequate way out and that is to end it now. (*Applause.*)

It is apparent that this can not be accomplished without serious sacrifices. Enormous sums have been expended upon ships under construction and building programs which are now under way can not be given up without heavy loss. Yet if the present construction of capital ships goes forward, other ships will inevitably be built to rival them and this will lead to still others. Thus the race will continue so long as ability to continue lasts. The effort to escape sacrifices is futile. We must face them or yield our purpose.

It is also clear that no one of the naval Powers should be expected to make these sacrifices alone. (*Applause.*) The only hope of limitation of naval armament is by agreement among the nations concerned, and this agreement should be entirely fair and reasonable in the extent of the sacrifices required of each of the Powers. In considering the basis of such an agreement and the commensurate sacrifices to be required, it is necessary to have regard to the existing naval strength of the great naval Powers, including the extent of construction already effected in the case of ships in process. This follows from the fact that one nation is as free to compete as another, and each may find grounds for its action. What one may do another may demand the opportunity to rival, and we remain in the thrall of competitive effort. I may add that the American Delegates are advised by their naval experts that the tonnage of capital ships may fairly be taken to measure the relative strength of navies, as the provision for auxiliary combatant craft should sustain a reasonable relation to the capital ship tonnage allowed.

It would also seem to be a vital part of a plan for the limitation of naval armament that there should be a naval holiday. It is proposed that for a period of not less than ten years there should be no further construction of capital ships. (*Applause.*)

I am happy to say that I am at liberty to go beyond these general propositions, and, on behalf of the American Delegation acting under

the instructions of the President of the United States, to submit to you
a concrete proposition for an agreement for the limitation of naval armament. (*Applause.*)

It should be added that this proposal immediately concerns the British
Empire, Japan and the United States. In view of the extraordinary conditions due to the World War affecting the existing strength of the navies
of France and Italy, it is not thought to be necessary to discuss at this
stage of the proceedings the tonnage allowance of these nations, but the
United States proposes that this matter be reserved for the later consideration of the Conference.

In making the present proposal, the United States is most solicitous to
deal with the question upon an entirely reasonable and practicable basis,
to the end that the just interests of all shall be adequately guarded and
that national security and defense shall be maintained. Four general
principles have been applied:

1. That all capital ship building programs, either actual or projected,
should be abandoned;

2. That further reduction should be made through the scrapping of certain
of the older ships;

3. That, in general, regard should be had to the existing naval strength
of the Powers concerned;

4. That the capital ship tonnage should be used as the measurement of
strength for navies and a proportionate allowance of auxiliary combatant
craft prescribed.

The principal features of the proposed agreement are as follows:

Capital Ships

United States. The United States is now completing its program of
1916 calling for 10 new battleships and 6 battle cruisers.

One battleship has been completed. The others are in various stages
of construction; in some cases from 60 to over 80 per cent of the construction has been done. On these 15 capital ships now being built over
$330,000,000 have been spent. Still, the United States is willing in the
interest of an immediate limitation of naval armament to scrap all these
ships.

The United States proposes, if this plan is accepted—

1. To scrap all capital ships now under construction. This includes 6
battle cruisers and 7 battleships on the ways and in course of building,
and 2 battleships launched.

The total number of new capital ships thus to be scrapped is 15. The
total tonnage of the new capital ships when completed would be 618,000
tons.

2. To scrap all of the older battleships up to, but not including, the
Delaware and *North Dakota*. The number of these old battleships to be
scrapped is 15. Their total tonnage is 227,740 tons.

Thus the number of capital ships to be scrapped by the United States, if this plan is accepted, is 30, with an aggregate tonnage (including that of ships in construction, if completed) of 845,740 tons.

Great Britain. The plan contemplates that Great Britain and Japan shall take action which is fairly commensurate with this action on the part of the United States.

It is proposed that Great Britain—

1. Shall stop further construction of the 4 new *Hoods,* the new capital ships not laid down but upon which money has been spent. These 4 ships, if completed, would have tonnage displacement of 172,000 tons.

2. Shall, in addition, scrap her predreadnaughts, second-line battleships, and first-line battleships up to but not including the *King George V* class.

These, with certain predreadnaughts which it is understood have already been scrapped, would amount to 19 capital ships and a tonnage reduction of 411,375 tons.

The total tonnage of ships thus to be scrapped by Great Britain (including the tonnage of the 4 *Hoods,* if completed) would be 583,375 tons.

Japan. It is proposed that Japan—

1. Shall abandon her program of ships not yet laid down, viz., the *Kii, Owari, No. 7* and *No. 8,* battleships, and *Nos. 5, 6, 7,* and *8,* battle cruisers.

It should be observed that this idea does not involve the stopping of construction, as the construction of none of these ships has been begun.

2. Shall scrap 3 capital ships: the *Mutsu* launched, the *Tosa* and *Kaga* in course of building; and 4 battle cruisers: the *Amagi* and *Akagi* in course of building, and the *Atoga* and *Takao* not yet laid down but for which certain material has been assembled.

The total number of new capital ships to be scrapped under this paragraph is 7. The total tonnage of these new capital ships when completed would be 289,100 tons.

3. Shall scrap all predreadnaughts and battleships of the second line. This would include the scrapping of all ships up to but not including the *Settsu;* that is, the scrapping of 10 older ships, with a total tonnage of 159,828 tons.

The total reduction of tonnage on vessels existing, laid down, or for which material has been assembled (taking the tonnage of the new ships when completed), would be 448,928 tons.

The Three Powers. Thus, under this plan there would be immediately destroyed, of the navies of the three Powers, 66 capital fighting ships, built and building, with a total tonnage of 1,878,043.

It is proposed that it should be agreed by the United States, Great Britain, and Japan that their navies, with respect to capital ships, within three months after the making of the agreement shall consist of certain ships, designated in the proposal and numbering for the United States 18, for Great Britain 22, for Japan 10.

The tonnage of these ships would be as follows: of the United States, 500,650; of Great Britain, 604,450; of Japan, 299,700. In reaching this result, the age factor in the case of the respective navies has received appropriate consideration.

Replacement. With respect to replacement, the United States proposes—

1. That it be agreed that the first replacement tonnage shall not be laid down until ten years from the date of the agreement;
2. That replacement be limited by an agreed maximum of capital ship tonnage as follows:

For the United States	500,000 tons.
For Great Britain	500,000 tons.
For Japan	300,000 tons.

3. That, subject to the ten-year limitation above fixed and the maximum standard, capital ships may be replaced when they are twenty years old by new capital ship construction;
4. That no capital ship shall be built in replacement with a tonnage displacement of more than 35,000 tons.

I have sketched the proposal only in outline, leaving the technical details to be supplied by the formal proposition which is ready for submission to the Delegates.

The plan includes provision for the limitation of auxiliary combatant craft. This term embraces three classes; that is: (1) auxiliary surface combatant craft, such as cruisers (exclusive of battle cruisers), flotilla leaders, destroyers, and various surface types; (2) submarines; and (3) airplane carriers.

I shall not attempt to review the proposals for these various classes, as they bear a definite relation to the provisions for capital fighting ships.

With the acceptance of this plan the burden of meeting the demands of competition in naval armament will be lifted. Enormous sums will be released to aid the progress of civilization. At the same time the proper demands of national defense will be adequately met and the nations will have ample opportunity during the naval holiday of ten years to consider their future course. Preparation for offensive naval war will stop now. (*Great applause.*)

SELECTION

"The Marines Have Landed": President Coolidge on Affairs in Nicaragua, January 10, 1927

In 1911 and 1912 the strength and influence of the United States helped to overthrow the government of Nicaragua and install one headed by Adolfo Diaz, who, in the interest of order and economic development, was more than willing to forgo a degree of Nicaraguan independence by granting the United

States broad powers in his country's affairs. Nicaragua reorganized its finances under American supervision and yielded control of the customs houses to an American citizen, thereby assuring the collection of duties and the application of the receipts to paying off foreign bondholders (both Americans and others) while at the same time removing one of the incentives for coups d'état. A "legation guard" of up to two thousand United States Marines remained in Managua, the capital, until 1925 and of course actually did more than guard the American legation. Under circumstances which President Coolidge explained in this message to Congress, the Marines returned to Nicaragua in early January, 1927, there to remain until January, 1933, in the closing weeks of the Hoover administration. So frequently did the Marines go to Nicaragua or another Central American or Caribbean republic that the journalistic cliché, "The Marines have landed and the situation is well in hand," became almost an American proverb.

President Coolidge was not coy about describing American motives in Nicaragua. "The proprietary rights of the United States in the Nicaraguan canal route . . . together with the obligations flowing from the investments of all classes of our citizens in Nicaragua, place us in a position of peculiar responsibility." One might argue that all classes of Americans failed to share equally in Nicaraguan investments, but it could hardly be claimed that the interests there were not endangered. "There is no question that if the revolution continues American investments and business interests in Nicaragua will be very seriously affected, if not destroyed."

The canal and investments brought Coolidge to take attitudes that were extraordinary for one chief of state to hold about another state. One can sense Coolidge's impatience with General Chamorro for his refusal to accept United States direction. "Notwithstanding the refusal of this Government and of the other Central American Governments to recognize him, General Chamorro continued to exercise the functions of President until October 30, 1926." Clearly, Coolidge also considered Mexico impertinent for supporting a Nicaraguan faction the United States opposed.

This selection, complete but for the elimination of some long quotations from treaties and other documents, may be found in the Congressional Record, Sixty-ninth Congress, second session, volume 68, part 2, January 10, 1927, pages 1324–1326.

To the Congress of the United States:

While conditions in Nicaragua and the action of this Government pertaining thereto have in general been made public, I think the time has arrived for me officially to inform the Congress more in detail of the events leading up to the present disturbances and conditions which seriously threaten American lives and property, endanger the stability of all Central America, and put in jeopardy the rights granted by Nicaragua to the United States for the construction of a canal. It is well known that in 1912 the United States intervened in Nicaragua with a large force and put down a revolution, and that from that time to 1925 a legation guard of American marines was, with the consent of the Nicaraguan Government, kept in Managua to protect American lives and property. In 1923 representatives of the five Central American countries, namely, Costa Rica, Guatemala, Honduras, Nicaragua, and Salvador, at the invitation of the United States, met in Washington and entered into a series of treaties. These treaties dealt with limitation of armament, a Central American tribunal for arbitration, and the general subject of peace and amity. The treaty last referred to specifically provides in Article II that the Governments of the contracting parties will not recognize any other government which may come into power in any of the five Republics through a coup d'état, or revolution, and disqualifies the leaders of such coup d'état, or revolution, from assuming the presidency or vice presidency. . . .

The United States was not a party to this treaty, but it was made in Washington under the auspices of the Secretary of State, and this Government has felt a moral obligation to apply its principles in order to encourage the Central American States in their efforts to prevent revolution and disorder. The treaty, it may be noted in passing, was signed on behalf of Nicaragua by Emiliano Chamorro himself, who afterwards assumed the presidency in violation thereof and thereby contributed to the creation of the present difficulty.

In October, 1924, an election was held in Nicaragua for President, Vice President, and members of the Congress. This resulted in the election of a coalition ticket embracing Conservatives and Liberals. Carlos Solorzano, a Conservative Republican, was elected President and Juan B. Sacasa, a Liberal, was elected Vice President. This Government was recognized by the other Central American countries and by the United States. It had been the intention of the United States to withdraw the marines immediately after this election, and notice was given of the intention to withdraw them in January, 1925. At the request of the President of Nicaragua this time was extended to September 1, 1925. Pursuant to this determination and notice, the marines were withdrawn in August, 1925, and it appeared at that time as though tranquillity in Nicaragua was assured. Within two months, however, further disturbances broke out between the supporters of General Chamorro and the supporters of the President, culminating in the seizure of the Loma, a fortress dominating the city of Managua. Once in possession of the Loma, General Chamorro dictated an agreement which President Solorzano signed the next day. According to the terms of this agreement the President agreed to substitute supporters of General Chamorro for certain members of his cabinet, to pay General Chamorro $10,000 for the expenses of the uprising, and to grant amnesty to all those who participated in it. Vice President Sacasa thereupon left the country. In the meantime General Chamorro, who, while he had not actually taken over the office of President, was able to dictate his will to the actual executive, brought about the expulsion from the Congress of 18 members, on the ground that their election had been fraudulent, and caused to be put in their places candidates who had been defeated at the election of 1924. Having thus gained the control of Congress, he caused himself to be appointed by the Congress as designate on January 16, 1926. On January 16, 1926, Solorzano resigned as President and immediately General Chamorro took office. The four Central American countries and the United

States refused to recognize him as President. On January 22 the Secretary of State addressed to the Nicaraguan representative in Washington the following letter:

Dear Doctor Castrillo:

In your communication of the 19th instant addressed to the Secretary of State you advise that President Solorzano having resigned his office General Emiliano Chamorro took charge of the executive power on January 17.

The hope expressed in your letter that the relations which have been close and cordial for so many years between Nicaragua and the United States will continue and grow stronger has been noted with pleasure. The Government and people of the United States have feelings of sincerest friendship for Nicaragua and the people of Nicaragua and the Government of the United States will, of course, continue to maintain the most friendly relations with the people of Nicaragua. This Government has felt privileged to be able to be of assistance in the past at their request not only to Nicaragua but to all countries of Central America more especially during the Conference on Central American Affairs which resulted in the signing of a general treaty of peace and amity on February 7, 1923, between the five Republics of Central America. The object of the Central American countries with which the United States was heartily in accord, was to promote constitutional government and orderly procedure in Central America and those Governments agreed upon a joint course of action with regard to the nonrecognition of governments coming into office through coup d'etat or revolution. The United States has adopted the principles of that treaty as its policy in the future recognition of Central American Governments as it feels that by so doing it can best show its friendly disposition towards and its desire to be helpful to the Republics of Central America.

It is therefore with regret that I have to inform you that the Government of the United States has not recognized and will not recognize as the Government of Nicaragua the régime now headed by General Chamorro, as the latter was duly advised on several occasions by the American minister after General Chamorro had taken charge of the citadel at Managua on October 25 last. This action is, I am happy to learn, in accord with that taken by all the Governments that signed with Nicaragua the treaty of 1923.

Notwithstanding the refusal of this Government and of the other Central American Governments to recognize him, General Chamorro continued to exercise the functions of President until October 30, 1926. In the meantime a revolution broke out in May on the east coast in the neighborhood of Bluefields and was speedily suppressed by the troops of General Chamorro. However, it again broke out with considerable more violence. The second attempt was attended with some success and practically all of the east coast of Nicaragua fell into the hands of the revolutionists. Throughout these events Sacasa was at no time in the country, having remained in Mexico and Guatemala during this period.

Repeated requests were made of the United States for protection, especially on the east coast. . . .

Accordingly, the Navy Department ordered Admiral Latimer, in command of the special-service squadron, to proceed to Bluefields. Upon arriving there he found it necessary for the adequate protection of American lives and property to declare Bluefields a neutral zone. This was done with the consent of both factions, afterwards, on October 26, 1926, reduced to a written agreement, which is still in force. In October, 1926, the good offices of the United States were sought by both parties for the purpose of effecting a settlement of the conflict. Admiral Latimer, commanding the special-service squadron, brought about an armistice to permit of a conference being held between the delegates of the two factions. The armistice was originally for 15 days and was later extended for 15 days more. At the request of both parties, marines were landed at Corinto to establish a neutral zone in which the conference could be held. Doctor Sacasa was invited to attend this conference but refrained from doing so and remained in Guatemala City. The United States Government did not participate in the conference except to provide a neutral chairman; it simply offered its good offices to make the conference possible and arranged a neutral zone at Corinto at the request of both parties during the time the conference was held. I understand that at this conference General Chamorro offered to resign and permit the Congress to elect a new designate to assume the presidency. The conference led to no result, since just at the time when it seemed as though some compromise agreement would be reached the representatives of Doctor Sacasa suddenly broke off negotiations.

According to our reports, the Sacasa delegates on this occasion stated freely that to accept any government other than one presided over by Doctor Sacasa himself would be a breach of faith with their Mexican allies. Hostilities were resumed on October 30, 1926. On the same date General Chamorro formally turned over the executive power to Sebastian Uriza, who had been appointed designate by the Congress controlled by General Chamorro. The United States Government refused to recognize Señor Uriza, on the ground that his assumption of the Presidency had no constitutional basis. Uriza thereupon convoked Congress in extraordinary session, and the entire 18 members who had been expelled during the Chamorro régime were notified to resume their seats. The Congress which met in extraordinary session on November 10 had, therefore, substantially the same membership as when first convened following the election of 1924. This Congress, whose acts may be considered as constitutional, designated Señor Adolfo Diaz as first designate. At this session of Congress 53 members were present out of a total membership of 67, of whom 44 voted for Diaz and 2 for Solorzano. The balance abstained from voting. On November 11 Señor Uriza turned over the executive power to Diaz, who was inaugurated on the 14th.

The Nicaraguan constitution provides in article 106 that in the absence of the President and Vice President the Congress shall designate one of its members to complete the unexpired term of President. As President Solorzano had resigned and was then residing in California, and as the Vice President, Doctor Sacasa, was in Guatemala, having been out of the country since November, 1925, the action of Congress in designating Señor Diaz was perfectly legal and in accordance with the constitution. Therefore the United States Government on November 17 extended recognition to Señor Diaz.

Following his assumption of office, President Diaz . . . November 15,

1926, requested the assistance of the United States Government to protect American and foreign lives and property. . . .

Immediately following the inauguration of President Diaz and frequently since that date he has appealed to the United States for support, has informed this Government of the aid which Mexico is giving to the revolutionists, and has stated that he is unable solely because of the aid given by Mexico to the revolutionists to protect the lives and property of American citizens and other foreigners. When negotiations leading up to the Corinto conference began, I immediately placed an embargo on the shipment of arms and ammunition to Nicaragua. The Department of State notified the other Central American States, to wit, Costa Rica, Honduras, Salvador, and Guatemala, and they assured the department that they would cooperate in this measure. So far as known, they have done so. The State Department also notified the Mexican Government of this embargo and informally suggested to that government like action. The Mexican Government did not adopt the suggestion to put on an embargo, but informed the American ambassador at Mexico City that in the absence of manufacturing plants in Mexico for the making of arms and ammunition the matter had little practical importance.

As a matter of fact, I have the most conclusive evidence that arms and munitions in large quantities have been on several occasions since August, 1926, shipped to the revolutionists in Nicaragua. Boats carrying these munitions have been fitted out in Mexican ports, and some of the munitions bear evidence of having belonged to the Mexican Government. It also appears that the ships were fitted out with the full knowledge of and, in some cases, with the encouragement of Mexican officials and were in one instance, at least, commanded by a Mexican naval reserve officer. At the end of November, after spending some time in Mexico City, Doctor Sacasa went back to Nicaragua, landing at Puerto Cabezas, near Bragmans Bluff. He immediately placed himself at the head of the insurrection and declared himself President of Nicaragua. He has never been recognized by any of the Central American Republics nor by any other government, with the exception of Mexico, which recognized him immediately. As arms and munitions in large quantities were reaching the revolutionists, I deemed it unfair to prevent the recognized government from purchasing arms abroad, and, accordingly, the Secretary of State has notified the Diaz Government that licenses would be issued for the export of arms and munitions purchased in this country. It would be thoroughly inconsistent for this country not to support the government recognized by it while the revolutionists were receiving arms and munitions from abroad.

During the last two months the Government of the United States has received repeated requests from various American citizens, both directly and through our consuls and legation, for the protection of their lives and property. The Government of the United States has also received requests from the British chargé at Managua and from the Italian ambassador at Washington for the protection of their respective nationals. Pursuant to such requests, Admiral Latimer, in charge of the special service squadron, has not only maintained the neutral zone at Bluefields under the agreement of both parties but has landed forces at Puerto Cabezas and Rio Grande, and established neutral zones at these points where considerable numbers of Americans live and are engaged in carrying on various industries. He has also been authorized to establish such other neutral zones as are necessary for the purposes above mentioned.

For many years numerous Americans have been living in Nicaragua, developing its industries and carrying on business. At the present time there are large investments in lumbering, mining, coffee growing, banana culture, shipping, and also in general mercantile and other collateral business. All these people and these industries have been encouraged by the Nicaraguan Government. That Government has at all times owed them protection, but the United States has occasionally been obliged to send naval forces for their proper protection. In the present crisis such forces are requested by the Nicaraguan Government, which protests to the United States its inability to protect these interests and states that any measures which the United States deems appropriate for their protection will be satisfactory to the Nicaraguan Government.

In addition to these industries now in existence, the Government of Nicaragua, by a treaty entered into on the 5th day of August, 1914, granted in perpetuity to the United States the exclusive proprietary rights necessary and convenient for the construction, operation, and maintenance of an oceanic canal. . . .

The consideration paid by the United States to Nicaragua was the sum of $3,000,000. At the time of the payment of this money a financial plan was drawn up between the Nicaraguan Government and its creditors which provided for the consolidation of Nicaragua's obligations. At that time the bondholders holding the Nicaraguan external debt consented to a reduction in interest from 6 to 5 per cent, providing the service of this loan was handled through the American collector of customs, and at the same time a series of internal guaranteed customs bonds amounting to $3,744,000 was issued by the Nicaraguan Government to pay off the claims which had arisen against it because of revolutionary disturbances from 1909 to 1912. The other outstanding external bonds, amounting on February 1, 1926, to about £772,000, are held in Great Britain. Of the guaranteed customs bonds, $2,867,000 were on February 1, 1926, still in circulation, and of these about $1,000,000 were held by Nicaraguans, $1,000,000 by American citizens, and the balance by nationals of other countries. The bonds held in the United States are held by the public in general circulation and, so far as the department knows, no American bankers are directly interested in the Nicaraguan indebtedness. This financial plan was adopted by an act of the Congress of Nicaragua on August 31, 1917. The National Bank of Nicaragua was made the depository of all Government revenues. The internal revenues were, as heretofore, to be collected by the Government. Collection of the internal revenue, however, was to be taken over by the collector general of customs, an American citizen appointed by the Nicaraguan Government and approved by the Secretary of State of the United States, if the product should average less than $60,000 a month for three consecutive months. This has never yet been necessary. The proceeds of the customs revenues were to be applied, first, to the payment of such sums as might be agreed upon in the contemplated contracts for the service of the foreign loan, the internal loan, and claims against the Nicaraguan Government. From the balance of the revenue $80,000 a month was to be used for the ordinary budget expenses and an additional $15,000 for extraordinary expenses.

Under this financial plan the finances of Nicaragua have been rehabilitated in a very satisfactory manner. Of the $3,744,000 of internal customs bonds issued in 1917 about $900,000 have been paid. Of the external debt, bonds issued in 1909, amounting to £1,250,000, there now remain only about £770,000. The total public debt of Nicaragua has been reduced from about $22,000,000 in 1917 to $6,625,203 at the beginning of 1926. Furthermore, the country in time of peace has ample revenues for its ordinary budget expenses and a surplus which has been used in extensive public improvements. The Nicaraguan National Bank and the National Railroad, controlling interests in which were formerly owned by American bankers, were repurchased by the Nicaraguan Government in 1920 and 1924, and are now wholly owned by that Government.

There is no question that if the revolution continues American investments and business interests in Nicaragua will be very seriously affected, if not destroyed. The currency, which is now at par, will be inflated. American as well as foreign bondholders will undoubtedly look to the United States for the protection of their interests.

It is true that the United States did not establish the financial plan by any treaty, but it nevertheless did aid through diplomatic channels and advise in the negotiation and establishment of this plan for the financial rehabilitation of Nicaragua.

Manifestly the relation of this Government to the Nicaraguan situation, and its policy in the existing emergency, are determined by the facts which I have described. The proprietary rights of the United States in the Nicaraguan canal route, with the necessary implications growing out of it affecting the Panama Canal, together with the obligations flowing from the investments of all classes of our citizens in Nicaragua, place us in a position of peculiar responsibility. I am sure it is not the desire of the United States to intervene in the internal affairs of Nicaragua or of any other Central American Republic. Nevertheless it must be said that we have a very definite and special interest in the maintenance of order and good government in Nicaragua at the present time, and that the stability, prosperity, and independence of all Central American countries can never be a matter of indifference to us. The United States can not, therefore, fail to view with deep concern any serious threat to stability and constitutional government in Nicaragua tending toward anarchy and jeopardizing American interests, especially if such state of affairs is contributed to or brought about by outside influences or by any foreign power. It has always been and remains the policy of the United States in such circumstances to take the steps that may be necessary for the preservation and protection of the lives, the property, and the interests of its citizens and of this Government itself. In this respect I propose to follow the path of my predecessors.

Consequently, I have deemed it my duty to use the powers committed to me to insure the adequate protection of all American interests in Nicaragua, whether they be endangered by internal strife or by outside interference in the affairs of that Republic.

CALVIN COOLIDGE.

The White House, January 10, 1927.

SELECTION

Prohibitionist Rhetoric and Strategy: The Reverend E. C. Dinwiddie of the Anti-Saloon League, 1915

From early 1920 until 1933 the government of the United States forbade the manufacture and sale of alcoholic beverages. Prohibition was a major issue of politics from well before the adoption of the Eighteenth Amendment to the Constitution (submitted to the states December 18, 1917, and ratified January 29, 1919) until its final repeal by the adoption of the Twenty-first Amendment (submitted to the states February 20, 1933, and ratified December 5, 1933). The Anti-Saloon League, established in 1895, was the most effective dry organization.

This selection, a report by the league's Washington lobbyist, officially called its national legislative superintendent, includes a great deal of typical prohibitionist rhetoric, reveals prohibitionist ways of thinking, and describes Anti-Saloon League strategy. In prohibitionists' speeches and writings their opponents were frequently termed "the liquor interests," the extent of whose iniquity was horrendous. "We are fighting a conscienceless enemy which is entrenched in the appetites and customs of vast multitudes of our people, and which has untold money at its command with which it does not hesitate to disseminate untruths, to corrupt elections, to intimidate the fearful in business and in politics, and to subsidize the press in order that its lease of life may be prolonged." At several points in his address the lobbyist revealed thought that was singularly partisan and somewhat fanatic. He seemed to believe, for example, that the supposedly improved health of American soldiers was attributable entirely to the abolition of the "official saloon in the United States Army, euphoniously [he probably meant euphemistically] called the 'canteen.'" In his comments about people who would not themselves "engage in the liquor traffic and accept the responsibility for its fiendish work" but who would vote for wets, he came very close to the fanatic position that whoever was not with him was against him.

The Reverend Mr. Dinwiddie made league goals and methods plain. Nation-wide prohibition, which required an amendment to the Constitution, was the primary goal. Until that goal was realizable, the league would work for lesser objectives. Through "a few comparatively small victories" the prohibitionists could make continual progress against "the liquor interests" and "build up and develop an invincible army before which the liquor forces could not stand." The league's basic weapon was the vote. "Our people, without distinction of party, should unfalteringly sustain the friends and punish the enemies of temperance reform. When a man in official position supports our cause, he should be sustained, irrespective of partisanship, as against an opponent who is unfriendly." He presented rather impressive evidence that the tactics worked. In 1915, he reported, about four-fifths of the nation was dry and about 55 per cent of the population lived in these dry zones.

Edwin Courtland Dinwiddie devoted his life to the Lutheran ministry and the fight against alcohol. From the time he became president of the Ohio Young Men's Prohibition League in 1888 at age twenty-one until he retired in the 1930s, he was an officer, paid or voluntary, in one antialcohol organization or another. He lobbied for national prohibition and, having won it, worked for strict enforcement. In 1928 he organized and directed a special National United Committee on Dry Planks and Dry Presidential Candidates. He vigorously but unsuccessfully fought repeal efforts. He was especially active in the international prohibition movement, the missionary division of the antiliquor fraternity.

The standard work on the Reverend Mr. Dinwiddie's organization is Peter H. Odegard, Pressure Politics: The Story of the Anti-Saloon League *(New York: Columbia, 1928). Dinwiddie's report, in slightly abridged form here, is from* Proceedings, Sixteenth National Convention of the Anti-Saloon League of America, Atlantic City, New Jersey, July 6–9, 1915, *pages 45–56.*

It is not my purpose to make a temperance or Prohibition speech on this occasion. This Convention has been treated to some masterly oratorical efforts denunciatory of the liquor traffic and filled with inspiration for more thorough conservation in the movement for its overthrow. It has seemed wise at this juncture to have a report of the state of our campaign—to recite some of the progress made—to tell of some of the victories won—in order that by the knowledge of their achievements our temperance forces may be encouraged to put forth yet more vigorous efforts and make still greater advances toward our goal which is the destruction by law of the legalized liquor traffic in the United States.

The significant national temperance victories along legislative lines during the last 25 years began with the successful issue of our campaign to outlaw the official saloon in the United States Army, euphoniously called the "canteen." This was the first legislative effort of the Anti-Saloon League of America in the national field, and it began with the institution of our Washington department in the fall of 1899. It was the misdirected effort in the first anti-canteen fight in Congress which hastened the decision of the National League to occupy this field.

Within six months after the establishment of our legislative headquarters at Washington, the Committee on Military Affairs of the national House of Representatives had favorably recommended the passage of the Bowersock bill, absolutely forbidding the selling or dealing in intoxicating liquors by any person within the military jurisdiction of the United States, and within 15 months after our Washington work was established an unambiguous, enforceable and salutary law was passed by Congress and signed by the President. Until within the last few years this law was assailed annually with great vigor and vehemence and with the backing of powerful moneyed interests who control a large section of the press and who sought an easy market for several million dollars' worth of their product which was closed to them by law. It is enough to say that recent official medical reports from the War Department show that notwithstanding the absence of the army saloon, the health of our soldiers was never better and the reports of the Judge Advocate General's department show a decided reduction in desertions and crimes.

There are many who predicted that this fight could not be won—(that we were destined to waste energy and resources in a vain effort to displace the army canteen). The success of the fight demonstrated the possibilities in a national legislative campaign, provided we operated along approved lines and were willing to advance cautiously and conservatively, keeping in touch with public opinion and not attempting more radical measures than the general temperance sentiment of the country would support. The passage of this legislation was particularly helpful in demonstrating to ourselves the power of united and well-directed public sentiment. Our people at once took courage and became inspired with the possibility of still further victories over the organized liquor traffic. This showed the wisdom of some of our foremost leaders, among whom was Dr. Isaac Funk, of New York, who in the early days of our national campaign encouraged the Superintendent in his belief that if we could win a few comparatively small victories and continually make progress all the while in our campaign against the liquor traffic, we should be able to build up and develop an invincible army before which the liquor forces could not stand. The results of the past 15 years of national warfare against the liquor traffic have completely demonstrated the soundness of this theory. In this connection it should be remembered that immediately following the passage of the anti-canteen law, the temperance forces of the country effectually refuted the old criticism that they were only iconoclasts and had no practical notions about putting anything better in place of the saloon. The very people who led the fight for the Prohibition of the army canteen immediately began the advocacy of a better ration for the United States Army and for saloon substitutes for the benefit of the enlisted men, and beginning with an initial appropriation of $500,000 in 1902, Congress has since generously responded to the requests of the temperance people year by year until three and two-third millions of dollars have been appropriated directly out of the Federal Treasury for the "erection, equipment, and maintenance" of suitable buildings at the army posts for recreative and social purposes for the enlisted men. Upon the initiative of the temperance forces of the United States, the government has practically declared that it is rich enough and proposes to be generous enough to supply the legitimate needs of its soldiery without compelling them to become beer drinkers and co-operative saloon-keepers in order to raise the money with which to purchase the comforts and necessities which confessedly they ought to have.

The year following the passage of the anti-canteen law, during the pendency of a bill regulating immigration into the United States, Congress prohibited liquor selling in the immigrant stations of the country and also in the National Capitol building and all the grounds appertaining thereto.

Only a year or two later Congress inserted a provision in the Sundry Civil Appropriations bill which forced the prohibition of the liquor selling canteen out of state and territorial soldiers' homes throughout the country by refusing federal aid to all such homes in which the sale of intoxicating liquor should be allowed. The following year, in making the appropriations for soldiers' homes, Congress decided to be entirely consistent in the matter, and so voted to prohibit liquor selling in all the national soldiers' homes over which the federal government exercises exclusive jurisdiction. Both of these enactments have resulted in untold good to the veterans, despite the unwarranted and untruthful reports that for many years were regularly circulated concerning the operation and effect of this legislation.

In 1906 Congress added several large Prohibition zones in the neighborhood of public institutions in the city of Washington, D. C., adding materially to the dry area of the national capital.

During the same year Congress passed a law which required collectors of internal revenue to furnish certified copies of lists of those who pay the federal tax as retail liquor dealers, so that if the state law permits this to be done, these lists can be used as evidence against blind tigers and other violators who sell liquor in defiance of state law, but who nevertheless pay the federal tax in order to escape punishment by the national government.

During the pendency of the statehood bill in 1905, at the behest of our forces in Oklahoma and Indian Territory, we secured the inclusion of a Prohibition provision by the Senate by a vote of 52 to 17. I call attention to this because of the cheap, critical and demagogical assertion which is so recklessly and persistently circulated, that the Congress of the United States, and particularly the Senate, has not responded to the judgment and sentiment of the country at large. I have no commission to defend either body, but I believe in telling the facts about men individually and legislative bodies, as such, as they actually exist, and I am glad to make the statement that the Congress of the United States whenever a fair temperance issue is gotten squarely before either body has never failed to represent the temper and judgment of the American people. In 16 years of service at the national Capital I recall no instance in either House or Senate—barring our constitutional amendment—where a proposition favorable to the temperance reform was clearly and squarely before the body, without other complications, that either the House or Senate voted such a proposition down. The statehood bill failed to pass in 1905 because of a difference between the two Houses with reference to the admission of Arizona, New Mexico, Oklahoma and Indian Territories. The following year the Enabling Act was passed to join Oklahoma and Indian Territories as one state, and at our request Congress required the new state of Oklahoma to take over upon itself the obligation of the federal government to maintain Prohibition in the Indian territory and in all those portions of Oklahoma territory which existed as Indian reservations January 1, 1906, for a period of 21 years—the time during which the Indians were forbidden by law to alienate their homesteads. This provision by Congress, which was a condition precedent to statehood, was made the basis of a state-wide fight by the temperance forces of Oklahoma in 1906 and 1907 which resulted in the adoption of state-wide Prohibition in the constitution of the new state by over 18,000 majority. This contest in Oklahoma was the first state constitutional fight waged in this country for 18 years, and the first successful one since the Dakotas were admitted with Prohibition in their constitutions in 1899, and Oklahoma therefore became the fourth state in the march of temperance progress in which state-wide Prohibition became effective. . . .

After long years of agitation and efforts to secure remedial legislation, Congress responded in the closing days of the Sixty-second Congress with the passage of the so-called Webb-Kenyon interstate liquor shipment bill which prohibits the shipment in interstate commerce of intoxicating liquors which are intended "to be received, possessed, sold, or in any manner used in violation of any law" of the destination state. The House of Representatives passed the Webb bill on February 8 by a vote of 239 to 64 against, and on the 10th of February the Senate by an overwhelming vote, but in which the yeas and nays were not recorded, passed the Kenyon bill. Inasmuch as unanimous consent was refused to substitute the Webb bill for the Kenyon bill in the Senate, under the skillful parliamentary leadership of Senator Gallinger, of New Hampshire, our friends in the Senate proceeded to perfect the Kenyon bill, and then, just before it was finally passed, substituted for it the language of the Webb bill. This had the effect of requiring the Kenyon bill to be passed by the House, the Webb bill having been referred under the rules of the Senate to its Committee on the Judiciary. In this way the enemies of the legislation had hoped to trick us and prevent final passage of either measure. The next morning the Judiciary Committee of the House authorized its chairman to ask in its name to take the Kenyon Senate bill from the Speaker's table and put it upon its passage without reference to the Committee, this being possible under section 2 of rule XXIV, of the House rules. The point of order was raised by the opponents of the legislation that this procedure was not permissible under this rule, inasmuch as there was no House bill on the calendar of the same general import as the Senate bill, or any relating to the subject at all. It is to the credit of Speaker Clark that in a common-sense ruling he held that the procedure was in order and strictly conformed to any reasonable construction of the rule, and the Senate bill was thereupon promptly passed by the House.

The President retained the bill in his possession for the 10 days allowed by the constitution and finally returned it to the Senate with his disapproval basing his veto upon the ground of its unconstitutionality. Within an hour after it had been received by the Senate, that body passed it over the President's veto by a vote of 63 to 21, and the following morning the House of Representatives likewise repassed the measure, "the objections of the President to the contrary notwithstanding" by a vote of 246 to 95, and thus it became a law. The Webb-Kenyon bill has been before the Supreme Court of a number of the states and in every case thus far, and notably in the states of Kansas, Iowa, Alabama, North Carolina and Delaware, it has been sustained as a valid exercise of the constitutional powers of Congress. Cases are now pending in the Supreme Court of the United States in which it is hoped the constitutionality and scope of the law will be definitely decided. In addition to the decisions of the state Supreme Courts referred to, the highest Federal Courts which have as yet passed upon the Webb-Kenyon law have decided in favor of its constitutionality—notably the Fourth Circuit Court of Appeals in a most able and convincing decision by Judge Woods of South Carolina. It is my steadfast belief that this legislation will be sustained by the courts and that under it it will be possible for each state to pass such valid and effective legislation as will practically put an end to the work of the bootleggers, blind tigers and blind pigs that have operated within their borders, hitherto chiefly under the protection and through the facilities afforded by interstate commerce because of the previous inaction of the federal Congress.

The same session of Congress which enacted the Webb-Kenyon interstate law likewise passed an anti-liquor code of laws for the District of Columbia. It displaced an old antiquated measure, enacted 20 years before, and chiefly in the interest of the liquor traffic, and was designed to give the national capital as good a code of regulatory laws short of actual Prohibition as it was possible to secure at that time. This measure, among many other important and helpful features, prohibits the granting of licenses in the residential sections of the District of Columbia; within 400 feet of an established church, school house, or college; within 300 feet of an alleyway occupied for residences or within 300 feet of any slum district, except upon unanimous vote of the three members of the Excise Board; it prevents the congestion of saloons on any street between two intersecting streets, limiting the number to four on both sides in any given square; forbids public drinking on cars or in waiting rooms of railroad and traction stations; arbitrarily limits the number of licenses, including hotels and clubs to 300—there being over 520 when the law was passed; provides a search and seizure law; strengthens the law against the sale of liquor to minors; prohibits sales on Sundays, legal holidays and inauguration days; provides against "fake" clubs; safeguards the prescribing of liquors by physicians and sales by druggists for medicinal purposes, and so on. This law has not been construed by the Excise Board which was appointed by the President of the United States as the proponents of the legislation and the members of the Senate and House had every right to expect. The board's construction of the law is now being tested in the courts, and agreeing with a special Senate Committee appointed to investigate the actions of the Excise Board of the District of Columbia, there is a general feeling that if the board does not resign, the President should ask for the resignation of these members and immediately appoint a board which will seek to interpret the law and enforce its provisions in a spirit of fairness instead of subserviency to the demands of the saloon crowd.

While it was not a matter of legislation but of departmental order, I cannot forego the opportunity of expressing my personal and official appreciation, and that of our temperance constituency throughout the nation, of Secretary of the Navy Daniel's order prohibiting the beverage liquor traffic and the use of intoxicating liquors "on board vessels or within any navy yard or station." This was a logical sequence to the order of Secretary

Long during the Spanish-American war when the canteen in the navy was abolished by departmental order, and these Secretaries deserve the highest praise for their wisdom and courage in promulgating such order in the interest of the service.

In the Army Appropriation bill for the fiscal year of 1914–1915 it was provided "that hereafter no officer or enlisted men in active service who shall be absent from duty on account of disease resulting from his own intemperate use of drugs or alcoholic liquors or other misconduct shall receive pay for the period of such absence, the time so absent and the cause thereof to be ascertained under such proceeding and regulation as may be prescribed by the Secretary of War."

Thus I have given you an epitome of the legal advances in national temperance reform during the past 15 years, and which certainly reflect credit upon the Congress of the United States, and should also serve to inspire us all to renewed activity and consecration in this fight until we shall finally have completely severed the relationship of the national government with this traffic, and written in the constitution itself nation-wide Prohibition, and in the statutes, laws to make such Prohibition effective.

In response to a nation-wide sentiment our national Convention in 1913 authorized and directed the initiation of a campaign to secure the submission of a national constitutional Prohibition amendment to the states. In harmony with that action a Committee of One Thousand—but which actually was a committee of over twice that number—assembled in Washington on the 10th of December, 1913, marched to the East front of the Capital and there presented to Hon. Morris Shepard, United States Senator from Texas, and the Hon. Richmond P. Hobson, member of the House of Representatives from Alabama, the draft of such an amendment. It was introduced on the same day by these gentlemen in their respective bodies of Congress, and immediately we began a campaign for the report of the amendment out of the committees to whom it was referred and its passage by the Congress itself. Extensive and exhaustive hearings were held before the Judiciary Committee of the House and before a sub-committee of the Judiciary Committee of the Senate. The House Committee reported the amendment without recommendation and it went on the calendar of the House in May, 1914. The sub-committee favorably reported the amendment to the full committee of the Senate but no action was taken by it. On December 22, 1914—just one year and twelve days after the formal introduction of our amendment—the House of Representatives took it up for consideration under a special rule, and after a day's session devoted to its discussion, running clear up to midnight, the House finally defeated the resolution by a vote of 197 for to 189 against, a two-thirds majority being required to submit an amendment to the national constitution to the states. Ten members were recorded as paired for the resolution and five against it. Some 30 members were absent or failed to vote. This result was a great surprise to the opponents of Prohibition as well as to some of its friends. Many believed that we should not have a majority in its favor. That the submission of a national Prohibition amendment should receive a clear majority vote the first time it was gotten before the national House of Representatives is a cause for sincere gratitude on the part of our temperance forces and constituted before the eyes of friends and enemies alike a great moral victory. So far as we are able to learn from any authoritative historical data, the original suggestion for a national constitutional Prohibition amendment, was made in the Grand Lodge of Good Templars in the state of Wisconsin over 40 years ago. The first presentation of such a concrete proposition in the National Congress was made by the Hon. Henry W. Blair, of New Hampshire, who introduced in 1876 and championed in several successive Congresses, with great ability, a Prohibition amendment. Upon several occasions such an amendment received favorable consideration and secured a favorable report from the Committee on Education and Labor of the United States Senate, but it was never brought to a vote in that body. Until this last year no national constitutional amendment resolution was ever so much as reported to the House by any committee to which it was referred.

The details of this contest on December 22 last, have been given through the secular, religious and temperance press of the country until our constituency is generally familiar with them. There is no necessity for their repetition on this occasion. Suffice it to say, the campaign for its adoption has been auspiciously begun, will be vigorously, systematically and universally prosecuted throughout the entire nation in the confident belief that under the Providence of God and with the consecrated help and enthusiasm of a united constituency, we shall move forward to complete success.

I have now given you in condensed form the record of the 15 years' achievements in the field of national temperance legislation. You will be treated to a resume of temperance progress in the various states of the Union by our accredited leaders in these different commonwealths, and it is not my intention nor within my province to speak along these lines at this time. In addition to the valuable national victories which we have won, it is a source of great gratification and of sincere thanksgiving, however, to know that whereas eight years ago at this time we had but three states in the Union with the state-wide prohibitory policy, we now have 18 which have either by constitutional or statutory enactment decided in favor of state Prohibition. Such has been our progress during recent years that under the various forms of Prohibition—local and state—probably not less than 80 per cent of the territorial area of the United States is free from the license saloon and probably over 55 per cent of our population is living in this dry territory. In this fight against the liquor traffic there is no royal road to success—there is no easy method which will insure success. We are fighting a conscienceless enemy which is entrenched in the appetites and customs of vast multitudes of our people, and which has untold money at its command with which it does not hesitate to disseminate untruths, to corrupt elections, to intimidate the fearful in business and in politics, and to subsidize the press in order that its lease of life may be prolonged. In this contest I am a firm believer in the "do everything" policy. I have been identified with the legislative department of our work since its inception. I believe in the enactment of law against this traffic. I believe in a complete reversal of the attitude of our government with relation to this business. I am an advocate of the severance of its every relation to the liquor traffic except that of uncompromising hostility. At the same time I recognize that to be effective, law must be supported by public sentiment, and I am in favor therefore of the development of a strong and active public sentiment against liquor selling and liquor drinking, and I favor the employment of every legitimate means for the creation of this sentiment. The platform, the press, the pulpit, the school, the home and the lodge room are all capable of being used to tremendous advantage in the development and maintenance of that militant public sentiment which is essential to our ultimate success. You know the arguments for Prohibition and you know the facts from experience where the policy has been tried by which those arguments can be sustained. There is just one to which I would like to direct the attention of the Convention in my closing words. Some people may think that moral arguments have lost their force in this fight. I do not think so. While it is true today we are assailing the saloon because of its great economic waste, and we are receiving large numbers of recruits from men of influence and position and wealth because of what they are beginning to realize liquor is doing economically in society, yet I believe that moral considerations are still potent with one great element in our country which is influential and powerful enough to decide this question at one election if it thoroughly resolved to do so. I readily concede that what I have in mind will not be effective with the non-Christian, but it ought to be with the Christian and churchmen of every denomination everywhere. I maintain that there is or should be such a thing as a "civic conscience" on this question, as on every other public, moral question. That "civic conscience" should be the composite of the individual consciences of the voters in the political unit where they reside, local, state or national. There are millions of men in this country that could not be induced to run a saloon or be identified actively or financially in any branch of the alcoholic liquor traffic. They are conscientiously opposed to it. They are not willing to make money out of it. They will not accept the personal, moral responsibility for what the saloon does to men and society, and yet great numbers of this class as citizens of the community or of the state will sanction the liquor traffic and practically give it their approval upon one pretext or another when they come to act as members of the body politic. My proposition is that no man who is not willing personally to engage in the liquor traffic and accept the responsibility for its fiendish work has a right as a member of society—as a citizen of the state—to authorize by his vote or influence another man or any number of them to carry on this business with the sanction of the law. This proposition should be pressed home upon the hearts and consciences of the Christian men and women of our country until we have secured the assent of the electorate in our churches to its undoubted truth. When these folk come to recognize it and act upon it there will be an end of the liquor traffic. Such is the mighty power and influence of the Christian Church in this country. The one needful thing in this great conflict of the Church with her arch enemy on earth is to get her membership interested in this question to the point of blood earnestness. When the Church really believes that the saloon ought to go and in her heart of heart intends that it shall go, THE SALOON WILL GO. The recognition of the principle which I have stated and the ordering of the lives of our Church constituency in conformity therewith is the quickest and surest method of which I have any knowledge to bring a "Sure Victory" over the liquor traffic.

There is just one other proposition to which I feel impelled to refer before I close. Next to the moral consideration by humanitarian and Christian people, the most important method to get results in this fight against the liquor traffic is for our people in all the political parties to make this issue the most important element in their political action. Our people, without distinction of party, should unfalteringly sustain the friends and punish the enemies of temperance reform. When a man in official position supports our cause, he should be sustained, irrespective of partisanship, as against an opponent who is unfriendly. When our people universally adopt and practice this principle of political action, the day of our final victory will be tremendously hastened. Great progress has been made along these lines during the past two decades, but there is still much to be done in bringing our people to see the importance of making this issue predominant and of displaying constructive political power in the interest of the friends and destructive political power against the enemies of this reform. Our experience during these latter years has thoroughly demonstrated the fact that the average man in public life in this country prefers to be on the right side of these moral questions, but he is tremendously concerned as to whether his vote in favor of such moral propositions is going to relegate him to the political junk pile. It is our business to see that the size of the political scrap-heap is not increased by the addition of our friends because they vote and labor in behalf of our propositions.

We have been making remarkable progress in this reform in recent years. Some of the old warriors, and great numbers of the new recruits are prone to ask the question as to how we will finally get the victory in this war. It is probable that no living man can tell the precise manner or time in which victory will be secured, but I think I hazard nothing in saying that we will best accelerate and insure it by pursuing the methods and adhering to the principles which have brought us the successes which we celebrate today. I can quite readily understand how a general in command of an army whose every onslaught is being repulsed and who is being constantly forced back, should seriously consider a change in his tactics or method of warfare, but I can see no reason for this in the case of an army that is winning battles, that is taking trenches and breastworks of the enemy, and which finds itself advancing victoriously toward its goal. The state and national victories of 20 years past have been along the non-partisan or omni-partisan lines which were laid down in the early days of the League's warfare, and with the successes of the past behind us, and with the prospect of a successful future before us, this is no time for our temperance army to alter its course or change its methods of attack. We can put into service new volunteers, we can employ new machinery in our warfare, we can redouble our efforts in both offensive and defensive fighting, but we do not need to discard our tried and proved methods. All we need is to keep our soldiers in fighting trim, to see that they do not lack the munitions of war, to use these and the most up-to-date inventions with increasing efficiency, to continue and increase our work of training young recruits to take the places of those who fall in the conflict, and for all those who fight in the field, and those who do the important work at home, to reconsecrate themselves to this great humanitarian service, and in the end, in His own time, we shall win the most significant, moral victory of the ages!

It is my firm conviction that the alcoholic liquor traffic, by its arrogance and insatiate greed, its waste of property, its production of poverty and crime, its lowering of industrial efficiency, its degeneration of the race, its menace of human rights and its destruction of human life, its defiance of restraints and its attacks on authority and law, its wreckage of homes, its curse of women and its heartless cruelty to children, its blight of the minds and its ruin of the bodies of men, its damnation of their souls, its blasphemy of God and its enslavement and mockery of the victims whom it plunders and despoils, is hastening the day of its complete and final overthrow.

SELECTION

The Difficulties of Enforcing Prohibition: The Wickersham Commission Report

Banning booze, as even the most zealous prohibitionists had to admit, was easier said than done. Just how well the Volstead Act (the enforcement measure enacted under the Eighteenth Amendment) was enforced, or precisely how much illicit traffic in alcoholic beverages there was, is impossible to ascertain. Reliable statistics do not exist, of course. There is a great deal of popularly believed folklore about the Prohibition Era; thus some would have us believe that getting a drink in the 1920s was as simple a process as it had been before the war or was to be again after repeal. In some places, violation of the liquor laws was open and widespread and enforcement was almost absent; in others, however, enforcement was fairly effective and drinking was clandestine. It is difficult to generalize about the national situation. This much is abundantly clear, however: The law called for universal and total abstinence, but in practice abstinence was somewhat less than universal and total.

In the 1928 presidential campaign Herbert Hoover supported the dry plank in his party's platform. He pledged strong enforcement of the law and called prohibition "a great social and economic experiment, noble in motive and far-reaching in purpose." After inauguration he decided more knowledge of the problem was necessary and, in May, 1929, created the National Commission on Law Observance and Enforcement, with George W. Wickersham as Chairman. Wickersham was an outstanding lawyer—Taft's Attorney General for four years, former president of the Bar Association of New York City, and president of the American Law Institute. The Wickersham Commission, as it usually was called, submitted its report to Hoover in January, 1931. In the report the commissioners demonstrated that they acutely and fully appreciated the difficulties inherent in prohibition enforcement, but they could not agree among themselves about a solution. Some, apparently, thought national prohibition should be abandoned and the matter left to the states. Others, apparently a majority, thought the law could be enforced with some changes and some modifications of enforcement practices. They did not agree among themselves how extensive these changes should be. In some respects the report was ambiguous, reflecting disagreement among its signers. President Hoover, in passing the report on to Congress, reaffirmed his belief that the Eighteenth Amendment should not be repealed. The report's probable effect, however, was to hasten repeal by furnishing further ammunition to the wets. Just thirteen months after the Commission reported, Congress submitted the repealing Twenty-first Amendment to the states.

A few minor points in this selection require clarification. In section 7 the report refers to the statutory definition of an intoxicating liquor as "clearly much below what is intoxicating in truth and fact." The Volstead Act defined as intoxicating any beverage that contained more than ½ per cent of alcohol by volume. That is approximately one-twelfth the alcoholic content of beer as it is made today. The interesting comments upon collection of Federal income taxes from prohibition violators, also in section 7, refer to the practice of indicting for evasion of income taxes gangster leaders whose organizations were engaged in bootlegging. The practice, of course, was no sanction of bootlegging. Al Capone, the most famous of the gangster chiefs of the Prohibition Era, went to prison for income tax evasion. The reference in section 8 to the little-known Increased Penalties Act is to a measure of March 2, 1929, more commonly called the Jones Act, which was intended to frighten violators of the prohibition laws by stiffer prison terms and fines. It actually had a contrary effect.

The full reference to this selection: National Commission on Law Observance and Enforcement, Report on the Enforcement of the Prohibition Laws of the United States, *Seventy-first Congress, third session, House document 722, 1931, pages 44–56.*

1. Corruption

As to corruption it is sufficient to refer to the reported decisions of the courts during the past decade in all parts of the country, which reveal a succession of prosecutions for conspiracies, sometimes involving the police, prosecuting and administrative organizations of whole communities; to the flagrant corruption disclosed in connection with diversions of industrial alcohol and unlawful production of beer; to the record of federal prohibition administration as to which cases of corruption have been continuous and corruption has appeared in services which in the past had been above suspicion; to the records of state police organizations; to the revelations as to police corruption in every type of municipality, large and small, throughout the decade; to the conditions as to prosecution revealed in surveys of criminal justice in many parts of the land; to the evidence of connection between corrupt local politics and gangs and the organized unlawful liquor traffic, and of systematic collection of tribute from that traffic for corrupt political purposes. There have been other eras of corruption. Indeed, such eras are likely to follow wars. Also there was much corruption in connection with the regulation of the liquor traffic before prohibition. But the present régime of corruption in connection with the liquor traffic is operating in a new and larger field and is more extensive.

2. The Bad Start and Its Results

Too often during the early years of prohibition were arrests made and prosecutions instituted without sufficient evidence to justify them. In very many instances, unwarranted searches and seizures were made, which resulted in the refusal by Commissioners to issue warrants of arrest, or in the dismissal of the prosecution by the courts. In many instances, the character and appearance of the prohibition agents were such that the United States attorney had no confidence in the case and juries paid little attention to the witnesses. Thus some of the most important causes were lost to the government. On the other hand, the prohibition agents were more concerned to secure a large number of arrests or seizures than to bring to the District Attorneys carefully prepared cases of actual importance. It is safe to say that the first seven years' experience in enforcing the law resulted in distrust of the prohibition forces by many of the United States attorneys and judges.

It must be said that enforcement of the National Prohibition Act made a bad start which has affected enforcement ever since. Many things contributed to this bad start.

(a) The Eighteenth Amendment was submitted and ratified during a great war. The National Prohibition Act was passed immediately thereafter. During a period of war the people readily yield questions of personal right to the strengthening of government and the increase of its powers. These periods are always characterized by a certain amount of emotionalism. This was especially true of the World War. These enlargements of governmental power, at the expense of individual right, are always followed by reactions against the abuses of that power which inevitably occur. Periods following great wars are generally characterized by social discontent and unrest which frequently culminate in peaceful or violent revolutions. We have been passing through this secondary phase.

The Eighteenth Amendment and the National Prohibition Act came into existence, therefore, at the time best suited for their adoption and at the worst time for their enforcement. The general reaction against and resentment of the powers of government was inevitable. It could not fail to find expression in opposition to those laws which affected directly and sought in large measure to change the habits and conduct of the people.

This attitude has been manifest in the non-observance and resistance to the enforcement of the prohibition laws.

The ratification of the Amendment was given by legislatures which were not in general elected with any reference to this subject. In many instances, as a result of old systems of apportionment, these legislative bodies were not regarded as truly representative of all elements of the community. When ratifications took place a considerable portion of the population were away in active military or other service. It may be doubted if under the conditions then prevailing the results would have been any different if these things had not been true, yet these circumstances gave grounds for resentment which has been reflected in the public attitude toward the law and has thus raised additional obstacles to observance and enforcement.

(b) In the second place, the magnitude of the task was not appreciated. It seems to have been anticipated that the fact of the constitutional amendment and federal statute having put the federal government behind national prohibition would of itself operate largely to make the law effective. For a time, there appeared some warrant for this belief. For a time, uncertainty as to how far federal enforcement would prove able to go, lack of organization and experience on the part of law breakers, and perhaps some accumulated private stocks and uncertainty as to the demand and the profits involved, made violations cautious, relatively small in volume, and comparatively easy to handle. But soon after 1921 a marked change took place. It became increasingly evident that violation was much easier and enforcement much more difficult than had been supposed. The means of enforcement provided proved increasingly inadequate. No thorough-going survey of the difficulties and consideration of how to meet them was undertaken, however, until violations had made such headway as to create a strong and growing public feeling of the futility of the law.

(c) A third cause was lack of experience of federal enforcement of a law of this sort. The subjects of federal penal legislation had been relatively few and either dealt with along well settled common-law lines, or narrowly specialized. There was no federal police power and the use of federal powers for police purposes became important only in the present century. The existing federal machinery of law enforcement had not been set up for any such tasks and was ill adapted to those imposed upon it by the National Prohibition Act. But it was sought to adapt that machinery, or to let it find out how to adapt itself, without much prevision of the difficulties. Inadequate organization and equipment have resulted.

(d) A fourth cause which had serious incidental effects was the attempt to enforce the National Prohibition Act as something on another plane from the law generally; an assumption that it was of paramount importance and that constitutional guarantees and legal limitations on agencies of law enforcement and on administration must yield to the exigencies or convenience of enforcing it.

Some advocates of the law have constantly urged and are still urging disregard or abrogation of the guarantees of liberty and of sanctity of the home which had been deemed fundamental in our policy. In some states concurrent state enforcement made an especially bad start with respect to searches and seizures, undercover men, spies and informers; and by the public at large the distinction between federal and state enforcement officers was not easily made. Moreover, the federal field force as it was at first, was largely unfit by training, experience, or character to deal with so delicate a subject. High-handed methods, shootings and killings, even where justified, alienated thoughtful citizens, believers in law and order. Unfortunate public expressions by advocates of the law, approving killings and promiscuous shootings and lawless raids and seizures and deprecating the constitutional guarantees involved, aggravated this effect. Pressure for lawless enforcement, encouragement of bad methods and agencies of obtaining evidence, and crude methods of investigation and seizure on the part of incompetent or badly chosen agents started a current of adverse public opinion in many parts of the land.

(e) Another cause was the influence of politics. No doubt this influence of politics is inevitable in any connection where very large sums of money are to be made by manipulation of administration, and where control of patronage and through it of interference or noninterference with highly profitable activities may be made to yield huge funds for political organizations and as means to political power. In the enforcement of prohibition politics intervened decisively from the beginning, both in the selection of the personnel of the enforcing organization and in the details of operation. This political interference was particularly bad some years ago in connection with the permit system. When inquiry was made into large scale violations, when permits were sought by those not entitled to them, when attempt was made to revoke permits which had been abused, recourse was frequently had to local politicians to bring to bear political pressure whereby local enforcement activities were suspended or hampered or stopped. Nor was this the only source of interference. For some time over-zealous organizations, supporting the law, brought pressure to bear with respect to personnel and methods and even legislation which had unfortunate results. Only in the last few years has enforcement been reasonably emancipated from political interference. . . .

3. The State of Public Opinion

From the beginning ours has been a government of public opinion. We expect legislation to conform to public opinion, not public opinion to yield to legislation. Whether public opinion at a given time and on a given subject is right or wrong is not a question which according to American ideals may be settled by the words, "be it enacted." Hence it is futile to argue what public opinion throughout the land among all classes of the community ought to be in view of the Eighteenth Amendment and the achieved benefits of national prohibition. So long as state cooperation is required to make the amendment and the statute enforcing it effectual, adverse public opinion in some states and lukewarm public opinion with strong hostile elements in other states are obstinate facts which can not be coerced by any measures of enforcement tolerable under our polity.

It is therefore a serious impairment of the legal order to have a national law upon the books theoretically governing the whole land and announcing a policy for the whole land which public opinion in many important centers will not enforce and in many others will not suffer to be enforced effectively. The injury to our legal and political institutions from such a situation must be weighed against the gains achieved by national prohibition. Means should be found of conserving the gains while adapting, or making it possible to adapt, legislation under the amendment to conditions and views of particular states.

Improved personnel and better training of federal enforcement agents under the present organization may well effect some change in public opinion, especially in localities where indignation has been aroused by crude or high handed methods formerly in vogue. But much of this indignation is due to the conduct of state enforcement, which affects opinion as to enforcement generally. A change in the public attitude in such localities should follow an overhauling of state agencies.

We are not now concerned with the various theories as to prohibition, or with public opinion thereon, except as and to the extent that they are existing facts and causes affecting law observance and enforcement.

It is axiomatic that under any system of reasonably free government a law will be observed and may be enforced only where and to the extent that it reflects or is an expression of the general opinion of the normally law-abiding elements of the community. To the extent that this is the case, the law will be observed by the great body of the people and may reasonably be enforced as to the remainder.

The state of public opinion, certainly in many important portions of the country, presents a serious obstacle to the observance and enforcement of the national prohibition laws.

In view of the fact, however, that the prohibition movement received such large popular support and the Eighteenth Amendment was ratified by such overwhelming legislative majorities, inquiry naturally arises as to the causes of the present state of public opinion. There appear to be many causes, some arising out of the structure of the law, the conditions to which it was to be applied, and the methods of its enforcement. Others, inherent in the principle of the act, may now be stated.

The movement against the liquor traffic and the use of intoxicating liquors for beverage purposes was originally a movement for temperance. The organizations which grew out of this movement and were potent in its development, were generally in their inception temperance organizations having as their immediate objectives the promotion of temperance in the use of alcoholic beverages and, as a means to this end, the abolition of the commercialized liquor traffic and the license saloon, which were the obvious sources of existing abuses. In many of those states where prohibition laws were adopted and saloons abolished, provision was made for the legal acquisition of limited amounts of alcoholic liquors for beverage purposes. It was only when the Eighteenth Amendment was adopted that total abstinence was sought to be established by fiat of law throughout the territory of the United States or even in many of those states which had adopted limited prohibition laws.

There are obvious differences, both as to individual psychology and legal principle, between temperance and prohibition. Temperance assumes a moderate use of alcoholic beverages but seeks to prevent excess. Even though the ultimate objective may be total abstinence, it seeks to attain that objective by the most effective regulation possible and by the education of the individual to the avoidance of excess and gradual appreciation of the benefits of abstinence. To those holding this view the field of legitimate governmental control over personal conduct is limited accordingly. Prohibition makes no distinction between moderate and excessive use. It is predicated upon the theory that any use of alcoholic liquors for beverage purposes, however moderate and under any conditions, is antisocial and so injurious to the community as to justify legal restraint. To those who entertain this view the effort to enforce universal total abstinence by absolute legal mandate is logical. There is, therefore, a fundamental cleavage in principle between those who believe in temperance and those who believe in prohibition which it is difficult to reconcile under the traditional American attitude toward the law already discussed. . . .

4. Economic Difficulties

Another type of difficulties are economic. Something has been said already of those involved in ease of production. The constant cheapening and simplification of production of alcohol and of alcoholic drinks, the improvement in quality of what may be made by illicit means, the diffusion of knowledge as to how to produce liquor and the perfection of organization of unlawful manufacture and distribution have developed faster than the means of enforcement. But of even more significance is the margin of profit in smuggling liquor, in diversion of industrial alcohol, in illicit distilling and brewing, in bootlegging, and in the manufacture and sale of products of which the bulk goes into illicit or doubtfully lawful making of liquor. This profit makes possible systematic and organized violation of the National Prohibition Act on a large scale and offers rewards on a par with the most important legitimate industries. It makes lavish expenditure in corruption possible. It puts heavy temptation in the way of everyone engaged in enforcement or administration of the law. It affords a financial basis for organized crime.

5. Geographical Difficulties

A different type of difficulties may be called geographical. For one thing the proximity of sources of supply from the outside along almost 12,000 miles of Atlantic, Pacific and Gulf shore line, abounding in inlets, much of it adjacent to unoccupied tracts offering every facility to the smuggler, speaks for itself. But in addition the chief sources of supply from the outside are immediately accessible along nearly 3,000 miles of boundary on the Great Lakes and connecting rivers. Likewise we must take account of 3,700 miles of land boundaries. Our internal geography affords quite as much difficulty. Mountainous regions, such swamp areas as the Dismal Swamp and the Everglades, islands in the great rivers such as the Mississippi, forested regions and barrens, are everywhere in relatively close proximity to cities affording steady and profitable markets for illicit liquor. Here also are the best of opportunities for unlawful manufacture.

6. Political Difficulties

What may be called political difficulties grow out of the limits of effective federal action in our polity, the need of state cooperation and the many factors operating against it, the tradition of politics and political interference in all administration, and the tendency to constant amendment of the law to be enforced.

It must be borne in mind that the federal government is one of limited powers. Except as granted to the United States or implied in those granted, all powers are jealously reserved to the state. Certain traditional lines of federal activity had become well developed and understood. Policing, except incidental to certain relatively narrow and specialized functions of the general government was not one of them. Importation, transportation across state lines, and the enforcement of excise tax laws were natural subjects of federal action. But prohibition of manufacture, distribution and sale within the states had always been solely within the scope of state action until the Eighteenth Amendment. This radical change in what had been our settled policy at once raised the question how far the federal government, as it was organized and had grown up under the Constitution, was adapted to exercise such a concurrent jurisdiction.

Nor was it merely that a radical change was made when the federal government was given jurisdiction over matters internal in the states. It was necessary also to adjust our federal polity to a conception of two sovereignties, each engaged independently in enforcing the same provision, so that, as it was supposed, wherever and whenever the one fell down the other might step in. Endeavor to bring about a nationally enforced universal total abstinence instead of limiting the power devolved on the federal government to those features of the enforcement of the amendment which were naturally or traditionally of federal cognizance, invited difficulty at the outset. But difficulties inhered also in the conception of the amendment that nation and state were to act concurrently, each covering the whole of the same ground actually or potentially; each using its own governmental machinery at the same time with the other in enforcing provisions with respect to which each had a full jurisdiction. . . .

7. Psychological Difficulties

A number of causes of resentment or irritation at the law or at features of its enforcement raise difficulties for national prohibition. A considerable part of the public were irritated at a constitutional "don't" in a matter where they saw no moral question. The statutory definition of "intoxicating" at a point clearly much below what is intoxicating in truth and fact, even if maintainable as a matter of legal power, was widely felt to be arbitrary and unnecessary. While there was general agreement that saloons were wisely eliminated, there was no general agreement on the universal regime of enforced total abstinence. In consequence many of the best citizens in every community, on whom we rely habitually for the upholding of law and order, are at most lukewarm as to the National Prohibition Act. Many who are normally law-abiding are led to an attitude hostile to the statute by a feeling that repression and interference with private conduct are carried too far. This is aggravated in many of the larger cities by a feeling that other parts of the land are seeking to impose ideas of conduct upon them and to mold city life to what are considered to be their provincial conceptions.

Other sources of resentment and irritation grow out of incidents of enforcement. In the nature of things it is easier to shut up the open drinking places and stop the sale of beer, which was drunk chiefly by working men, than to prevent the wealthy from having and using liquor in their homes and in their clubs. Naturally when the industrial benefits of prohibition are pointed out, laboring men resent the insistence of employers who drink that their employees be kept from temptation. It is easier to detect and apprehend small offenders than to reach the well organized larger operators. It is much easier to padlock a speakeasy than to close up a large hotel where important and influential and financial interests are involved. Thus the law may be made to appear as aimed at and enforced against the insignificant while the wealthy enjoy immunity. This feeling is reinforced when it is seen that the wealthy are generally able to procure pure liquors, where those with less means may run the risk of poisoning through the working over of denatured alcohol, or, at best, must put up with cheap, crude, and even deleterious products. Moreover, searches of homes, especially under state laws, have necessarily seemed to bear more upon people of moderate means than upon those of wealth or influence. Resentment at crude methods of enforcement, unavoidable with the class of persons employed in the past and still often employed in state enforcement, disgust with informers, snoopers, and under-cover men unavoidably made use of if a universal total abstinence is to be brought about by law, and irritation at the inequalities of penalties, even in adjoining districts in the same locality and as between state and federal tribunals—something to be expected with respect to a law as to which opinions differ so widely—add to the burden under which enforcement must be conducted.

Resentment is aroused also by the government's collecting income tax from bootleggers and illicit manufacturers and distributors upon the proceeds of their unlawful business. This has been a convenient and effective way of striking at large operators who have not returned their true incomes. But it impresses many citizens as a legal recognition and even licensing of the business, and many who pay income taxes upon the proceeds of their legitimate activities feel strongly that illegitimate activities should be treated by the government as upon a different basis.

Any program of improvement should seek to obviate, or at least reduce to a minimum, these causes of resentment and irritation.

It will be perceived that some of them are due to differences of opinion as to total abstinence and could only be eliminated by bringing about a substantial unanimity on that subject throughout the land, or by conceding something to communities where public opinion is adverse thereto. Others are due largely to inherent features of all enforcement of law which have attracted special attention in connection with a matter of controversy. These may be met in part by improvements in the machinery of enforcement, by improvements in the general administration of criminal justice, and by unifying or reconciling public opinion. Still others are due to unfortunate but to no small extent remediable incidents of enforcement. Federal enforcement has been steadily improving in this respect. If state enforcement agencies in many jurisdictions could be similarly improved, the effect ought to be seen presently in a more favorable public opinion.

8. The Strain on Courts, Prosecuting Machinery, and Penal Institutions

Our federal organization of courts and of prosecution were ill adapted to the task imposed on them by the National Prohibition Act. Serious difficulties at this point soon became apparent and enforcement of national prohibition still wrestles with them. The program of concurrent federal and state enforcement imposes a heavy burden of what was in substance the work of police courts upon courts set up and hitherto employed chiefly for litigation of more than ordinary magnitude. In the first five years of national prohibition, the volume of liquor prosecutions in the federal courts had multiplied by seven and federal prosecutions under the Prohibition Act terminated in 1930 had become nearly eight times as many as the total number of all pending federal prosecutions in 1914. In a number of urban districts the enforcement agencies maintain that the only practicable way of meeting this situation with the existing machinery of federal courts and prosecutions is for the United States Attorneys to make bargains with defendants or their counsel whereby defendants plead guilty to minor offenses and escape with light penalties. Hence a disproportionate number of federal liquor prosecutions terminate in pleas of guilty. In the year ending June 30, 1930, over eight-ninths of the convictions were of this character. Since enactment of the Increased Penalties Act, 1929, prosecutors have proceeded by information for minor offenses in most cases, thus facilitating the bargain method of clearing the dockets. During the year ending June 30, 1930, whereas for the federal courts as a whole 41.4 per cent of the convictions resulted in sentences to some form of imprisonment, in three urban districts in which there was obvious congestion the percentages were 6.3, 3.9 and 5.0, respectively. The meagerness of the result in proportion to the effort shows the seriousness of the difficulty under which the enforcement of national prohibition has been laboring. But this is not all. The bargain method of keeping up with the dockets which prevails of necessity in some of the most important jurisdictions of the country, plays into the hands of the organized illicit traffic by enabling it to reckon protection of its employees in the overhead. In some of our largest cities sentences have been almost uniformly to small fines or trivial imprisonment. Thus criminal prosecution, in view of the exigencies of disposing of so many cases in courts not organized for that purpose, is a feeble deterrent. The most available methods of enforcement have come to be injunction proceedings and seizure and destruction of equipment and materials.

Lawyers everywhere deplore, as one of the most serious effects of prohibition, the change in the general attitude toward the federal courts. Formerly these tribunals were of exceptional dignity, and the efficiency and dispatch of their criminal business commanded wholesome fear and respect. The professional criminal, who sometimes had scanty respect for the state tribunals, was careful so to conduct himself as not to come within the jurisdiction of the federal courts. The effect of the huge volume of liquor prosecutions, which has come to these courts under prohibition, has injured their dignity, impaired their efficiency, and endangered the wholesome respect for them which once obtained. Instead of being impressive tribunals of superior jurisdiction, they have had to do the work of police courts and that work has been chiefly in the public eye. These deplorable conditions have been aggravated by the constant presence in and about these courts of professional criminal lawyers and bail-bond agents, whose unethical and mercenary practices have detracted from these valued institutions.

SELECTION

The Religious Issue in the 1928 Election:
The Charles Marshall–Governor Smith Exchange
of Letters in "The Atlantic Monthly"

The United States differs from most other Western nations in many ways, not the least of which is that it is unusually heterogeneous in religion. Notwithstanding this religious pluralism, no major political party nominated other than a Protestant for the Presidency until 1928 or seriously considered doing so until 1924. At the 1924 Democratic convention, Governor Alfred E. Smith of New York, a Roman Catholic, narrowly missed the nomination. He received the nomination on the first ballot at the 1928 convention.

Smith's Catholicism figured prominently in the campaign and the election results. He lost in several traditionally Democratic states with overwhelming Protestant populations. For example, in the South he lost Florida, Texas,

Tennessee, North Carolina, and Virginia as well as all the Border states. On the other hand, in the big cities of the North and East, where Catholic populations were concentrated, Smith ran considerably better than had previous Democratic presidential candidates. The total vote for John W. Davis, the Democratic nominee in 1924, in the nation's twelve largest cities was about 1.3 million less than that cast for Coolidge; in 1928 Smith carried these cities by a small margin. For a generation after the election, it was a commonplace among politicians that a Catholic presidential candidate could not win.

Actually, the religious factor in the vote for or against Smith, while certainly significant, cannot be separated from other factors. Smith was a son of Irish immigrant parents, was of urban lower-class origins, and, in the parlance of the time, was a "wringing wet" on prohibition. He thus fit the stereotype of a Catholic held by many rural and small-town Protestant prohibitionists, and whether religion or ethnic background or metropolitan manners or convictions on alcohol was the controlling factor in bringing some normally Democratic voters to oppose him is quite impossible to determine.

A reasonable person might detect traces of religious bigotry in the Charles Marshall letter to Smith, but the exchange was on an infinitely higher level of intelligence, tolerance, and honesty than most of the words used in the 1928 campaign on the religious issue. A weekly newspaper of Aurora, Missouri, the New Menace, for example, published inflammatory and bigoted articles and editorials and repeated the old charges of immorality in convents and of plans for Catholic insurrection that went as far back as the Know-Nothing movement of the mid-nineteenth century.

Al Smith (1873–1944) needs little introduction. He was in the New York State Assembly from 1903 to 1915, served two years as sheriff of Manhattan, and in 1917 was elected president of the Board of Aldermen of New York City. He was elected Governor of New York four times, in 1918, 1922, 1924, and 1926. Charles Clinton Marshall is considerably more obscure. He was a retired lawyer of New York City, an Episcopalian, and an old-stock American (member of the Sons of the American Revolution). With this letter to Smith Marshall began a second career as a writer on church history and on religion in constitutional law.

The full letters, here cut by about half, may be found in The Atlantic Monthly, volume 139, April and May, 1927, pages 540–549 and 721–728. Marshall's April contribution was entitled "An Open Letter to the Honorable Alfred E. Smith"; Smith's reply was "Catholic and Patriot: Governor Smith Replies." The best account of the 1928 campaign is Edmund A. Moore, A Catholic Runs for President: The Campaign of 1928 (New York: Ronald, 1956).

Marshall's Letter

Sir:—

The American people take pride in viewing the progress of an American citizen from the humble estate in which his life began toward the highest office within the gift of the nation. It is for this reason that your candidacy for the Presidential nomination has stirred the enthusiasm of a great body of your fellow citizens. They know and rejoice in the hardship and the struggle which have fashioned you as a leader of men. They know your fidelity to the morality you have advocated in public and private life and to the religion you have revered; your great record of public trusts successfully and honestly discharged; your spirit of fair play, and justice even to your political opponents. Partisanship bids fair to quail before the challenge of your personality, and men who vote habitually against your party are pondering your candidacy with sincere respect; and yet—through all this tribute there is a note of doubt, a sinister accent of interrogation, not as to intentional rectitude and moral purpose, but as to certain conceptions which your fellow citizens attribute to you as a loyal and conscientious Roman Catholic, which in their minds are irreconcilable with that Constitution which as President you must support and defend, and with the principles of civil and religious liberty on which American institutions are based.

To this consideration no word of yours, or on your behalf, has yet been addressed. Its discussion in the interests of the public weal is obviously necessary, and yet a strange reticence avoids it, often with the unjust and withering attribution of bigotry or prejudice as the unworthy motive of its introduction. Undoubtedly a large part of the public would gladly avoid a subject the discussion of which is so unhappily associated with rancor and malevolence, and yet to avoid the subject is to neglect the profoundest interests in our national welfare.

American life has developed into a variety of religious beliefs and ethical systems, religious and nonreligious, whose claims press more and more upon public attention. None of these presents a more definite philosophy or makes a more positive demand upon the attention and reason of mankind than your venerable Church, which recently at Chicago, in the greatest religious demonstration that the world has ever seen, declared her presence and her power in American life. Is not the time ripe and the occasion opportune for a declaration, if it can be made, that shall clear away all doubt as to the reconcilability of her status and her claims with American constitutional principles? With such a statement the only question as to your proud eligibility to the Presidential office would disappear, and the doubts of your fellow citizens not of the Roman Catholic Church would be instantly resolved in your favor.

The conceptions to which we refer are not superficial. They are of the very life and being of that Church, determining its status and its relation to the State, and to the great masses of men whose convictions deny them the privilege of membership in that Church. Surely the more conscientious the Roman Catholic, and the more loyal to his Church, the more sincere and unqualified should be his acceptance of such conceptions.

These conceptions have been recognized before by Roman Catholics as a potential obstacle to their participation in public office, Pope Leo XIII himself declaring, in one of his encyclical letters, that 'it may in some places be true that for most urgent and just reasons it is by no means expedient for (Roman) Catholics to engage in public affairs or to take an active part in politics.'

It is indeed true that a loyal and conscientious Roman Catholic could and would discharge his oath of office with absolute fidelity to his moral standards. As to that in general, and as to you in particular, your fellow citizens entertain no doubt. But those moral standards differ essentially from the moral standards of all men not Roman Catholics. They are derived from the basic political doctrine of the Roman Catholic Church, asserted against repeated challenges for fifteen hundred years, that God has divided all power over men between the secular State and that Church. Thus Pope Leo XIII, in 1885, in his encyclical letter on *The Christian Constitution of States,* says: "The Almighty has appointed the charge of the human race between two powers, the ecclesiastical and the civil, the one being set over divine, and the other over human things.'

The deduction is inevitable that, as all power over human affairs, not given to the State by God, is given by God to the Roman Catholic Church, no other churches or religious or ethical societies have in theory any direct power from God and are without direct divine sanction, and therefore without natural right to function on the same basis as the Roman Catholic Church in the religious and moral affairs of the State. The result is that that Church, if true to her basic political doctrine, is hopelessly committed to that intolerance that has disfigured so much of her history. This is frankly admitted by Roman Catholic authorities.

Pope Pius IX in the famous Syllabus (1864) said: 'To hold that national churches, withdrawn from the authority of the Roman Pontiff and altogether separated, can be established, is error.'

That great compendium of Roman Catholic teaching, the *Catholic Encyclopedia,* declares that the Roman Catholic Church 'regards dogmatic intolerance, not alone as her incontestable right, but as her sacred duty.' It is obvious that such convictions leave nothing in theory of the religious and moral rights of those who are not Roman Catholics. And, indeed, that *is* Roman Catholic teaching and the inevitable deduction from Roman Catholic claims, if we use the word 'rights' strictly. Other churches, other religious societies, are tolerated in the State, not by right, but by favor.

Pope Leo XIII is explicit on this point: 'The (Roman Catholic) Church, indeed, deems it unlawful to place the various forms of divine worship on the same footing as the true religion, but does not, on that account, condemn those rulers who, for the sake of securing some great good or of hindering some great evil, allow patiently custom or usage to be a kind of sanction for each kind of religion having its place in the State.'

That is, there is not a lawful equality of other religions with that of the Roman Catholic Church, but that Church will allow state authorities for politic reasons—that is, by favor, but not by right—to tolerate other religious societies. We would ask, sir, whether such favors can be accepted in place of rights by those owning the name of freemen?

Furthermore, the doctrine of the Two Powers, in effect and theory, inevitably makes the Roman Catholic Church at times sovereign and paramount over the State. It is true that in theory the doctrine assigns to the secular State jurisdiction over secular matters and to the Roman Catholic Church jurisdiction over matters of faith and morals, each jurisdiction being exclusive of the other within undisputed lines. But the universal experience of mankind has demonstrated, and reason teaches, that many questions must arise between the State and the Roman Catholic Church in respect to which it is impossible to determine to the satisfaction of both in which jurisdiction the matter at issue lies.

Here arises the irrepressible conflict. Shall the State or the Roman Catholic Church determine? The Constitution of the United States clearly ordains that the State shall determine the question. The Roman Catholic Church demands for itself the sole right to determine it, and holds that within the limits of that claim it is superior to and supreme over the State. . . .

The Roman Catholic Church, of course, makes no claim, and never has made any claim, to jurisdiction over matters that *in her opinion* are solely secular and civil. She makes the claim obviously only when the matter in question is not, *in her opinion,* solely secular and civil. But as determination of jurisdiction, in a conflict with the State, rests solely in her sovereign discretion, no argument is needed to show that she may in theory and effect annihilate the rights of all who are not Roman Catholics, sweeping into the jurisdiction of a single religious society the most important interests of human well-being. The education of youth, the institution of marriage, the international relations of the State, and its domestic peace, as we shall proceed to show, are, in certain exigencies, wrested from the jurisdiction of the State, in which all citizens share, and confided to the jurisdiction of a single religious society in which all citizens cannot share, great numbers being excluded by the barriers of religious belief. Do you, sir, regard such claims as tolerable in a republic that calls itself free?

And, in addition to all this, the exclusive powers of the Roman Catholic Church are claimed by her to be vested in and exercised by a sovereignty that is not only created therefor by the special act of God, but is foreign and extraterritorial to these United States and to all secular states. This sovereignty, by the highest Roman Catholic authority, that of Pope Leo XIII, is not only superior in theory to the sovereignty of the secular State, but is substituted upon earth in place of the authority of God himself.

We quote Pope Leo in his encyclical letter on *The Christian Constitution of States:* 'Over the mighty multitude of mankind, God has set rulers with power to govern, and He has willed that one of them (the Pope) should be the head of all.' We quote Pope Leo in his encyclical letter on *The Reunion of Christendom:* 'We who hold upon this earth the place of God Almighty.'

It follows naturally on all this that there is a conflict between authoritative Roman Catholic claims on the one side and our constitutional law and principles on the other. Pope Leo XIII says: 'It is not lawful for the State, any more than for the individual, either to disregard all religious duties or to hold in equal favor different kinds of religion.' But the Constitution of the United States declares otherwise: 'Congress shall make no law respecting an establishment of religion or prohibiting the free exercise thereof.'

Thus the Constitution declares the United States shall hold in equal favor different kinds of religion or no religion and the Pope declares it is not lawful to hold them in equal favor. Is there not here a quandary for that man who is at once a loyal churchman and a loyal citizen? . . .

Nothing will be of greater satisfaction to those of your fellow citizens who hesitate in their endorsement of your candidacy because of the religious issues involved than such a disclaimer by you of the convictions here imputed, or such an exposition by others of the questions here presented, as may justly turn public opinion in your favor.

Yours with great respect,
CHARLES C. MARSHALL

Smith's Reply

Charles C. Marshall, Esq.

Dear Sir:—

In your open letter to me in the April *Atlantic Monthly* you 'impute' to American Catholics views which, if held by them, would leave open to question the loyalty and devotion to this country and its Constitution of more than twenty million American Catholic citizens. I am grateful to you for defining this issue in the open and for your courteous expression of the satisfaction it will bring to my fellow citizens for me to give 'a disclaimer of the convictions' thus imputed. Without mental reservation I can and do make that disclaimer. These convictions are held neither by me nor by any other American Catholic, as far as I know. . . .

I should be a poor American and a poor Catholic alike if I injected religious discussion into a political campaign. Therefore I would ask you to accept this answer from me not as a candidate for any public office but as an American citizen, honored with high elective office, meeting a challenge to his patriotism and his intellectual integrity. Moreover, I call your attention to the fact that I am only a layman. The *Atlantic Monthly* describes you as 'an experienced attorney' who 'has made himself an authority upon canon law.' I am neither a lawyer nor a theologian. What knowledge of law I have was gained in the course of my long experience in the Legislature and as Chief Executive of New York State. I had no such opportunity to study theology. . . .

Taking your letter as a whole and reducing it to commonplace English, you imply that there is conflict between religious loyalty to the Catholic faith and patriotic loyalty to the United States. Everything that has actually happened to me during my long public career leads me to know that no such thing as that is true. I have taken an oath of office in this State nineteen times. Each time I swore to defend and maintain the Constitution of the United States. All of this represents a period of public service in elective office almost continuous since 1903. I have never known any conflict between my official duties and my religious belief. No such conflict could exist. Certainly the people of this State recognize no such conflict. They have testified to my devotion to public duty by electing me to the highest office within their gift four times. You yourself do me the honor, in addressing me, to refer to 'your fidelity to the morality you have advocated in public and private life and to the religion you have revered; your great record of public trusts successfully and honestly discharged.' During the years I have discharged these trusts I have been a communicant of the Roman Catholic Church. If there were conflict, I, of all men, could not have escaped it, because I have not been a silent man, but a battler for social and political reform. These battles would in their very nature disclose this conflct if there were any.

I regard public education as one of the foremost functions of government and I have supported to the last degree the State Department of Education in every effort to promote our public-school system. The largest single item of increased appropriations under my administration appears in the educational group for the support of common schools. Since 1919, when I first became Governor, this item has grown from $9,000,000 to $82,500,000. My aim—and I may say I have succeeded in achieving it—has been legislation for child welfare, the protection of working men, women, and children, the modernization of the State's institutions for the care of helpless or unfortunate wards, the preservation of freedom of speech and opinion against the attack of war-time hysteria, and the complete reorganization of the structure of the government of the State.

I did not struggle for these things for any single element, but in the interest of all of the eleven million people who make up the State. In all of this work I had the support of churches of all denominations. I probably know as many ecclesiastics of my Church as any other layman. During my long and active public career I never received from any of them anything except cooperation and encouragement in the full and complete discharge of my duty to the State. Moreover, I am unable to understand how anything that I was taught to believe as a Catholic could possibly be in conflict with what is good citizenship. The essence of my faith is built upon the Commandments of God. The law of the land is built upon the Commandments of God. There can be no conflict between them.

Instead of quarreling among ourselves over dogmatic principles, it would be infinitely better if we joined together in inculcating obedience to these Commandments in the hearts and minds of the youth of the country as the surest and best road to happiness on this earth and to peace in the world to come. This is the common ideal of all religions. What we need is more religion for our young people, not less; and the way to get more religion is to stop the bickering among our sects which can only have for its effect the creation of doubt in the minds of our youth as to whether or not it is necessary to pay attention to religion at all.

Then I know your imputations are false when I recall the long list of other public servants of my faith who have loyally served the State. You as a lawyer will probably agree that the office of Chief Justice of the United States is second not even to that of the President in its influence on the national development and policy. That court by its interpretation of the Federal Constitution is a check not only upon the President himself but upon Congress as well. During one fourth of its history it has been presided over by two Catholics, Roger Brooke Taney and Edward Douglass White. No one has suggested that the official conduct of either of these men was affected by any unwarranted religious influence or that religion played with them any part other than it should play in the life of every God-fearing man.

And I know your imputations are false when I recall the tens of thousands of young Catholics who have risked and sacrificed their lives in defense of our country. These fundamentals of life could not be true unless your imputations were false.

But, wishing to meet you on your own ground, I address myself to your definite questions, against which I have thus far made only general statements. I must first call attention to the fact that you often divorce sentences from their context in such a way as to give them something other than their real meaning. I will specifiy. . . .

Again, you quote from the *Catholic Encyclopedia* that my Church 'regards dogmatic intolerance, not alone as her incontestable right, but as her sacred duty.' And you say that these words show that Catholics are taught to be politically, socially, and intellectually intolerant of all other people. If you had read the whole of that article in the *Catholic Encyclopedia* you would know that the real meaning of these words is that for Catholics alone the Church recognizes no deviation from complete acceptance of its dogma. These words are used in a chapter dealing with that subject only. The very same article in another chapter dealing with toleration toward non-Catholics contains these words: 'The intolerant man is avoided as much as possible by every high-minded person. . . . The man who is tolerant in every emergency is alone lovable.' The phrase 'dogmatic intolerance' does not mean that Catholics are to be dogmatically intolerant of other people, but merely that inside the Catholic Church they are to be intolerant of any variance from the dogma of the Church.

Similar criticism can be made of many of your quotations. But, beyond this, by what right do you ask me to assume responsibility for every statement that may be made in any encyclical letter? As you will find in the *Catholic Encyclopedia* (Vol. V, p. 414), these encyclicals are not articles of our faith. The Syllabus of Pope Pius IX, which you quote on the possible conflict between Church and State, is declared by Cardinal Newman to have 'no dogmatic force.' You seem to think that Catholics must be all alike in mind and in heart, as though they had been poured into and taken out of the same mould. You have no more right to ask me to defend as part of my faith every statement coming from a prelate than I should have to ask you to accept as an article of your religious faith every statement of an Episcopal bishop, or of your political faith every statement of a President of the United States. So little are these matters of the essence of my faith that I, a devout Catholic since childhood, never heard of them until I read your letter. Nor can you quote from the canons of our faith a syllable that would make us less good citizens than non-Catholics. In fact and in truth, I have been taught the spirit of tolerance, and when you, Mr. Marshall, as a Protestant Episcopalian, join with me in saying the Lord's Prayer, we both pray, not to 'My Father,' but to 'Our Father.'

But I go further to demonstrate that the true construction of your quotations by the leaders of Catholic thought is diametrically the opposite of what you suggest it to be.

Your first proposition is that Catholics believe that other religions should, in the United States, be tolerated only as a matter of favor and that there should be an established church. You may find some dream of an ideal of a Catholic State, having no relation whatever to actuality, somewhere described. But, voicing the best Catholic thought on this subject, Dr. John A. Ryan, Professor of Moral Theology at the Catholic University of America, writes in *The State and the Church* of the encyclical of Pope Leo XIII, quoted by you:—

'In practice, however, the foregoing propositions have full application only to the completely Catholic State. . . . The propositions of Pope Pius IX condemning the toleration of non-Catholic sects do not now, says Father Pohle, "apply even to Spain or the South American republics, to say nothing of countries possessing a greatly mixed population." He lays down the following general rule: "When several religions have firmly established themselves and taken root in the same territory, nothing else remains for the State than to exercise tolerance towards them all, or, as conditions exist to-day, to make complete religious liberty for individual and religious bodies a principle of government." '

That is good Americanism and good Catholicism. And Father Pohle, one of the great writers of the Catholic Church, says further:—

'If religious freedom has been accepted and sworn to as a fundamental law in a constitution, the obligation to show this tolerance is binding in conscience.'

The American prelates of our Church stoutly defend our constitutional declaration of equality of all religions before the law. Cardinal O'Connell has said: 'Thus to every American citizen has come the blessed inheritance of civil, political, and religious liberty safeguarded by the American Constitution . . . the right to worship God according to the dictates of his conscience.'

Archbishop Ireland has said: 'The Constitution of the United States reads: "Congress shall make no laws respecting an establishment of religion, or prohibiting the free exercise thereof." It was a great leap forward on the part of the new nation towards personal liberty and the consecration of the rights of conscience.'

Archbishop Dowling, referring to any conceivable union of Church and State, says: 'So many conditions for its accomplishment are lacking in every government of the world that the thesis may well be relegated to the limbo of defunct controversies.'

I think you have taken your thesis from this limbo of defunct controversies.

Archbishop Ireland again said: 'Religious freedom is the basic life of America, the cement running through all its walls and battlements, the safeguard of its peace and prosperity. Violate religious freedom against Catholics, our swords are at once unsheathed. Violate it in favor of Catholics, against non-Catholics, no less readily do they leap from the scabbard.'

Cardinal Gibbons has said: 'American Catholics rejoice in our separation of Church and State, and I can conceive no combination of circumstances likely to arise which would make a union desirable to either Church or State. . . . For ourselves we thank God that we live in America, "in this happy country of ours," to quote Mr. Roosevelt, where "religion and liberty are natural allies." '

And referring particularly to your quotation from Pope Pius IX, Dr. Ryan, in *The State and the Church,* says: 'Pope Pius IX did not intend to declare that separation is always unadvisable, for he had more than once expressed his satisfaction with the arrangement obtaining in the United States.'

With these great Catholics I stand squarely in support of the provisions of the Constitution which guarantee religious freedom and equality. . . .

I summarize my creed as an American Catholic. I believe in the worship of God according to the faith and practice of the Roman Catholic Church. I recognize no power in the institutions of my Church to interfere with the operations of the Constitution of the United States or the enforcement of the law of the land. I believe in absolute freedom of conscience for all men and in equality of all churches, all sects, and all beliefs before the law as a matter of right and not as a matter of favor. I believe in the absolute separation of Church and State and in the strict enforcement of the provisions of the Constitution that Congress shall make no law respecting an establishment of religion or prohibiting the free exercise thereof. I believe that no tribunal of any church has any power to make any decree of any force in the law of the land, other than to establish the status of its own communicants within its own church. I believe in the support of the public school as one of the corner stones of American liberty. I believe in the right of every parent to choose whether his child shall be educated in the public school or in a religious school supported by those of his own faith. I believe in the principle of noninterference by this country in the internal affairs of other nations and that we should stand steadfastly against any such interference by whomsoever it may be urged. And I believe in the common brotherhood of man under the common fatherhood of God.

In this spirit I join with fellow Americans of all creeds in a fervent prayer that never again in this land will any public servant be challenged because of the faith in which he has tried to walk humbly with his God.

Very truly yours,
ALFRED E. SMITH